FROM THE ABYSS OF LONELINESS TO THE BLISS OF SOLITUDE

FROM THE ABYSS OF LONELINESS TO THE BLISS OF SOLITUDE

Cultural, Social and Psychoanalytic Perspectives

Edited by

*Aleksandar Dimitrijević
and Michael B. Buchholz*

First published in 2022 by
Phoenix Publishing House Ltd
62 Bucknell Road
Bicester
Oxfordshire OX26 2DS

Copyright © 2022 to Aleksandar Dimitrijević and Michael B. Buchholz for the edited collection, and to the individual authors for their contributions.

Cover image: *Tresor* by Eleni Paltoglou-Blümel. Reprinted with the kind permission of the artist.

The rights of the contributors to be identified as the authors of this work have been asserted in accordance with §§ 77 and 78 of the Copyright Design and Patents Act 1988.

All rights reserved. No part of this publication may be reproduced, stored in a retrieval system, or transmitted, in any form or by any means, electronic, mechanical, photocopying, recording, or otherwise, without the prior written permission of the publisher.

The publisher has endeavoured to obtain all of the copyrights for the illustrations. Notwithstanding, if unintentionally there are any outstanding claims from a copyright holder can they please contact the publisher.

British Library Cataloguing in Publication Data

A C.I.P. for this book is available from the British Library

Paperback ISBN-13: 978-1-80013-109-5

Typeset by Medlar Publishing Solutions Pvt Ltd, India

www.firingthemind.com

Contents

Acknowledgements	ix
About the editors and contributors	xi
Editors' introduction	xvii

Part I
Philosophy and culture

Introduction to Part I   3
Aleksandar Dimitrijević

1. The hidden sociality of the solitary subject: phenomenological
   and psychoanalytical reflections on loneliness   5
   Jagna Brudzińska

2. "And live alone in the bee-loud glade"? Asceticism, hermitage,
   and the technologies of the self   19
   Colum Kenny

3. Lone wolves' loneliness—about a special variant of terrorism   31
   Michael B. Buchholz

vi CONTENTS

4. Historical roots of solitude and private self (with continual reference to Shakespeare) 57
   Aleksandar Dimitrijević

Part II
Art and literature

Introduction to Part II 71
Michael B. Buchholz

5. Loneliness and solitude: historical transformations of meaning and their expression in art, especially in music 77
   Helga de la Motte-Haber

6. Myth of the solitary artist 103
   Aleksandar Dimitrijević

7. Places of loneliness 121
   Karin Dannecker

8. Seven kinds of loneliness: mental pain, language, and interaction in David Rabe's play *Hurlyburly* 147
   Dominic Angeloch

Part III
Developmental psychology and health

Introduction to Part III 169
Michael B. Buchholz

9. Loneliness and imaginary friends in childhood and adolescence 173
   Inge Seiffge-Krenke

10. Loneliness and insecure attachment 185
    Aleksandar Dimitrijević

11. Epidemiology of loneliness 201
    Eva M. Klein, Mareike Ernst, Manfred E. Beutel, and Elmar Brähler

CONTENTS   vii

12. Loneliness and health
    Gamze Özçürümez Bilgili   213

13. Loneliness and the brain
    Gamze Özçürümez Bilgili   227

Part IV
Psychoanalysis

Introduction to Part IV   241
Aleksandar Dimitrijević

14. The silent cry, the maze of pipes, the mice, and the cellar:
    the many voices of infantile loneliness   243
    Patrizia Arfelli

15. Landscapes of loneliness: engaging with Frieda Fromm-Reichmann's
    pioneering work   255
    Gail A. Hornstein

16. Loneliness and being alone: the contributions of two British analysts   267
    Lesley Caldwell

17. Traumatic aloneness in children with narcissistically preoccupied parents   279
    Jay Frankel

18. The clinical encounter with the lonely patient: trauma and the empty self   295
    Charles Ashbach

19. Shame and its cover-up: the self-enclosed prison of isolation   307
    Peter Shabad

20. Strengthening the human bond: in psychotherapy, "doing We"
    is more important than intervention   319
    Michael B. Buchholz

Index   341

Acknowledgements

This book about loneliness was finished in a mere eleven months. What is far more important is that working on it did not include a single trace of loneliness. Not only have the two of us met regularly and worked in good humour and providing inspiring feedback and support to one another, but the same was the spirit of our exchange with many people we would like to thank here explicitly.

Jay Frankel and Salman Akhtar were the first with whom we discussed the project and individual ideas, and they provided many important recommendations and suggestions. James Anderson also helped with fruitful ideas.

Before the actual beginning, Carolina Gehrke Gus, then still a student-assistant, helped us with initial literature searches, organisation of databases, and useful suggestions.

From the very first meeting, we felt Kate Pearce understood our project, and throughout our working process, she kept showing extraordinary flexibility and support, always having the quality of the book as her first priority. We could not have wished for a better publisher.

We are, naturally, most thankful to our contributors, who granted us their years of experience, knowledge, time, and patience in dealing with our requests for revisions. Some of them are also old friends, and we are particularly happy to have made new ones while thinking together.

Alma Schlegel, also a student-assistant, read all the accepted versions, formatted reference lists, and pointed out the passages that could have been written more clearly.

Throughout it all, we were also supported by a host of invisible friends who are not mentioned anywhere in the book: Rembrandt, Aby Warburg, A. C. Bradley, Mikhail Bulgakov, Miroslav Timotijević, Herbert Stein …

To all of them, our most sincere thanks.

About the editors and contributors

Editors

Michael B. Buchholz is professor of social psychology at International Psychoanalytic University (IPU), Berlin (Germany). He is a psychologist and social scientist and a fully trained psychoanalyst. He is head of the doctorate programme at IPU and chair of the social psychology department. He has published more than twenty books and more than 350 scientific papers on topics like analysis of therapeutic metaphors and therapeutic conversation, including supervisory process, and he has contributed to psychoanalytic treatment technique, theory, and history. He has conducted conversation analysis studies on group therapy with sexual offenders, about therapeutic "contact scenarios" and on therapeutic empathy. His actual interests are the study of therapeutic talk-in-interaction using conversation analysis. Together with Anssi Peräkylä (Helsinki) he is editing a "Frontiers in psychology" research topic "Talking and Cure—What's really going on in psychotherapy".

Aleksandar Dimitrijević, PhD, is a clinical psychologist and psychoanalyst. He works as a lecturer at the International Psychoanalytic University and in private practice in Berlin. He has given lectures, seminars, university courses, and conference presentations throughout Europe and in the US. He is author of many conceptual and empirical papers about attachment theory and research, psychoanalytic education, and psychoanalysis and the arts, some of which have been translated into German, Hungarian, Italian, Slovenian, Spanish, and Turkish. He has also edited or co-edited eleven books or special journal issues, the most recent of which are *Ferenczi's Influence on Contemporary Psychoanalytic Traditions* (with Gabriele Cassullo and Jay Frankel, 2018) and *Silence and Silencing in Psychoanalysis* (with Michael B. Buchholz, 2020).

Contributors

Dominic Angeloch, Priv.-Doz. Dr. phil., is managing editor of the German monthly psychoanalytic journal *Psyche* and lecturer in comparative literature at the Goethe-University, Frankfurt am Main, Germany. He studied philosophy, Romance languages, and general and comparative literature in Heidelberg, Paris, and Berlin. He gained his doctorate with a thesis on the methodology of psychoanalytic aesthetics and Gustave Flaubert at the LMU, Munich: "*Die Beziehungzwischen Text und Leser. Grundlagen und Methodik psychoanalytischen Lesens. Mit einer Lektüre von Flauberts 'Éducation sentimentale'*" (Gießen 2014). His habilitation was on "Experience and Poetics of Knowledge. On Conditions of the Transformation of Experience into Literature and of Literature into Experience in Wilfred Bion and George Orwell" at Goethe-University, Frankfurt (2020). The first of two books out of this context appears in March 2022: *Die Wahrheit Schreiben. George Orwell: Entwicklung und Methode seines Erzählens* (Edition Tiamat, Berlin). For a list of publications and activities see: https://uni-frankfurt.de/85325555/PD_Dr__Dominic_Angeloch.

Patrizia Arfelli, MD, is a child neuropsychiatrist, and an adolescent and child psychoanalytical psychotherapist, Tavistock trained. She worked as department head in the Inpatient Adolescent Division of the Child Neuropsychiatry Division of Turin University, where she received extensive experience working with suicidal patients. She was also a court consultant in cases of abused children, and was a lecturer at the Postgraduate School of Clinical Psychology, Turin University. She is currently a lecturer in child neuropsychiatry at the Department of Psychology, Aosta University. She translated into Italian Eric Rayner's *The Independent Mind in British Psychoanalysis*, and *The Inner World and Joan Riviere* edited by Athol Hughes. She works in private practice with children, adolescents, and parents, and is particularly interested in traumatised and deprived patients and in adoptive children and families.

Charles Ashbach, PhD, is a clinical psychologist in private practice in the Philadelphia area. He is a founding faculty member of the International Psychotherapy Institute (IPI) and director of the IPI Philadelphia affiliate, Philadelphia Psychotherapy Study Center (PPSC). He is co-author of the book *Object Relations, the Self and the Group* as well as co-author of *Suffering and Sacrifice in the Clinical Encounter*. His interests include the reworking of the concept of narcissism, the psychoanalytic study of war, and the problem of intense resistance.

Manfred E. Beutel is director of the Department of Psychosomatic Medicine and Psychotherapy at the University Medical Center Mainz (since 2004), including the postgraduate training programme for psychodynamic psychotherapy (since 2010). His main research interests include psychotherapy research, psycho-oncology, and determinants of health and illness in the general population.

ABOUT THE EDITORS AND CONTRIBUTORS xiii

Elmar Brähler is scientific advisor at the Department of Psychosomatic Medicine and Psychotherapy at the University Medical Center Mainz (since 2013). Earlier he was director of the Department of Medical Psychology and Sociology at the University of Leipzig. Some of his main research areas are psychodiagnostics and gender-specific and social aspects of health and illness.

Jagna Brudzińska is professor of philosophy at the Institute of Philosophy and Sociology of the Polish Academy of Sciences where she is head of the Research Group "Philosophical Anthropology and Social Philosophy". At the Husserl-Archive of the University of Cologne she is research fellow and editor of the critical edition of Edmund Husserl's last work, *Experience and Judgment*, for the book series Husserliana. Her main research fields are Husserlian phenomenology, modern theory of subjectivity, theoretical psychology, psychoanalysis, and social theory. She is author of: *Bi-Valenz der Erfahrung. Assoziation, Imaginäres und Trieb in der Genesis der Subjektivität bei Husserl und Freud* (Springer, 2019); co-editor of *Founding Psychoanalysis Phenomenologically. Phenomenological Theory of Subjectivity and the Psychoanalytical Experience* (Springer, 2011), and author of numerous articles. She is also a professional psychologist working in the area of psychoanalysis and qualitative research.

Lesley Caldwell is a psychoanalyst of the BPA in private practice in London. She is honorary professor in the Psychoanalysis Unit at University College London where she has taught and supervised on master's and doctoral programmes and from 2010 to 2016 coordinated the unit's interdisciplinary programme. With Helen Taylor Robinson, she is joint general editor of *The Collected Works of D. W. Winnicott* (OUP, 2016) and is responsible for the more than one hundred extra entries added to the online edition of the *CW* and freely available as Volume 12 on the OUP website. Her most recent publications address the body, analytic communication and silence, and transitionality.

Karin Dannecker, Prof. Dr. phil. habil., director of the art therapy MA programme at the Weißensee Kunsthochschule, Berlin. She works clinically as art therapist with psychiatric and psychosomatic patients. She has researched and published about the efficacy of art therapy. Her books include *Kunst, Symbol und Seele* (Peter Lang, 2015, 4th edition), *Psyche und Ästhetik. Die Transformationen der Kunsttherapie* (Medizinisch Wissenschaftliche Verlagsgesellschaft, 2021, 4th edition). She is the editor of *Internationale Perspektiven der Kunsttherapie* (Nausner & Nausner, 2003); *Art Therapies and New Challenges in Psychiatry* (Routledge, 2018); co-editor of *Kunst Außenseiter Kunst* (together with Wolfram Voigtländer) (Kunsthochschule Weißensee, 2011), *Warum Kunst?* (together with Uwe Herrmann) (Medizinisch Wissenschaftliche Verlagsgesellschaft, 2017).

xiv ABOUT THE EDITORS AND CONTRIBUTORS

Mareike Ernst is a research psychologist at the Department of Psychosomatic Medicine and Psychotherapy at the University Medical Center Mainz and principal investigator of the project TASC ("Together against suicidal ideation and behavior in cancer patients"). She is also a psychodynamic psychotherapist in training. Her main research areas are early adversity, psychooncology, psychotherapy research, and suicide prevention.

Jay Frankel, PhD, is an adjunct clinical associate professor, and clinical consultant, in the New York University Postdoctoral Program in Psychotherapy and Psychoanalysis; associate editor, and previously executive editor, of the journal *Psychoanalytic Dialogues*; co-author (with Neil Altman, Richard Briggs, Daniel Gensler, and Pasqual Pantone) of *Relational Child Psychotherapy* (Other Press, 2002); co-editor (with Aleksandar Dimitrijević and Gabriele Cassullo) of *Ferenczi's Influence on Contemporary Psychoanalytic Traditions* (Routledge, 2018); and author of three dozen journal articles and book chapters, and numerous conference presentations, on topics including the work of Sándor Ferenczi, trauma, identification with the aggressor, authoritarianism and mass submission to authority, the analytic relationship, play as inherent to the therapy process, child psychotherapy, relational psychoanalysis, and others.

Gail A. Hornstein is professor emerita of psychology at Mount Holyoke College, Massachusetts, USA. Her research centres on the contemporary history and practices of psychology, psychiatry, and psychoanalysis, and her articles and opinion pieces have appeared in many scholarly and popular publications. She is author of two books: *To Redeem One Person Is to Redeem the World: The Life of Frieda Fromm-Reichmann*, which questions standard assumptions about treatment through the story of a pioneering psychiatrist, and *Agnes's Jacket: A Psychologist's Search for the Meanings of Madness*, which shows how the insights of people diagnosed with psychosis can challenge fundamental assumptions about mental health, community, and human experience. Her *Bibliography of First-Person Narratives of Madness in English*, now in its fifth edition with more than 1,000 titles, is used internationally by educators, clinicians, and peer organisations. She directs the Hearing Voices Research Project (a national research and training effort in the US, supported by the Foundation for Excellence in Mental Health Care), and speaks widely about mental health issues across the US, UK, and Europe.

Colum Kenny, BCL, PhD, is a barrister and professor emeritus at Dublin City University, where he developed a module in belief and communication. During 2020 he created the website earthact.ie, a resource for self-starting climate groups. He has been a member of the Irish broadcasting regulator and a founding board member of the EU Media Desk in Ireland, His books include *Moments that Changed Us: Ireland after 1973* (Gill & Macmillan, Dublin, 2005) and *The Power of Silence: Silent Communication in Daily Life* (Karnac, London, 2011, & Geulnurim, Seoul, 2016).

ABOUT THE EDITORS AND CONTRIBUTORS   xv

Eva M. Klein, PhD, is a psychoanalytic psychotherapist and research psychologist, and a Post-Doc in the DFG research training group "Life Sciences—Life writing" at the University Medical Center Mainz. Her main research areas of interest are migration and mental health, the role of recalled childhood experiences in psychopathology, and the psychometric evaluation of questionnaires in the general population.

Helga de la Motte-Haber, who studied psychology and later musicology, gained a doctorate at the University of Hamburg. From 1972 to 1978 she held a professorship at the Pädagogische Hochschule in Cologne, and from 1978 to 2004 at the Technische Universität, Berlin. In 2005 she was honorary professor of the University of Music in Hannover. In 1983 she founded the German Society of Psychology of Music. In 2015 she was awarded an honorary doctorate by the Hochschule für Musik und Darstellenden Kunst. She has written books on the psychology of music, sound art, and the music of the twentieth century.

Gamze Özçürümez Bilgili is a psychiatrist and a psychoanalytic psychotherapist. She is a professor and head of the Department of Psychiatry at Başkent University Faculty of Medicine, and guest lecturer at International Psychoanalytic University, Berlin. She is past secretary general of the Psychiatric Association of Turkey (2011–2013). She has been in training at Istanbul Psychoanalytic Association since 2013, and a member of Istanbul Psychoanalytic Association and Ankara Contemporary Psychoanalytic Psychotherapies Association. Her main fields of research and publication are psychoanalytic psychotherapy, psychoanalytic theory and literature, psychosomatics, trauma, mood disorders, refugee mental health, and consultation liaison psychiatry.

Inge Seiffge-Krenke is professor of developmental psychology and has worked at several German and international universities. Her research interests include stress, coping, relationship development, identity, and psychopathology. She was the head of several international studies on these topics that took place in twenty-one countries. Trained as a psychoanalyst for children, adolescents, and adults, and working in diverse in- and outpatient institutions, it is particularly important for her to integrate developmental and clinical perspectives in her research.

Peter Shabad, PhD, is clinical associate professor in the Department of Psychiatry at Northwestern University Medical School. He is on the faculty of the Chicago Institute for Psychoanalysis and the core faculty of the Chicago Center for Psychoanalysis (CCP). He is an associate editor at *Psychoanalytic Dialogues*. Dr Shabad is co-editor of *The Problem of Loss and Mourning: Psychoanalytic Perspectives* (IUP, 1989) and is the author of *Despair and the Return of Hope: Echoes of Mourning in Psychotherapy* (Aronson, 2001). Dr Shabad is currently working on a new book entitled *Seizing the Vital Moment: Passion, Shame, and Mourning*, to be published by Routledge. He is the author of numerous papers and book chapters on diverse topics such as the psychological implications of death, loss and mourning, giving and receiving, shame, parental envy, resentment, spite, and regret. Dr Shabad has a private practice in Chicago in psychoanalysis and psychoanalytic therapy.

Editors' introduction

Loneliness is one of a handful of phenomena experienced by everyone and the cause of a host of troubles in everyday lives of millions of people around the globe. It is undeniably connected to emotional pain, social maladjustment, health conditions, especially cardiovascular, and life expectancy—all in the negative. Orphanages from Communist Romania have proven, hopefully for the last time, that growing up in social isolation has disastrous consequences for children's development, both cognitive and emotional. A Harvard-based study (Waldinger, 2015) that followed subjects from early childhood into their mid-eighties found that the best predictor of happiness in old age was the quality and richness of social life in middle age.

It is an uncanny coincidence that this book was co-edited and written partly during the pandemic and lockdowns of 2020 and 2021. So many people suffered from loneliness, while others enjoyed their solitude, and many epidemiological studies were published about the ways the pandemic increased the experience of this tormenting mental state. Although loneliness has always been here and bothered many individuals, it now came to the foreground and it seems everyone became aware of its importance.

Aristotle, and John Bowlby, and everyone in between, had the same attitude towards the issue of loneliness: that it is against human nature, dangerous, tolerable only by a select few. We often feel that it is a form of punishment and develop strategies to avoid it; countless works of art are devoted to describing how it changes us. We must not forget, however, all those creative spirits who search for temporary aloneness that will provide a setting for concentration and dedication. Be it an ascetic attempt to control the body and purify the soul or the scientific or artistic absorption by the newest inspiration, many have felt that only inner solitude and social isolation can provide the subtlest and most fragile concentration necessary for bringing the work to fruition. Solitude also has the aura of a state not many people are capable of attaining,

xviii   EDITORS' INTRODUCTION

and they are, probably at the same time, revered and envied. We do not really know how to develop it, despite many religious and spiritual approaches that have spent centuries in refining effective yet cautious approaches to it. And it seems particularly under threat now, when our everyday lives are bombarded by countless messages and superficial contacts.

Psychoanalytic consulting rooms are equally full of loneliness as the world around them is, if not even more. Psychoanalysts listen about the pain of loneliness every day and are offering themselves as "companions in solitude" to help their patients learn how to use their alone time in the most beneficial way. There is a widespread belief that loneliness is the most fundamental problem every mental health patient suffers from, although its manifestations may differ. At least three classical psychoanalytic papers were devoted to loneliness, yet they were all written in the late 1950s. Is there anything contemporary psychoanalysis can add to this?

Sadly, psychoanalysts write very little about loneliness and even less about solitude. It is an interesting phenomenon that Freud barely mentioned loneliness, and many dictionaries of psychoanalysis do not have entries for either loneliness or solitude. In the *International Dictionary of Psychoanalysis* (Mijolla, 2005), we, surprisingly, found not more than ten mentions of "loneliness", but not a separate entry, and the situation is similar in Salman Akhtar's *Comprehensive Dictionary of Psychoanalysis* (2009). Both concepts are also barely present on the PEP-Web when one looks for papers explicitly focused on them, although it is more frequently mentioned: "There are few publications that are dedicated to studying loneliness but it remains a powerful descriptor in our literature" (Lynch, 2013, p. xv).

Two collections of psychoanalytic essays were published in the last ten years, *Loneliness and Longing: Conscious and Unconscious Aspects* from 2012, edited by Willock et al., and *Encounters with Loneliness: Only The Lonely* from 2013, edited by Richards et al. At the time of writing this text, they were quoted eight times each. We believe this is not a consequence of the quality of these two books, as they both offer inspiring insights, but of the surprising lack of interest among the potential audience.

This is particularly strange given that we have recently become aware that loneliness can also plague analysts, who might try to avoid it through overworking, abuse, or self-harm. To the best of our knowledge, Freud never described himself as lonely. But psychoanalysts of subsequent generations described their place behind the couch as lonely (Buechler, 1998, 2012; Greene & Kaplan, 1978; Schafer, 1995). Four chapters of the *Encounters with Loneliness* book are devoted to the psychoanalytic training process (pp. 159–219), and three chapters of *Loneliness and Longing* to the traumatised analyst's loneliness (pp. 175–209). Even more striking are the findings by Sharon Klayman Farber, who interviewed a large number of psychotherapists only to find that

> practicing psychotherapy can impede one's ability to form healthy, fulfilling personal relationships when the relationships with one's own patients [become] the sole source of fulfilling relationships … more prone to mental illness, substance abuse, sexual actingout, and suicide. (2017, p. 37)

It is difficult to believe that psychotherapists are not alarmed by this and are not looking for solutions. Another problem is parochialism. Both the above-mentioned collections of essays by large groups of psychoanalysts (2012, 2013) take into account almost no research data about loneliness. In the same vein, the comprehensive *Handbook of Solitude* (Coplan & Bowker, 2014) includes only one chapter about psychoanalysis (Galanaki, 2014) with hardly any references to contemporary trends, and the most important loneliness researcher does not even mention psychoanalysis in a book of more than 300 pages (Cacioppo & Patrick, 2008). At the same time, the most prominent loneliness scholar is a philosopher (Mijuskovic, 2019), and a branch of philosophical analysis focused on aloneness, named monoseology, is being developed (Domeracki, 2020).

We thus hope to offer a comprehensive treatise of loneliness and solitude, firmly founded in cultural and philosophical contemplations, always consulting epidemiological, developmental, social, and neuroscience research, while retaining a clinical psychoanalytic focus. To achieve that, we tried to provide answers to five questions, which we will summarise here.

What loneliness, what solitude?

One question comes to the fore at the very opening: Is loneliness a psychological phenomenon or an effect (and if so, of what)? Can you avoid loneliness or is it an anthropological condition, impossible to escape (Pohlmann, 2011)? And does loneliness exist in nature, independent of humans?

Many different terms are used when it comes to this topic and throughout this book: aloneness, loneliness, solitude, isolation, withdrawal, seclusion, privacy—these are only some of them. We would like to begin by disentangling them. Luckily, in English, that is not a demanding task, as different terms exist for different states.

The term *aloneness* means that someone is, temporarily or permanently, isolated from other people and does not have anyone to communicate with at that moment. This is a factual and psychological category and does not say anything about possible emotional reactions or wishes to change that situation.

Loneliness is not the state of being alone, though it is often mistaken as such. It is a painful feeling of estrangement or social separation from meaningful others; an emotional lack that concerns a person's place in the world. Although these two states frequently overlap, one can be alone and feel no pain about it or experience utter loneliness while surrounded by people.

At the opposite end, *solitude* is aloneness sought, sometimes even planned and desired, so that one can devote oneself to union with nature, creative activity, or religious ecstasy. The same person can experience aloneness one time as painful (loneliness) and another time as blissful (solitude).

Why loneliness, why solitude?

The first reason to study loneliness and its effects is that it is a widespread, almost universal phenomenon and source of suffering. Recently, even governments have realised that loneliness is a problem they have to try to solve. In the UK, two years before the pandemic, in 2018, a Ministry of Loneliness was established, only a couple of decades after Margaret Thatcher brought forward the idea that "there's no such thing as society", when only self-interest seemed to count, and the "self-against-society" configuration became prominent. Indeed, people living in more individualistic societies report that they experience higher levels of loneliness (Barreto et al., 2021).

The "quantity" goes hand in hand with "quality"—loneliness is painful, difficult to endure, exhausting, both psychologically and physiologically. We now have a very clear picture of its disastrous effects on somatic health (and one chapter of this book is devoted to that) and it has long been obvious that loneliness can be both an important cause and a common consequence of mental disorders. Again, policymakers have to do something about this because loneliness turns out to be very costly if you count the number of work absences, hospitals days, or indeed mortality rates. Many questions open for researchers as well, like what is the reason for loneliness to be so harmful, or how come human kind still has not developed better ways to prevent all this turmoil?

The situation with solitude is, one more time, completely the opposite, in that it is scarce, cherished, and might be instrumental for personality development and creativity. Despite all this, it is not understood nearly well enough and it is even more rarely supported. We can only hypothesise, but it seems that learning how to "guard" one's own and other people's solitude would bring abundant fruit.

Where loneliness, where solitude?

It is also interesting that loneliness can have clear spatial and temporal boundaries. Prisons, for example, are institutions where social isolation, to the level of solitary cells, is used as a form of punishment. And even when some forms of social bond are developed between prisoners, the feelings of loneliness are pervasive, together with shame, alienation, and humiliation. The reasons for this are obvious—this form of aloneness is almost never chosen, there is always an element of coercion in coming to prisons and staying there until "the end of time". The most horrifying examples of this are certainly the Nazi concentration camps and Soviet Gulags, both described by many survivors. The case can be frighteningly similar with psychiatric asylums, as many have witnessed since the memoirs, studies, or novels by the likes of Artaud, Goffman, and Ken Kessey; foster homes, especially for children who are repeatedly forced to move from one to the other; boarding schools, which are believed to cause a specific psychiatric syndrome; migrants in a queue before the administration opens in an early morning hour. Although some people join monasteries, military barracks, or refugee camps voluntarily, not only are some forced to do so but also long-term stays in any of them may lead to chronic isolation and loneliness. There are also unexpected places of loneliness, like hotel rooms, where touring actors and singers, especially after long applauses and feelings of narcissistic fulfilment, have to face empty and impersonal spaces again and again.

At many places of loneliness, the greatest torment is described as not being able or allowed to experience solitude, never having any privacy in the constant presence of unknown others. A recommendation related to this was made couple of decades ago (Deleuze, 1993, p. 188): the problem is not to make people talk, but to provide them with empty spaces of solitude and silence from which they would finally have something to say. The powers of oppression do not prevent people from talking; on the contrary, they force them to do so. But all of a sudden there is so much talking that no one listens and no one knows what to say. An actual therapeutic task for our age could be named—hearing silencing.

There are, however, places of solitude as well. The most readily available is (still) nature, which many use as a retreat, no matter their underlying idea. Stillness, quiet, silence, absence of people and human products—all of this can have recuperating effects on us. Others choose monasteries or other religious institutions to look for a moment of solitude in their search for God or the divine, spiritual, transcendent. And in every hectic and noisy large city, we can nowadays finds many artists' ateliers and scientists' labs, where people isolate even from the beloved ones to be able to focus all their energy on creative work. As a rule, these places have special emotional value because they bear reminders of some valued moments or hopes of their repetition.

What may seem paradoxical is that some of the most relevant places of loneliness today are the internet and social media. The "social" media destruction of human networks produces the loneliness against which social media seem to be the cure. A recent study (Guntuku et al., 2019) compared Twitter messages of 6202 users using the word "lonely" or "alone" with another group of messages matched by age and gender, but without these words. Linguistic analyses were applied to compare both groups with respect to language markers of mental health and whether these markers could predict the frequency of words like "loneliness" and "alone". Using these words indicated eating or sleep disorders, psychosomatic symptoms, and, more generally, open exchange of interpersonal difficulties; correlations between such disorders and the "loneliness"-vocabulary was high.

When loneliness, when solitude?

Does loneliness have a history? Yes, it does, and even twofold—cultural and personal.

Historic changes started during the Early Modern Age, when the focus on personal, private, solitary grew very quickly, particularly through self-portraits, autobiographies, and soliloquies, but also due to the development of sciences, transportation, and large cities. Western societies are said to favour what has been called (political) individualism (Macpherson, 1962); they developed a language for loneliness which frames this new emotional state (Alberti, 2019). Today, we realise that loneliness can be understood by referring to "individualism" only

EDITORS' INTRODUCTION

insufficiently.[1] Individualism also came with a high price. Two centuries were guided by unrestrained exploitation of nature. Epistemic separations of subject and object, established in Europe since the mid-seventeenth century can no longer be used as sharply, and today we gradually realise that this configuration included a "self against the natural world" and we have academic voices that allow us to think of nature as an actor (Latour & Schwibs, 2018).

As this kind of alarm cries have been raised over several years (Latour & Schwibs, 2018), a similar kind of reasoning is produced by psychoanalytic authors (Bollas, 2021; Lemma, 2005) who include in their subtle psychological considerations a rich perception and attentiveness towards political fights and societal changes influencing patients deeply although they are hardly aware of it. One of the created distinctions is the difference between "being seen or being watched" (Lemma, 2009). The wish to be seen meant to be recognised, to be made real in the perceiving eye of a loving person, and psychoanalysts learned from Heinz Kohut the importance of small children's deep desire "to be seen" and to see the gleam in the eye of the mother when she perceives her child. The word "mother", then, served as a substitute for a small social world in which even older children, adolescents, and adults want to be "seen" in order to realise a contact. The idea is that people are endowed with a kind of *sensory membrane* (Berardi, 2011), which is set in vibration by others' gazes (and other forms of exchange) that cannot be expressed in words.[2]

Contemporary social media extended the possibilities of communication in a hitherto completely unknown way, but they cannot replace the role and function of the significant other. They replace "seeing" by "watching"—but all too often by persons completely anonymous. The "significant other", a central term of the early social interaction theory (G. H. Mead, 1932) was considered the constituent of individuality. It had a forerunner under the poetic name of a "soulmate" or a "companion" (Braten, 2013), someone to be found complementing one's own incompleteness. This metaphor of completing one's self has traces in distant history. It meant the coherent fitting of soul, body, and state, and can be found in the myth by Aristophanes as retold in Plato's *Symposium*. Man and woman in ancient times, Aristophanes tells us, formed a unit, so full of happiness and joy that the gods became envious and split this unit into two. We mention it here to show why "communication" alone excludes the "significant other" and leads to loneliness. "To communicate" has changed its meaning and is widely understood as delivering sheer information via digital media, while Latin *communicare* meant "to share" one's presence with others.

It is also possible to think that the experience of loneliness changes with age in an individual's life. Although we can never reach complete autonomy from others, it does seem that with time our dependent needs become less urgent or less a matter of life and death. In the beginning, another person regulates our hunger, warmth, cleanliness, as well as the state of

---

[1] The Japanese example of Hikikomori (Teo et al., 2014)—young adolescents who stay for months or even years in their homes—shows that individualism is only one component on a path to understanding loneliness.

[2] Infant researchers named this "together-knowledge" (Braten, 2013, p. 158).

our nascent self—or its very existence. This function then becomes internalised and turns into a progressively more mature capacity to enjoy time on one's own (albeit in the presence of the invisible form of the other inside oneself). This is, however, a very optimistic (and perforce superficial) description of a process that can go awry at countless corners. Some children indeed grow up in overwhelming aloneness (which we usually call neglect). They can be in the physical presence of parents who are divorced, self-obsessed, depressed, drunk, work double shifts, or they are separated from parents partly or altogether. The consequence of this can be the lack of social skills necessary for sharing inner experiences with others (outward loneliness, as it were) and the incapacity to understand one's own behaviour, choices, or decisions, which can result in a specific type of inner loneliness. Sometimes children invent a phantasy comrade in order to overcome the agony of being alone.

But loneliness can haunt us long after the childhood is over. The largest ever survey about loneliness (46,054 subjects from 237 countries—Barreto et al., 2021) found that it has its most painful effects on young men from individualistic countries and that it decreases with age. So it seems that young men lack some socio-emotional skills to establish bonds that prevent the feeling of isolation that most people acquire over time. Alternatively, it could be that by old age other people become less important and we turn to other priorities or preparations to die.[3]

Finally, loneliness may be more frequent or resonate more prominently at specific points of our lives. At the times of loss, we may miss the beloved intensely and lose hope that overcoming loneliness will ever be possible; while recovering from mental disorders, and especially if stigmatised, we may feel that no one can or indeed wants to understand us; in the cases of political persecution or silencing, victims may feel abandoned even by the one-time closest friends and be incapable of showing who they actually are.

How loneliness, how solitude?

The simplest illustration for a How-question is to think of people who feel lonely—and others have withdrawn from them. To understand them, we will use the so-called "P-theory" (Causadias, 2020), which focuses on the following four elements in order to better analyse culture:

- "*People* refer to population dynamics, social relations, and culture in groups, including families, communities, and nations" (Causadias, 2020, p. 315)
- As already discussed, there are *places* where loneliness is strongly experienced
- *Participation* rules widely determine one's loneliness. In the evening outside a discotheque, the bouncers sort out who is allowed in and who is not; not observing a dress code leads to

---

[3] Storr (1988, pp. 168–184) has noticed a specific form of solitude among creative persons in old age, which he calls "the third period", when the works are 1) less concerned with communication, 2) unconventional in form, 3) show no need to convince, and are 4) "exploring remote areas of experience which are intrapersonal or suprapersonal rather than interpersonal".

exclusion; people in certain neighbourhoods never get to have their children attend certain schools or universities

- *Practices* of imposition on young girls in a school class have been carefully described (Goodwin, 2006, pp. 223ff.). Coming from a certain neighbourhood and community engagement with lower socio-economic status are reasons enough for the feeling of loneliness to increase.

Among many possible examples, we will focus here on the so-called lone-wolf terrorists. The name of lone-wolf is an ideological right-wing invention to endow these people with an aura of heroism. However, researchers show that these people announce their deeds and more often than not communicate to their companions via the internet that they are on the way and express wonder that nobody reacts to their threats. School bombers behave similarly: they tend to show their weapons to classmates the day before the action, announce their deeds and talk via the internet. There is a strong impression that they all plead to be stopped.

Power is one of the core features in understanding *how* loneliness (and many other social phenomena) is produced. "Power is executed over people, in places, by practices" (Causadias, 2020, p. 318), and it defines human relationships in many direct and indirect ways, in fine-grained levels and a rich variety of frames, and often results in the production of (hidden) shame. When it comes to loneliness, the role of power has already been briefly mentioned here. The experience of aloneness crucially depends on whether it is voluntary or imposed. If I choose, or even better, organise it myself, it can be an enjoyable solitary time. But if others decide and enforce on me that I have to spend long or unlimited or unpredictable time in a camp, prison, asylum, I may try to protest and rebel but will most probably end up humiliated and lonely.

Treating loneliness, enhancing solitude?

What then can we offer those haunted by loneliness? And are there ways to support or protect solitude, in oneself and in others?

Can loneliness be cured like a malady or is it an overall human condition? Some strongly recommend to "do nothing" (Odell, 2019), to refrain from attention economy, to switch off your computer, not start a day with reading emails—and to regain the ability to observe bees in a garden, to hear the birds sing, to listen to the rain, to enjoy nature's beauty and silence in a forest. Yes—but there are devastated and destroyed landscapes where no birds sing, and no raindrops fall. They are silent but this silence frightens us. No simple solutions and quick fixes were discovered throughout the history of human kind for a problem as complex as loneliness. Whatever stands opposite to loneliness—friendship, love, family, community, psychotherapy, you name it—are phenomena equally complex to understand and fragile to sustain in one's actual social life.

The other consequence of the invention of modern loneliness, which was previously outlined here, is that in modern days even solitude is often understood in a medical fashion and has lost its positive connotation. And this includes treatment programmes. Today there are thousands of self-help books that promise to help readers find their special one; there are also numerous books, guides, and programmes set up to support lonely people in their search for love, and even suicide-pacts arranged by those who do not succeed (Alberti, 2019, p. 79). Practising psychotherapy today is confronted with the strong influence of such suicide-pacts offered in the "social" media. "Involuntary celibates" (INCELs) aggressively fight against the assumed injustice of being excluded from "access" to women they find attractive.

These five questions pose great challenges to scientists, practitioners, and actually everyone who faces loneliness or enjoys solitude. This book is an attempt to shed light on these multifaceted phenomena that are everywhere around us yet remain under-investigated. We hope that the following twenty chapters will contribute to their profound understanding, help the lonely, be it patients or analysts, become better able to voice their loneliness, and support those in search of solitude that may be instrumental in reaching new insights.

References

Akhtar, S. (2009). *Comprehensive Dictionary of Psychoanalysis*. New York: Routledge.

Alberti, F. B. (2019). *A Biography of Loneliness: The History of an Emotion*. Oxford: Oxford University Press.

Barreto, M., Victor, C., Hammond, C., Eccles, A., Richins, M. T., & Qualter, P. (2021). Loneliness around the world: Age, gender, and cultural differences in loneliness. *Personality and Individual Differences*, *169*: 110066.

Berardi, F. (2011). *After the Future*. Oakland, CA: AK Press.

Bollas, C. (2021). *Three Characters: Narcissist, Borderline, Manic Depressive*. Bicester, UK: Phoenix.

Braten, S. (2013). *Roots and Collapse of Empathy. Human Nature at Its Best and at Its Worst. Advances in Consciousness Research*. Amsterdam, the Netherlands: John Benjamins. Retrieved from http://gbv.eblib.com/patron/FullRecord.aspx?p=1249354 (last accessed August 19, 2021).

Buechler, S. (1998). The analyst's experience of loneliness. *Contemporary Psychoanalysis*, *34*(1): 91–113.

Buechler, S. (2012). Someone to watch over me. In: B. Willock, L. C. Bohm, & R. C. Curtis (Eds.), *Loneliness and Longing: Conscious and Unconscious Aspects* (pp. 13–27). London: Routledge.

Cacioppo, J. T., & Patrick, W. (2008). *Loneliness: Human Nature and the Need for Social Connection*. New York: W. W. Norton.

Causadias, J. M. (2020). What is culture? Systems of people, places, and practices. *Applied Developmental Science*, *24*(4): 310–322.

Coplan, R. J., & Bowker, J. C. (Eds.) (2014). *The Handbook of Solitude: Psychological Perspectives on Social Isolation, Social Withdrawal, and Being Alone*. New York: Wiley-Blackwell, 2021.

Deleuze, G. (1993). *Unterhandlungen (übers. von Gustav Roßler)*. Frankfurt, Germany: Suhrkamp.

Domeracki, P. (2020). Three rival versions of a correlation between solitude and communitiveness in a monoseological discourse. *Paedagogia Christiana*, *45*(1): 23–36.

Farber, S. K. (Ed.) (2017). *Celebrating the Wounded Healer Psychotherapist: Pain, Post-traumatic Growth and Self-disclosure*. Abingdon, UK: Routledge.

Galanaki, E. (2014). The origins of beneficial solitude: psychoanalytic perspectives. In: R. J. Coplan & J. C. Bowker (Eds.), *The Handbook of Solitude: Psychological Perspectives on Social Isolation, Social Withdrawal, and Being Alone* (pp. 58–74). New York: Wiley-Blackwell, 2021.

Goodwin, M. H. (2006). *The Hidden Life of Girls. Games of Stance, Status, and Exclusion*. Malden, MA: Blackwell.

Greene, M., & Kaplan, B. L. (1978). Aspects of loneliness in the therapeutic situation. *International Review of Psychoanalysis, 5*: 321–330.

Guntuku, S. C., Schneider, R., Pelullo, A., Young, J., Wong, V., Ungar, L., Polsky, D., Volpp, K. G., & Merchant, R. (2019). Studying expressions of loneliness in individuals using Twitter: An observational study. *BMJ Open, 9*(11): e030355. https://doi.org/10.1136/bmjopen-2019-030355.

Latour, B., & Schwibs, B. (2018). *Das terrestrische Manifest*. Berlin: Suhrkamp.

Lemma, A. (2005). The many faces of lying. *International Journal of Psychoanalysis, 86*: 737–753.

Lemma, A. (2009). Being seen or being watched? A psychoanalytic perspective on body dysmorphia. *International Journal of Psychoanalysis, 90*: 753–771.

Lynch, A. A. (2013). Introduction. In: A. K. Richards, L. Spira, & A. A. Lynch (Eds.), *Encounters with Loneliness: Only the Lonely* (pp. xiv–xx). Astoria, NY: International Psychoanalytic Books.

Macpherson, C. B. (1962). *The Political Theory of Possessive Individualism: Hobbes to Locke*. Oxford: Oxford University Press.

Mead, G. H. (1932). *Mind, Self and Society*. Chicago, IL: University of Chicago Press.

Mijolla, A. D. (Ed.) (2005). *International Dictionary of Psychoanalysis (vol. 1)* [*Dictionnaire international de la psychanalyse: enhanced American version*.] Detroit, MI: Thomson/Gale.

Mijuskovic, B. L. (2019). *Consciousness and Loneliness: Theoria and Praxis*. Leiden, the Netherlands: Brill.

Odell, J. (2019). *How to Do Nothing: Resisting the Attention Economy*. New York: Melville House.

Pohlmann, F. (2011). Einsamkeit. Anthropologische Erkundungen eines Gefühlszustandes. *Merkur—Deutsche Zeitschrift für europäisches Denken, 65*(740): 44–55.

Richards, A. K., Spira, L., & Lynch, A. A. (Eds.) (2013). *Encounters with Loneliness: Only the Lonely*. Astoria, NY: International Psychoanalytic Books.

Schafer, R. (1995). Aloneness in the countertransference. *Psychoanalytic Quarterly, LXIV*: 496–516.

Storr, A. (1988). *Solitude: A Return to the Self*. New York: Free Press.

Teo, A. R., Stafflebam, K. W., & Kato, T. A. (2014). The intersection of culture and solitude: the Hikikomori phenomenon in Japan. In: J. C. Bowker & R. J. Coplan (Eds.), *The Handbook of Solitude: Psychological Perspectives on Social Isolation, Social Withdrawal, and Being Alone* (pp. 445–460). Chichester, UK: John Wiley & Sons.

Waldinger, R. (2015). What makes a good life? Lessons from the longest study on happiness. *Harvard Study of Adult Development, 28*(8). Retrieved from https://ecole-commercer.com/IMG/pdf/80_years_study_hapiness_harvard.pdf.

Willock, B., Bohm, L. C., & Coleman Curtis, R. (Eds.) (2012). *Loneliness and Longing: Conscious and Unconscious Aspects*. New York: Routledge.

Part I

Philosophy and culture

Introduction to Part I

Aleksandar Dimitrijević

Loneliness and solitude long predate psychoanalysis, both as universal human experiences and as variously defined and approached concepts. Philosophers, poets, playwrights—so many people have written about loneliness that it can even be seen as a primary reason for writing. And this seems to have been the case all around the globe and in different epochs. Add to this all those unpublished—often using definitions hidden from everyone—diaries, journals, unsent letters, and tearful nights, unreciprocated passions, bodily aches, ascetic lives, neglectful childhoods (and so much more), and it will immediately become evident that everyone knows what loneliness is and wants to avoid, shorten, overcome, or suppress it. The trope is slightly different when it comes to solitude, which is often idealised and romanticised, but again always noted, discussed, revered, a cause of envy as much as adoration.

Not only have psychoanalysts been strangely silent about loneliness and solitude, but also their contributions are not solidly founded on these diverse traditions of "loneliness research" or narratives about it. For instance, the three seminal psychoanalytic papers about loneliness (see Chapters 15 and 16 of this volume) are all written without a single serious attempt to establish a dialogue with other approaches to the phenomenon. One is even tempted to think that all major problems of psychoanalytic theory stem from its chronic loneliness, even isolation.

This book opens, therefore, with several chapters that elucidate the history of our understanding of loneliness and provide context for the psychoanalytic ones. Our contributors dive into different sources of knowledge to bring back to us the pearls of insight about the bliss of solitude and the perils of loneliness. Be it philosophy, literature or film analysis, musicology, or epidemiology and neuroscience, the perspectives and information provided will prove invaluable for every future contemplation about loneliness.

The first section is titled "Philosophy and culture" and consists of four chapters. In the first one, Jagna Brudzinska uses her double expertise as a philosopher and psychoanalyst both to demonstrate the genealogy of philosophical interpretations of loneliness from Plato to St Augustin, from Jaspers to Husserl (who is the focus of her research and editorial activities), and to draw connections to the contemporary theories of intersubjectivity.

With his unprecedented reliability, Colum Kenny reviews numerous approaches to solitude in religious and ascetic traditions from different continents and historical periods. His apparent interest is in W. B. Yeats, but he elaborates on the risk of monastic isolation, the search for the middle way, and returns to the inspiring legacy of Thomas Merton.

Michael Buchholz is not only a seasoned clinical psychoanalyst but also a prolific social scientist and professor of social psychology. In his first chapter in this book, he focuses on a widely discussed and urgent problem of the (possible) psychological basis of terrorist acts. Because many perpetrators fit the popular image of a "lone wolf", loneliness has often been seen as an actual cause of these homicidal (and often suicidal at the same time) acts. Buchholz here not only reviews different interpretations of this phenomenon, but also concludes with a list of possible ways to overcome this loneliness.

In the final chapter of this section, Aleksandar Dimitrijevic searches for the historical beginnings of the now widespread experiences of preserving a private self and solitude. With its large cities, social networks, and (forthcoming) sociable robots, contemporary Western society represents a paradox of the impossibility of finding solitude and the simultaneous haunting dread of loneliness. It may, thus, be difficult for us to imagine the world of the twelfth century when, as historians claim, solitude became possible for the first time, to become prominent only at the time of Montaigne, and reach its peak in Hamlet's soliloquies.

These four chapters are planned to draw the most expansive horizon of "loneliness studies". Building on it, the next section will portray some segments of artistic and literary representations of loneliness and solitude.

CHAPTER 1

The hidden sociality of the solitary subject: phenomenological and psychoanalytical reflections on loneliness

Jagna Brudzińska

Already with Socrates, Western philosophy reaches the insight that the path towards truth goes through loneliness. However, only in modernity the figure of *solus ipse* is claimed as the absolute measure of everything and every knowledge. The individual ego is burdened with the solitary exploration and explanation of the world and thereby faces sociality as an unsolved problem. In the twentieth century, both phenomenology and psychoanalysis achieve a re-evaluation. They discover the primary intersubjective structure of the ego. They observe that the ego is inhabited by others, even in its primary loneliness. On the one hand, phenomenology discovers the primary intersubjective structure of the ego and thereby overcomes the traditional singularity of the individual consciousness. On the other hand, psychoanalysis discloses such relationality even in the dimension of the unconscious. For both, the primary bodily condition of the human subject is crucial as a requirement for individualisation. My aim in this chapter is to clarify the phenomenon of loneliness in its constitutive relation to sociality.

In the following, I offer a philosophical perspective on the intimate interlocking between loneliness and sociality. In order to come closer to this connection, I design a philosophical-historical perspective that makes no claim to completeness. Many theses can only be outlined symptomatically. The chapter rather makes an attempt to show how the leitmotif of solitary sociality and social loneliness runs through the entire history of Western philosophy, and at demonstrating its high hermeneutic value.

Through pain to truth

Western philosophy is firmly rooted in the ideal of self-knowledge. Socrates (469–399 BC) linked the search for truth to insight into one's own inner self and declared the Delphic oracle's

"Know thyself" to be the obligatory guide for a blissful life (i.e. Plato, 370 BC). But what or who is the self? Already the pre-Socratic philosophy uncovers and aims at exploring the inner dimension of the human being and its connection to the socio-political situation of ancient polis. Sophism, in particular, makes its mark here. For the Sophists, paradigmatically in the doctrine of the affects, which Gorgias of Leontini summarised in his speeches to Helena in the fifth century BC, the human being is internally filled with affects, which are subject to influences and manipulations (Poulakos, 1983). Speech, as logos, when used skilfully, is able to influence the passions of man. Language is therefore an effective power. This discovery is tremendously important when it comes to the socio-political contexts of Attic democracy. Sophistic is the art of oratory that aims to exert powerful influence in the leading of the polis' life. It is the art of rhetoric that teaches how to deal with the emotions, propagating the positive valuation of the pleasant and pleasurable over pain and suffering (Kerferd, 1981).

It is precisely this valuation, however, that prompts Socrates to his philosophical and socio-political radical critique, as expressed in *Gorgias*, one of Plato's (380 BC) early dialogues. Socrates decouples truth from the simple experience of pleasure and ties it to virtue. Virtue can certainly be achieved through pain and does not require the satisfaction of personal needs, neither as a presupposition nor as its goal. According to Socrates, accepting pain and suffering is morally preferable to acting wickedly. Famously, this insight is brought to full fruition in his own dramatic decision to die for the truth. For the first time in Western philosophy, Socrates chooses the path of loneliness as morally valuable. But this is a special form of solitude: the path of the solitary search for truth as the path of research and exploration of the inner horizon. This is the first time that truth is not sought in the outer world, but in the inner man. It is a truth that demands absolute honesty and is intertwined with the moral quality of the subject.

For Socrates, being honest with oneself means critically questioning his own motives and remaining uninfluenced by external conditions and temptations. In our times, this call for self-knowledge as a path of ethical and moral renovation of the human being is clearly stated concerning the horrors brought about by the First World War by Edmund Husserl in his 1923 essays for the Japanese journal *Kaizo* (Husserl, 1922–37).

The motif of anti-opportunism is so strong in this context that it determines Socrates's own fate. This is the most significant representation of what it means that truth can only ever have a moral nature. Truth is not a business of pure theory but is always rooted in the practice of life. It demands the involvement and engagement of the whole man. Whereas sophistry discovers the permeability and thus also the manipulability of the human being and makes use of it, the Socratic ideal demands a permanence of the human character which is best appreciated in the strenuous loneliness of the search for truth. This paves the way for the demand for autonomy of individual existence.

The high song of loneliness

The Socratic ideal bears fruit in Christianity. Here, a philosophy of inwardness develops, in which both the idealisation of suffering as a path to truth and the further exploration of human inwardness and spirituality progress. In the fourth century AD St Augustine represents a decisive stage in this process. His motto *Noli foras ire, in te ipsum redi, in interiore homine habitat veritas* ("Do not wish to go out; go back into yourself. Truth dwells in the inner man") (Augustine, 390; Byers, 2013) will be an important inspiration for Husserl who will quote this famous passage in the *Cartesian Meditations* (1929), the work dedicated to the phenomenological theory of intersubjectivity. For Augustine, truth lies in the full expansion of the human soul, which, however, is not only a mundane interiority, but includes the divine infinity within itself. This is Augustine's paradoxical thinking: the individual and the thus necessarily limited human soul includes the universality of God. This paradox does not solve the problem of loneliness, but it takes it into a new dimension. It is not a condemnation and a blame; it is not a mere inevitability of human life. By becoming aware of his inner self, man rises above himself and attains participation in the greater reality of God. The path of the philosopher that leads through inwardness is a solitary path, but it does not end with death, as it did with Socrates. Rather, it is at once painful and healing. It is a path full of promise. It is the only path of salvation.

In this sense, taking up the philosophy of the Stoa, Boethius (523–4) speaks of the consolation of philosophy (Donato, 2013). From the northern Italian prison where he was awaiting execution, he formulates a high song of aloneness, just as the Canticle sings the high song of love in the Bible. He has been painfully excluded from worldly business, but at the same time he experiences himself as liberated from it. He has conquered the time of inner life and thus eternity by losing everything else. The catastrophic loss and exclusion from public life also affects his relationships with others. Due to his sentence, Boethius has lost the respect of his community and the recognition that can come from fellow human beings. But in his disgrace he is not merely alone: loneliness is in his experience not a mere external condition. Boethius is alone, and only this gives him the freedom to drive his soul towards the sublime. This vertical movement towards God must always struggle against the weight of mundane desires and needs. Among these is the need to escape loneliness. But only solitude ultimately proves to be the path to the perfection of human existence. Only this path leads to authentic bliss.

The connection between loneliness, truth, and virtue, which in Socrates finds expression in the sacrifice of death, reaches a new climax here. The practical dimension is not only involved in the severity of punishment and martyrdom, but also takes the form of bliss. The connection between solitude and bliss is asserted. Solitude means here not mere isolation of the individual self—or, if we want to use a modern term, individual ego. Rather, solitude includes love and God and thus holds a promise of bliss.

The theoretical and ontological loneliness

The connection between loneliness and bliss represents the weak point of modernity and this depends on the peculiar modern conception of subjectivity. Modern philosophy discovers the ego as the centre of consciousness and the reference point of all experience and knowledge. The ego is exalted in its potency and declared to be the measure of all things and all truth. In the concept of self-consciousness, philosophy locates the ultimate ground not only of cognition but also of human dignity (Düsing, 1997). This corresponds with profound social changes. The challenges of the modern world confronted thinkers with egoic crises, crises that regard the ego itself. The result is an isolation that is not automatically compensated for by an increase in practical autonomy. Rather, a significant separation of the theoretical from the practical dimension of life takes place. Self-knowledge is declared a merely theoretical enterprise. Descartes's thinking I becomes the guarantor of knowledge independent of its possibility of achieving individual happiness (Descartes, 1641).

A paradoxical movement emerges. On the one hand, modern philosophy discovers the singular I, the ego, which from now on is to become the title of human interiority. On the other hand, cognitive consciousness is interpreted primarily theoretically. Therefore, the cognitive consciousness loses its practical reference. The I becomes empty of content. As *solus ipse*, it advances in the Enlightenment to an abstract theoretical principle of cognition. It loses its intersubjective reference. Accordingly, the ego must "deduce" its decisions and solutions to the questions of right and wrong only from itself in a sober, affect-free reflection. Practical autonomy becomes coupled to the cold, pitiless loneliness of the ego. The powerful ego is lonely. Every disturbance from outside, every influence remain alien to it.

For explaining this dense isolation of the egoic subjectivity, G. W. Leibniz coined the term "monad" (Leibniz, 1714). The monad indicates a subjectivity understood as a microcosm, as a universe on its own (Di Bella, 2005). The monad has no windows, Leibniz states. And yet it is in deep communication with other monads (Puryear, 2010). The entire creation is reflected in it. Here, Leibniz confronts us with the riddle of communitarisation (*Vergemeinschaftung*). The fact of real, empirical sociality is not self-explanatory. Rather, the thesis of the reciprocal mirroring of the monads opens up a large field of research that has not lost its topicality to this day. The mirroring thesis is currently highly influential within neurobiological research. It was the discovery of the so-called mirror neurons which has been praised since the beginning of the twentieth century, both in science and in the media and society, as a milestone in research into the social structure of the human brain and neurobiological access to the foreign subject (Gallese, 2001, 2002; Rizzolatti et al., 2001). However, neurobiological descriptions are not able to explain the intersubjective sense of the constituting functions of mirroring and its meaning for the genesis of the subject (Brudzińska, 2014a). Phenomenology and psychoanalysis also refer to the concept of mirroring. In his *Cartesian Meditations* Husserl extensively deals with the problem of communalisation. He mentions here the phenomenon of mirroring as an explicitly motivational process. He stresses that monads do not simply reflect each other. They rather affect and motivate each other, even if in a pre-reflexive way. Mirroring is for Husserl no neutral reflection (Husserl, 1929–35, p. 191). Subjects bear each other (Husserl, 1929–34). In psychoanalysis it is Jacques Lacan who refers to the metaphor of the mirror. For him the mirror stage of the human infant (6–18 months) is crucial for the building of the ego (Lacan, 1977). However, primarily new psychoanalysis describes concrete mechanisms that can be interpreted as powerful mirroring of others. These imitative mechanisms seem to be decisive for the shaping of the self in the form of a primary intersubjectivity (Gaddini, 1969; see also Brudzińska, 2019).

For Leibniz, to whom the metaphor of mirroring can be traced back, the question about the genesis of the self is not yet present. In his view, albeit being locked in itself, the monad is not isolated. This puts loneliness in a new light. Loneliness is not only the experience and the choice of the truth-seeking ego, but the ontological situation of an ego posited amid other egos. Loneliness is not the result of an individual decision; it is rather ontologically anchored in the structure of the monad. Neither a factual encounter nor a real exchange takes place between monads. Thus, loneliness is inescapable. At the same time, it is not a conscious form of loneliness. Focused on its theoretical attitude towards reality, the monad is not aware of its essential isolation. Being located and interwoven in a universal mirroring system, it leaves its structural loneliness unthematic. Embedded in the universal mirroring, the monad does not face its ontological lack of communication, and loneliness remains an ineliminable ontological feature.

The loneliness of the will

Abandoning Leibniz's speculative assumptions, at the culmination of modernity Immanuel Kant sharpened the thesis of the transcendental subject taken in its solipsistic position. The pure ego of Kant's critique of reason, which appeared in 1781, is stripped of every empirical, social, and communal sphere and functions alone and only as a principle of autonomy (Kant, 1781). The question of loneliness or communication with others no longer even arises. An egoic power reigns over experience. Such power not only accompanies, but, as Kant puts it, *must* accompany all experiences of the ego (transcendental I). It is an unbreakable necessity, grounded in the very structure of reason.

Thus, egoic omnipotence reaches its climax in the history of the Occident. Kant's ego principle is invulnerable. The invincible ego becomes the principle not only of theoretical but also of practical autonomy. In the practical sphere, the power of the ego takes the form of a merciless inner judge. The modern separation of theory and practice is seemingly overcome. However, for Kant, it is not a matter of a union or equivalence in the mutual relationship of the practical and theoretical use of reason. Rather, practical autonomy is subordinate to theoretical autonomy and must justify itself before it (Kant, 1788).

Such an intensification of the thesis of the powerful ego meets with effective resistance in the nineteenth century. The strong self-transparent and self-confident ego is called into question. Schopenhauer's and Nietzsche's reflections challenge the idealist paradigm. These authors overtly contest the compulsive corset imposed on the *solus ipse*. They sense and give voice to the unconscious dark forces of the human soul that remain inaccessible to reflection or even threaten it. As Sigmund Freud put it a generation later, they show that the ego is not the master in its own house. The process of disempowerment of the strong, impenetrable ego was set in motion.

However, as has been sketched above, the strength of the ego was linked to its loneliness, its inner impenetrability. Does this progressive disempowerment of the ego automatically mean a breaking of loneliness? The ego is questioned in its omnipotence and deprived of its power. It shows its weakness and its inner opacity. But in doing so, it discovers a new form of strength: the potency of its own will (Schopenhauer, 1819). Schopenhauer succeeds in finding a metaphysical ground to the egoic subjectivity in its blind striving will. Here, the inversion of the relationship between practice and theory in modernity takes place. Following this lead, Schopenhauer calls into question the naive belief in the ego as a pure centre of ideas. The ego does not really have control over what it wills itself. Its will does not obey reason and does not follow its representations. The subject does not "know" what she or he wants but experiences the world through wills and desires. The practical principle of pure will as a blind and initially aimless life instinct dominates and determines every cognitive achievement. This domination of an all-pervading will does not only empower the subject. It also provides the ground for its suffering and isolation. The striving I does not escape loneliness, it does not escape itself, it struggles in building up relationships with others. The discovery of the power of the will brings with it a new form of suffering. The ego experiences the intertwining between desire and suffering, between powerful will and unbroken loneliness.

Loneliness and individuality

Schopenhauer's thoroughly metaphysical speculation bears its fruits into the twentieth century. The connection between ego and loneliness thus seems to be independent of whether the I is intended as a strong or weak subject, whether it is a powerful and controlling instance or an ego at the mercy of unknown powerful forces. In the twentieth century, Karl Jaspers formulates: "To be 'I' is to be lonely" (Jaspers, 1916–17, p. 390). By simply being, the I is a lonely instance; it always establishes a distance, draws a circle around itself. Although he did not see himself as an existentialist, but as a philosopher of existence, Jaspers expresses in this passage the basic existentialist feeling of the twentieth century. Loneliness is no longer simply the consequence of a personal decision. To be lonely or not to be lonely is not a choice. At the same time, loneliness is not an ontological character of subjectivity, as observed regarding Leibniz's monad. Rather, loneliness is a fundamental situation of human existence, insofar as this can be assessed as an egoic existence. Only by giving up one's own ego can one possibly escape loneliness, thereby however accepting to live an inauthentic life.

Here, we face an interesting circularity. According to Jaspers, loneliness only exists for egoic individuals. The egoic individual, however, only exists in society. Being lonely therefore requires and presupposes, according to Jaspers, the horizon of community. Loneliness as an individual phenomenon is experienced in a structure of tension. On the one hand, there operates the striving for individuality and thus the urge towards loneliness; on the other hand, the individual condition is the ground for suffering and thus provokes the urge out of loneliness. Loneliness is thus never understood in a unipolar way, but always in relation to and in tension with the social situation of the human being. Only those who are connected to society can also be lonely. To be excluded from society means an inner death and the extinction of the individuality of the ego.

Based on such a radical claim, Jaspers distinguishes between two forms of loneliness: a heroic solitude and a suffered, involuntary loneliness. Heroic solitude recalls Socrates's sacrifice for truth and Boethius's affirmation of the sublime in the experience of aloneness. According to Jaspers, a heroically solitary person is the one who fulfils his or her achievement and destiny despite contrary expectations placed upon him or her by society. A heroically solitary person goes against the tide of conformity, renounces immediate recognition, lives up to his individuality, thus accepting his responsibility not only for himself but also for society. In the philosophy of Martin Heidegger, this heroic solitude is placed under the demand of authenticity of the person in his history.

The opposite pole to this is "suffered loneliness". Jaspers's implicit valuation is unmistakable here. The person who merely suffers loneliness gives up his individuality instead of realising it. He reduces his being to a merely social, for example, externally determined and dependent one. In the words of Martin Heidegger, the one who merely suffers loneliness becomes an impersonal "man" of history (Heidegger, 1927).

This strong value polarisation culminates in the following paradox. Man becomes lonely in a negative sense when he or she allows himself or herself to be determined by society. Conformism leads to a painful kind of sociality that brings with it loneliness or, better, inner isolation. The tension Jaspers creates between heroic and suffered loneliness seems very dramatic. We are almost confronted with Kierkegaard's Either/Or (1843), as herald of an insoluble conflict. From a psychoanalytical point of view, it appears here as a conflict between autonomy and dependency or even between control and subordination. However, such an evaluation of autonomy as a positive form of loneliness and dependency as a negative form tears the horizon of human development and therefore reduces its potential. The phenomenological-existentialistic reflection seems here to deteriorate into an idealisation of the independency of the human being. Does this solution do justice to our existential situation? Jaspers himself attempts to answer the question by describing various ideal-typical forms of intersubjective understanding as coping mechanisms for loneliness, stressing thereby the tension between love and power as regulation sources of human relationships. All these forms, however, are set at the level of a mature individual who is capable of self-reflection.

After all, for Jaspers, loneliness is not simply there, it is constituted, it arises. To feel lonely, a person must grasp his or her social existence as a self-conscious individual. We are dealing here with a highly reflexive phenomenon. Phenomenologically speaking, loneliness here becomes the correlate of the self-consciousness of a fully developed individual. With this statement, on the one hand, we reach the limits of the classical paradigm of the singularity of the ego, and on the other hand, we uncover the limits of the dominating reflective model of self-consciousness. It is phenomenology and psychoanalysis that make it possible to go beyond these two barriers, to think of "egological" singularity in a new way, and to grasp deeper processes of personality

Egological and primary intersubjectivity

As far as the social location of human subjectivity is concerned, Edmund Husserl (1929–35), in his phenomenology of the person, distinguishes between egoistic and social attitudes. He states that human life is of two kinds: "Man lives either asocially or socially" (p. 511). The same activities can be performed either as a member of society or in isolation, withdrawn into one's own private sphere. Whether it is a walk or a meal, we can do it alone and in our private sphere, or in the company of others, in the exchange of society.

In this relationship, however, for Husserl, belonging to a co-world is a primary condition. Only by starting from an original common world can the question of the difference between a private and a common sphere arise. Phenomenology sets itself the task of questioning the genesis of this common world and not simply taking it as a fact.

According to common understanding, phenomenology starts from an already individuated subject (ego) and asks about the communitarisation of such individuated ego (cf. Yamaguchi, 1982; Zahavi, 1996). The term "communitarisation" refers to the way in which an already individuated subject comes into contact with others. The focus lies on the way in which the ego realises its connection with others (Husserl, 1929, §55). To elucidate such a process, we need to ask: how does it come about that we are individuated subjects at all or, better, that we become such? This is the characteristic question that genetic phenomenology—as a new approach developed by Edmund Husserl (Brudzińska, 2021)—pursues and that involves a radical reversal of our perspective: we no longer ask how the ego is able to discover other egos in its world and break out of loneliness; rather, we ask how an ego becomes an individual in the first place, how does it discover and determine itself, how does it develop the ability not only to be alone, but to relate to its loneliness?

This is a question also tackled by modern psychoanalysis. In the last section, I will discuss Donald W. Winnicott's (1958) powerful contribution about the capacity to be alone. Before that, however, we need to introduce a last meaningful phenomenological notion that can provide a decisive contribution to the interpretation of loneliness.

In his research manuscripts dating from the 1930s, within the framework of the genetic-phenomenological approach, Edmund Husserl formulated the thesis of "primary intersubjectivity" of the human subject (Husserl, 1929–35, pp. 154–155). With this expression, he suggests that the subject or ego is always characterised by intersubjectivity at its core. The ego is not a self-contained monad, and the other does not appear ex post in the history of the subject's experience. Rather, every human being interacts with others from the very beginning of its existence. This has a profound effect on the process of subjective individuation. Even more, individuation could not take place at all without this primary, highly performative context.

Husserl is, of course, bound to the philosophical tradition of the thinking ego-subject, but he considers such a subject in a new way. By coining the somewhat paradoxical term "egological intersubjectivity", he highlights profound and powerful intersubjective connections that determine the ego in its concretion. The egological subject is not only originally dependent on others, as implied by the notion of primary intersubjectivity, but is entangled with the other in multiple ways.

Adaptation to others here is no longer interpreted as the devalued phenomenon of coping with the negative experience of loneliness, or, in Jasper's words, of merely suffering loneliness. Rather, Husserl unfolds primary sociality as a universal structure of intersubjectivity that carries each ego in its own egological self-organisation. It is the one indissoluble structure of being-for-one-another (Husserl, 1929–35, p. 191).

Husserl explains that the original being-for-one-another does not consist of a mere representation of the other in its own inner world. Contact with the other is also not exhausted in a mere reflection or representation. In this sense, Leibniz's (1714) monadic conception is overcome. Rather, we are dealing with a specific kind of efficacy that points back to relations of mutual dependence within personal experience. On this basis, the ego is, from the beginning, only "relatively" itself. It only partially owns itself: it can only be what it is as a "member" (*socius*) of a primary social context.

The social structure, in turn, is not simply made up of independent members and does not consist of a complete set of subjects. It is not a juxtaposition of separate elements within a neutral structure, but involves integral moments linked into an original social unity. To understand this structure, reference to Kurt Lewin's model of the field can be helpful (Lewin, 1951). The elements within the field can be explained only in terms of their internal relationality and not as independent parts of a whole. Modern psychoanalysis still works with this model, but with reference to the understanding of the psychoanalytical situation as a dynamic field in which several actors are involved (Baranger & Baranger, 2008).

From a genetic-phenomenological point of view, the primary social unit presents itself as a pre-egological form of life that is characterised by an instinctive-affective and bodily organised interrelation of tendencies, needs, desires, and drives. My thesis is that this social structure can best be imagined as the interaction of emotively acting, originally plural consciousnesses (Brudzińska, 2014b). Such a consciousness cannot be reduced to a singular and reflexive consciousness but refers to an emotive subjectivity that corresponds to Husserl's notion of a "concrete personal subject" (Husserl, 1912–16, pp. 216–217). The concrete personal bodily subject forms a constantly developing context that is in permanent reflective and pre-reflective, bodily, instinctive, and affective exchange and involvement with other subjects and with the surrounding world (Husserl, 1912–16, pp. 194ff.). The person as such is a comprehensive, psychic context that constantly arrives at its own individuation through reciprocal motivation, which can only be understood from the experienced inner perspective. This description clearly excludes the characterisation of the person as a self-contained monad. Rather, the person appears here as an affective structure constantly achieving her own individuation through reciprocal motivation in relation with others. As such, she can only be understood from the experienced inner perspective. This understanding is no solitary enterprise; it rather needs a responsive other who is able to co-perform one's own experiences.

Being alone and being lonely

Philosophical-historical reconstruction has so far attempted, albeit sketchily, to show how Western thought has defined the difference between being alone and being lonely. The first—being alone—is a merely external and contingent determination. With Husserl, we can speak of withdrawal into the private sphere. Being lonely, on the other hand, is a subjective experience that can also take place in the company of others. In the framework created by the concept of primary intersubjectivity, this difference can be rethought. Being alone and being lonely are no longer two independent phenomena but belong together in a dynamic that becomes understandable against the background of the individuation of the ego.

Starting from the thesis of primary intersubjectivity and the understanding of the ego as a primarily relational structure, it becomes clear that not simply being alone, but also the capacity to be alone is the result of a constitutive process. The capacity to be alone must not be theoretically presupposed. It is not given a priori and is not simply determined by the fact that we are bodily separated subjects. Rather, it is a subjective ability that must first be developed in experience. Whether this succeeds does not simply depend on the individual concerned, but on a complex developmental process in which the immature ego responds to a holding environment that adequately answers its needs. Only gradually does the ego develop a demarcation, its own membrane that encompasses its inner organisation.

Donald W. Winnicott (1958), who has devoted an important study into this process, emphasises that the basis of the capacity to be alone is the experience of being alone in the presence of the other. With this concept of aloneness, we are no longer in the external situation of a Robinson Crusoe. Rather, we are dealing with a primary intersubjective process considered from the experienced inner perspective—as an unconscious process. The immature ego participates in the capacity of the other to provide support. An infant with a still very weak ego organisation receives support and protection. Only then can he gradually explore the world and discover his needs. In this process, the psychic membrane grows, which allows us to distinguish between our own needs and those of others. This is an ability that is a lifelong challenge for us, precisely because of our original intersubjective genesis. These processes are not self-reflective, of course, but are essentially bodily and inscribe themselves firmly in our corporeality.

Winnicott emphasises that in this process the ego-supporting, facilitating environment is gradually internalised. The support experienced is incorporated into the emerging ego structure. Only then can physical aloneness become psychologically bearable and transform into the experience of solitude. Being alone no longer means being in the void. Rather, in the inner solitude and in the associated developed capacity to be alone, one is confronted with the internalised objects of primary intersubjectivity. Thus, in the experience of being lonely, I am no longer alone.

Solitude becomes a dimension in which I experience the effect of my inner others and live through them. My capacity for loneliness depends on the quality of these primary object relations. When alone, I am then hopeful or fearful, I can live it and use it as a positive source for my creativity or fear it as a horror scenario and suffer a breakdown. The decision to act heroically or merely to suffer is not an individual decision of a strong and in principle autonomous ego. Rather, it is related to my developmental history and the history of my object relations.

The most important of those objects have left traces that have enabled or prevented me from experiencing loneliness. This does not mean that the human being lacks all freedom. However, the spaces of his possibility are not ideally open, but always predetermined by the concrete path of development (Khan, 1983; Winnicott, 1967). Loneliness seems to be one of these spaces of possibility, which the ego does not create alone, but always in the intimate work of development, involved with others, who in turn have to be able to get entangled with me and to resonate authentically in our entanglement.

References

Augustine (390). In: L. O. Mink (Ed.) & J. H. S. Burleigh (Trans.), *Of True Religion*. Ann Arbor, MI: University of Michigan Press, Gateway Editions, 1959.

Baranger, M., & Baranger, W. (2008). The analytic situation as a dynamic field. *International Journal of Psychoanalysis*, 89(4): 795–826.

Byers, S. (2013). *Perception, Sensibility, and Moral Motivation in Augustine: A Stoic Platonic Synthesis*. Cambridge: Cambridge University Press.

Boethius (523–4). In: P. G. Walsh (Trans.), *The Consolation of Philosophy*. Oxford: Oxford World's Classics, 2002.

Brudzinska, J. (2014a). Mitvollzug und Fremdverstehen. Zur Phänomenologie und Psychoanalyse der teilnehmenden Erfahrung. *Phänomenologische Forschungen*: 45–76.

Brudzinska, J. (2014b). Becoming a person in the life-world. *Paradigmi. Rivista di Critica Filosofica*, 3: 91–110.

Brudzinska, J. (2019). Imitation and individuation. The creative power of phantasy. *Social Imaginaries*, 5(1): 81–95.

Brudzinska, J. (2021). The genetic turn. Husserl's path toward the concreteness of experience. In: H. Jacobs (Ed.), *The Husserlian Mind* (pp. 129–139). New York: Routledge.

Descartes, R. (1641). In: G. Hefferman (Trans.), *Meditations on First Philosophy*. Notre Dame, IN: University of Notre Dame Press, 1990.

Di Bella, S. (2005). *The Science of the Individual: Leibniz's Ontology of Individual Substance*. Dordrecht, the Netherlands: Springer.

Donato, A. (2013). *Boethius' Consolation of Philosophy as a Product of Late Antiquity*. London: Bloomsbury.

Düsing, K. (1997). *Selbstbewusstseinsmodelle. Moderne Kritiken und systematische Entwürfe zur konkreten Subjektivität*. Munich, Germany: Wilhelm Fink.

16 FROM THE ABYSS OF LONELINESS TO THE BLISS OF SOLITUDE

Gaddini, E. (1969). On imitation. *International Journal of Psychoanalysis, 50*(4): 475–484.

Gallese, V. (2001). The "shared manifold" hypothesis. From mirror neurons to empathy. *Journal of Consciousness Studies, 8*: 33–50.

Gallese, V. (2002). The roots of empathy: the shared manifold hypothesis and the neural basis of intersubjectivity. *Psychopathology, 36*: 171–180.

Heidegger, M. (1927). *Being and Time.* J. Macquarrie & E. Robinson (Trans.). Oxford: Basil Blackwell, 1962.

Husserl, E. (1912–16). *Ideas Pertaining to a Pure Phenomenology and to a Phenomenological Philosophy. Second Book. Studies in the Phenomenology of Constitution.* R. Rojcewicz & A. Schuwer (Trans.). Dordrecht, the Netherlands: Kluwer, 1989.

Husserl, E. (1922–37). *Fünf Aufsätze über Erneuerung.* In: T. Neon & H. R. Sepp (Eds.), *Aufsätze und Vorträge (1922–1937).* Dordrecht, the Netherlands: Kluwer, 1989.

Husserl, E. (1929). *Cartesian Meditations.* D. Cairns (Trans.). The Hague: Martinus Nijhoff, 1960.

Husserl, E. (1929–34). In: D. Lohmar (Ed.), *Späte Texte über Zeitkonstitution (1929–1934): Die C-Manuskripte.* Dordrecht, the Netherlands: Springer, 2006.

Husserl, E. (1929–35). In: I. Kern (Ed.), *Zur Phänomenologie der Intersubjektivität. Part III: 1929–1935.* The Hague: Martinus Nijhoff, 1973.

Jaspers, K. (1916–17). Einsamkeit. In: K. Saner (Ed.), *Revue Internationale de Philosophie, 37*: 390–409.

Kant, I. (1781). *Critique of Pure Reason.* P. Guyer & A. W. Wood (Eds., Trans.). Cambridge: Cambridge University Press, 1999.

Kant, I. (1788). *Critique of Practical Reason.* M. J. Gregor (Trans.). Cambridge: Cambridge University Press, 1997.

Kerferd, G. B. (1981). *The Sophistic Movement.* Cambridge: Cambridge University Press.

Khan, M. M. R. (1983). *Hidden Selves: Between Theory and Praxis of Psychoanalysis.* London: Hogarth.

Kierkegaard, S. (1843). *Either/Or.* H. V. Hong & E. H. Hong (Trans.). Princeton, NJ: Princeton University Press, 2013.

Lacan, J. (1977). The mirror stage as formative of the function of the I. In: A. Sheridan (Ed.), *Écrits, a Selection* (pp. 1–7). London: Tavistock.

Leibniz, G. W. (1714).The principles of philosophy, or, the monadology. In: R. Ariew & D. Garber (Eds., Trans.), *Philosophical Essays.* Indianapolis, IN: Hackett, 1989.

Lewin, K. (1951). *Field Theory in Social Science.* New York: Harper.

Plato (380 BC). *Gorgias.* T. Irwin (Trans.). Oxford: Clarendon Press, 1980.

Plato (370 BC). *Phaedrus.* Cambridge: Cambridge University Press, 1952.

Poulakos, J. (1983). Gorgias' Encomium to Helen and the Defense of Rhetoric. *Rhetorica: A Journal of the History of Rhetoric, 1*(2): 1–16.

Puryear, S. (2010). Monadic interaction. *British Journal for the History of Philosophy, 18*(5): 763–796.

Rizzolatti, G., Fogassi, L., & Gallese, V. (2001). Neurophysiological mechanism underlying the understanding and imitation of action. *Nature Neuroscience, 2*: 661–670.

Schopenhauer, A. (1819). *The World as Will and Representation, Vol. I.* J. Norman, A. Welchman, & C. Janaway (Trans.). Cambridge: Cambridge University Press, 2010.

Winnicott, D. W. (1958). The capacity to be alone. *International Journal of Psychoanalysis, 39*: 416–420.

Winnicott, D. W. (1967). The location of cultural experience. *International Journal of Psychoanalysis, 48*(3): 368–372.

Yamaguchi, I. (1982). *Passive Synthesis und Intersubjektivität bei Edmund Husserl.* The Hague: Kluwer.

Zahavi, D. (1996). *Husserl und die transzendentale Intersubjektivität. Eine Antwort auf die sprachpragmatische Kritik.* Dordrecht, the Netherlands: Kluwer.

CHAPTER 2

"And live alone in the bee-loud glade"? Asceticism, hermitage, and the technologies of the self

Colum Kenny

On London's busy Fleet Street, the Irish poet W. B. Yeats noticed a small water fountain in a shop window. This set him daydreaming amid the noisy traffic, yearning for the peace of a small wooded island that he had known across the sea in County Sligo, Ireland. He was inspired to write his poem "The Lake Isle of Innisfree", which begins:

> I will arise and go now, and go to Innisfree,
> And a small cabin build there, of clay and wattles made:
> Nine bean-rows will I have there, a hive for the honey-bee,
> And live alone in the bee-loud glade.
>
> And I shall have some peace there, for peace comes dropping slow,
> Dropping from the veils of the morning to where the cricket sings …

During his teenage years in Sligo, Yeats had fantasised about conquering bodily desire and withdrawing to seek wisdom on Innisfree. He admired the Massachusetts philosopher and poet Henry David Thoreau of Walden Pond (O'Donnell & Archibald, 1999, pp. 85, 139). However, his lines about Innisfree also echo a well-known ancient Gaelic poem, ostensibly written by an early Irish Christian who yearned to be a hermit:

> I wish, O Son of the living God, O ancient, eternal King,
> For a hidden little hut in the wilderness that it may be my dwelling.

20 FROM THE ABYSS OF LONELINESS TO THE BLISS OF SOLITUDE

An all-grey lithe little lark to be by its side,
A clear pool to wash away sins through the grace of the Holy Spirit.

—Meyer (1913, p. 30)

The south-western Atlantic coast of Ireland is dotted with the remains of small stone cells, known because of their shape as "beehive huts". In these huts hermits once lived ascetic lives. They recited from memory the biblical 150 psalms ("the three fifties") and lived on a sparse diet. Some huts are in clusters that once constituted small communities of individual hermits who were grouped around an oratory shaped like the inverted hull of a boat (basic "eremitic monasteries"), and some stand alone (Henry, 1956–57, pp. 45–46, 157–158).

If both Yeats and the monks longed for solitude, their respective lifestyles were very different. This reflects the fact that there is more than one kind of hermitage, and that there are relative levels of asceticism as well as a number of purposes for which people seek solitude. Each purpose may be useful in its own way, each aloneness sought as a means of enriching the spirit and enlivening the heart. A hermit, loosely speaking, can be religious or secular.

The construction of hermitages reflects a variety of objectives and relationships with the "Other"—depending on how one imagines that other. A hermitage is a technology for framing the use of solitude to some end. Reaching that end involves a silent dialogue, in some cases with one's "self" or one's conscience, in others with what is envisaged as a spirit, artistic muse, or divinity. Yet many who have attempted even a relatively short retreat from the busy world to a place of *hermitage* (from the Greek word meaning somewhere deserted) have soon found that the noise of internal mental dialogue can become deeply disturbing. Not least for that reason, religious traditions recommend or even require hermits to consult with and be supervised by a master or other person experienced in such matters. Understood thus, the term "hermit" does not designate a hyper-individualist. At the same time, it is not necessarily antithetical to or incompatible with being a "self-actualiser" as Abraham Maslow conceived that category, even if Maslow's biographer recently implied this to be the case (Hoffman, 2020, pp. 908, 925, 929).

Locked down

Asceticism is often associated with hermitages, although "the simple life" of which stressed city dwellers dream or for which the well-fed and well-heeled poet Yeats yearned is likely to be considerably less ascetic than that of a monk in a beehive hut or that of one of the early "desert fathers" of North Africa. Asceticism on the part of the weary citizen may be minimal, a case of enjoying temporary simplicity due to being in a remote place. In a similar way, the Zen aesthetic, to which an interior decorator may aspire, seldom involves those who inhabit that space submitting themselves to the regular ascetic discipline or prolonged meditation practice that a stern Zen roshi might require.

The coronavirus pandemic has resulted in governments adopting policies that "lock down" their populations, restricting movement and requiring or requesting people to stay at home and not to mix generally with others. This has led to fears about the psychological toll of isolation, and some have suggested that people generally can learn from hermitic religious and cultural practices how to use creatively the solitude of forced withdrawal. For example, according to the *New York Times*, in November 2020, a married couple, living in rural USA, has created Raven's Bread Ministries: an online service for "hermits and lovers of solitude whatever their religious affiliation or spiritual affinity". The wife previously lived as a hermit for six years in a primitive cabin in West Virginia. Before then she had spent thirty years as a Poor Clare nun in Canton, Ohio. The husband was a member of the Glenmary Home Missioners for twenty years. The *New York Times* reported:

> [The couple] believe that anyone could benefit from incorporating some eremitic fundamentals—such as being rooted in place, practicing austerity and committing to a daily schedule that prioritizes prayer or meditation—to help them make sense of their isolation into their lives, regardless of personality type, religiosity, or life circumstances. (Osgood, 2020)

More specifically, the authors of a recent Brazilian study assert a strong correlation between resilience and the use of religious and spiritual practices by lay people, writing that "our findings corroborate with the opinion of previous authors" that religiosity and spirituality seem to have an important role in reducing suffering, influencing health outcomes, and minimising the consequences of social distance. However, the field of religion and spirituality is vast, and these authors acknowledge that one of the few other studies that investigated the influence of religious and spiritual practices on health outcomes during the COVID-19 pandemic included 303 members of North American religious communities but found no association between religious commitment and distress or anxiety (Lucchetti et al., 2020). Whether the explanation for the latter result is a low variability of responses due to the nature of the group itself or to some other factor such as the religious maturity of the sample is moot.

While isolated persons generally may indeed learn lessons from monasticism and from hermits, the difference is so fundamental between a hermit who has actively chosen to live alone in spartan conditions, and a citizen forced to stay indoors, or a convicted criminal confined unhappily in jail that it is difficult to believe it can be equated in anything but a figurative sense. While locked-down citizens and prisoners may understand and accept the reality of their conditions in such circumstances, striving to make the best of things and praying for support, they cannot reasonably be expected to embrace the particular forms of solitude that they endure. Hermits welcome theirs existentially.

Hermitages

One may be an ascetic without being a hermit. Common qualities of philosophical or religious asceticism—in classical, Christian, or Eastern traditions for example—do not require one to live apart or alone in a hermitage. Thus, fasting, celibacy, prayer, visualisation, and voluntary poverty may be practised anywhere. Nor is living alone necessarily in itself an ascetic practice. Millionaires may be recluses in the midst of plenty and comfort. Moreover, a study of practices of eremitism and reclusiveness in the USA argues that these are inseparably linked to the US ideals of individualism and freedom (Bergmann & Hippler, 2017), and the latter motivations seem quite different in tone from the religious and spiritual wellsprings of hermitage and reclusiveness in other cultures.

One may retreat from the world for misanthropic reasons, perhaps to live alone in a forest as some half-crazed militant plotting vengeance who occasionally emerges to mail poison or explosives to an intended victim. However, it is more usual to find the term "hermit" used positively to encompass those who choose or design that which Foucault describes as

> technologies of the self which permit individuals to effect by their own means or with the help of others a certain number of operations on their own bodies and souls, thoughts, conduct, and way of being, so as to transform themselves in order to attain a certain state of happiness, purity, wisdom, perfection, or immortality. (Foucault, 1988, p. 18)

If to one person this choice is driven by the imperative "to thine own self be true", to another the call is "to be true to God"—to listen as the Jewish prophet Elijah did in the cave at Horab for the Lord to pass by (1 Kings 19: 9–15). Preparing oneself for an encounter with the ineffable may be understood by some to demand constant denial of "the self", in the sense of forsaking physical desires or personal status, although clearly from other verses of that early Irish monk who was mentioned above, it is a way of life that sometimes has its own attractive conditions and the hermitage itself is not always an arid desert:

> Quite near, a beautiful wood around it on every side,
> To nurse many-voiced birds, hiding it with its shelter.
>
> A southern aspect for warmth, a little brook across its floor,
> A choice land with many gracious gifts such as be good for every plant.
> —Meyer (1913, p. 30)

If to one person the chosen place of solitude is somewhere to encounter God or is a generator of artistic and intellectual creativity, to another it is a forum for "letting go", for meditation without concern about results. In all cases, an isolated hermitage is fraught with the dangers of solipsism and even mental derangement. For this reason alone—besides other factors such as the exercise of power and the imposition of orthodoxy or such as a philosophical belief in the intrinsic value of community—Christian authorities have been wary of approving of the solitary hermitical path for any individual. William Johnston writes that "Most religious traditions have sought to initiate their devotees into mystical silence rather than allowed them to wander freely into the deeper caverns of the mind" (Johnston, 1974, p. 94). His opinion, that the best measure for distinguishing the mystic from the neurotic is a person's adaptability both to community living by humble service and to the habits of hard work, or even drudgery, is a common one among supervisors of spiritual practices.

Christian hermits

Christ himself is said to have retreated to the desert where he fasted for forty days and forty nights, being confronted and tempted by demons ("the devil"). He is said to have replied, in words that summoned his followers to hear God and that have sustained generations of ascetics: "Man shall not live on bread alone, but on every word that comes from the mouth of God" (Mathew 4: 1–11).

Later some Christian hermits, or "anchorites" as they were also known, fled society to live remotely for much longer than forty days. The most renowned pioneer of that way of life is remembered as a saint, Anthony the Great of Egypt. He flourished about the year 300 (Ryan, 1972, pp. 3–53). The eremitic way spread extensively from Egypt into Palestine, then through the Sinai Peninsula, Mesopotamia, Syria, and Asia Minor. Eventually it reached Europe. Monasteries frequently grew up around the cell of a hermit, formed as the hermit attracted disciples. Later, close to these monasteries, isolated cells might be built where members of their communities who were deemed capable of living in solitude could retire if they wished. The crucial word is "close", for those who felt the want of solitude were still expected by Christian authorities to reside near an oratory or a monastic church. In that respect the Irish monk above complied with orthodoxy, desiring near his hut in the woods

> A few men of sense—we will tell their number—
> Humble and obedient to pray to the King [God] ....
>
> A pleasant church and with the linen altar-cloth, a dwelling for God from Heaven;
> Then, shining candles above the pure white Scriptures.
>
> —Meyer (1913, p. 30)

The institutional Christian church preferred hermits to be attached ultimately to disciplined communities. Neither its councils nor monastic rules were particularly encouraging of those who were desirous of leading an eremitic existence:

> To guard against the serious dangers of this kind of life, monastic institutes were founded that combined the advantages of solitude with the guidance of a superior and the protection of a rule. Thus, for example, we had the Carthusians and the Camaldolese [religious orders] at Vallombrosa and Monte Vergine. Nevertheless there still continued to be a large number of isolated hermits, and an attempt was made to form them into congregations having a fixed rule and a responsible superior. (Besse, 1910, p. 280)

Discipline and supervision were undoubtedly a means of exercising power over individuals who might otherwise spread unorthodox or heretical opinions, but they were also necessary to ensure that those who sought spiritual guidance were not abused or confused and those who sought wisdom did not sink in a sea of subjectivity and self-delusion. The ultimate objective of hermitic practice was the same as that of communal or "cenobitic" monastic practice, which is not the glorification or elevation of the individual onto an actual or metaphoric pillar but the service of the whole Christian community in compassion, following the example of Jesus.

Thomas Merton

The contrast between the ostensible attraction of a religious life spent alone in a hermitage and that passed within a monastery alongside fellow seekers of what Foucault calls "a certain state of happiness, purity, wisdom, perfection, or immortality" was notably personified during the twentieth century by Thomas Merton. An English convert to Catholicism, Merton entered the Trappist monastery of Gethsemani in Kentucky and wrote a renowned early autobiography, *The Seven Storey Mountain*. He gradually grew to have a public role, critical of the US war in Vietnam and other public policies and was a pioneer in developing the relationship between Catholic intellectuals and Buddhists. Among his guests in Kentucky, before Merton's untimely death in 1968, was the Dalai Lama. Merton pressed his superiors hard for permission to stay sometimes in a small building about two kilometres from the main monastery. He did not get to spend very long there but even such periods, when he was allowed to separate from the community at that hermitage, in some ways accentuated his sense of individuality, as he wrote:

> Though I realize that I am not the ideal of an absolute hermit, since my solitude is partly that of an intellectual and poet, still it is a very real inclination for solitude and when I have continuous solitude for a more or less extended period, it means a great deal and is certainly the best remedy for the tensions and pressures that I generate when I am with the community ... this little bit of solitude helps me to appreciate the real values that do exist in the common life, though they certainly manage to get hidden when I get too much of them. (Furlong, 1980, p. 271)

Merton's move towards isolation shared more of the character of Yeats's desire for solitude in a bee-loud glade than it did of the desert fathers who forsook all pleasures of the flesh. Indeed, Merton found that his new arrangement afforded him some opportunities to mix with men and women outside the monastic community that he would not have enjoyed otherwise. Solitude might calm certain tensions and pressures, as he found, but it could also spark a set of noisy internal struggles.

For some Christian religious practitioners there is a paradoxical understanding of the call to solitude. This involves seeing hermitage as a state of mind or soul even when one is in the midst of daily life, and that regards such an "invisible" retreat as akin to Christ's long and generally unremarked, unaccounted existence at Nazareth before his public life began about the age of thirty. Charles de Foucauld, who founded a caring religious order, the Little Brothers of Jesus, and who is said to have not made a single convert to Christianity before his violent death in North Africa, personified the fifteenth-century advice of the German Thomas à Kempis in the *Imitation of Christ*: "Strive to be unknown". The prior general of the order that de Foucauld founded, whose members work "in the world" but who also periodically withdraw to solitude, later wrote:

> Jesus was like everybody else; the Gospel proves this indisputably. He kept his secret so well that not one of the inhabitants of the village, not one of His relatives—outside of Joseph and Mary—ever suspected at any moment that He might be different from other men. (Voillaume, 1972, p. 27)

This insight touches on aspects of religious isolation and hermitage that cannot be fully explored in a short essay, but that include the belief of some religious people that being generally "unknown" to others as an individual while knowing and being known to God is a sufficient reason for being and is somehow helpful to the wider world. It involves too a perception that the "desert" may be found anywhere, even—or especially today—in large cities where the very presence of a self-contained spiritual practitioner in a neighbourhood or workplace may bear witness to spirituality as much as ever did a medieval monk in a stone beehive hut on the remote west coast of Ireland. For those who do not share religious faith even in the broadest sense, it can be hard to grasp that such beliefs are deeply experienced as authentic rather than merely held as intellectual propositions.

Hinduism

While the hermit is an exception in Christian communities, and not only among the entire Christian population but even among monks and nuns, the condition of being a hermit was seen in the Hindu tradition as a potentially desirable experience for any person. The ancient Dharmasutra of Vasistha specified four stages of life, being those of the student (Brahmacarya), the householder (Grihasta), the hermit (Vanaprastha), and the ascetic (Sanyasa). These constitute a path towards fulfilment of one's purpose on earth, but the last two are quite aspirational in the context of usual patterns of daily existence. The path of the hermit, as explained in the ninth chapter of Vasistha Dharmasutra, is intended for one's middle age and might attract some people. One suspects that it would not entirely entice very many followers in practice. The hermit is to be meek, dressing in garments made of grasses or skin, to avoid settlements, gather wild growing roots and fruit (only), and remain chaste and bathe at morn, noon, and eve. He (and it is men who were envisaged, although wives might consent to go along) may accept alms of roots and fruit but no other kind and shall kindle a fire according to a specific ritual. After six months of living in this manner "he shall dwell at the root of a tree, keeping no fire and having no house" (Bühler, 1882, pp. 45–46). One assumes that observance of the latter rule depends on climate. Some Christian hermits have been inspired by Hinduism (Aguilar, 2019, p. 29–56).

There is frequently a transactional dimension to hermitage. It is not a pointless retreat or a giving up, but a way of storming heaven, or a mode of winning the muse's attention for a poet or writer, or even simply a good opportunity for the troubled mind to process thoughts. In laying aside activities or possessions and in retreating, one is thus advancing. And yet in the Indian tradition the hermit is told that one shall only give, not receive (Vasistha, 9 (8)), and in the Christian tradition that one asks "not my will, but Yours [God's] be done" (Luke 22: 42), and in Buddhist practice that one strives mightily without expectation of personal reward or even an evident result. Somehow in sacrificing one's selfish ambitions, ego, and tastes compassionately for a greater reality one is satisfied.

The great spiritual traditions are not naive about the possibility of self-delusion or derangement along the way of the hermit, their adherents having seen various forms of obsession and neurosis that can result in even people of impeccable intention becoming a danger to themselves or others. Looking after oneself is part of the technology of being a successful hermit, with that caring Socratic principle adopted or adapted into the Christian tradition. While busy lay people might think of all who take up residence in an austere monastery as hermits, monks themselves are very conscious of the difference between living in a monastic community and seeking permission from a religious order to abide principally on one's own.

In a study of Latin-American monasticism Ludueña (2005) has addressed an area of possible misconception on the part of academic researchers who adopt what they consider to be purely secular or "scientific" methodologies in their study of religious communities. Focusing on ascetic technologies in a Benedictine monastery, principally silence and *lectio divina* (a "divine reading", usually from the Bible), he argues that the adoption of vernacular technologies of the self through adaptation-participation can bridge ontologies between the fieldworker and the "Other's" culture by producing intimacy with the object of study. While non-believers may not share the beliefs of monks, they can at the very least enter into practices that monks employ in relation to the numinous during the process of experiencing what monks ultimately perceive as "God". This ethnography respects distinctive forms of experiential knowledge, even if these are alien to the observer:

> The *lectio* [*divina*] is a reading that is profoundly meditated and thought about. Indeed it is in the contemplation of God's Word through reading and rereading a paragraph ("rumination" is the native category for this) that the process the monks call "hearing" takes place. In fact, hearing can be understood as a cognitive process whereby God talks to religious men. God does it through signs which are invested with specific meaning by monks. The activity is an internal, introspective, and strictly individual dialogue with the numinous. The hearing is carried out in these spaces of meditated reading in the loneliness and silence of the cell. (Ludueña, 2005, p. 151)

Even more than the monk in community, a hermit enters wholeheartedly into the experience of direct communication with the numinous or divine. Martin has explored the extent to which such technology of the self requires or results in rejection of "the world", of usual pleasures and responsibilities. He did so in the context of the Syrian Thomas tradition that is found expressed in various apocryphal or other texts relating to that apostle's supposed missionary activities in India (Martin, 1988, pp. 51–63).

It is worth stressing that in the Western tradition a monk's or hermit's life in solitude is not seen to justify a solipsistic abdication of responsibilities to other people. It is not a narcissistic indulgence but has meaning insofar as it helps others, perhaps simply by example but frequently by charitable behaviour. Similarly, in Buddhist traditions, the bodhisattva foregoes nirvana in order first to help others realise their potential.

Buddhist hermits

The tension between hermitic and cenobitic or communal monastic lifestyles is found not only in Christianity. In Buddhism too, some highly dedicated spiritual practitioners live outside the normal monastic structures. In a recent study of solitude in Buddhism and psychoanalysis, one author writes of rivalries between the organised monkhood known as the *sangha* and so-called "forest monks" and other hermits: "The latter tend to regard the former (the *sangha*) as having compromised entirely too much with the illusory world of attachment, while the former regard the latter more or less as crackpots who ignore the fact that the Buddha taught neither asceticism nor sensuality but a middle way" (Paul, 2011, pp. 300–301).

Milarepa, whose life story many Tibetans greatly love, is said to have sung of the joys of solitude. The words attributed to him are reminiscent of those verses on hermitage by the medieval Irish monk and by W. B. Yeats quoted above:

> This is a delightful place, a place of hills and forests.
> In the mountain meadows, flowers bloom;
> In the woods dance the swaying trees …
> Birds sing tunefully,
> Bees fly and buzz …
> I, Milarepa, happily abide
> Meditating upon the void-illuminating mind.
>
> —Chang (1999, pp. 74–75)

Like the Jewish Elijah who had a transcendent experience as he emerged from reflection in a cave, Milarepa found it fruitful to retreat and meditate:

> … in six well-known caves open to view, in six unknown caves, in six secret caves, and in two others, making twenty in all. In addition there were four widely known large caves

and four unknown large caves. This includes all my places of meditation, except for some smaller caves where conditions were favourable. (Lhalungpa, 1977, p. 146)

The outcome of Milarepa abiding among the birds and bees, and moving from cave to cave is clear:

As a result of my meditation I have achieved total awakening wherein the object meditated upon, the action of meditating, and the subject who meditates merge into one, so that now I no longer know how to meditate. (Lhalungpa, 1977, pp. 146–147)

The mature meditator delights in such ostensible paradoxes, eradicating the "stains of discernment" through an experience that only becomes clouded again by words. For that person the retreat into solitude provides an opportunity to taste rather than just to talk about reality.

In the Japanese tradition, temples dedicated to the merciful bodhisattva Kannon arose where holy men had built huts as permanent abodes for spiritual practice. The austere Shôku for example, quite like the Irish monks who sat in their beehive huts or stood in cold streams reciting psalms, remained inside his hut reciting and copying the Lotus Sûtra (MacWilliams, 2000, p. 392). Harpur sees parallels between medieval Irish "hermit poets" and the early Chinese poet Li Bai as well as Zen haiku masters (Harpur, 2020, p. 120). In the Buddhist tradition, as in the Christian, hermitages attracted both ascetic followers of the first hermit and lay people looking for inspiration.

Conclusion

Hermitage is a term used broadly to refer to a place of withdrawal from the busy world, a place such as a cave or a hut in the wilderness, although hermitages have no essential form and are not necessarily remote and may be less austere than caves and huts sometimes are. The use of a hermitage encompasses withdrawal for creative or religious/spiritual purposes. World religions have long seen a role for hermitages as one of the means, or technologies of the self, whereby some of their adherents may experience the numinous and can develop or grow spiritually. Hermits generally are not encouraged to eschew community entirely and are expected to benefit others somehow. Their hermitic existence is justified by their loyalty to a higher spirit with which they enter into an internal dialogue. The objective of such hermits is not to be alone or isolated from the world in a misanthropic manner but to enhance both themselves and humanity generally. Those who are not religious or who are religious but not inclined to life in a hermitage may benefit from understanding the techniques of religious hermits.

References

Aguilar, M. (2019). *The Way of the Hermit*. London: Jessica Kingsley.

Bergmann, I., & Hippler, S. (2017). *Cultures of Solitude: Loneliness–Limitation–Liberation*. Bern, Switzerland: Peter Lang.

Besse, J. (1910). Hermits. In: *The Catholic Encyclopedia, Volume 7* (pp. 280–288). New York: Appleton.

Bühler, G. (Ed.) (1882). *The Sacred Laws of the Aryas, Part 2: Vasishta and Baudhayana*. Oxford: Clarendon.

Chang, G. (Ed.) (1999). *The Hundred Thousand Songs of Milarepa*. Boston, MA: Shambhala.

Foucault, M. (1988). Technologies of the self. In: L. H. Martin, H. Gutman, & P. H. Hutton (Eds.), *Technologies of the Self: A Seminar with Michel Foucault* (pp. 16–49). London: Tavistock.

Furlong, M. (1980). *Merton: A Biography*. London: Collins.

Harpur, J. (2020). The hidden glimmering: solitude, wilderness, and the divine in early medieval Irish poetry and the poetry of Li Bai. *New Hibernia Review, 24*(2): 120–131.

Henry, F. (1956–57). Early monasteries, beehive huts and dry-stone houses in the neighbourhood of Caherciveen and Waterville (Co. Kerry). *Proceedings of the Royal Irish Academy, Section C: Archaeology, Celtic Studies, History, Linguistics, Literature, 58*: 45–166.

Hoffman, E. (2020). The social world of self-actualizing people: reflections by Maslow's biographer. *Journal of Humanistic Psychology, 60*(6): 908–933.

Johnston, W. (1974). *Silent Music: The Science of Meditation*. New York: Harper & Row.

Lhalungpa, L. P. (1977). *The Life of Milarepa*. New York: Dutton.

Lucchetti, G., Góes, L. G, Amaral, S. G., Ganadjian, G. T., Andrade, I., Almeida, P. O., Mendes do Carmo, V., & Manso, M. E. G. (2020). Spirituality, religiosity and the mental health consequences of social isolation during Covid-19 pandemic. *International Journal of Social Psychiatry*: November 2. https://journals.sagepub.com/doi/full/10.1177/0020764020970996.

Ludueña, G. A. (2005). Asceticism, fieldwork and technologies of the self in Latin American Catholic monasticism. *Fieldwork in Religion, 1*(2): 145–164.

MacWilliams, M. W. (2000). The holy man's hut as a symbol of stability in Japanese Buddhist pilgrimage. *Numen, 47*(4): 387–416.

Martin, L. H. (1988). Technologies of the self and self-knowledge in the Syrian Thomas tradition. In: L. H. Martin, H. Gutman, & P. H. Hutton (Eds.), *Technologies of the Self: A Seminar with Michel Foucault* (pp. 51–63). London: Tavistock.

Meyer, K. (1913). *Ancient Irish Poetry*. London: Constable.

O'Donnell, W. H., & Archibald, D. A. (1999). *The Collected Works of W. B. Yeats, Volume 3*. New York: Charles Scribner's Sons.

Osgood, K. (2020, November 28). What we can learn from solitude. *New York Times*. https://nytimes.com/2020/11/28/style/self-care/hermits-solitude.html.

Paul, R. A. (2011). Solitude in Buddhism and in psychoanalysis: The case of the great Tibetan yogi Milarepa. *American Imago, 68*(2): 297–319.

Ryan, J. (1972). *Irish Monasticism: Origins and Early Development*. Dublin: Four Courts Press.

Voillaume, R. (1972). *Seeds of the Desert: The Legacy of Charles de Foucauld*. St Albans, UK: Anthony Clarke.

CHAPTER 3

Lone wolves' loneliness—about a special variant of terrorism

Michael B. Buchholz

Turning and turning in the widening gyre
The falcon cannot hear the falconer;
Things fall apart; the centre cannot hold;
Mere anarchy is loosed upon the world,
The blood-dimmed tide is loosed, and everywhere
The ceremony of innocence is drowned;
The best lack all conviction, while the worst
Are full of passionate intensity.

—Yeats & Watts, 1921, p. 158

Thinkers aren't thinking, Abraham, teachers aren't teaching. The writers don't write, they stand onstage and play with themselves instead, emulating Mailer and Ginsberg. We've lost a generation. Young men walk into my office and declare their intention to live in a geodesic dome and tend bees, or compose choral music in Esperanto. To do *happenings*. Tradition's kaput. Nothing's good enough, not since Warhol, that schmuck with earlaps. It isn't interesting enough to be merely a man or a woman, even.

—Lethem, 2004, p. 47

Introduction

Nothing could better demonstrate why researchers have enormous difficulties to define terrorism than the ammonium nitrate explosion in Lebanon, August 4, 2020. According to newspaper records from various sources it was a detonation, creating another "ground zero". However, the conditions of how it was created could not be more different than those from 9/11. It was not a terrorist attack by a group of young jihadist men fighting against capitalist government and its symbols—but of comparable dimensions in effect. In Lebanon not a single terrorist or group instigated this disaster. It was the result of a corrupt government (Blakeley & Raphael, 2016), destructively expropriating their own country, whose power, paired with sloppiness, took them by surprise and destroyed their dominance. Neither a single person nor a group caused or meant it as attack: it was a result and symbol of a government that exploited a country in mafia-like manner after dividing the territory according to religious affiliations. The dismantling of the state took place long before the port disaster—which acts as a symbol for long-lasting terroristic actions of a state against its population.

Two questions arise: How to define terror and terrorists? And who defines? Speaking before the UN in 1974 Yasser Arafat said that what some people call a terrorist is named a freedom fighter by others. The connection to failed dialogue was documented by the empty seats of the Israeli representatives (Laster & Erez, 2015). Some authors name 110 definitions of terrorism (Bloom & Horgan, 2019), but no internationally agreed-upon one exists. Recently, Laster & Erez (2015) proposed a definition:

> Most commentators now agree that the constituent elements of terrorism include (a) the intentional use of violence (b) against noncombatant targets (including both civilians and iconic symbols) (c) to create fear, terror, psychic harm (d) by virtue of the widest possible publicity coverage for the group, cause, individual (e) pursuing political, religious, or ideological objectives. Needless to say, these objectives are achieved by inflicting the greatest possible damage, including loss of life, on mostly indiscriminate victims. (Laster & Erez, 2015, p. 85)

It is not too difficult to apply such a definition to the Lebanon explosion—but roles are changed. Before the explosion, Salman Akhtar (2017) wrote one of the best psychoanalytic papers about terrorism, beginning with these definitional difficulties. He adds further examples. George Washington, Menachem Begin, or Subbash Chandra were named "terrorists" by the British government before they became presidents of their country; the US took Nelson Mandela for one of the most dangerous terrorists; six years later he received the Nobel Peace Prize. In 1994 Yasser Arafat received the Nobel Peace Prize, after being held a terrorist by so many. What a terrorist is lies in the proverbial eye of the beholder, the author concludes (Akhtar, 2017).

I am writing here as a clinical psychoanalyst, social scientist, and former professor for social psychology at IPU (International Psychoanalytic University, Berlin). I am not an expert in terrorism research. The question I began with was what psychoanalysis can *contribute* to terrorism studies. However, I learned the important lesson to take another stance: what can be *learned*? What emerges for psychoanalytic theorising from what can be known about terrorism and terrorists? Walking through this thorny territory I hope to gain a better understanding of what the word "lone" means for at least some of these men. My result is that their loneliness is best defined as a psychosocial "zero zone", better understood in a social-psychology framework than in an individualistic framework of personal grievances only. I use "zero zone" as a metaphor for a mental state the political equivalent of which is "ground zero". Something so devastated and empty that the hope that something could still thrive and grow back is itself extinguished. Society is at the utmost periphery. The members of society, living people, are on the one hand to be addressed as recipients of a message, on the other hand they are thought to be killed: "in order to get our message before the public, We've had to kill people" reads a line in the 35,000 lines of the Unabomber Manifesto,[1] written by Ted Kaczynski (graduating with a PhD from Harvard at the age of twenty) in the loneliness of the Montana mountains.[2]

The most important role in studying lone wolves is that of bystanders. The bystanders' emotional or social withdrawal from protecting and guiding young men in trouble creates a silent zone. Their expectation to observe a bombastic disaster makes them excited but silent, aroused but tense, which leads them to the threshold of the "zero zone" with no return. Both, bystanders' withdrawal and expectations, are social psychological factors contributing to the zero zone of loneliness. I will try to work out some details of this hypothesis.

Problems of defining terrorism

The difficulties to define terrorism (Ganor, 2002) present a strong methodological warning against attempts to describe a terrorist's psychopathology individualistically. There are other difficulties with a clinical-only view.

Individual psychopathology as origin?

First, to attribute a mental disorder to someone comes close to excusing it by taking agency and moral responsibility from the shoulders of the perpetrator (Leuschner, 2013; Reemtsma, 2008). I include a short example from a study of two psychoanalytic authors in this field:

> One of the fundamental principles of psychoanalytic theory is that of *psychic determinism*, the notion that one's conscious thoughts and actions are shaped and controlled by unconscious forces and that manifest symptoms and behaviors contain unconscious and multiple symbolic meanings. (Meloy & Yakeley, 2014, p. 349, italics added)

---

[1] Kaczynski, T. (1995) Industrial society and its future (Unabomber's Manifesto). This essay first appeared in *The New York Times* and *The Washington Post* on September 19, 1995. It was published under the pseudonym FC, for *Freedom Club*.

[2] It was his brother David, who detected characteristics of Ted's way of writing in the publication of the "manifesto" and his alerting a law enforcement agency that led to the arrest of Ted.

Psychoanalyst J. Reid Meloy and Jens Hoffmann directed attention to threat assessment (Meloy & Hoffmann, 2014), editing papers on computerised content analysis of terrorist propaganda (Sanfilippo et al., 2014), or communicative techniques in interviewing imprisoned perpetrators (Meloy & Mohandie, 2014).

If one's social action could be fully explained *by determination* from unconscious forces, which powerfully exert uncontrollable influences on one's behaviour, it follows that this Unconscious takes responsibility from the person's agency. It is not an individual's agency, then, that is responsible, but unconscious determination. This assumption runs the risk of being read as a cop-out.

Second, many psychoanalysts maintain to strongly believe in deterministic views, while such a confession is otherwise broken by contradictions with other statements. A *strong* concept of determinism cannot allow for any kinds of innovation or change in an individual's life. A *weak* concept of determinism which is delivered after a fact loses all explanatory power. Studying mental disorders in lone wolves is one thing—using mental disorders as explanations within a deterministic framework disqualifies determinism, but not role and function of childhood experiences. These authors quickly give up professing to hold deterministic views, as "… terrorism represents a meaningful communication enacted through violence" (Meloy & Yakeley, 2014, p. 349).

To view terrorism as meaningful communication opens a path away from determinism but does not exclude the role of traumatic experience and personal grievance mixed up with political grievance. To communicate meaningfully means making use of highly relevant social tools—symbols, language, the internet—which supposes a choice of which tool is used, and which communication is delivered. To have a choice is the opposite of determinism. The unanswered question remains: who is addressed by "communications enacted through violence"?

Third, a communicative point of view does not only ask a) who is addressed?, b) what is the message?, but can ask meaningfully c) who talks? (Cushman, 2010). One answer, often found, is the identification with charismatic leaders conveyed through media communication. Consequently, this leads to moral disappointment combined with in-group solidarity, which a lone wolf gives up in favour of social closure while deepening ideological training in a process of radicalisation. Another answer is the vicarious identification with some perceived social injustice: "Importantly, one does not need to experience unjust events first-hand in order to feel sufficiently motivated to become a terrorist" (Silke, 2003, p. 43).

Franz Fuchs and Ted Kaczynski, the Unabomber, are prototypes. They closed themselves off against the influences of the outside world deeply and chose reclusion into wilderness (Spaaij, 2012). Franz Fuchs became depressive and, as he failed to find a partner, wanted to commit suicide. Volkert von der Graaf became depressive and his attempt to kill himself failed. However, it is difficult to judge the order of actions. Was depression the cause of the withdrawal? Or was criticism of social conditions (political grievances) the cause of the retreat into wilderness, isolation, and loneliness? In the case of van der Graaf the court concluded that his depressive disorder was *not* responsible for the assassination of Dutch politician Pim Fortuyn.

Fourth, it seems that some authors admit to determinism, but then, are not able to redeem it completely. They uphold the opinion that "terrorism represents a meaningful communication enacted through violence" (Silke, 2003, p. 43) which opens a social psychological line of reasoning. "Among lone wolves, if there has not been the personal experience of trauma, there is often a vicarious identification with it" (Meloy & Yakeley, 2014, p. 349).

The authors allude to what is known as the "copycat effect" (Coleman, 2004). To imitate an action is mediated by very influential, wrongly named "social" media—the social psychological dimension overrules determinism. Who *decides* to imitate whom? In fact, even in cases such as Anders Behring Breivik, experts disputed seriously the role of psychopathology and came to contradictory conclusions (Bromark, 2014). Empirical studies of twenty-seven lone wolves (Eby, 2012) showed that the assumption of psychic problems of the perpetrators can be documented only in less than half of the cases. Similar conclusions were drawn by Spaaij (2012). There is no single disposition of lone wolf psychopathology,[3] although they suffer from personal grievances and have high rates of social incapacity.

Fifth, two white supremacists, Tom Metzger and Alex Curtis, popularised the term "lone wolf" in the 1990s. The term was used in a communicative way to encourage others to commit solo acts for tactical reasons. A picture of the lonesome hero was created which even infiltrated theories by creating a type. It was a purposefully introduced name to parallel actions with the pre-1914 anarchistic tradition. The field of "critical terrorism studies" (Jackson, 2016) makes this distinction between "naming" (epistemological) and "ascribing existence" (ontological) the core of theories and studies.

The name "lone wolf terrorist" has seductive powers to think of individual biographical causes, which has roots in anarchist tradition (Jensen, 2014). In 1877 Russia, Vera Zasulich, one of the first figures, observed a severe injustice: a servant was publicly flogged by a governor in rage because he was not greeted by taking off the hat. However, the governor's unjustified deed was not prosecuted. Vera Zasulich, who observed both, the bad deed by the governor and the silence of justice, decided to act. She appeared in the governor's rooms and shot him down. Afterwards she silently waited to be arrested and later the court acquitted her. Her attack on the responsible governor was not psychologically, but ethically motivated. She wanted to re-establish social balance.

The same holds true for Clayton Wagner who became a US anti-abortionist in the 1970s after his pregnant daughter Emily was forced to go to work prematurely, causing her to give birth to a stillborn child at twenty-four weeks (McCauley & Moskalenko, 2014). Giving an impressive comparison of these two individual fates, in different countries and different times, these authors ascribe to them a strong role of conscience. This was stimulated by a strong emotional experience, resulting in serious grievance. Both fought against what they thought to be a serious social injustice. They stirred up consciousness but did not want to stir up a community or society with anxiety or horror. They were lonely, at least their actions were.

The New Right uses the image of the lonesome, heroic fighter as a call for quite different acts: actively inviting identification with such an image, and thus not acting out of ethical considerations, but only suggesting ethical motives. This picture of heroic tradition suggests

---

[3] A contrasting standpoint is taken by Gallagher (2017), an experienced Irish police officer.

a people living in harmony, destroyed by globalisation and immigration of non-white races. The picture thus portrays an ethical justification to fight and commit terroristic attacks. But it is no more than a myth. Critical terrorism researchers state that the heroic picture of the ethically justified lonesome hero is meant to animate identificatory processes by talking about "lone wolves". One can observe that the far right has lost its ethical overtones (Gallagher, 2017). There is a gap between the (heroic) "name" and the (brutal) "facts"; using the name risks unwanted identification with the hero-picture of lone-wolves. This is why Hankiss (2018) gives up the term "lone wolves". Nevertheless, these authors propose to study lone wolves in a social psychological framework. Other authors, far from right-wing ideology, go a step further and see an "age of lone wolf terrorism" on the horizon (Hamm & Spaaij, 2017).

Identifying the paradox

We have to turn to the paradox that strong social influences are disguised as social withdrawal. I conclude that there is a flaw in psychoanalytic determinism, which is overruled by social effects, above all communication including "who talks?". The communicative power of using historical "names", or inventing new ones, in order to justify "heroes" is beyond determinism as well as the possibility to *decide* for and against serious ethical doubts. In short, to understand lone wolves, methodological individualism and determinism in psychoanalytic theorising must be given up. Or better, to view both as resulting from the years of Freud's, and many other practitioners', lonesome work behind the couch; maybe it is time for an update, not an abandonment, in psychoanalytic theory (Stepansky, 2009).

Researchers have found psychopathology in about 42 per cent of lone wolves (Eby, 2012; Spaaij, 2012), but they add that psychopathology has weak explanatory power; most of them were studied by psychiatrists. Often enough a serious diagnosis could be documented. A hint, hidden in a footnote, by a well-informed researcher, has the power to loosen the knot: "One can, for instance, also explore terrorism in a framework of (social) psychology. This is especially appropriate when one is dealing with 'lone wolf' terrorists" (Schmid, 2011, p. 34).

If you distinguish between "inside" (psychic life) and "outside" (social life), this sounds like a paradox—how to study "lone" wolves by *social* psychology, then? An answer to this question can be found in a "provisional definition" of terrorism at which Timothy Shanahan arrives after a careful discussion of other definitional attempts:

> "Terrorism" is the strategically indiscriminate harming or threat of harming members of a target group in order to influence the psychological states of an audience group in ways the perpetrators anticipate may be beneficial to the advancement of their agenda. (Shanahan, 2016, p. 239)

It is the only definition I could find which points so directly to psychological effects. Centre stage of this definition is "to influence the psychological states of an audience …" and that the perpetrators "anticipate" how mental states of an audience are altered. These *social psychological abilities* are required if you want to achieve something that involves other people. Both, anticipation and influencing the psychological state of other people, qualify for competent navigation in a social field. It is part of what I will call "social mind". This definition does not aim to include *motives* for violating or killing others. The aim is to "influence the psychological states of an audience group"; killing and violating others is *a means to this end*. This emphasis in Shanahan's definition is a breakthrough.

Its value can be best illustrated by the 9/11 Twin Towers attack in 2001. The perpetrators artfully anticipated the media's response. Twenty minutes after the first attack, when cameras were installed and worldwide attention was secured, the second attack followed—and the footage spread around the world quickly. The media's own will to report was *used cleverly*. To influence psychological states does not only mean to know about individual psychology. You must know about groups and their communicative behaviour and tools. You must be psychologically minded in order to maximise effects. You must fully understand how mass communication operates to navigate so skilfully (which, of course, is not meant in an admiring manner). You must be a social mind attacking other social minds.

Shanahan's definition, after seriously discussing other proposals, illustrates what has been overlooked: a) there is a lot of (diabolic) psychological and social-communicative competence in terroristic perpetrators; b) the targets are not those who die or are mutilated (this would be a military attack), the target is the audience, set into a traumatic state. This, often enough, is done via media reports. Can we refer to social psychological references, which help to understand this skilful navigation of social minds in social areas? Here I want to mention Randall Collins's approaches. He worked on violence in the tradition of Goffmanian social theorising and of psychoanalyst Earl Hopper, who wrote about his work with severely disturbed and aggressive participants in therapeutic group settings.

Elements of a "social mind"—theory of violence

Since the impulses were explained by Collins (2008), it became clear that a situationistic approach to violence wins all drive-conceptions. Nevertheless, Collins's theory is compatible with hormonal analyses (Mazur, 2009) of people's experience in violent situations, covers differences in men and women (Cocoradă, 2012), and can be combined with economic analyses of terror financing (Myres, 2012). I cannot present this theory here in its entirety, a brief summary must suffice.

Collins and Hopper

Humans have a choice to act violently, but Collins strongly explained that this is more feared than executed. Why? Because everybody knows how it feels to be beaten in the face, to be shot, or to be attacked by a knife. Knowing—not from experience, but from imagination. One can know these experiences without having experienced them; the reason is that you have a sensitive body. This is why most people are inhibited to use even milder forms of verbally violating the rules of conduct—because the risks of escalation are deeply felt and can be contained by embodied knowing (Young, 2010) of how it feels to be shamefully exposed, falsely accused, or exposed to the risks of ridicule. These effects increase in front of an audience and this component of humiliation is calculated by the perpetrators unconsciously. Their social mind acts upon an unconsciously working social mind (Hopper, 2003a). Hopper's psychoanalytic considerations aim at understanding this dimension of social mind. In a related methodological approach, he explores a similar territory of experience as Collins does.

Most often these mutual but silent assumptions suffice to avoid any form of violence. Collins concludes that people have an *inhibition* to act violently. Societies develop a rich ritual repertoire to protect against violent risks. Such rituals protect against violent outbursts. To act violently makes everybody lonesome; there is a strong threat of exclusion. In Hopper's terms: a group before, during, and after an attack changes its social mind from aggregation to massification and back to aggregation (Hopper, 2003b). An *aggregation* is an assembly of single individuals; in a *mass* there is a higher state of fusion and loss of individuality. For example, people at a bus stop form an aggregation in Hopper's terminology, people in a football arena are a mass. An audience wildly applauding a piano soloist in a concert hall behave like a mass, but while approaching the wardrobe they quickly re-individualise and change into an aggregation with much lower levels of felt social cohesion. Both, aggregation and masses, can be distinguished from *mobs*, which assemble with a direct aim to act violently. Aggregates defend, in Hopper's view, against the dangers of fusion and confusion, masses defend against the dangers of separation and loneliness. Both, fusion/confusion and separation/loneliness, are considered to be "derailed" forms of social mind. Hopper observes further differences between masses and aggregates in norms, communicative styles, interaction. I will not further pursue this argument here. It suffices to mention that he observes alterations between aggregation and mass as two states of social mind—depending on situations. Problems may arise if a participant cannot fluently oscillate between these altered states.

This may be the case in the following circumstances: within a *mass* people feel less responsibility, but after an attack (hooligans after a football match), when returned to aggregation, on the way home, individual responsibilities and guilt can no longer be avoided and denied. These defences can only remain present through the fatal and fateful decision to continue life as a violent perpetrator to defend against guilt or guilt-feelings. To maintain a supposed "identity" and projective defences ("I—as a white Christian man—hate Jews, Muslims, black people, etc."), then, works as a defensive ideology against awareness of having violated basic dimensions of social mind. Psychoanalyst Christopher Bollas thinks of ideologies of this kind as "calcified paranoia" (Bollas, 2018). All in all, social-mind theory leaves it to an (unconscious) decision to act violently, or not.

What is an unconscious decision?

In Freud's texts, one repeatedly encounters the idea that patients in treatment should arrive at a state to *decide* for or against the continuation of neurosis. This means that there must have been a prior unconscious decision for neurosis, denial, subsequent rationalisation, selective perception, and also for repression and other defence mechanisms emanating from the ego. His often-used term "object *choice*" points to a similar direction of this thinking.

In the case of violence, guilt can thus remain averted, projection (that others "started it" or did not deserve better) can be used, and a rationalising phantasy of belonging to a superior type of mankind may be constructed. Such identity formations, then, belong to defensive structures.

In Western tradition there are at least two standard "models" for "identity". One is derived from the Cartesian "I think, therefore I am!". Descartes created this formulation under the horrible circumstances of the Thirty Years War in Europe, while he lost a child and the (unmarried) mother. Nevertheless, "*Cogito, ergo sum*" is said to be the optimistic version of constituting modern Ego.

The other version is seldom mentioned in this debate, although met in Shakespeare's drama *Richard III*. Richard kills all his rivals and manages the unspeakable infamy of soliciting the hand of the wife of one he has murdered—while he leans over the dead man's corpse. She lets herself be won over by a man, who, through his deformities and ugliness, felt empowered to commit all these outrages. What could have enraptured her, what could have won her over? What might be going on? Why does love not stand in the way of such a deformity of itself? And how brutal, how clear-sighted, when Shakespeare makes this same Richard exclaim: "What do I fear? Nobody here. Richard loves Richard, which means: I am I."

The difference between "I think, therefore I am" and "I am I" is obvious. The preface "I think …" is silenced, more precisely to think yourself as an act of self-founding. Shakespeare teaches us that this act of "subjecticide" (as Bollas names it) needs justification; in Richard's case, delivered by his ugliness entitles him to all his cruelty.

Shakespeare and Descartes are considered antagonistic poles of modern self-constitution, both cannot ignore "thinking". But how great the difference is: in Descartes it is reflection, in Richard it is arbitrary justification (opposed against guilt).

Freud (1923b) enters this field of antagonisms in his structural theory, where he ascribes to the Ego the potential to execute defences. The Ego is seen as the operation centre of access to the world; but he describes also its potential to distort perception and thinking. Acting violently, then, is not to be thought as based in "(volcano) outbreaks" (a metaphor astonishingly often found in Kernberg's work). It is based in unconscious decisions which seek relief from (feelings of) guilt by hurting the social mind.

Acting violently in view of both authors, then, must be *trained*, as, for example, hooligans or soldiers are. Humans are not "driven", they have options. If soldiers are isolated from their comrades or if hooligans are without bystanders' support they are thrown back to levels of individualisation where topics of individual responsibilities urgently return. Their decision to act violently while being a member of a mass is felt as what it is: a mental configuration that cannot be justified if they are alone. Here is an opportunity used by intervention programmes for young adults. Hopper's theory is helpful to detect paths into violence and why it is difficult to give up one's paranoia in favour of metanoia (which means "reverse").

I would like to say more about the social mind, which includes an unconscious knowing of what one has done, how it feels for another person, and what effects in others are produced by one's own actions. This knowing must not be formulated, but it guides even violent acts. Wittgenstein delivered an illustration in his thought experiment of "the beetle in the box".

> Suppose everyone had a box with something in it: we call it a "beetle". No one can look into anyone else's box, and everyone says he knows what a beetle is only by looking at his beetle. —Here it would be quite possible for everyone to have something different in their box. One might even imagine such a thing constantly changing. (Wittgenstein, 1953, § 293)

Discussing the headline of "private language argument", it is clear that the "beetle" might be a funny metaphor for a self. To *know* of it cannot be strictly distinguished from *believing* in it; but to violate this belief is a strong challenge for sociality. Beliefs of that kind unite many aspects of society. The most simple illustration is a sheet of paper, which "represents" the worth of money—but what you see is a coloured sheet of print. However, if the belief in its worth decays (what we name inflation) it has devastating effects on social life. Social mind is built in an analogous fashion. You can know it, you can feel it, you internally predict others' behaviour (Huron, 2006), you understand how to categorise utterances as fun or not, you know when to tell a dirty joke (Sacks, 1978) or how to understand forgetfulness as an interactive resource (Goodwin, 1987), and you know how and when to "repair" social bonds (Albert & de Ruiter, 2018). Further, you assume that others know all of this and more as well.

Collins, derived from Goffman, thinks in a similar way. Presenting many video-documented observations, Collins concludes that humans have no inborn competence to act violently; on the contrary, they fear it. They are ritualistically connected to each other through their culture and these rituals belong to a domain of unconscious social mind, the utterances of which can be observed and described. On the other hand, our cultural concepts are impregnated by movies: watching the saloon-fights in a Western, enjoying violent scenarios (e.g. Quentin Tarrantino) or computer games. In real life, Collins documents, things are much more different. People in violent-laden situations show anxiety, not rage, on their faces. Consequently, it is wrong to claim that the veneer of civilisation is thin against the powers of mighty unconscious drives. A theory which can describe *situations* where people *decide* for violence and/or terroristic attacks seems more useful.

Collins describes certain situational circumstances that must be realised in order to make participants act violently. For example, if you have two groups in a confrontation, what people experience emotionally is what Collins terms "confrontational tension and fear" (ct/f). They feel a high level of expectable embodied tension, documented by incompetent attempts at an attack followed by a fast retreat; they fear embodied confrontation, documented by displaying anxious faces, but no rage. The rage is on the faces of bystanders. Group members fight their tendency to leave by fuelling their mood. Not only by the use of alcohol, but by rhythmic calling and clapping of hands, a common activity which alters their mental states into higher cohesion, like in a mass. It is as if their social mind unconsciously "knows" what is required if you want to act violently. Here, rhythm is a necessary means for massification.

Then, if a member in one group happens to stumble and fall, the emotional situation mutates into a rushed one, because the other group senses a chance to roll over. This is the situational moment for manifestations of violent outbursts. Examples of such situations can be found in military battlegrounds, as, for example, in the My Lai massacre (Greiner, 2007), after football or other sport events, between police and demonstrators, and so on. The situational condition, Collins concludes, for the outbreak of manifest violence is a moment of weakness. Grasped by a fast social mind as a moment of chance for success and an end to confrontational tension. As members of a mass they are protected, but lonely; as fighters, when the risks seem to be clarified, a chance is scented to "re-member" and to leave alive and unviolated.

Collins makes violence, directed at enemy targets, a "military" perspective, a topic of discussion. Terroristic attacks, however, as Shanahan's definition distinguishes, are directed at the audience. We can now add: terrorist attacks are directed at the social mind of the audience by spreading fear and terror in survivors. It is the communicative value of the action that counts. It threatens the audience by being brought into a state of fearful isolation. The threat is loneliness, as nobody can predict who will survive and who will not. The attack goes against social cohesion and continues to an indeterminable endpoint in time. This is why, after an attack, those in positions of responsibility immediately and publicly declare via the media that we will not let it get us down. The media try to restore belief in the ritualistic cohesion system of social life.

Collins's and Hopper's theories share the assumption of a social mind aiming at restoring social life (by everyday rituals) and knowing what is required for this aim. Both researchers explain where this knowledge is derived from through using its opposite:[4] even a minimal participation in social life—survival after birth—as one of the first lessons, teaches you what pain is. Quickly you understand that other human beings know, as well as you do, what pain is and neither language nor rational thinking are necessary to *know* it. To avoid inflicting harm on others (on all levels) acts as a precondition for social life. Therefore, "doing harm" is indissolubly connected with a violation of this basic dimension of your own social mind. It provokes anxiety as you cannot predict whether your social bonds will be restored or not, whether a response will be violent or not, whether you will be "re-membered" or not. This fear increases the value of connectedness and you "know" that to care for another's survival means to care for

---

[4] Remember the distinction between "knowing" and "knowledge" introduced by Polanyi (1969). Knowledge refers to a supply of phrases that can be formulated; it is a more or less static and stable conception which can be taught in courses and learned from people. "Knowing" refers to a "tacit" dimension; for example, a craftsman feels whether a material is fit or not, a nurse "knows" how to find the vein for an injection, a therapist "knows" when to speak and when better to remain silent. It is a more volatile dimension that cannot be learned, it is "personal" knowledge. "Knowing" is much more difficult to teach, thus, most often beginners are instructed to "observe" what the expert does. This is how children learn how to tie their shoe-laces; it could not be well described in words. Personal knowing, acquired by experience and "observing", is bound to a sense of resonance, balance, "feeling": dimensions not addressed in acquiring "knowledge". Veen et al. (2020) take up these topics.

your own. However, there are contexts (e.g. school, or worse, preschool family life), in which you are sometimes forced into compliance with violent actions. Or, there are societies where governments operate in terrorist manners. Here, everything must be reversed from positive to negative and you need to learn to put trust *into* violence (Reemtsma, 2008). The big surprise for historians was that terror ended from one day to the next as Stalin died (Conquest, 2008). Forced compliance into violence gradually could then be given up and a social mind was gradually restored.

While military attacks are directed against enemies, terroristic attacks address an audience. They communicate a message, the overall content of which is "fear". Following Hamm and Spaaij (2017), I want now to outline the process of radicalisation in lone wolves to focus on a further social dimension: enablers and bystanders.

How to model radicalisation

Hamm and Spaaij (2017) deduce their model from a database of 106 cases (p. 159). All data is derived from publicly available sources, not from police files or law enforcement institutions, or from secret services. They structure this material qualitatively, following their training as social scientists. Results are rich and impressively show what can be known in full detail. Their work is widely appreciated.

This is not the place to outline the whole book. I refer to the radicalisation model (p. 159) which consists of six steps. Those later called lone wolves have (1) some *personal grievance* of a very common kind. As the majority of them are men, they do not find a girlfriend, their school career deteriorates, they lose a job and begin to use drugs, too much alcohol, withdraw from social life, spend much time during the day in their bed sleeping and awake in the evening. Most of them find (2) *online sympathisers*, others join *extremist groups*, which support them in recoding their personal misery into political grievance. Via these social connections they find (3) *enablers* who recommend certain texts to read, introduce them to further radical forums from where they are supplied with weapons or explosives (or instructions). Enablers help to plan an action which is then reliably "readable" for others; sometimes parents or teachers observe a fundamental change in the subject's behaviour. They sometimes intervene (e.g. by blocking use of a car), sometimes not; most often they withdraw, abhorred. The next step (4) in the radicalisation process is named *broadcasting intent*. Most lone wolves communicate what their intent is within a period of a few days to a few hours in advance. Some of this broadcasting intent reads as if they want to be stopped. However, the overall experience is that their online "friends" suddenly do not respond anymore, they withdraw in silence. A *triggering event* (5) is then reported in many cases and finally (6) *terrorism* is executed. This model describes longer and shorter periods of time in which many transformations from one stage to the other are involved. "That is, individuals do not 'snap' and become radical" (p. 160). The model rewinds to step 1, which opens the potential for copycat actions and confirms the mixture of personal and political grievances. The model is not meant to work in a linear mode; single actors can skip a stage. It is a heuristic device which is valuable as plans and intentions are "witnessed by others—friends, family members, co-workers, students, civic leaders, police and retail gun store clerks". They are the "social environment" whose non-activity contributes to the actors' loneliness. The authors conclude that "… they can lead to intervention" (p. 160).

They point out, that pre-9/11 terrorists (a quarter of their database) had a strong origin in criminal activities with uncanny abilities to operate under the radar of law enforcement for long periods of time. A prominent example was James Earl Ray who, in April 1968, assassinated Martin Luther King and eluded capture for nearly thirty years while thwarting a huge amount of law enforcement people. The authors observe: "But that talent seems to be a thing of the past" (p. 162). This is a diagnosis of "times, they are a changing" (Bob Dylan)—I will come back to the change of time. Post-9/11 lone wolves do not have that criminal past, they do communicate their actions in advance, they broadcast their intent widely. For the purpose of illustration I chose one case here.

Jerrod Loughner—a "zero zone" of loneliness

In everything I want to propose here, there is no denial of traumatic experiences causing psychopathology in lone wolves. But from cognitively cultivating extremist *beliefs* it is a far step to extremist, violent *action*. We deal with a lot of interwoven factors; the radicalisation model is meant only as a heuristic device. First, just a few brief illustrations.

Sirhan Sirhan, who in 1968 killed Robert Kennedy, was sexually abused by his father. The experts quarrelled whether he was schizophrenic or a case of borderline personality disorder. His actual motivation (Meloy & Yakeley, 2014) however was revenge against Robert Kennedy who had voted in the US Senate to sell fighter jets to Israel during the Six Days War. The assassination was executed on the anniversary. Anniversaries and special dates play a communicative role. They are meant to bring something across to the community. A message often overheard. We find places in time (anniversaries), we detect practices (of revenge), we take sides or not (with Sirhan's Palestinian people), and we can conclude that he was a person who suffered from personal and political grievances.[5] He counts as one of those lone wolves "who have been able to turn the tides of history" (Hamm & Spaaij, 2017, p. 10). He produced a lot of followers, for example, the Iranian extremist Hussein Kholya or the Palestinian Rahid Baz. The first hijacked a flight from Texas to Mexico in 1983, the second killed fifteen Jewish boys on the Brooklyn Bridge in 1994. Within the pre-9/11 era these perpetrators are considered "paradigmatic cases" (Hamm & Spaaij, 2017, p. 31). Some are kept in historical memory. Sirhan ended another person's political career. These perpetrators fought on one side of the Palestinian–Israeli war. They sought advantageous places for military attacks, and they could imagine participating in order to influence the outcome of the war. This complex changed after 9/11.

---

[5] I mention places, practices, participation, and people, in order to lead readers to Causadias (2020) presenting the "p-theory" as a very useful concept to describe the "fuzzy concept" of culture.

In the post-9/11 era, Jerrod Loughner's assassination of Congresswoman Gabrielle Giffords in Tucson, in January 2011, presents a similar constellation. Here I select it as an example to show what is overlooked when the analysis starts with "motivation". I present a description from Meloy and Yakeley (2014):

> As he (Loughner) appeared to decompensate further into psychosis, he became increasingly disruptive in his classes at Pima Community College, and on one occasion in the spring of 2010, he said this as recorded by campus police (PCC police report, September 23, 2010):
>
> > "He very slowly began telling me in a low and mumbled voice that under the Constitution which had been written on the wall for all to see, he had the right to his freedom of thought and whatever he thought in his head he could put on paper. By placing his thoughts in his homework assignment his teacher 'must be required to accept it' as a passing grade."
>
> > Here again the nexus between ideology and paranoia is suggested as dominant forces outside the self are perceived to be attempting to control his thoughts and are linked to an esoteric belief system; moreover, unknown to the police at that time, Loughner was nurturing a grievance toward Congresswoman Gabrielle Giffords from three years earlier when she did not answer his written question, "What is government if words have no meaning?" He carried out her attempted assassination and a mass murder in January, 2011. (pp. 360 *ff*.)

Only this kind of clinical *description* delivers the impression that Loughner's psychosis determined the assassination. Here we have a fuller plot of these circumstances (Hamm & Spaaij, 2017).

In August 2007 Loughner met Giffords for the first time at an event where she spoke to Girl Scouts. When Giffords invited the audience to pose questions, Loughner asked: "What is government if words have no meaning?" This provocative unanswerable question was clearly detected as nonsensical by Giffords, who changed her language to Spanish and turned to other participants. Hamm and Spaaij (2017) do not analyse this question.

One can make an attempt though. The entire assertion is that words have no meaning, framed in a "what … if …"-clause. Words without a meaning can be found in jokes, in children's play, or can be labelled as psychotic. But this utterance here is neither childish nor nonsensical. It is some kind of a diagnosis that Loughner poses to government representative Gabrielle Giffords. Who is the object of such diagnosis? Giffords responded *as if* she had understood Loughner's words: she responds with withdrawal to an obviously meaningless question. *His* words have no meaning is the diagnosis he cries out and her response confirms. It is the question of a social mind who feels that social bonds threaten to be lost. To connect this aspect with "government", however, leads to the conclusion that analysis cannot end here. For Loughner, it is the world he lives in which is threatened by a loss of meaning-while-speaking and, as language and words are the highest level of social bonding and social mind, he announces that under such dire circumstances no government has the right to anything.

We will never be able to decide about the "real meaning" of this question. But, conversation analysts (Schegloff et al., 1977) and linguists (Hampe & Grady, 2005) strongly confirm previous infant observations (Braten & Trevarthen, 2007): meaning is not only generated in the mouth of the speaker but also in the ears of the listener. Listening is a selective process: there are numerous ways of answering, ritual practices familiarise us with standardised responses, social life is released and social minds, too. We have a repertoire. However, in treatment, gifted analysts (Langs, 1983; Mitchell, 1988; Searles, 1987) have taught us how non-standardised responses change meanings. In a more technical manner, talk-in-interactions are organised in a broad framework as pair sequences, where the response indicates to the speaker how their first declaration is understood by the respondent. The aspect of convergence of various types of research is mentioned only briefly but underlines how important the response to a question is: it has the potential to change the question's meaning.

The implicit assertion of Loughner's question, whether words have no meaning, is, by lack of a response, unfortunately confirmed. From my "philosophical armchair", years later, I try to imagine what would have happened if Giffords could have answered: "Oh, if words have no meaning, I would not have neither heard nor understood your question. But I have. And this shows that words have meaning."

Later, Loughner complained to his friends, not that Giffords had blamed him—blaming would have required that he was perceived; Loughner complained that Giffords had *mistreated* him.

Nevertheless, he was registered as a participant of Giffords' event organisation and mailing list. So, he received a standard letter sent by Gifford's office, thanking him for his participation. When he found the letter, three years later, he scrawled "Die bitch" and "assassination plans have been made" onto it. This letter was lying around opened. This illustrates what is meant by personal and political grievances being mixed up.

What is known about his biography is summarised in the following: Loughner was born in 1988 as an only child; in schooldays he played the saxophone in the school band, wrote short stories, and was connected to the alternative music scene. Without strong political beliefs, he experienced what a friend called a "mental downfall" after the break-up of a romantic relationship with a girl. He started abusing drugs, vodka, and magic mushrooms, became interested in "conscious dreaming", and, due to failed exams, had to leave school after his junior year. He defaced a street sign, was arrested, and rejected from joining the army because of former drug use. But then he left the party scene, changed to a better lifestyle which made him lose weight. However, after giving up drugs and alcohol, at the age of twenty, other problems intruded into his awareness more pervasively. On the internet he wanted to revive his interests in controlled dreaming and mind control, but instead he found inspiring anti-government ideas—step 2 in the radicalisation process. Then, the movies by Alex Jones "became Loughner's enabler" (Hamm & Spaaij, 2017, p. 138). Jones claimed that the US government was an accomplice, not only in faked moon landings, but in the Oklahoma City bombing, and even in the 9/11 attacks. These conspiracy theories offered a political interpretative frame for personal grievances and can be linked to Loughner's resentment against Gabrielle Giffords and her political ideas. Giffords was a rising "shooting star" in the Obama administration, highly intelligent, fluent in five languages; many predicted a stellar career for her. Consequently, Loughner saw her as a representative of a tyrannical system, executing too much control on individual living. Giffords became a target because she was accessible, because she represented "the system", and because she was a woman. Women, in his mind, should not be endowed with too much power.

As Loughner was in Giffords's administrative mailing list, he was one of some 20,000 addressees who were informed about a next announcement. "This was the triggering event" (Hamm & Spaaij, 2017, p. 145). The woman he hated most would come close to where he lived! The day before the attack he wrote to his friends on Myspace: "I'll see you on National TV!" and then "This is a foreshadow … why doesn't anyone talk to me?" The day before the attack he filmed himself, posing with his Glock against his bare buttocks. He prepared a topic of conversation for his afterlife. The next day, the date of the attack, he posted on Myspace for a last time (Hamm & Spaaij, 2017, p. 145): "Good bye friends. Please don't be mad at me. The literacy rate is below 5%. I haven't talked to one person who is literate. I want to make it out alive. The longest war in the history of the United States. Goodbye. I'm saddened with the current currency and job employment. I had a bully at school. Thank you. P.S.—plead the fifth!"—I comment on these posts in the next paragraph.

The next day Loughner went to Giffords's meeting, stood up and shot her in the face, killing five more people. When he eventually tried to reload his gun, he was overwhelmed. He had no flight plan. This was the end of the Tucson massacre.

The zero zone of lone wolves' loneliness

Loughner's questions and writings, as already quoted, demonstrate that these men are not "lone" in a psychological sense only. His asking "… why doesn't anyone talk to me?" reads like a documentation of being fully ignored, in a moment of planning one of the most cruel terrorist attacks of the time.

In February 2020 in Germany, a young man forcefully drove his car into a large group of people. A few days before this attack, he is said to have broadcast dark but anticipatory words to a neighbour: "Soon, the newspapers will report about me." One of the most read German newspapers, the *Frankfurter Allgemeine Zeitung* (FAZ), reported this conversation in a court case on September 28, 2020. "Broadcasting intent" is recognised by journalists.

Lone wolves act on *personal and political grievances*, are surrounded by *enablers*, and inspired in a *warrior subculture*. Nevertheless, they have serious doubts which nearly all of them try to *broadcast*. This term of the radicalisation model means: they try to communicate—without response. Perceiving loneliness from a social psychological viewpoint, the most important thing is that they are not responded to, even ignored!

It is similar to a clinician's knowledge about people planning suicide; after the attempt, people often remember remarks which announce a more or less hidden, but now clearly intelligible, intention to commit suicide. Non-respondents, then, experience deep feelings of guilt, not to have paid attention—experiencing this as participation. The *broadcasting of intent* is well known from school shootings (Leenaars & Reed, 2016; Leuschner, 2013), from Breivik's attack in Norway in 2011, from the Christchurch attack, and many others. School shooters often announce their deed in advance, make remarks about their intentions verbally or via the internet, invite classmates in order to show them their newly acquired weapons. Often, the non-resonant behaviour of "bystanders", their ignorance to what is communicated to them, operates as a *trigger,* creating a *silent zone* of loneliness.

Announcing a planned action includes obligatory self-commitment. To withdraw from it, afterwards, one risks being considered a coward. The *silent zone* is created as the bystanders do not do what the maintenance of social mind and social structure would require them to do: prevent the execution of the act. Social mind theory would assume bystanders to know that withdrawal non-responsiveness heightens the pressure of the culprit's self-commitment; thus, bystanders exert an enormous influence by non-intervention. Social psychology handbooks inform about this type of role and function of bystanders in many other areas of research.

However, what Loughner communicated in these quotes is not only a silent zone, it is a zero zone. While silence can be broken by someone's response and a return to social life, and communication is an option, a zero zone leaves no such option. There is no return.

I will describe what I understand by zero zone in three steps: first, a short analysis of Loughner's communications; second, the role of bystanders; third, the internet and real abstraction.

Loughner's communication

Loughner's postings start with a "goodbye" to "friends", most of whom he had never met personally. He broadcast his intentions widely. In his postings on Myspace he mentioned the name of Gabrielle Giffords, he photographed his 9mm Glock, attached the picture. Some people from his personal environment, fellow students, and officials, were alarmed by his announcements, words, and behaviour. Obviously, they remained inactive. Hamm and Spaaij are right to call Loughner a "walking time-bomb" (p. 145). They read his messages as a "dire warning" which is undoubtedly correct, but only for reasonable people who want to prevent such horrible events. Is "warning" consistent with "Goodbye, friends"? Considering it a "warning" does not portray the full picture.

There is another way to categorise his message. One aspect is, he did not only warn that others were in danger, he also informed that he would carry out an event where he would have to survive ("to make it out alive"). The only thing not mentioned is what the event will be. It is only hinted at and that is what excites the imagination. It is "something" they are invited to, an *invitation* to attend a spectacle of cruelty in which he risks sacrificing himself.

FROM THE ABYSS OF LONELINESS TO THE BLISS OF SOLITUDE

The gladiators in ancient Rome exclaimed: "Hail, Caesar, those about to die salute you!" (*Ave Caesar! Morituri te salutant!*). This old formulation begins with words of greetings, just as Loughner's does. Gladiators were forced to participate in actions of mutual killing. The people in the stands wanted "bread and games" (*panem et circenses*). They wanted entertainment through watching others fight and die. Here, it is Loughner who calls out to be doomed to death. Like an ancient gladiator, there is a minimal chance of survival: he wants "to make it out alive". He names political grievances, "current currency and job employment", and a personal grievance to have had a "bully at school". He invites his friends to a self-initiated spectacle of cruelty: the miracle to be solved is why nobody read this as a warning. My answer is that it was read as an *invitation* by his "friends", and as "people in the stands" (behind their online screens) they could silently wait to read or hear about what happened in the next news broadcast. Again, we cannot decide definitely between "warning" or "invitation". Such double categorisation (Deppermann, 2011; DiMaggio, 1997; Douglas & Hull, 1992; Lepper, 2000; Potter & Reicher, 1987) is often found in communication; I mentioned pre-suicidal messages which often read accurately—after the incident. This is my privileged position, of course. Indecisive communications, based on double categorisation, have the effect of placing the responsibility on the listeners. It is for them to interpret what was said.

They decided to say nothing. Did they "not participate"? Non-participation does not equal non-communication. The readers received an announcement which evokes expectations: why did nobody give Loughner a call or inform police or other law enforcement? My proposition is that what appears as passivity is the active influence of bystanders.

The role of bystanders

"This lack of communication among bystanders marks the final, tragic lesson of the Tucson massacre," Hamm and Spaaij (2017, p. 149) conclude. Their book delivers evidence that lone wolf attacks can be stopped by others; it's not the lone wolf alone who succeeds or does not. The role of bystanders overcomes methodological individualism. The 2011 Norwegian lone wolf, Anders Breivik, for example, was observed by a pedestrian while he entered his van in police uniform with a pistol in his hand. The pedestrian alerted the police; however, he could only speak to a tape which was not listened to until ninety minutes later. This gave Breivik the time to flee from Oslo to the youth summer camp on Utoya island, where he shot seventy-six young people dead (Sandberg, 2015). Although Loughner broadcast his intent, no police were present to protect Giffords. Alaska's governor Sarah Palin had a "target list", for use in political advertising against the Democratic Party, which Giffords was on. Giffords was depicted in the crosshairs of a gun's telescopic sight. She must have been known as a politician she was at risk. Facebook executive Randi Zuckerberg said many people on the social networking site are wondering whether Sarah Palin is to blame. In the year before the Tucson massacre, Sarah Palin wrote: "It's time to take a stand" on the map. Giffords had reacted to announcements like these and remarked: "When people do that, they've got to realise there are consequences to that action."[6] Later, of course, Palin's team denied and disavowed everything.

In line with the thinking presented here, one can see that there is some "broadcasting intent" which does not come from the perpetrators but from the bystanders.

Hamm and Spaaij (2017) add a long and detailed chapter about the influence of the FBI. Several years ago, the FBI started a programme where agents "test" possible lone wolves in order to provoke them to become active. They keep an eye on young men in trouble, contact them as "brothers" and offer to introduce them to "brothers" in higher positions, who "really know" what "could be done". After some time, when the young man is "ready for action" he is offered full equipment—and when he places the "bomb" (which will never explode) in a large building, other agents enter the scene and arrest the perpetrator. The authors are far from accusing the FBI in general, but they present rich material. One of the seduced people later said: "It was like an invitation." And Hamm & Spaaij (2017, p. 217) add: "In this and other cases, the FBI seemed to create the very enemy it was hunting."

This remark addresses an event in September 1975. When attention turns to the post-9/11 attacks, Hamm and Spaaij (2017) speak of FBI "mythmaking". The problem is: how will the FBI ever recognise the endpoint of terrorism when defending against it contributes to its enaction?

Studying these cases in detail forces one to stop thinking in deterministic and individualistic terms. It is time to include the broadcast of intent, on the internet and in social life, uttered by vulnerable and "easily susceptible men on the margins of society" (p. 260), in theory and intervention programmes. More attention should be directed to active enablers, passive bystanders, and to the communication in the media.

Internet and real abstraction

Lone wolves live the ideal of leaderless resistance (Sageman, 2008), generating worldwide advertisements (ISIS) and audiences. Sageman studied 172 Salafi Jihadists; his research included seventeen variables, grouped in three categories: social background, psychological make-up, and circumstances of joining the Jihad. He described how young men, before 2004, were recruited by face-to-face engagement in local halal restaurants. Since then an enormous expansion of communication and interaction in internet forums has evolved.

Sageman observes that the age of terrorists has decreased. Before 2003 his sample had an average age of twenty-six: now they are about twenty years of age. "At the same time, gender separation among terrorists is starting to disappear because of the Internet." This observation initiated a productive series of studies (Bromark, 2014; Cunningham, 2003; Gan et al., 2019; Jacques & Taylor, 2008).

---

[6] Taken from: https://abcnews.go.com/Politics/sarah-palins-crosshairs-ad-focus-gabrielle-giffords-debate/story?id=12576437, December 18, 2020.

Social affiliation plays a prominent role in the process of radicalisation. Sageman proposed a "bunch of boys" theory. According to this theory, young men collectively decide to join a terrorist organisation. A second pathway was described as being through joining childhood friends:

> I described how the interactivity among a "bunch of guys" acted as an echo chamber, which progressively radicalized them collectively to the point where they were ready to collectively join a terrorist organization. (Sageman, 2008, p. 116)

Strong social affiliation is one of the predispositions he observes in his rich material. What he notes there is how the internet alters these influences. However, there are even more changes now: there is a higher degree of activity in chat rooms and forums and the degree of women's participation has increased. Another alteration must be considered. The passive websites might be important for (self-)radicalisation but they "merely reinforce already made-up minds". A new and very influential phenomenon is the high degree of interactivity "and rapidly changing human relationships in ways of which we are not yet fully aware" (p. 114).

> The intensity of feelings developed online rival those developed offline. Some terrorist experts are skeptical that online relationships can generate the intensity of trust and emotions required to sacrifice oneself for cause or comrades. However, many psychological studies have compared the strength of positive feelings that people develop toward each other online and offline. It seems that online feelings are stronger in almost every measurement than offline feelings. This is a robust finding that has been duplicated many times. (Sageman, 2008, p. 114)

People who have exchanged their views intensively online, quickly build strong bonds when meeting for the first time offline; some hurry to marry, because they believe they have a deep understanding of the other—before ever having met face-to-face. What can be observed in terrorist circles is not so different from what can be observed in "normal" life. To arrange dates online tops offline meetings not only in frequency, but in form, mutual assessment, and language codes.[7] This does not only hold true for love, but for collective suicides as well.

On the other hand, online meetings and relationships are associated with low costs for ending a relationship. You can simply cut the connection. The internet's anonymity protects offline risks. Both higher and faster levels of interactivity and intimacy, as well as lack of civility, are not yet fully recognised within society offline. Sageman warns that, beyond the topic of terrorism, "… offline society has not come to the kind of communicative compromise that took centuries to develop in face-to-face communications" (p. 115). He sees what I would call an

---

[7] New changes in terminology, like "friends" and "*social*" networks" have intruded into everybody's everyday speech. Students observing the social milieu are using data generated through online assessment technologies.

"erosion of social mind". Conversation analysts have begun to study the influence of technological changes (Hutchby, 2001).

Sageman is sensitive to historical distinctions. In his book there is an interesting passage:

> This new medium of communication is changing people's relationships as well. The previous major revolution in communication—the invention of movable type printing by Johannes Gutenberg around 1450—resulted in the Reformation, the Counter-Reformation, the various religious wars that plagued Europe, the universal spread of education (once books were available, there was a reason to learn to read), the dramatic rise of mail (now that people knew how to read and write, they could write letters to each other), the Enlightenment (including the rise of science, which was mediated through books), and many far more subtle changes. Interpersonal relationships that were developed and sustained by written means of communication differed from those dependent on oral means of communication, making people more introspective and giving rise to the novel and the scientific study of introspection (psychology, for example). Computer-mediated communication, which seems to collapse time and eliminate space, has the potential to transform human relationships faster and to an even greater degree. (Sageman, 2008, p. 115)

Such revolutions in technology have been described by a German founder of sociology, Georg Simmel. I quote from the English translation of his book with the uncommon title *The Philosophy of Money* (1900):

> As soon as one realizes the extent to which human action in every sphere of mental activity operates with abstractions, it is not as strange as it may seem at first glance that not only the study of the economy but the economy itself is constituted by a real abstraction from the comprehensive reality of valuations. (Simmel & Frisby, 2009, p. 78)

The term "real abstraction" addresses not only a mode of scientific description, but a reality of historical movements. Some spheres of life separate themselves from one another and constitute themselves as abstract realities. When one no longer exchanges things in kind (natural goods) but makes monetary payments, money acquires the status of a real abstraction. It is a real thing which can be seen and touched, but it operates as an abstraction. In 1877 Japan's taxes were still calculated in rice and in Western Europe salt was at an earlier time used to calculate payments (hence *salary*). Later, money superseded any other currency (Schwartz, 2017). This is how Sageman uses Gutenberg's invention of the mid-fifteenth century: his analogy illustrates that the same is happening with the internet, just on a higher level. Interactivity, conversation, exchange, all take place to a large extent without corporeality. Letters, the telephone, etc., used to be intermediate steps. These technological tools gradually lost their voice or face-to-face connection more and more. Today, Hamm and Spaaij (2017, p. 158) are completely right:

> Virtually all lone wolves have an affinity with some person, community, or group, be it online or in the real world. This is a significant finding because it contests the policy assumption that lone wolf terrorists do not communicate with others or follow in the violent tradition of others. They clearly do.

They "do communicate", but just in this abstract fashion, which we saw at the end of Jarred Loughner's disastrous case. There is communication, there are friends, but that doesn't aid support to step beyond the borders of a zero zone of loneliness, it intensifies it. The real abstraction of disembodied internet communication nourishes unsurmountable doubts of being alive or not. This might be another fraction of his encoded question to Gabrielle Giffords: "What is government if words have no meaning?" In particular, people who understand the information technology of the internet know that in this real abstraction words have no meaning, can have none.

The end of lone-wolf age?

Of course, there is a message. Many authors, at this point, have mentioned hope: that a multi-step radicalisation model makes lone wolves recognisable and understandable to a certain degree. At least, detectable by attentive relatives, neighbours, friends—in real life. It seems as if in a socially dense community, no crime could happen without at least one single person being informed about it. Not listening and non-responding produce the social vacuum we call loneliness. This is not to blame "society" or single bystanders. It just makes the social production of unbearable loneliness visible. Julia Ebner (2017, pp. 78 ff.) describes jihadists and right-wing terrorists as equivalent. Loneliness, in both groups, is produced by the highly attractive offer to define yourself anew in every moment by abstraction from real personal meetings, from temporality, from communicating bodies, from trusted circumstances. The price of this is disembodiment. One cannot arbitrarily invent new identities for oneself or commit oneself to new narratives without limit.

The question arises as to if there is an end to lone-wolf terrorism? Hamm and Spaaij (2017) write as if they assume that a new age has begun. Others are more doubtful. Four waves of modern terrorism were clearly distinguished by Rapoport (2016). A wave is defined as

> a cycle of activity in a given time period—a cycle characterised by expansion and contraction phases. A crucial feature is its international character; similar activities occur in several countries, driven by a common predominant energy that shapes the participating group's characteristics and mutual relationships. (p. 4)

The four distinct waves of modern terrorism were: the anarchist wave (nineteenth century), anti-colonial wave (1930–1960), New Left wave (mid-1960s to early 1990s), and religious wave (until today). Here we can learn how terrorism evolves over time. Rapoport describes these waves as lasting for about forty years before new strategies and forms appear.

This distinction has been a strong guideline in terrorism history and research. Meanwhile, some authors (Gallagher, 2017) are doubtful. In what way should the "loneliness" of lone wolves be responded to? As a multi-faceted event …

- As a social phenomenon of (mostly) young men in desperate states. In this case, neighbours, relatives, and families should be more carefully guided in responding to their utterances, withdrawals, and other behaviours sensitised by the radicalisation model.
- Their mental disorders cannot be described as the sole factor, but only embedded in a multitude of other factors; one of them is the role of silent bystanders.
- Their mysteriously encrypted public statements should be more carefully listened to as indicators of a radicalisation step accompanied by a new stage of desperate loneliness.
- Political opponents should do nothing that could justify radical actions.
- A model of lone wolf radicalisation should be complemented by a model of opponents' public statements radicalisation.
- Access to arms and explosives should be better controlled.
- Up to now the internet has not been seen clearly enough as a real abstraction that devastates social life by devaluing the "social mind".
- "Social mind" was a social achievement acquired over centuries, the violation of which was always considered a risk for more than the local event only.

In all these areas social research is on the way and urgently required. We should not lose sight of the main terrorist threat coming from right-wing extremists, not from violent Muslim extremists (Kurzman & Schanzer, 2015).

References

Akhtar, S. (2017). The tripod of terrorism. *International Forum of Psychoanalysis, 26*(3): 139–159.

Albert, S., & Ruiter, J. P. de (2018). Repair: the interface between interaction and cognition. *Topics in Cognitive Science, 10*(2): 279–313. https://doi.org/10.1111/tops.12339.

Blakeley, R., & Raphael, S. (2016). Understanding Western state terrorism. In: R. Jackson (Ed.), *Routledge Handbook of Critical Terrorism Studies* (pp. 339–359). London: Taylor & Francis.

Bloom, M., & Horgan, J. (2019). *Small Arms: Children and Terrorism.* Ithaca, NY: Cornell University Press.

Bollas, C. (2018). *Meaning and Melancholia: Life in the Age of Bewilderment.* London: Routledge.

Braten, S., & Trevarthen, C. (2007). Prologue: From infant intersubjectivity and participant movements to simulation and conversation in cultural common sense. In: S. Braten (Ed.), *On Being Moved: From Mirror Neurons to Empathy* (pp. 21–35). Amsterdam, PA: John Benjamins.

Bromark, S. (2014). *Massacre in Norway: The 2011 Terror Attacks on Oslo and the Utøya Youth Camp.* Lincoln, NE: Potomac, University of Nebraska Press.

Causadias, J. M. (2020). What is culture? Systems of people, places, and practices. *Applied Developmental Science, 24*(4): 310–322.

Cocorada, E. (2012). Gender differences in the micro-violence connected to the assessment process. *Procedia—Social and Behavioral Sciences, 33*: 183–187.

Coleman, L. (2004). *The Copycat Effect: How the Media and Popular Culture Trigger the Mayhem in Tomorrow's Headlines*. New York: Simon & Schuster.

Collins, R. (2008). *Violence—A Micro-Sociological Theory*. Princeton, NJ: Princeton University Press.

Conquest, R. (2008). *The Great Terror: A Reassessment* (40th anniversary edn.). Oxford: Oxford University Press.

Cunningham, K. J. (2003). Cross-regional trends in female terrorism. *Studies in Conflict & Terrorism, 26*(3): 171–195. https://doi.org/10.1080/10576100390211419.

Cushman, P. (2010). So who's asking? Politics, hermeneutics, and individuality. In: R. Frie & W. J. Coburn (Eds.), *Psychoanalytic Inquiry: Volume 32. Persons in Context: The Challenge of Individuality in Theory and Practice* (pp. 21–40). New York: Routledge.

Deppermann, A. (2011). The transformation of descriptions into categorizations. *Human Studies, 34*(2): 155–181.

DiMaggio, P. (1997). Culture and cognition. *Annual Review of Sociology, 23*: 263–287.

Douglas, M., & Hull, D. (Eds.) (1992). *How Classification Works: Nelson Goodman among the Social Sciences*. Edinburgh, UK: Edinburgh University Press.

Ebner, J. (2017). *The Rage: The Vicious Circle of Islamist and Far-Right Extremism*. London: I. B. Tauris.

Eby, C. A. (2012). *The Nation that Cried Lone Wolf: A Data-driven Analysis of Individual Terrorists in the United States Since 9/11*. Monterey, CA: Naval Postgraduate School.

Freud, S. (1923b). *The Ego and the Id. S. E., 19*: 12–68. London: Hogarth.

Gallagher, M. J. (2017). The 2016 "lone wolf" tsunami—is Rapoport's "religious wave" ending? *Journal of Strategic Security, 10*(2): 60–76.

Gan, R., Neo, L. S., Chin, J., & Khader, M. (2019). Change is the only constant: the evolving role of women in the Islamic State in Iraq and Syria (ISIS). *Women & Criminal Justice, 29*(4–5): 204–220. https://doi.org/10.1080/08974454.2018.1547674.

Ganor, B. (2002). Defining terrorism: Is one man's terrorist another man's freedom fighter? *Police Practice and Research, 3*(4): 287–304.

Goodwin, C. (1987). Forgetfulness as an interactive resource. *Social Psychology Quarterly, 50*: 115–131.

Greiner, B. (2007). *Krieg ohne Fronten. Die USA in Vietnam* (Vol. 648). Bonn, Germany: Bundeszentrale für politische Bildung, Hamburger Edition.

Hamm, M. S., & Spaaij, R. (2017). *The Age of Lone Wolf Terrorism: Studies in Transgression*. New York: Columbia University Press.

Hampe, B., & Grady, J. E. (Eds.) (2005). *Cognitive Linguistics Research: Vol. 29. From Perception to Meaning. Image Schemas in Cognitive Linguistics*. Berlin: Mouton de Gruyter.

Hankiss, A. (2018). The legend of the lone wolf. *Journal of Strategic Security, 11*(2): 54–72.

Hopper, E. (2003a). *The Social Unconscious: Selected Papers*. Philadelphia, PA: Jessica Kingsley.

Hopper, E. (2003b). *Traumatic Experience in the Unconscious Life of Groups. The Fourth Basic Assumption: Incohesion: Aggregation/massification or (ba) I:A/M* (Vol. 23). London: Jessica Kingsley.

Huron, D. (2006). *Sweet Anticipation—Music and the Psychology of Expectation: A Bradford Book*. Cambridge, MA: MIT Press.

Hutchby, I. (2001). *Conversation and Technology: From the Telephone to the Internet*. Cambridge: Polity.

Jackson, R. (Ed.) (2016). *Routledge Handbook of Critical Terrorism Studies*. London: Taylor & Francis.

Jacques, K., & Taylor, P. J. (2008). Male and female suicide bombers: Different sexes, different reasons? *Studies in Conflict & Terrorism*, *31*(4): 304–326. https://doi.org/10.1080/10576100801925695.

Jensen, R. B. (2014). The pre-1914 anarchist "lone wolf" terrorist and governmental responses. *Terrorism and Political Violence*, *26*(1): 86–94. https://doi.org/10.1080/09546553.2014.849919.

Kurzman, C., & Schanzer, D. (2015, June 16). The growing right-wing terror threat. *New York Times*. https://nytimes.com/2015/06/16/opinion/the-other-terror-threat.html.

Langs, R. (1983). *Unconscious Communication in Everyday Life*. New York: Jason Aronson.

Laster, K., & Erez, E. (2015). Sisters in terrorism? Exploding stereotypes. *Women & Criminal Justice*, *25*(1–2): 83–99. https://doi.org/10.1080/08974454.2015.1023884.

Leenaars, J., & Reed, A. (2016). *Understanding Lone Wolves: Towards a Theoretical Framework for Comparative Analysis*. The Hague: International Center for Counter-Terrorism.

Lepper, G. (2000). *Categories in Text and Talk: A Practical Introduction to Categorization Analysis*. London: Sage.

Lethem, J. (2004). *The Fortress of Solitude*. New York: Vintage.

Leuschner, V. (2013). Exzessive individuelle Gewalt. "School Shootings" und "Lone Wolf Terrorism" als soziale Phänomene. *Berliner Journal für Soziologie*, *23*(1): 27–49. https://doi.org/10.1007/s11609-013-0212-9.

Mazur, A. (2009). A hormonal interpretation of Collin's micro-sociological theory of violence. *Journal for the Theory of Social Behavior*, *39*(4): 434–447.

McCauley, C., & Moskalenko, S. (2014). Toward a profile of lone wolf terrorists: What moves an individual from radical opinion to radical action. *Terrorism and Political Violence*, *26*(1): 69–85. https://doi.org/10.1080/09546553.2014.849916.

Meloy, J. R., & Hoffmann, J. (Eds.) (2014). *International Handbook of Threat Assessment*. Oxford: Oxford University Press.

Meloy, J. R., & Mohandie, K. (2014). Assessing threats by direct interview of the violent true believer. In: J. R. Meloy & J. Hoffmann (Eds.), *International Handbook of Threat Assessment* (pp. 388–398). Oxford: Oxford University Press.

Meloy, J. R., & Yakeley, J. (2014). The violent true believer as a "lone wolf"—psychoanalytic perspectives on terrorism. *Behavioral Sciences & the Law*, *32*(3): 347–365. https://doi.org/10.1002/bsl.2109.

Mitchell, S. A. (1988). *Relational Concepts in Psychoanalysis: An Integration*. Cambridge, MA: Harvard University Press.

Myres, G. (2012). Investigating in the market of violence: Toward a micro-theory of terrorist financing. *Studies in Conflict & Terrorism*, *35*(10): 693–711.

Polanyi, M. (1969). *Knowing and Being: Essay by Michael Polanyi*. M. Green (Ed.). Chicago, IL: University of Chicago Press.

Potter, J., & Reicher, S. (1987). Discourses of community and conflict: The organisation of social categories in accounts of a "riot". *British Journal of Social Psychology, 26*: 25–40.

Rapoport, D. C. (2016). The four waves of modern terrorism. In: S. M. Chermak & J. D. Freilich (Eds.), *Library of Essays on Transnational Crime. Transnational Terrorism* (pp. 3–30). London: Routledge.

Reemtsma, J.-P. (2008). *Vertrauen und Gewalt. Versuch über eine besondere Konstellation der Moderne.* Hamburg, Germany: Hamburger Edition.

Sacks, H. (1978). Some technical considerations of a dirty joke. In: J. Schenkein (Ed.), *Studies in the Organization of Conversational Interaction* (pp. 249–270). New York: Academic Press.

Sageman, M. (2008). *Leaderless Jihad: Terror Networks in the Twenty-first Century.* Philadelphia, PA: University of Pennsylvania Press.

Sandberg, S. (2015). Terrorism as cultural bricolage: the case of Anders Behring Breivik. In: D. Ziegler, M. Gerster, & S. Krämer (Eds.), *Framing Excessive Violence: Discourse and Dynamics* (pp. 77–96). Basingstoke, UK: Palgrave Macmillan.

Sanfilippo, A., McGrath, L., & Bell, E. (2014). Computer modeling of violent intent: a content Analysis Approach. In: J. R. Meloy & J. Hoffmann (Eds.), *International Handbook of Threat Assessment* (pp. 224–235). Oxford: Oxford University Press.

Schegloff, E. A., Jefferson, G., & Sacks, H. (1977). The preference for self-correction in the organization of repair in conversation. *Language, 53*: 361–382.

Schmid, A. P. (2011). The definition of terrorism. In: A. P. Schmid (Ed.), *The Routledge Handbook of Terrorism Research* (pp. 39–98). London: Routledge.

Schwartz, B. (2017). How is history possible? Georg Simmel on empathy and realism. *Journal of Classical Sociology, 17*(3): 213–237. https://doi.org/10.1177/1468795X17717877.

Searles, H. F. (1987). *My Work with Borderline Patients.* London: Jason Aronson.

Shanahan, T. (2016). The definition of terrorism. In: R. Jackson (Ed.), *Routledge Handbook of Critical Terrorism Studies* (pp. 223–246). London: Taylor & Francis.

Silke, A. (2003). Becoming a terrorist. In: A. Silke (Ed.), *Terrorists, Victims and Society: Psychological Perspectives on Terrorism and Its Consequences* (pp. 29–54). Chichester, UK: Wiley.

Simmel, G., & Frisby, D. (Eds.) (2009). *The Philosophy of Money.* London: Routledge.

Spaaij, R. (2012). *Understanding Lone Wolf Terrorism: Global Patterns, Motivations and Prevention.* Dordrecht, the Netherlands: Springer.

Stepansky, P. E. (2009). *Psychoanalysis at the Margins.* New York: Other Press.

Veen, M., Skelton, J., & La Croix, A. de (2020). Knowledge, skills and beetles: Respecting the privacy of private experiences in medical education. *Perspectives on Medical Education.* Advance online publication. https://doi.org/10.1007/s40037-020-00565-5.

Wittgenstein, L. (1953). *Philosophical Investigations.* Oxford: Blackwell.

Yeats, W. B., & Watts, C. T. (1921). *The Collected Poems of W. B. Yeats.* Ware, Herts, UK: Wordsworth Editions, 2008.

Young, C. (2010). Narrative embodiments: Enclaves of the Self in the realm of medicine. In: A. Jaworski & N. Coupland (Eds.), *The Discourse Reader* (2nd edn., pp. 407–418). London: Routledge.

CHAPTER 4

Historical roots of solitude and private self (with continual reference to Shakespeare)[1]

Aleksandar Dimitrijević

The world without and before solitude

In contemporary Western societies, the ideas of solitude and private self are almost taken for granted. We have developed systems for protecting our privacy and exhibiting it only when, we believe, we decide to do so. We entertain highly speculative theories about personality parts that are gladly, or out of necessity, shared with others and those that remain concealed or revealed only to intimate friends. In stark contrast to this, contemporary media are often used as a means to aggressively peek into someone's privacy to an unprecedented level. That can all lead to an illusion that solitude and private self—together with the sense of identity, uniqueness, autonomy—have, both ontogenetically and historiogenetically, been with us since forever, that we are born with them, and they simply "unfold" under favourable circumstances.

Just as these beliefs are intuitively acceptable, they are fundamentally incorrect. It was not always like that, and it is not like that at all points on the globe, even now. For instance, on the island of Bali, the individual self plays a minimal role and does not have the inner dimension—members of some communities there do not use personal names, or their names change with age and social or family roles (Gergen, 1991, pp. 8–10). Other indigenous communities do not have words for inner states, or use only a couple of nouns and/or adjectives. And there are still places in which one person is never alone, neither at home nor while working.

Luckily for us, it is now possible to follow the gradual change and the introduction of the ideas of solitude and private self through the history of Western civilisation. The purpose of

---

[1] Many thanks to Tobias Blümel, historian, who advised me on how to improve a previous version of this chapter.

this chapter will be to review the historians' findings about this development, and to offer yet another reading of Shakespeare all focused on solitude and privacy.[2]

An excellent illustration to begin with is the tragic destiny of Oedipus (though in a sense different than usually discussed by psychoanalysts). Once he learns about his responsibility for the plague that has hit the city of Thebes—that is, killing his father and marrying his mother— Oedipus asks for the worst imaginable punishment. He becomes homeless, and takes the status of a person who does not belong to a polis, because he knows something that will be confirmed by Socrates: in the process of defining and maintaining who you are, exile is deadlier than poison. The praxis of ostracism was considered by Greek communities of that era the cruellest of all punishments. It could lead directly to death or slavery, but also to the loss of personal identity, which was utterly dependent on the social one: belonging to a polis, or in Athens to a specific neighbourhood inside the polis, and one's home, was more essential than what we nowadays call the actualisation of one's self. In accord with that, travel that led to an extended stay in foreign lands brought an indelible sense of uprootedness and social and personal inadequacy. This was even worse when living there permanently. For evidence, one need look no further than Aristotle's inferior status in Athens.

It was only slightly different in the first centuries of Christianity, both before and after Constantine, when the conception of prayer was that it should take place inside a person, in solitude, and not as a group ritual. In his review of the history of the relationship between Christianity and the sense of interiority, Foucault (1988, p. 35) describes three stoic "technologies of the self": revealing oneself in letters to friends, exploration of one's consciousness, and ascesis. He emphasised Christian believers' attempts to recognise themselves as sinners, admitting their sins, and basing their activities on that (p. 40). However, this change was in no way sufficient, since it had affected a minimal number of pious members of European societies, mostly ascetic, desert monks (Ariés & Duby, 1988, pp. 449–455), and wandering knights (Huizinga, 1924, pp. 84–141). Large masses, no matter how pious, especially in the Byzantine empire, have not encountered any of this.

The everyday life of ordinary people of that epoch, however, could in no way include isolation or solitude. As recently as the twelfth century, it was utterly impossible to meet a person alone in the street or on the road. If anyone were found alone, they would be considered psychotic, a criminal, or an actor,[3] and laws did not punish an attack on them or the rape of

---

[2] The review of the historical roots of solitude and private self is based on the following texts: Ariés & Duby, 2001; Baumeister, 1986, 1987, 1998; Bound Alberti, 2019; Brockmeier, 2001; Danziger, 1997; Gergen, 1991, ch. 2; Huizinga, 1924; Kristeva, 1995; Seigel, 2005.

[3] After the fall of the Roman Empire, the first theatre was opened in England in 1567. During the intermittent eleven centuries, actors were treated as heathens and vagabonds, and there were few jobs for an educated person stigmatised as working in theatre. Actors were often arrested, whipped, and put into shackles. A special "Law about the homeless" put into practice in England in 1604, to replace an older law that allowed for selling the homeless as slaves, applied to actors as well (Greenblatt, 2005, pp. 74–88).

a woman found alone outside her home. This applied in France and Central Europe (Ariés & Duby, 1988) and in England (Greenblatt, 2005, p. 87).

Solitude became an important, and sometimes central topic in human relationships, artistic representations, and philosophical elaborations, during a clearly defined historical moment. But the change towards the personal and social worlds that we find familiar today was contingent on many diverse factors.

Societal changes that led to the emergence of solitude

Solitude and clear distinction between the private self and social roles were not widely practised even in the late Middle Ages. When, between 1050 and 1200, private religiousness became more prominent, and the poetry of French troubadours more widely known,[4] tides started changing. Only by the beginning of the fifteenth century, significant societal changes gave birth to a different type of individual.

Primus inter pares among these changes was undoubtedly the increased insistence on the empirical approach to sciences. Bacon and Galileo introduced the standards of observation, replicability, and measurement, the telescope showed that the world was incomparably vaster than people had earlier believed, and in 1543 Copernicus had, after long hesitation, published a book that advocated the heliocentric system. The evidence that the Earth and humans were not at the centre of the universe lead to the rejection of the image of the world in which everything was strictly fixed, defined, and unchangeable in the ontological and, consequently, social realms.

Science brought another source of massive changes essential for this chapter's topic: the possibility of fast transportation. In the feudal age, it was still considered that everything and everyone were in their appropriate places, and that movement could only be unnatural or forced (Ferguson, 1999, p. 171). In the Middle Ages, individuals moved to find more fertile land, for trade, or for pilgrimage. In the early modern age, many individuals were leaving without the idea of return but motivated by their need to change or improve themselves, so much so that it is justified to say that movement was the central experience of modernity (p. 171).

As the centre of all these changes, cities grew enormously, and living in them became more prestigious. Already in the sixteenth century, in places like Naples, Venice, and London, people did not know most of their neighbours, did not produce their food or sew their clothes. Urbanisation brought about small, nuclear families, distance from nature, and a clear separation between private and professional spaces. In its turn, that led to individualism, experiencing oneself as a remote unit whose aim was to be self-defining and self-improving.

Especially noteworthy was the idea of European colonisers that the Americas were a "New World" that they were supposed to organise and shape in their own fashion, a notion that would remain alive at least until the end of the nineteenth century, as witnessed in Whitman's poetry.

---

[4] For details see chapters 8–10 in Huizinga, 1924.

60   FROM THE ABYSS OF LONELINESS TO THE BLISS OF SOLITUDE

This idea would lead to the possibility of crossing the ocean and leading a life significantly different from one in England, France, or Spain.[5] Many had discovered that it was possible to leave behind the identity and moral code one had in the "Old World" and build entirely new ones.

The change was also brought about by negative developments. One of those was the plague, which around 1350 and throughout the following century killed a large percentage of the European population, caused economic and social problems, even fears that the year 1500 would bring the end of the world. It also made people isolate, avoid social contacts, and become self-reliant.

In predominantly Catholic countries, an important role was played by the Inquisition, a permanent Church-based judicial institution (Thomsett, 2010). Formed in 1227 by Pope Gregory IX, the Inquisition treated non-believers, heretics, Jews, conversos, witches, and scientists with "the point of view that heresy and other crimes against God or the Church deserved a death sentence emerged around the end of the 4th century" (p. 4). The situation was at its worst in Spain, during the Reconquista of the second half of the fifteenth century, especially under the Grand Inquisitor Tomás de Torquemada. This situation instilled fear into millions, many fled or converted, but possibly everyone had to reconsider their faith, identity, loyalty, what to claim publicly and what to keep inside themselves or utter only *sotto voce*.

Another innovation of that era was the rise of Protestantism, which left far-reaching consequences, primarily through the insistence on inner faith instead of rituals that gathered large masses of believers (Bell, 2007): "Preaching of the 15th century encouraged people to make religion personal: to see Christ's sufferings in the mind's eye, to test them upon the heart" (p. 169); "… an inward turn: rather than rely on an uncertain Church, each individual must perform his own spiritual self-examination" (p. 184). The new religion also rejected the idea of purgatory and praying, which was believed to help the dead, further severing connections among people. The first attempts to understand mental disorders arising not as a result of witchcraft but as delusions, appeared, albeit outside clerical institutions. This spurred interest in psychological phenomena and the exploration of the inner world (Dimitrijević, 2015).

The Reformation also inspired the translations of the Bible into languages people used in their everyday lives. This process started with Luther's famous emancipation of the German language in the fifteenth century and reached England around 1520 (Greenblatt, 2005, p. 90). This meant that individual believers could perform the service previously reserved for priests, which made them incomparably more independent subjects than ever in the history of Christianity. This meant that mammoth, centralised clerical systems were not necessary any more, but also that talking to God became equal to talking to oneself.

Printing was introduced around 1440 and within several decades the availability of books and literacy grew exponentially. Already in the age of Shakespeare, some books enjoyed such wide reception that they had several editions (Shapiro, 2005, p. 340). McLuhan (1962) even

---

[5] This relocation of large groups of emigrants again had a predecessor in the unique experience of Marco Polo's travel to Asia in 1272.

claimed that Gutenberg had invented solitude: printed books had made it possible for people to seek aloneness, read in isolation, explore their interiority.

New artistic genres started appearing in that same period. While in the early memoirs there was no clear distinction between public and private (Ariés & Duby, 1988, p. 468), authors now came to believe it made sense for them to describe their lives, attitudes, and worldviews. With Augustine's *Confessions* (397–400) as the long-held and major influential predecessor, autobiographies with a broad spectrum of stories about oneself, independent of history or apologetics, became a genre per se and not an incident during the Early Modern age (Ariés & Duby, 1988, p. 471).

In the fourteenth century, ordinary people's faces started appearing in portraits, and paintings did not have to represent religious content. Giotto introduced linear perspective (Drury, 2000, p. 8), and different technical innovations made psychological portraiture possible: "The use of oil paint and surface effects made it possible to make the pupil of the eye shine like a mirror, a luminous presence that inhabited the portrait as the soul inhabits the body" (Ariés & Duby, 1988, p. 564).

In the 1380s, painters began signing their works—feeling they were the creators and almost godlike—and representing their faces (Bell, 2007, p. 168). Many still portrayed themselves as just one of the characters in a group (like Michelangelo, probably, in the *Last Judgement* fresco of the Sistine Chapel), usually the one with whom the observer could establish eye contact (like Raphael in the *School of Athens*). It may seem peculiar today that humanity had to wait until the end of the fifteenth century for the first self-portraitist. No one before Dürer contemplated painting himself as the painting's main subject systematically.[6] Dürer painted his image for the first time when he was thirteen years old (Honour & Fleming, 2002, p. 468) and repeated this seven more times throughout his life. He "created a visual form for the solitary, private self" (Bell, 2007, p. 184) and that is why "[H]is three self-portraits in oil are milestones in the history of introspection that bridge the divide between the Middle Ages and the Renaissance" (Ariés & Duby, 1988, p. 494).

The birth of solitude

All the changes mentioned above brought forth the idea for broad masses of people of forming a personal identity, and the possibility of changing that identity over one's lifetime—two issues unknown before the Renaissance.

The coming centuries were marked by more extensive social mobility—among social classes and through radical changes of manners and place of living. The number of manufacturing workshops and the level of production multiplied. Money circulated much faster, and individuals moved up and down the social hierarchy in unprecedented ways. More than ever, life

---

[6] Dürer was also the first painter who systematically signed his drawings and paintings (Honour & Fleming, 2002, p. 468).

became defined by the capacity to innovate and initiate rather than by the inherited societal position. This process brought about new professions and required specialisation and different forms of education, while previously professions were few, and schools and specialisations barely existed.

In 1980, Stephen Greenblatt, under the strong influence of Foucault, described the process of self-fashioning. He claimed that the Renaissance upper classes dressed, posed, and presented themselves publicly in certain ways that were prescribed by different levels of European society, and described in books. This had a circular effect on the reshaping of culture and arts. Some individuals also realised they could fashion themselves in individual ways, paying little or no attention to the societal norms,[7] and without the experience of being fixed at one place in their communities (Baumeister, 1987, p. 169). They won the possibility of defining themselves based on their inner experience, and without having to use other frames of reference, which was practically unthinkable in previous historical periods although it is now taken for granted. New personalities started appearing wherever new narratives, new names, or newly obtained recognition became possible. This situation gives people more liberty in looking for their idiosyncratic life pathways, bringing, at the same time, incomparably higher risks and responsibilities related to life-altering decisions.

Increasingly important became the idea of inner space, "personality depth", the importance of personal vocation, emphasis on emotionality and free will. Some came to understand the self as belonging to a person, as a personality trait, influenced by the environment, yet malleable, and always unique, unrepeatable, autonomous.

The emergence of the private self was closely connected with the simultaneous emergence of solitude. Although it may be difficult to imagine today, no one was ever left on their own until the end of the seventeenth century (Baumeister, 1987, p. 169). All the members of one large family were always together either in the field, around the fireplace, or in the public space (Ariés & Duby, 1988, pp. 351 ff.). The idea of private space did not exist. No one had, for instance, a room of one's own (much less a key for it), and even the King of France slept in the same room with twenty other persons. It was only by the end of the Middle Ages that "rooms for solitude" or "rooms for thinking" were "invented" (Ariés & Duby, 1988, pp. 536 ff.). As in another of Dürer's famous works, the appearance of these rooms coincided with a real epidemic of melancholy in the Renaissance (Morris, 1998, p. 53),[8] and this connection should not surprise us. First, the Renaissance brought about the insistence on humans instead of on the metaphysical and transcendent, which made the artists and philosophers more interested in humankind and consequently in themselves. Second, mourning also brings associations to

---

[7] One of Greenblatt's best literary illustrations is Shakespeare's Iago, among other reasons, because he exclaims "Virtue! A fig!"

[8] For another illustration see "pleurers", mourners, above and around the tomb of an early fifteenth-century Duke of Burgundy (Bell, 2007, p. 158).

solitude and the inner personal space where sadness is experienced, and to a process through which personality is being formed and developed (Freud, 1917e).

Individual lives became changeable, and in the space of one generation, all customs would alter to the level of incomprehension and condemnation. For instance, the use of carriages on a mass scale in the sixteenth and seventeenth centuries made people of older generations worried that wheels would lead to children forgetting how to walk (Greenblatt, 2005, p. 166). Moreover, if one can define oneself through the individual experience of the inner world, then every fundamental change of this experience can lead to a new identity.

Solitude started becoming a topic books were written about. The earliest one we know of is Petrarch's *The life of Solitude* written between 1346 and 1356 and published a century later. The most famous and influential was Montaigne's *Essay on Solitude* of 1571. Still, the term was to enter a dictionary only in 1656, when Thomas Blount defined it as "an one; an oneliness, or loneliness, a single or singleness" (after Bound Alberti, 2019).

During that same period, another new word entered Western European languages. When it comes to English, in the time that roughly corresponds to Shakespeare's childhood, the term "self", for the first time, did not come to refer to something negative, as it was used to refer to the opposite of the only acceptable God's will. It started entering many compound nouns, and besides the adjective form with the meaning "same", it became a noun in its own right. Its root is in the substantialisation of the reflexive pronoun (oneself, myself) and implies a subject with the capacity to reflect on his or her condition. In German *Das Selbst* appeared simultaneously, while the French *le soi* is somewhat later (Baumeister, 1986, pp. 40–41). That testifies to the growing need to think about oneself as an individual and about the inner life, to such an extent that in Shakespeare, less than half a century later, "self" is a common word. For instance, Regan says about herself, "I am of that self metal made as my sister" (*King Lear*, 1.1.69),[9] Polonius advises his son "to thine own self be true" (*Hamlet*, 1.3.78), and the noun appeared several times in the Sonnets as well (e.g. 4.11; 10.13; 62.12).

Shakespeare's "invention of the human"

As the embodiment of all the changes described above, and the very source of many of them, stands the oeuvre of William Shakespeare, who lived in the turbulent times of transformation of the feudal into the capitalist order, from Renaissance into Reformation, from Catholicism into the English form of Protestantism, and the resurrection of theatrical art. Shakespeare witnessed the old world and its insistence on the principle of order in nature, society, and the universe, and rejected it in his plays more strikingly than anyone else was able to.

It is also evident that psychological models prevalent in Shakespeare's time cannot explain his characters. He is the first master of the description of solitude and private self in the history of literature and his characters are the first ones in whom the personal transcends the societal

---

[9] I am quoting Shakespeare after *The Norton Shakespeare, Second Edition*, 2007.

and historical aspects. Contrary to the tragic tradition of antiquity, Shakespeare's heroes, at least in his mature phases, are not destroyed by external forces, they are agents in the sense contemporary psychology recognises: they initiate actions and influence them all the time; they are tragic because of their inner traits and motivations (Bradley, 1904).

This capacity could partly have come from Shakespeare's personal experiences, as he witnessed religious conversions, refashioned himself in London, and was very proud of becoming a nobleman. It is crucially important that before starting to write, he had collected ample theatrical experience and wrote not only as a great poet but with a stupendous feeling for the stage. As an actor, Shakespeare had to identify with the inner states of fictitious characters to alter his identity, possibly several times during the same performance. One is even tempted to accept the ironic belief that for Shakespeare the stage was a socially acceptable laboratory for exploring the nascent experience of the private self.

All the aspects of Shakespeare's originality—cognitive acuity, linguistic energy, and power of invention (Bloom, 1994, p. 43)—converge to this same purpose of expressing new identity patterns. To find this expression, for *Hamlet* alone he needed 600 words he had never used before, among which 170 did not exist in English and he had to create them (Shapiro, 2005, pp. 320–321). Other technical innovations include completely new figures of speech and the "strategic opacity"—intentional and systematic attempts to leave his characters' motivation unclear (Greenblatt, 2005, pp. 324 ff.). It is impossible for us to resolve the mystery of Iago's urge to destroy lives around himself, especially when it comes to a woman who has never done him any wrong, and he himself cannot help us understand this even at the very end.[10] We are not able to tell what makes Lear divide the kingdom and demand expressions of love from his daughters; and, of course, there is nothing more famous in the whole of Shakespeare than the debate raging over the last two centuries related to the reasons for Hamlet's delay of the revenge required of him. This last example is so provocative that *Hamlet* is compared to Rorschach ink blots (Nuttall, 2007, p. 201), the projection here indicating our implicit agreement that literary characters contain different levels of motivation, feelings, attitudes, disorders—the inner life of a real person of our times.

That became possible when Shakespeare learned how to put on stage protracted moments of "empty time", gaps in plot, periods when the hero explores his mind and thus stops the development of action.[11] The earliest example of this is *Julius Caesar*, where Brutus, the real hero of the tragedy, introduces the term *interim*[12] and explains it as a result of the dialogue between what is nowadays called unconsciousness and consciousness:

---

[10] This is what Coleridge famously referred to as the "motive-hunting of motiveless malignity".

[11] As a rule, these moments are followed by very intense action, like the appearance of supernatural beings, sword fights, or comic sequences, which shows us that Shakespeare was aware of how unaccustomed his audiences were to this "soul-searching".

[12] The term is already present in the *Sonnets* (56.9) and *Love's Labour Lost* (1.1.169). There, however, it refers to a mere pause (see Crystal & Crystal, 2002, p. 243).

> Between the acting of a dreadful thing
> And the first motion, all the interim is
> Like a phantasma, or a hideous dream:
> The Genius and the mortal instruments
> Are then in council; and the state of man,
> Like to a little kingdom, suffers then
> The nature of an insurrection.

—(2.1.63–69)

The term *interim* refers to the period between the rise of the motive and the execution of action it urges us to perform, which makes possible different psychological contents: re-evaluation of the motive itself, searching for the adequate form of action, emergence of the possible feelings of guilt, or even attempts at sublimation. That takes place in solitude, and all major Shakespeare characters are indeed loners (Shapiro, 2005, p. 333). In both cases, Hamlet is the most striking example: his exploration of what motivates him overshadows the plot (see Greenblatt, 2005, pp. 302–303), and he is generally perceived as one of the loneliest characters in the history of literature.

Shakespeare's soliloquies also bring viewers and readers the impression that characters talk about something that has just occurred in their minds, something they find alien and surprising. That inaugurates Shakespeare's representation of characters uttering something unconnected and giving us an impression that we are not in the presence of a theatrical character that is supposed to say a line someone wrote, but that we are watching or reading confessions of a person free-associating and having direct access to that person's inner psychological processes.

In *Hamlet*, the soliloquies become the most essential and exciting parts of the play, although they occur when there is no action on the stage, but the protagonist talks to himself. The numbers of soliloquies and lines in them are much higher here than in any other Shakespeare play. We can also infer their importance from the last moments of the play. When Horatio summarises the tragic outcomes, we find his story ridiculously short and superficial, almost banal. The reason for this is simple: contrary to us, Horatio was not privileged to have heard a single soliloquy, and without them, he does not have a clue about what happened around him.

In Shakespeare's major tragedies, the loss of social status means the loss of personal identity. For instance, Othello's problems begin when he, contrary to his initial intention, substitutes "the sea for a house", the adventurous life of a soldier for marriage (1.2.25–28). In his greatest tragedy, Shakespeare describes the breakdown of a king who gives away everything to his daughters, who will turn out to be ungrateful. Although it is a simplification to reduce Lear's madness to just one cause, I would like to suggest that it unfolds not because he loses his possessions or even his entourage, but because now he does not have his social, public self any more, and he did not learn—had no one to learn from—how to constitute the private, individual identity. The only option he is familiar with is to find himself with the help of references others give him:

66   FROM THE ABYSS OF LONELINESS TO THE BLISS OF SOLITUDE

> KING LEAR:
> Doth any here know me?—Why, this is not Lear:
> Doth Lear walk thus? Speak thus? Where are his eyes?
> Either his notion weakens, or his discernings
> Are lethargied—Ha! waking? 'tis not so.—
> Who is it that can tell me who I am?
> FOOL:
> Lear's shadow.
>
> —(1 4. 232–237)

There is no way for Lear, or anyone else at that time, to assert their identity unless someone else reveals it to them. This connection is evident in the very title of the tragedy about the character who is the epitome of the phenomena discussed here. While "Hamlet" refers to personal identity (which is complicated by the fact that he bears the same name as his father), "The Prince of Denmark" is the definition of his social identity. Finally, "or" underlines the tension between the two, the necessity to choose one or the other. Due to this tension, Hamlet is alien to his time, as well as to everyone who surrounds him. Since the very beginning, and particularly after his conversation with the Ghost—and even though the two Hamlets share nothing but the name, his father is equally alien to him as is his uncle (Bloom, 1998, pp. 387–390)—all old relationships are disrupted, and the whole play is plagued by mistrust and eavesdropping. *Hamlet*, thus, conveys a story about a person forced to discover and develop his inner self in complete loneliness.

During his first appearance on the stage, Hamlet describes to his mother that he has something inside himself, which was a revolutionary statement. Talking about his expression of mourning his father's death, he says:

> Seems, madam! Nay, it is; I know not "seems".
> 'Tis not alone my inky cloak, good mother,
> Nor customary suits of solemn black,
> (…)
> For they are actions that a man might play:
> But I have that within which passeth show;
> These but the trappings and the suits of woe.
>
> —(1.2.76–86)

Shakespeare's vision has thus become the prime inspiration for the apotheosis of solitude and interiority within Romanticism, as well as to Freud's efforts to study those scientifically.[13]

---

[13] Eight of Shakespeare's plays are mentioned in *The Interpretation of Dreams* alone. It was already claimed "Shakespeare was the original psychologist, and Freud a belated rhetorician" (Bloom, 1998, p. 714), and that the unconscious of psychoanalytic theory is always structured like Shakespeare's language (Armstrong, 2005).

Conclusion

Shakespeare's oeuvre contains the first description—and, Harold Bloom (1998) claimed, *invention*—of the basic principles of identity formation, emotional expression, establishing relationships, worldview; so much so that we, no matter whether conscious or not, follow in his characters' footsteps. Just five years after Shakespeare's death, Robert Burton included in his list of the melancholy types the *Solitario*, admitting though that there were good sides about it as well. He was followed by Milton who wrote about divorce and prescribed marriage as a remedy against loneliness. Still, loneliness was described only in its physical aspect, with no mention of emotional suffering even in *Robinson Crusoe*.

Not until the end of the eighteenth century did loneliness get the meaning we give it today. We can find it in Rousseau's *Confessions* of 1769 and *Reveries of the Solitary Walker* of 1776–78. High tide was set in motion by Johann Georg Zimmermann, who published in 1784, in German, no less than a four-volume book. The English translation, *Solitude Considered with Respect to Its Dangerous Influence upon the Mind and Heart*, was published in the abridged edition, of a mere 380 pages, and became very popular, going through many editions and reprints.

We all may need a reminder that loneliness has a history, and is a relatively new concept that we are still trying to adapt to, especially given the current pandemic of loneliness. The term only appeared in the nineteenth century and in the future there might again be a time when we will not need it in the same sense that we do now.

References

Ariés, P., & Duby, G. (Eds.) (1988). *A History of Private Life. Vol. 2: Revelations of the Medieval World.* Cambridge, MA: Harvard University Press.

Armstrong, P. (2005). *Shakespeare in psychoanalysis.* London—New York: Routledge.

Baumeister, R. F. (1986). *Identity: Cultural Change and the Struggle for Self.* New York: Oxford University Press.

Baumeister, R. F. (1987). How the self became a problem: a psychological review of historical research. *Journal of Personality and Social Psychology, 52*(1): 163–176.

Baumeister, R. F. (1998). The self. In: D. T. Gilbert, S. T. Fiske, & G. Lindzi (Eds.), *The Handbook of Social Psychology, Volume 1.* 4th edn. (pp. 680–740). New York: McGraw-Hill.

Bell, J. (2007). *Mirror of the World: A New History of Art.* London: Thames & Hudson.

Bloom, H. (1994). *The Western Canon: The Books and School of the Ages.* New York: Riverhead.

Bloom, H. (1998). *Shakespeare: Invention of the Human.* New York: Riverhead.

Bound Alberti, F. (2019). *A Biography of Loneliness.* Oxford: Oxford University Press.

Bradley, A. C. (1904). *Shakespearean Tragedy.* London: Macmillan, 1978.

Brockmeier, J. (2001). From the end to the beginning. Retrospective teleology in autobiography. In: J. Brockmeier & D. Carbaugh (Eds.), *Narrative and Identity: Studies in Autobiography, Self and Culture* (pp. 247–280). Amsterdam, the Netherlands: John Benjamins.

Crystal, D., & Crystal, B. (2002). *Shakespeare's Words: A Glossary and Language Companion*. London: Penguin.

Danziger, K. (1997). The historical formation of selves. In: R. D. Ashmore, & L. Jussim(Eds.), *Self and Identity: Fundamental Issues* (pp. 137–159). Oxford: Oxford University Press.

Dimitrijevic, A. (2015). Being mad in early modern England. *Frontiers in Psychology, 6*: 1740. doi: 10.3389/fpsyg.2015.01740.

Drury, E. (2000). *Self Portraits of the World's Greatest Painters*. London: Parkgate.

Ferguson, H. (1999). Freud and the dynamics of modernity. In: A. Elliot (Ed.), *Freud 2000* (pp. 169–203). New York: Routledge.

Foucault, M. (1988). Technologies of the self. In: L. H. Martin, H. Gutman, & P. H. Hutton (Eds.), *Technologies of the Self: A Seminar with Michel Foucault* (pp. 16–49). London: Tavistock.

Freud, S. (1917e). Mourning and melancholia. *S. E., 14*: 237–258. London: Hogarth.

Gergen, K. J. (1991). *The Saturated Self: Dilemmas of Identity in Contemporary Life*. New York: Basic Books.

Greenblatt, S. (1980). *Renaissance Self-Fashioning: From More to Shakespeare*. Chicago, IL: University of Chicago Press.

Greenblatt, S. (2005). *Will in the World: How Shakespeare Became Shakespeare*. New York: W. W. Norton.

Honour, H., & Fleming, J. (2002). *A World History of Art*. 6th edn. London: Laurence King.

Huizinga, J. (1924). *The Waning of the Middle Ages*. London: Edward Arnold, 1987.

Kristeva, J. (1995). *New Maladies of the Soul*. New York: Columbia University Press, 1997.

McLuhan, M. (1962). *The Gutenberg Galaxy*. Toronto, Canada: University of Toronto Press.

Morris, D. B. (1998). *Illness and Culture in the Postmodern Age*. Berkeley, CA: University of California Press.

Nuttall, A. D. (2007). *Shakespeare the Thinker*. New Haven, CT: Yale University Press.

Seigel, J. (2005). *The Idea of the Self: Thought and Experience in Western Europe since the Seventeenth Century*. New York: Cambridge University Press.

Shapiro, J. (2005). *1599: A Year in the Life of William Shakespeare*. London: Faber and Faber.

Thomsett, M. C. (2010). *The Inquisition: A History*. Jefferson, NC: McFarland.

Part II

Art and literature

Introduction to Part II

Michael B. Buchholz

In this section, Helga de la Motte-Haber takes you, the reader, on an extensive journey through times and arts. Starting with the observation that "la solitude" in French does not make the distinction this book tries to elaborate on, this author guides us through the territory of related vocabulary in German and English and we follow the birth of a distinction between the modern subject ("sub-iectum" which originally meant subjection or submission) and its world which was inhabited by the spirit of the divine. Medieval mysticism, strongly represented by Meister Eckhart's "divine spark" glimmering in everybody's eternal soul, left the task to everyone to contact the divine within oneself. However, this was a tremendous challenge for the Church, severely threatening its basis as a powerful institution. If every human being was said to own the divine, how could a mighty institution which wanted to define the divine and bring it to non-believers tolerate this? Therein is embedded an interesting story worth telling here.

The writings of the ancient Greek philosopher Aristotle were transmitted to Latin Christianity by Islamic authors like Alfarabi, Ibn Sina (in Latin Avicenna) and Ibn Rushd (in Latin Averroes). This tradition taught the natural bliss of the mind (Flasch, 2006, pp. 53 ff.), which included the idea, a Christian version going back to Augustine, that the human soul can discover its divine origin in itself. These authors talked of human intellectuality ("intellectus"). So, the human mind is much more strongly connected with God in and by itself than was assumed by all those who thought that the divine teaching is to be brought to unbelievers through and by the word laid down in books. However, the teaching that no external gift of divine grace mediated by the institution of the Church was required to know God had to be considered hostile by the Church.

Illustration 1. Lippo Memmi 1378 in Santa Catarina in Pisa

Illustration 2. Bennozo Gozzoli 1374, Louvre (Paris)

Instead of soul or mind, psychoanalysts have taught us to talk of "trueself". In this ancient tradition, this bliss of the mind (or soul, or self) was not reserved for Christians alone.

Lessing, in his Ring Parable ("Nathan the Wise", 1779), took up this idea of the unity of the experience of God, independent of teachings of the "book religions". It was a special type of experience found in Islamic and Jewish mysticism and poetry as well as in Christian and ancient traditions. We could have been spared many disputes between the book religions had this view prevailed. But it contradicted the teachings and power claims of the Church. In the year 1277, the bishop of Paris (where Thomas Aquinas taught) prohibited the teaching that our mind could reach the knowledge of the first cause by itself (Stein, 2009). The Council of Vienna in 1311 condemned teaching that human spiritual nature can find natural bliss by itself. And finally, the corresponding teaching of Meister Eckhart was forbidden by Pope John XXII in 1329. This prohibition was philosophically justified and prepared by Thomas Aquinas. The victory of institutional power is represented in the Dominican church of Santa Caterina in Pisa by Lippo Memmi, painted in the third decade of the thirteenth century, showing Holy Thomas with "the book", the Bible, in his hands, surrounded by other saints with books in their hands, setting his feet on Arabic philosopher Averroes (with a turban on his head), crushed by the victory of Church and Thomas. A similar painting by Benozzo Gozzoli hangs in the Louvre in Paris. Meister Eckhart died in 1328 in Avignon, before he could be caught by the Catholic Inquisition—but his conviction of the glimmering spark became a pervasive light for creativity to overcome forms of loneliness.

Tacitly, our author de la Motte-Haber also represents the idea of unity. We follow her guiding us from Zen master Daisetz Suzuki to Schopenhauer and John Cage, and her overwhelming ability to show us how similar ideas were expressed by other composers in music. Her tremendous knowledge is displayed in fascinating details and by richly presenting us musical pieces—this chapter is not only to be read. It is to be heard. Readers are well advised to take time and take a full treasure box of music records to listen to again and again while reading. De la Motte-Haber's contribution brings readers closest to the experience that there is a deep spiritual dimension in loneliness with which artists and philosophers have managed to get in touch and to put us in touch with this experience. It creates a connection with this dimension of humanity for psychotherapists as well; sharp demarcations between arts, philosophy, and music are abolished or, at least, weakened. Intensive reading makes one feel that the price we have paid over the centuries is a kind of melancholia, audible in *Hamlet* and in Schubert, in the *Passions* by J. S. Bach or Handel's *Messiah* and modern composers, and we read about it in countless philosophical texts. Freud takes the topic up in his paper about "The 'uncanny'" (1919h) and de la Motte-Haber accomplishes the wonderful feat of showing us how close Mozart's *Don Giovanni* is to Freud. Again, take time to read!

The invisible loyalty bond between creativity and loneliness is outlined in Aleksandar Dimitrijević's contribution, too. In their private lives, artists often pay a price for following the creative call. Marriages end in divorce, children are neglected, and many composers, like Beethoven, have lived in isolation. The fundamental question arises: how could these men and women nevertheless know so much of human existence that violinist Hilary Hahn once remarked that Beethoven's Violin Concerto articulates all aspects of human life? How was this possible? Dimitrijević points out something related: that in his Ninth Symphony, Beethoven used Schiller's cry of joy "all people will be brothers" as the counter to loneliness. Loneliness could be overcome in composing such an overwhelming piece of music and we hear this message today although two centuries separate us from Beethoven—we hear, we are touched emotionally in depth, and then we understand. Like de la Motte-Haber, Dimitrijević also cannot avoid setting out the deep relationships between music and poetry, and he can extend this train of thought even further to child development. The lifelong task is to find your own voice by diving deeply into the mysterious experience of inspiration—in solitude. Rilke knew much about that. He could hear inspiring voices, and this was not psychotic. The "true self", a philosophical term first used by the philosopher Plotinus in the second century of our time and later taken up by psychoanalyst Donald W. Winnicott (without knowing the work of Plotinus), is what is to be found. Or is it better to say: "… to be created"? But it is not a "thing", it's an experience transcending the limits of any individual. You cannot aim at wanting to achieve it; at best, you can prepare to endure it. In this respect, some early psychoanalysts felt that the concept of narcissism has a religious dimension. Dimitrijević offers lines of thinking as an invitation to continue thinking about it more, of course without turning to piety. Again, he finds how creative minds are often lonely and that they draw their strength from loneliness. He is attracted by Rilke's term "Weltinnenraum" (the "inner space of the world") and this points strongly to our ecological problems. There is no "outside" of our world, and others, like sociologist Niklas Luhmann, have proposed to accept that we can only do "global domestic politics" ("Welt-Innenpolitik"). Dimitrijević concludes that the seeming antagonism of creativity and loneliness stems from the same root: you cannot have one of them without the other. This is more than a moral guideline; it is to be respected because it is true.

Karin Dannecker continues the thread of thought presented here. The Beatles wondered where these masses of lonely people come from—bringing the aporetic experience of loneliness *in* masses before our eyes. For Dannecker, loneliness and art are deeply connected, as we learned from the previous chapters; she adds the observation of places of loneliness and their symbolic meanings. Such a place is in front of your TV screen, where about half the population spend hours of time each day as their main company. She reviews movies where the experience of loneliness is portrayed artistically. Suddenly, when we lie on couches, as Wordsworth is quoted as saying, we experience the bliss of solitude—and a line can be drawn to psychoanalysis. The couch has sometimes been described as the only place left in modern life where such bliss is given a chance. Dannecker refers to psychoanalysts who understood the couch in this special way—like the artist, a patient on the couch communicates to him- or herself and to the attentive listener. This experience is impressively documented in paintings by patients in art therapy treatment. One patient's paintings of a house (as the metaphor for this experience of inside-outside) are also impressively complemented by corresponding paintings of artists. What children sometimes reveal is true: houses have faces. They are not only objects as opposed to subjects: they can be experienced (and painted) as actors, they respond.

Dominic Angeloch, a literary scholar close to psychoanalysis, alludes to the "seven deadly sins"; the chapter heading "Seven kinds of loneliness" is not a clinical exposition of depressive variants. He uses the play *Hurlyburly*, premiered on the stages of New York and Chicago in 1984, and meant by its author David Rabe as a kind of mirror for the audience: "Look, this is how you enacted just that loneliness you are so deeply suffering from!" How is this loneliness produced? The sober answer Rabe delivers, which is clearly analysed by Angeloch, is: by talk. The never-ending talk—parties, TV, meetings without meeting, neighbours over fences, talk-talk-talk. Why does it produce loneliness as it is intended to document everyone as connected, in a way face-open, so friendly to everybody? Rabe's answer comes out when you listen to the play, the actor's voices, here presented—and then analysed by Angeloch as a never-ending nightmare of signifiers without reference and without a chance ever to be signified; they are produced to simulate talk, until all meaning disappears. It is impressive how this jumps into the reader's eye when reading what Rabe copied, obviously from lived experience, into his play. It is a horror-mirror of everyday experience. It produces "attacks on linking"—although it is meant to link people—as psychoanalyst Wilfred Bion's term is used. We are introduced into a world of talk neither with a reference to one's personal life nor with addressing the other in communicative intent. The characters have no history and when something shines up as conveying a history it is immediately denied. If somebody seems to meaningfully refer to what has been said before, this link is immediately interrupted. Angeloch makes a distinction using conversation analysis. A narrative cannot avoid presenting two versions of your self: a "told self", about whose experience you talk, and a "performative self", doing the telling. Rabe's actors never succeed in presenting a full narrative, because they "summarise" their experience in exclaiming repeated phrases like "weird, weird, weird"—but what was it that is named as weird? You cannot find that out. The performance of a teller cannot come to an end because the teller is qualified by comments, offered a cigarette or a drink, or distracted otherwise. All meaningful conversation is destroyed. On the surface, nobody seems to suffer from that, but there is a pervading sense of loneliness. Angeloch undertakes the difficult task of singling out the details of people—we do that in so many opportunities. We can follow an artistic play and its skilful analysis of how loneliness is made. It is the counterpart of loneliness the other authors in this section have singled out. The result is that we have two cornerstones of a loneliness: desired-for in connection with a creative process and a produced loneliness by a describable way of talking-destroying-connection. Adapting Rabe's view, we could also name this modern despair, and Angeloch's analysis shows how it is made.

References

Freud, S. (1919h). The "uncanny". *S. E., 17*: 217–272. London: Hogarth.

Flasch, K. (2006). *Meister Eckardt. Die Geburt der "Deutschen Mystik" aus dem Geist der arabischen Philosophie (The Birth of "German Mysticism" from the Spirit of Arabic Philosophy)*. Munich, Germany: C. H. Beck.

Lessing, G. E. (1996/1779). *Nathan der Weise (Nathan the Wise)*. In *Werke*, vol. 2. Darmstadt: Wissenschaftliche Buchgesellschaft.

Stein, H. (2009). *Die wiederentdeckte Einheit (The Rediscovered Unity)*. Aachen, Germany: Shaker-Verlag.

CHAPTER 5

Loneliness and solitude: historical transformations of meaning and their expression in art, especially in music

Helga de la Motte-Haber

The French word *solitude* does not distinguish between the experience of being alone and a related unpleasant experience of isolation. The same applies to the German concept of *Einsamkeit*. English, however, having adopted and adapted the French term *solitude*, permits a distinction between this happy aloneness and an unpleasant state of *loneliness* or *lonesomeness*. The word *lonely* in English dates back to the sixteenth century. William Shakespeare used the word *alone* in his *Sonnets* (in No. 29), which were inspired by Petrarch, in: "I all alone beweep my outcast state." *Alone* gave rise to *lonely*. The word *solitary* had already existed in Middle English, based on the Latin *solitudo*. The German term *einsam* (which may be rendered variously as "lonely", "solitary", "isolated", "desolate", "remote", "lone"), with sporadic usage documented since the fourteenth century, is derived from the word *eine* ("a"), which could indicate *allein* ("alone", "by oneself"; "sole") and was modified to conform with the existing word *gemeinsam* ("common", "shared", "together"). The term *einsam* gained currency through Martin Luther's translation of the Bible. The experience of solitude or loneliness is common to all cultures, as studies such as Jan Assmann's 2000 examination of ancient Egyptian literature have shown. Laments about forsakenness featured vocal signs of grief, comparable in the European context to sighing on a falling minor second. And acoustic metaphors were used to express dejection. For a funeral march, a gravely advancing, halting dotted rhythm is often employed. George Frideric Handel's funeral march from the oratorio *Saul*, mostly arranged for a brass ensemble, is a popular choice when a funeral calls for particular reverence.

There were limitations to the present study concerning the selection of musical works. Mainly vocal music whose text suggests a relevant interpretation has been included. Musical works for the stage, however, have been considered only in exceptional cases. While they often contain representations of loneliness or solitude, it would not have been possible to examine them comprehensively within the limited scope of an essay. It was more feasible to do this with individual pieces. Melancholy and longing, the companions of loneliness and solitude, are certainly expressed in instrumental music as well, especially as the lament bass used by Claudio Monteverdi was adopted from vocal music. Instances of this include Wolfgang Amadeus Mozart, String Quartet, KV 465; Beethoven, op. 53 (piano sonata No. 21, "Waldstein"); and Fryderyk Chopin, op. 28 (24 preludes). The painful first movement of the String Quintet, op. 163, by Franz Schubert, which is followed by an elegiac, melancholic second movement, can in fact be interpreted as epitomising desolation. Omission for the sake of achieving a certain unity and coherence in the text was particularly difficult in this instance.

It was a personal decision to differentiate the concept of loneliness or solitude against the background of circumstances specific to particular eras or in the context of broader philosophical approaches. It made sense to embed it in the relevant contemporary context, because *solitude* and *loneliness* are not basic emotions like grief or joy. They are historically variable concepts that often pertain to existential questions.

One broader consideration was the locus of the experience of loneliness or solitude: in the midst of the world, or effectively subject to conditions in an isolated cell or within oneself. Particularly in connection with one's own self, the question arose—inspired by reflections on nature—of one's position in relation to the cosmos. The introductory examples serve to create a framework for this essay. It is only in the course of the following reflections that they are brought into connection with music.

Definitions of loneliness or solitude before the invention of the concept of the subject in European culture

Reflections on solitude and loneliness generally begin with references to the medieval mysticism of Meister Eckhart (1260–1328) and specifically to his sermon on "Von der *Abgeschiedenheit*" (1300) ("seclusion"; as used by Eckhart, often translated as "detachment"). His ideal was not the hermit. He did not consider seclusion in the wilderness or the cell essential for a spiritual experience of God, but only an inner detachment from the external things that can dominate everyday life. He compared behaviour with a door moving back and forth on a static hinge: the external person is linked to things swaying back and forth; as an internal person he remains calmly detached, like a hinge that remains motionless in one spot as the door swings. Arthur Schopenhauer's preoccupation with medieval mysticism and his reading of Eckhart enabled him to describe immovable detachment as liberation from the will. Eckhart had also concluded that detachment free of any desire admitted no space for even the smallest thing; it is akin to nothingness. Schopenhauer had recognised the affinity of this thinking to Buddhism, as had Daisetz Teitaro Suzuki, who prompted John Cage's intensive reception of Meister Eckhart. Readings from Eckhart's writings are a popular feature of Ars Antiqua concerts today. Meister Eckhart has also been brought up in the present context because he foreshadowed a form of the modern concept of the subject, which emerged only in the modern era and led to a contemplation of the self, the inner person, which would come to typify solitude or loneliness.

But expressions of subjective states associated with a sense of the pleasant or unpleasant are found throughout history. Thus, in the Middle Ages, monks of certain orders were required to live cloistered lives in a monastic cell. The sickness of monks living in isolation, *acedia*, a state of weariness or listlessness and sadness (*tristitia*), was a sin that demanded penance. *Tristitia* was understood as a kind of depression or melancholy, as distinguished from outright sorrow or grief (*maeror, luctus*). One of the most important abbots of the nascent Order of Cistercians, Bernardus Claraevallensis (Saint Bernard of Clairvaux), was only too familiar with this malady of solitude (*solitudo*) and isolation (*reclusio*). As a Cistercian, emerging from a reform movement of the Benedictine order, his attitude differed from that of the life-affirming Dominican Eckhart. If God was with you, the Cistercians believed, you were not alone, even in the seclusion of a monastic cell. The contemplation of God as a purely spiritual contemplation was central for the Cistercians. In his treatise *De vita solitaria*, in the volume *Epistula ad Fratres de Monte Dei* published in 1144 by his biographer Guillaume de Saint-Thierry, Bernard of Clairvaux thus expressly instructed the monks on the necessity of isolation—for it was only through this meditative contemplation that one could arrive at the blissful certainty of truth.

Loneliness or solitude is to be understood here as a condition to which one is subjected. It does not raise the question, as it did for Eckhart, of individual identity. The subject is understood quite literally as a *sub-iectum*. It is subject to a dependence that cannot be influenced. In the Middle Ages, this view of human existence, which can certainly still be witnessed today, was able to be coupled with prophetic powers. The numerous preachers of repentance saw themselves as mouthpieces of God. Following the example of the apostles, they lived as itinerant monks. The social isolation as outsiders that came with homelessness could become a form of spiritual asceticism. It was already the case that important prophets had mostly received their prophecies and instructions in a wilderness, or, like Moses, received the commandments on the summit of a mountain. The founding of monasteries enabled this solitude in nature to be replaced by the stillness of the study. Various representations of the church father Hieronymus, who translated the Bible into Latin (the Vulgate), are interesting in this regard. He is mostly depicted in his study. But Albrecht Dürer, who had portrayed him on multiple occasions, also chose one scene in a wasteland. This suggests an equivalence between different places of seclusion. Medieval illustrators mostly considered the confines of a study appropriate for representations of poets or musicians. But seclusion did not carry negative connotations. The divine inspiration hoped for in solitude lent isolation a positive quality.

The experience of loneliness or solitude underwent a new interpretation with the notion in humanism of the innermost self. Francesco Petrarca was probably not well acquainted with Saint Bernard's *Epistula* when he wrote his 1346 treatise *De vita solitaria*, in which he contrasted worldliness with inwardness or introspection. It was a matter of self-examination. His personal experience, which as a scholar he cultivated with many books, is placed above the busyness of the city, where the goal is the acquisition of wealth. According to Joachim Küpper (2002, p. 79), the reference in the second book is to Bernhard von Clairvaux and his meditative contemplation of the divine in nature: a notion that inspired Petrarch to view nature as a source of inspiration for the poet. For the richness of the inner experience was augmented by contemplation of the landscape. In 1336, driven by the desire to become acquainted with the high altitudes of the place, he had climbed Mont Ventoux together with his brother and some servants. As he descended, however, he turned his gaze inwards, and it seemed to him that without greatness of spirit, nothing else was great.

The unity of the *vita activa* and the *vita contemplativa*, as called for by Meister Eckhart, underpinned Michel de Montaigne's 1580 essay "On Solitude". The true *solitude* of being by oneself did not require one to lead a hermit's existence—though one could best enjoy it alone, it was also possible in the midst of the cities or at the royal court. His recommendation (p. 103) that one be content with oneself represents a new and unique variant of the concept of solitude. It implies introspection, thus predicating a notion of the modern ego/self and of self-enquiry.

This brief overview shows that, though it appears at first blush very simple, the concept of solitude or loneliness can be defined in very different ways. Circumstances related to society and typical of the time in question are caught up in it, as are individual sensibilities in which the development of the modern concept of the subject is reflected. While views of solitude and loneliness can be seen to have evolved over time, certain conceptions also recur in different guises. This is true of a notion arising in the eighteenth and nineteenth centuries, if not earlier, of a state of being subjected to the dark, confused feeling that was described as an "unconscious". What was new here was the emphasis on the uncanny, which was more frightening than the idea of memento mori so frequently invoked in the past.

In the following historical study of music, seclusion in the midst of society only becomes apparent at the turn of the twentieth century, most clearly in Gustav Mahler's song "I am lost to the world". Here, however, unlike with Meister Eckhart, self-denial is not entirely free of pain. But the inspirations of Hildegard of Bingen do correspond very well to the medieval notion of subjection and, with negative implications, the melancholy expressed by the minnesingers. This kind of state of being at the mercy of forces outside oneself appears again in connection with the "English malady", again negatively connoted, in the music of John Dowland. Nature as a source of inspiration, as in the writings of Petrarch, and the discovery of oneself when alone in nature, became the central theme in the nineteenth century. But nature could also become an experience of horror and dread.

In submission to a spiritual, artistic experience of God

Any creativity on the part of the artist, as in later eras, was inconceivable in the Middle Ages. Though it speaks of self-awareness when monks, freezing cold and feeling forsaken, noted this in the margins of the oldest musical manuscripts (c. 920) of the monastery of St. Gall, they could scarcely have conceived of the Alleluia Jubilus they were notating as emanating from anything other than a divine inspiration. The human self was not a constitutive entity. Instead, it was moved or overcome by a force considered divine. Wolfram von Eschenbach, about whom little more is known than what he himself mentioned in passing, addressed just such a necessity of divine inspiration as imperative in his epic *Willehalm* (c. 1300), of which only fragments survive.

LONELINESS AND SOLITUDE 81

He considered himself both illiterate and artless, and prays in the opening text to the triune God to give him the ability to tell the following story. He hoped for a "transmission" to his soul. In his famous poem *Parzival* (1200–10), too, he reiterated his insufficient ability as a "scribe". In the work of Richard Wagner, who drew on Wolfram, Parsifal is still depicted as a pure simpleton. Similarly, Pope Gregory I (Saint Gregory the Great), to whom the Gregorian chant had long been attributed, was not considered its author. He is shown in medieval representations dictating to a monk skilled in notation the words that a dove, the symbol of the Holy Spirit, imparts to his ear. The oldest depiction of the church father Hieronymus was likewise depicted with such a dove of inspiration.

Music played an important role in the medieval mysticism of Hildegard of Bingen. Hildegard seems to have come from a musical family; her brother was a cathedral organist, but she herself did not have any systematic education or training. She called herself an "indocta", an unlearned person. She required the assistance of one of the monks who was able to write in neumes to record her inspirations. Music seems to have been extremely important to her. She created more than seventy musical works, whose magical melodies, rich in free-floating melismas, are recorded in neumic notation. Hildegard saw music as a realisation of the harmony of the heavens that she experienced in her visions, devotion to which dissipated all earthly fears of failure. Music constitutes a small but significant part of her visions. She describes these in an extensive body of writing which, though of a general nature, also contributes to an understanding of her musical inspirations. She described the origin of her visions, including the acoustic ones, beginning in 1151, in the prologue of her first work (*Scivias*, Rupertsberg manuscript, German translation by Maura Böckeler, 1954). There are indications here of a conception of music that differed from the traditional understanding insofar as she no longer viewed it as being founded on a universal order of numbers. The repetition of the heavenly assignment in certain passages of this prologue—say and write what you see and hear—is reminiscent of a musical form with a refrain. It was not, as in later times, a personal inspiration, but a simple act of receiving: "You therefore, o mortal, who receive this, not in the disquiet of deceit but in the purity of simplicity, having been directed toward the revealing of hidden things—write what you see and hear." Hildegard spoke of the one who received as of a forsaken nullity: "O weak mortal, both ash of ash and rottenness of rottenness, say and write what you see and hear."

In the aforementioned prologue she associated her inspirations with her personal biography:

> But I, although I did see and hear this, nevertheless [...] refused to write for a long time— not out of obstinacy but as an office of humility—until I lay on a bed of sickness, struck down by God's lash [...] I set my hand to write [...] receiving the strength to lift myself out of my illness.

A depression accompanying the feeling of nullity seems to have played a role—in other words, one facet of the spectrum of loneliness. In 1163 she wrote again in the prologue of her book *De operatione Dei* (alternative title: *Liber divinorum operum*): "I—wretched and frail creature that I am—began then to write with a trembling hand [...]: I saw it with the inner eye of my spirit

82   FROM THE ABYSS OF LONELINESS TO THE BLISS OF SOLITUDE

and grasped it with my inner ear. [...] And once again I heard a voice from heaven instructing me. And it said, 'Write down what I tell you!'" She felt she was a prophet called by God, and in 1147/8, with Bernard of Clairvaux intervening on her behalf, she received the right from Pope Eugene III to present herself publicly as such. Unlike visual representations of her botany, those of her musical inspiration depict her in a monastic cell. In the most famous illustration, Hildegard is virtually imprisoned, with the monk doing the musical notation only just able to peer in. Fiery flames from above demonstrate that her melodies emanate directly from God. She herself considered herself to be a medium.

Loneliness as a state of exclusion—the melancholic lament of the *Minnesang*

In the twelfth and thirteenth centuries, loneliness was a central theme of the chansons sung by the troubadours of southern France, who initially spread throughout northern France (where they were known as *trouvères*). Through the marriage of Eleanor, Duchess of Aquitaine, with the Duke of Normandy, the future king of England, this sung love poetry took on in what was then French-speaking England as well. Eleanor's son, Richard the Lionheart, was one of the first singers. At around the same time, this chivalric court culture became widespread in Germany in the form of the *Minnesang*, or minnesong. The novelty of this art form was that rather than Latin, it used the vernacular. There are numerous manuscripts in existence, some with notes (square notation), which, however, show only the sequence but not the rhythm. The famous *Codex Manesse* reproduces only the lyrics. The poetry had precedence; there were musical contrafacta, that is, borrowed melodies. Central motifs included unfulfilled desire, loneliness, and longing. They were love songs in the form of laments concerning an unattainable lady, generally of high standing. The troubadour Jaufré Rudel dreamt of a woman beyond the ocean, an *amour de loin* (love from afar). Here, aloneness was not a state of isolation or confinement that could be conducive to creativity. It was rather the experience of being excluded. Walther von der Vogelweide (*Bin ich dir unmaere ...*), associated this with the observation: "*Minne entouc niht eine/si sol sîn gemeine*" ("Love is no good alone,/it is meant to be shared"). Being alone ultimately excludes love. Rostanh Berenquier (*Tot ainsi con es del balasicz ...*) found complete isolation easier to bear than his lovesickness: "It is better for me, as I see it now/that grief pierce my heart and kill me,/or that I become a recluse in a tower/than suffer such bitter, heavy grief."

Are we to assume that the author, who was at the same time always the singing performer, identified with the content of his recital? Is this an adumbration of the later idea of the subject? It is more likely that the doctrine of *inventio* from ancient rhetoric applied, in other words, that clearly defined rules were used governing how one was to proceed in creating a song. But this does not exclude the possibility of psychoanalytical interpretations postulating a compensatory function of this entertaining cultural practice of courtly life. The troubadours never sang of marital love. At the time, marriage was rarely a matter of love, but rather one of political expediency. The troubadours sang of something that was considered unattainable. Ulrich Müller

LONELINESS AND SOLITUDE 83

(1986, pp. 283–315) saw this as a compromise between the drives of the id and the demands of the ecclesiastical superego.

Melancholia

The difference between mourning and melancholia was the subject of a treatise by Sigmund Freud (1917e). The grieving individual experiences a loss, while the melancholic cannot fully comprehend what he has lost. He turns against himself, tormenting his ego, which has taken the place of an Other. While melancholia does share some of the characteristics of mourning or grief, it is unspecific, implies disappointments, low self-esteem, depressed states, and laments that are accusations. The minnesong is thus melancholy, but not sad in the sense of mourning or grief. And yet the madness of melancholy has been associated since time immemorial with mania, that is, also viewed as a source of creativity.

In the late sixteenth century and the seventeenth century, melancholy seems to have been an illness that primarily afflicted men in England. The specifically English malady was the subject of several publications by authors including Edmund Spenser, John Donne, and Nicholas Robinson. Robert Burton's book *The Anatomy of Melancholy* (1621) in particular was published in a great many editions. Burton sought to find an explanation from a religious, philosophical, and medical perspective, the latter with reference to the ancient theory of the humours. The idea of melancholy was already very present in Shakespeare's *Hamlet* and influenced the poetry of John Milton.

The music of John Dowland may be the prototypical expression of a melancholic attitude. A famous lutenist who also wrote lively dances, his music is nevertheless typified by an expression of melancholy. "Semper Dowland, semper dolens" ("always Dowland, always doleful") was the caption he gave to a lute pavane that he also arranged for a consort piece titled *Lachrimae, or seven tears* (1604). His songs, mostly accompanied by the lute, an intimate, soulful instrument, are the epitome of lamentation. They are suffused by sombre melancholia in the Freudian sense. They are sometimes set very dissonantly, as in the song expressing the desire: "In darkness let me dwell." The lyrics are attributed to him. The most famous song, "Flow my tears,/ fall from your springs!/Exiled for ever, let me mourn" (1600), emerged from the *Lachrimae Pavane* (1596), which he composed during his highly paid position in the service of the Danish king. Dowland imitated the image of tears with the repetition of four descending tones in A minor. It may have been the case, as biographies have suggested, that Dowland suffered from depression. But it cannot be ruled out that he may have suffered from the zeitgeist and also from the fact that he, who was later to convert to Catholicism, was "exiled". Was he afflicted by the English melancholia? It is mostly associated with the prevailing political circumstances, which afforded the well-educated middle classes few opportunities for professional advancement and thus resulted in general dissatisfaction. Though England did have a parliament early on, the kings often paid little heed to it. Many monarchs sought to restore absolutist rule. Even the republicanism brought about by Oliver Cromwell's revolution was short-lived. Though he refused to be crowned king, he ruled with an iron fist.

Henry Purcell, it would seem, was not afflicted by the English malady. He was in the service of the English court. From 1680 onwards, his tasks included composing an ode in honour of the monarch each year—among other things, the funeral music for Queen Mary. His sacred music (anthems and hymns) certainly included pieces that dealt with the tormented ego of the melancholic: "O, I'm sick of life" (after Job). But Henry Purcell's "O solitude, my sweetest choice!" is much more difficult to interpret. Written in 1685, it is a standalone work for a high singing voice (soprano or countertenor and basso continuo). The text from 1617 was originally by Marc Antoine Girard de Saint-Amant and is used in the English translation by Katherine Philips. This poem made Girard de Saint-Amant famous overnight in France. Purcell's setting is the embodiment of melancholy and longing. To be performed slowly with the expression of melancholic gravity of the key of C minor, an almost beseeching aspect emerges through the repetitions of a ground bass pattern which are accompanied by the singing voice and seem to continue without a break. Purcell's theme was a form of solitude as withdrawal from the world—the desire to be remote from tumult and noise. A similar message can be found in *The Fairy-Queen* (1692), an adaptation of Shakespeare's *A Midsummer Night's Dream*: "Come, come, come, let us leave the Town/And in some lonely place,/Where Crouds and Noise were never known,/Resolve to spend our days." But Purcell is not talking about the kind of process of self-discovery that preoccupied Michel de Montaigne. The restless thoughts to which reflection gives rise are odious to him. Purcell composed a dream of a flight to Arcadia, represented by nature. Girard de Saint-Amant was an important precursor of the pastoral poetry of the Baroque. His work did not yet feature the Virgilian idyll populated by herdsmen which would soon take centre stage; instead, in Purcell's work, too, the mere sight of trees and mountains is sung of as a wishful nocturnal dream. In a minor key—a paradise lost. But Arcadia soon found its way into musical pastorals, including in the early works of Wolfgang Amadeus Mozart. It became an important motif of Italian and French baroque painting, with the addition of memento mori motifs.

Gloom and desolation

Meditations on the transience of human life were often associated not only with melancholy, but with a feeling of misery or despair. Andreas Gryphius's famous sonnet *Einsamkeit* (1650)—"Within this loneliness of more than barren lands"—still invoked the traditional notion of the redemptive wilderness, but no longer in the sense of the ascetic life of a hermit. Instead, he speaks of skulls, birds, such as owls that cannot sing, or of "picked and bleached bones". It is not mild melancholia that is the subject here, but black depression or gloom. The contemplation of nature, in which man is placed as the highest being, yet as part of the universe, inspires in him the depressing thought: "How not upon firm ground our hope and hoping stands." The idea of the memento mori, which was ubiquitous throughout the religious wars of the seventeenth century, is at the heart of this sonnet. In Gryphius's work this awareness of transience does not yet take place exclusively, but certainly already to some extent, through reference to a self. In the final verse, the poem turns from the contemplation of the barrenness of nature to a self-awareness, explicitly described as fruitful, of a twofold nature. It is attributed to one's own "spirit", which, however, is held by God. Gryphius was a Lutheran. This explains the dual function of loneliness in his sonnet. It is on the one hand a subjective emotional state attributed to a self; a state which, however, must at the same time be reconciled with a God-given mental power of judgement.

During the Counter-Reformation, melancholy became a typical illness in Germany, too, though it was mainly attributed to the Protestants in reference to the depressed mental state of acedia, as a sinful temptation by the devil. But the Protestants viewed it not only as a test of their faith, but also as a personal challenge that could not be overcome through penance and good works alone. It was a self-interrogation as a fundamental reflection on the constituents of life. It was meant to lead to insight, as it says in a poem by Paul Gerhardt: "You are certainly not the governor/who has to control everything./God sits in government/and controls everything well", and also "he will set free your heart/from the burden so heavy". In Georg Philipp Telemann's musical adaptation, "Entrust your way and what grieves your heart" (1653) is one of the best-known songs in the Protestant hymnal. The subject matter raised here by Paul Gerhardt also applied to the beginnings of German tragic drama, which was emerging at this time. Walter Benjamin (1928) considered rumination and interrogation to be its typical characteristics and differentiated it in this way from ancient tragic drama. But he also noted that the instances of acedia, of melancholia, had remained astonishingly dark in German tragic drama. And he contrasted this with the way in which they are overcome in the Christian spirit in William Shakespeare's *Hamlet*.

The melancholy of the tormented self, attributed to the Protestants and finding unique expression in Passion music, was grounded in human fallibility, which was always a given due to original sin. Luther, however, had accorded grace an important place in his teaching with reference to the epistles of Paul (see Galatians 5:13). *Sola gratia*, by grace alone, cannot be earned through good works, confession, or other human endeavour; it is a gift from God. The possibility of undeserved mercy was enshrined in the legal system of most Western societies.

Johann Sebastian Bach associated the idea of grace with a musical testament to the supreme solitude. The passage in question is from the *St Matthew Passion* (1729), a double-choir work (Choir I devoted largely to the lament, Choir II instructive for the congregation). The first line from the 22nd Psalm is used to express the most profound desolation, when Jesus on the cross cried out: "Eli, Eli, lama sabachthani?" ("My God, my God, why hast thou forsaken me?"). Bach, like the librettist Picander, presumably knew the entire psalm, which later (verse 24) reads: "but when he cried unto him, he heard". The feeling of aloneness is powerfully portrayed in the *St Matthew Passion*, textually through the splitting of the beginning of the psalm, musically through the use of the Phrygian mode, a church mode which, in addition to minor, long remained reserved for lamentation. In the time around 1700, Phrygian was considered a mode that could leave no one untouched. In Bach's work, it is represented in terms of tonality as a transition from B flat minor to E flat minor. These were the keys of the blackest melancholy, and also of death, until well into the nineteenth century. The Phrygian mode enabled Bach to articulate this desolation very clearly as a question with the use of the ascending whole tone, because, like spoken words, the ascending whole tone conveys an impression of openness. It is only in the context of the entire work that this question acquires greater relevance. It concerns the impossibility of infallible subjective judgement, the resulting melancholy, and the possibility of grace. To understand this, we need to look at the first part of the *Passion*. The greatest dramatic effect is achieved where Choir number 1 emerges from the anonymity of lamentation to assume agency. It expresses subjective experience, something which is mostly the domain of the arias. Eleven times, representing the disciples with the exception of Judas, the choir asks in the first person who the traitor is: "Lord, is it I?" Without the usual introductory remark by the evangelist, the choir then goes straight into a chorale (text by Paul Gerhardt, based on a well-known melody): "It is I. I should atone". No further justification is required to see this passage as an appeal to the conscience of the individual and ultimately as the individual's confession of guilt. But this is followed in the very next verse by the idea of mercy: "You take upon your back the burdens that oppress me." In the passage "My God, why hast thou forsaken me?" it is again given to a chorale to respond, namely from the ninth verse of the song, "Sacred Head, Now Wounded". It contains the promise of mercy: "When I must once and for all depart, then do not depart from me." In contrast to the positive conclusion of the 22nd Psalm and to the text of the chorale, however, Bach composed the idea of *sola gratia* opening on the dominant. The Passion in the style of an oratorio emerged as an important form in connection with Protestantism for the replacement of the Mass. Self-interrogation, personal responsibility for decisions, conscience, and penance are important requirements for the profession of faith. With the Passions, Bach sought to instill in the listener an appreciation of these; and the plea for mercy is also to be seen in this context, given human fallibility. But only God can grant it. Following their first performances, Bach's oratorios would only become influential again after their revival in 1829 by Felix Mendelssohn-Bartholdy. After this, they were no longer viewed as *Gebrauchsmusik*—music intended primarily for practical use and performance—but rather as autonomous works.

George Frideric Handel's *Messiah* (1741), on the other hand, was performed more than fifty times. It is based on the prophecies of the prophet Isaiah of the coming Messiah, compiled and arranged by Charles Jennens. Around halfway through the work, in the second part, there is a nadir of despair, brought on by taunts and derision: "He looked for some to have pity on Him but here was no man, neither found He any to comfort Him." For this tenor accompagnato in a slow tempo, based on Psalm 69:20: "Thy rebuke hath broken His heart", Handel, too, used harmonic means to express desolation and despair. No unifying key is stipulated for these eighteen measures. Instead, the piece meanders between various keys from the initial A flat major to the distant B major. Melancholy and grief make this setting of loneliness one of the most powerful passages of this oratorio. As a setting of the *Heilsgeschichte*—the history of the world interpreted as showing forth the working of God's grace—Handel had often performed it during Lent. Later, in England, however, it was more frequently performed during Advent. Unlike a Passion, the focus is not on the memento mori. Handel's *Messiah* was not conceived as a sacred work, and it could not have been performed at church services according to the precepts of the Anglican Church, which were influenced by the teaching of Calvin. Evidently there were, however, subsequently some rare performances in churches.

The rise and fall of *solitude* in the Enlightenment

Solitude was viewed negatively in the eighteenth century. This is surprising, given the fact that an aesthetics of feeling and sensation (*Empfindungsästhetik*) was typical of this period. But of course, this era was also no stranger to feelings of grief and sadness, of elegy and lament, and of pain, and hence dissonances considered gloomy and grim. The *Piano fantasy with accompaniment of a violin* (1787) by Carl Philipp Emanuel Bach is "to be played mournfully and very slowly". It was not until the beginning of the nineteenth century, however, that the clavichord, which was C. P. E. Bach's main instrument, came to be described not only as melancholic, but as lonely as well. Mozart's song *An die Einsamkeit* (KV 391) ("To Loneliness" or "To Solitude"), part of his early body of work, is to be performed "sadly, yet serenely" and is rooted in the tradition of the *Empfindsamer Stil* ("sensitive style"). Written in 1780, more than one hundred years after Purcell, it still invokes solitude as a gentle and soothing comforter, even as it conjures the image of the grave. The expression of desolation and despair of the seventeenth century seems to have been lost.

The dominant tradition was the philosophical rationalism of Christian Wolff, who believed that only animals, but not humans, could live alone. In *Rational Thoughts on the Social Life of the Human Being* (1721, p. 2), he wrote of the necessity of socialisation for human improvement, as man "cannot perfect his own state in solitude to the extent that he can when he lives among people". François Voltaire reasoned similarly in his *Dictionnaire philosophique, portatif* (1764, p. 336), arranged by keyword, in the entry for *Virtu*: The solitaire/loner lacks virtue (virtu). He is selfish: "he will be good to himself, but not to us". Voltaire was a staunch opponent of Jean Jacques Rousseau's idea that education served only to bring about man's social enslavement.

Like Rousseau of Swiss origin, the physician and writer Johann Georg Zimmermann explored the subject of *Einsamkeit* in four volumes written in 1784–85. By implication, he was also addressing the question of how the law of reason of the Enlightenment, into which the theory of natural law had been remodelled, could be reconciled with Rousseau's view. Zimmermann soon gained international renown. An abridged English translation was published in 1799 (vol. 2) and 1800 (vol. 1) with the title *Solitude* and the author's name given as "Zimmerman". New editions quickly followed. A French translation, likewise abridged, was published in 1788. Zimmermann had already written two books on solitude prior to this (1756, 1773). The many editions suggest the significance of the theme.

Zimmermann defined solitude as a form of solitariness and quiet in which one could give oneself over to one's own thoughts and ideas. Looming above solitude was always the black spectre of melancholia, which he associated with dreadful woods, impassable mountains, and dealing with the dead. The frontispiece of the first edition was a memento mori print. This sense of the uncanny was something he shared with his friend Johann Caspar Lavater. But for Zimmermann solitude was more than just melancholy; it was also a prerequisite for creative development and his appreciation of nature. He described it generally with an abhorrence of vain worldly pursuits (1800, pp. 11–12): "[B]ut to acquire the advantages which solitude is capable of affording, the mind must not be impelled to it by melancholy and discontent, but by a real distaste to the idle pleasures of the world." Zimmermann believed, however, that this turning away from the vain thirst for entertainment of his era should be pursued only for a time. He believed it was necessary to return to the society of others. He stressed the necessity of this at just as much length as he did the necessity of solitude. This demand for a balance between individual withdrawal and a return to human companionship constitutes a central idea of his oeuvre. Here he was in opposition to the widespread rejection of solitude found for instance in the work of Wolff and Voltaire, and he sought to reconcile the Enlightenment theory of the law of reason with the ideas of Jean Jacques Rousseau (see also Alina Timofte, 2014), who had defined the original condition of man as being devoid of civilisation. Rousseau had described solitude as an existential condition, as in his *Reveries of the Solitary Walker*; in the fifth "walk" (1782, p. 441), in which he watched and listened to the movement of the waves one evening on the shore of a lake, "to make me pleasurably aware of my existence, without troubling myself with thought". The French Enlightenment philosophers did not share his opinion. Nevertheless, Zimmermann's work became a best-seller in its time, and even Goethe had a copy of the four-volume edition. A similar understanding of the connection between culture and nature is found a little later in the work of Immanuel Kant in the context of his reflections on Rousseau.

Uncanny fantasies: repressed places of *loneliness*

The rejection of solitude in the age of Enlightenment resembles a process of repression whose defence mechanisms do not function sufficiently flawlessly to prevent uncanny images from rising up before one's mind's eye, especially on long and lonely nights. The painted nightmares of Henry Fuseli are one example of this. In accordance with him, his friend Johann Caspar Lavater (1776, vol. 2, p. 20) placed the imaginings that came to him in his "lonely cabinet" in quotation marks, as if they were not his own. Lavater interpreted (p. 286) one of the shadowy images he described as the ruined human nature of a murderer. Lavater saw this murderer in his mind's eye: "in solitary midnight hours, when sleep escaped him, and his conscience still attempted in vain the final warnings". Solitude, Zimmermann had said, had a greater effect than reason on the imagination, because it led to the constant production of new associations. This would also seem to apply to his friend Lavater.

Uncanny imaginings can be brought on not only alone in times of darkness like midnight, but also by remote places, whose stillness can be conducive to meditation and serve as a memento mori. The graveyard is the privileged site for this. Thomas Gray's very well-known "Elegy Written in a Country Church Yard" (1751) with its renunciation of the world ("Far from the madding crowd's ignoble strife") seems almost to stand in the tradition of a romantic concept of solitude. This all changed, however, with the emergence of the gothic novel. Yet graveyards and charnel houses with representations of the danse macabre had already been a place for fear and trembling long before this. As time passed, however, burial grounds were increasingly relocated to the outskirts of the villages and towns. On the one hand, these sites set apart were to be dedicated to silent devotions and prayer. But there was also a desire to keep the tremulous fear instilled by death and the Last Judgement away from everyday life. Another reason given for the separation of the graveyards was that of hygiene, in case of any possible toxic effluvia from corpses. Views such as these added to the eerie air of the cemeteries. As coffins were only introduced in the modern era towards the end of the eighteenth century, people were also afraid that the corpses could be dug up by dogs. The idea that this geographical separation of death from everyday life corresponded to a process of repressing the uncanny is nothing new. Sigmund Freud's reflections on death in his essay on "The 'uncanny'" ("Das 'Unheimliche'", 1919h) have made it possible to explain this process by the fact that the primeval, animistic notion of the return of the dead still held sway. Incidentally, the nineteenth-century paintings of graveyards by the likes of Caspar David Friedrich and Carl Gustav Carus, representing places of longing, do not stand in any contradiction to Freud's view. For according to Freud, fictions differ from the experience of reality anyway, which explains why the uncanny reveals itself in a different form in art. With their dead trees, ruins, or snow-covered landscapes these images convey not only stillness, solitude, and loneliness, but also uncanny elements that touch on a child's repressed fear of the dark.

One musical testament to nocturnal horror emanating from a deserted, sequestered place where you have the feeling you could be ambushed by ghosts, is the graveyard scene in *Don Giovanni* (1787) by Wolfgang Amadeus Mozart. It dominates the second act, at least from the moment when the opera's protagonists find themselves in the house in which Don Giovanni has murdered the Commendatore. The sextet (*Sola, sola in buio loco*) expresses the sense of solitude and fear: "Alone, in this dark place I feel my heart beating loudly, and such a fear assails me." Don Giovanni decides to go with his servant to the cemetery to the Commendatore's grave. The stone statue of the deceased man appears to the servant to be animate, nodding and speaking. Although Don Giovanni considers such talk to be foolishness, he ironically invites the statue to dinner. Another spun-out scene begins with a scream and a knocking; the servant does not want to open the door; Don Giovanni opens it himself. A rest lasting one and a half measures, then suddenly a diminished seventh chord appears, repeated three times, in a violent fortissimo, syncopated and with the rhythm of a funeral march—a brief pause—the stone statue has accepted the invitation. The sudden appearance of these dissonant chords, underscored by the trombones, has an incredible impact; no listener will be able to forget this passage. The four tones of the diminished seventh chord have a tension that wants to contract inward to a triad. But as the layering of minor thirds does not define a key, any note could also be a leading tone that leads in another direction to another chord. Rather than resolving this diminished seventh chord, Mozart follows it with a seventh chord, again loudly repeated, which leads, as a dominant, to the grave and solemn D minor and to the "speech" of the ghostly Commendatore. Don Giovanni, not only a murderer, but a lascivious womaniser as well, passes up the opportunity to improve himself that is held out to him by the Commendatore and descends at the end into the flames of hell. The final chord in a triumphant D major harks back to the D minor. The atmosphere invoked in *Don Giovanni* through image and action by Mozart's librettist Lorenzo Da Ponte, at a site that many would prefer to repress, captures the uncanny aspect of the scene

An epitome of sublimity and the pain of yearning

As early as the Renaissance and the Baroque era, the diminished seventh chord was frequently used to express horror, pain, and death. Franz Schubert relied on this effect in his *Winterreise* (in "The Crow"), as did Robert Schumann in *Dichterliebe* ("A Poet's Love", in the song "I do not chide you"). Ernst Theodor Hoffmann (1810, p. 36) described Ludwig van Beethoven's juxtaposition of diminished seventh chords in the Fifth Symphony (from bar 168) as "It appears as if the breast, burdened and oppressed by the premonition of tragedy, of threatening annihilation, in gasping tones was struggling with all its strength for air." Hoffmann repeated this idea but added that it also evokes the pain of an infinite longing that encompasses love, hope, and joy. It is an "indeterminate longing" that does not allow for affects denoted by words as vocal music does. Beethoven could have understood the diminished seventh chord in the sense of E. T. A. Hoffmann. Sometimes (e.g. Piano Sonata No. 28, op. 101), Beethoven used also the playing instruction "*sehnsuchtsvoll*" (infinite longing). Richard Wagner later maximised the directionless striving of this sound with the Tristan chord but it is made up in the verbal context of the musical theatre.

In his late works, Beethoven intensified the musical expression to the limits of the possible. Intense feelings can find echo in it. Personal feelings of listeners attach to his music, and all the more so because music takes hold without one knowing why. Sigmund Freud rejected music for that reason (1914b). The unusually long Adagio (appassionato e con molto sentimento) of the *Hammerklavier Sonata* op. 106 is one of those pieces that can touch on an existential state of mind, although in the lament of the F sharp minor the friendly D major passage leaves a trace. In contrast to the contrapuntal first movement, this movement focuses on the harmonic-melodic process. The unison beginning shows how much Beethoven thought in terms of sound rather than tones. Also, the nuanced means of presentation contribute to this impression (una corda, mezzo voce, crescendo … espressivo, tutte corde, con grand espressione …). Since its first performance, the expression of this movement has been understood as an apotheosis of pain, albeit not in the sense of personal expression but as the epitome of sublimity. This does not mean, however, that such music cannot open up dimensions of experience in the listener (also of loneliness) for which he cannot draw on his everyday reality.

Beethoven, however, dedicated the Piano Sonata op. 81a, the so-called *Les Adieux sonata*, composed on the occasion of the flight of his archduke friend from the Napoleonic war, to an individual experience of loneliness. The three movements of this sonata are to be understood programmatically: Farewell, Absence, and Reunion. They are preceded by a slow introduction whose opening horn fifth announces the departure. From this introduction is derived—melodically (sigh motive) and rhythmically—the slow second movement of Absence. The term dissonance seems to me inappropriate for the sonority with which in eight measures this slow introduction moves (with a diminished seventh chord) from C minor to C sharp major and then to a subdominant transition to the first movement, the farewell. The harsh sounds, starting twenty-five measures before the end of this first movement, were thought by the publisher to be an error and omitted. These dissonances show that Beethoven was looking for new means of expression. The Sonata op. 81a can be interpreted in terms of feelings associated with loneliness. And yet it, too, is a testimony to that yearning which, in the sense of E. T. A. Hoffmann, simultaneously embraces pain and torment as well as joy and love.

Infinite yearning—the dark absolute in nature and humankind

It is scarcely possible to make a sharp distinction between different eras, and they have also been defined differently at different times in history. Thus E. T. A. Hoffmann, in his aforementioned analysis, ascribes Beethoven's music to the Romantic movement. Indeed, Beethoven was a precursor, but his pantheism was not very closely connected with natural philosophy, which gained a strong influence.

The experience of reality changed in the eighteenth century with the development of measuring instruments (the microscope, the thermometer) and scientific discoveries including that of gravity, of magnetism, and of air or a vacuum. Advances in knowledge were a condition for the rationalism of this time. People were also seeking to penetrate physical and psychological processes. As a result, however, the obscure or dark thoughts postulated by Wilhelm Leibniz assumed new significance. At the end of the eighteenth century, these were attributed by Ernst Platner to a separate, dark psychological entity, the unconscious, which, however, manifested only energetically in drives. And did not the scientific evidence of forms of invisible kinetic energy also have such a dark ground? The effects of the newly discovered, inexplicable forces, especially magnetism, were fascinating. It seemed that there was in matter an absolute, supra-individual basic principle at work, which, by the end of the eighteenth century at the latest, appeared to be the anima mundi, of which the human soul also partook.

A new form of pantheist-inspired natural philosophy emerged in this context on the basis of Neoplatonic philosophy, which had already experienced a revival in humanism, and which provided the inspiration in the seventeenth century for the Cambridge Platonists' new conception of nature. Anthony Ashley Cooper, 3rd Earl of Shaftesbury, took up this tradition. In *Characteristics of Men, Manners, Opinions, Times* (1711, Vol. III, p. 345), he wrote:

> O mighty Nature! [...]. Supreme Creator! Thee I invoke, and thee alone adore. To thee this Solitude, this Place, these Rural Meditations are sacred. [...]. I sing of Nature's Order in created Beings, and celebrate the Beautys which resolve in Thee, the Source and Principle of all Beauty and Perfection.

Alone, in a state of meditation, nature appeared holy. Furthermore, Cooper's deism implied the equation of all living beings with nature.

Johann Georg Sulzer, who spoke English, may have been familiar with Cooper's thought. His (Sulzer) comprehensive encyclopedia *General Theory of the Fine Arts* (1774, vol. 2, p. 653), whose influence is still felt today, described in great detail impressions of the countryside and their artistic depiction:

> A quiet region full of charm, the gentle rippling of a brook, and the whispering of a little waterfall—a lonely place never entered upon by other human beings—awakens a gentle, shivering sense of solitude, and at the same time seems to fill us with awe of that invisible force at work in this abandoned spot.

It is typical of the aesthetics of his time that he was concerned first and foremost with impressions, with sensations, that are inspired by inanimate nature. But Sulzer also attributed to nature an aesthetic power. Unlike Cooper, however, he associated nature's charm with the shiver of solitude; and, somewhat like E. T. A. Hoffman, this shiver with infinite yearning. This twofold quality became typical of German Romanticism and, in the nineteenth century, of English and French Romanticism as well. This shiver was attributed to something obscure and monstrous, inexplicable and defying definition, an existential terror that appeared to locate the shivering sense of solitude within the self.

Sigmund Freud had undertaken a careful consideration of E. T. A. Hoffmann in his essay on the uncanny, which, as something unfamiliar and frightening that could not be grasped by the intellect, aroused fear and trembling. In his initial, provisional definition, however, he drew on Friedrich Wilhelm Joseph Schelling. Quoting somewhat imprecisely (probably from an entry in an encyclopedia), he described as uncanny everything that is a mystery and ought to remain concealed. Unlike Freud, however, Schelling did not view the unconscious as something personal; it prevailed as the anima mundi in all matter. The numerous studies on Freud's relationship to Schelling have failed to take adequate account of this distinction. Parallels between Freud and Schelling are evident above all in the emphasis they both placed on the importance of the unconscious for the production of art.

The darkness of which Schelling also speaks concerns the absolute nature of being that underlies all manifestations of existence, of nature, of man, and of art. But even in the eighteenth century, this numinous experience was already linked to remote and solitary landscapes, as, for example, in England, where it was associated with the experience of the "delightful horror" of the sublime following the first crossing of the Alps by John Dennis in 1688. Sulzer's associating it also with the charm of the gently rippling brook in a lonely landscape constituted a broadening of the notion that still obtained in the nineteenth century. Nature was thus no longer a heavenly place or a barren wilderness, it was no longer disposed for human benefit; it had become an expression of the immaterial anima mundi, a pantheistic, infinite, dark and monstrous absolute that was at work in everything. In Romanticism, art reflected this notion of animate nature.

But this was also an era with another preoccupation, the fairy tale. Yet here, too, nature played the crucial role: "From olden tales it flings out/A beckoning white hand [...]. Where all the trees have voices/And sing their choral chants" (Heinrich Heine, "Lyrical Intermezzo", 1823).

Natural philosophy in artistic thought: England and France

The development of music in Germany was unique, but romantic thought developed in England and France as well, so a brief look at poetry is in order, to avoid national bias. In England in particular, the popularity and wide reception of Schelling's writings meant that there was a distinct similarity between English and German Romanticism. Schelling's conceptual distinction between phenomenal nature as *natura naturata* and *natura naturans* with its animating *anima mundi* is cited by Samuel Taylor Coleridge in his lecture "On Poesy or Art" (1818). The English writer and lawyer Henry Crabb Robinson played an important role in the dissemination of knowledge about Germany. Today it is widely known only of Samuel Taylor Coleridge, who had studied in Germany for a time, that he engaged in intensive reading of Schelling's writings (Burwick, 1990). Nature for him could be a refuge experienced in quiet solitude, through which its spiritual character is able to unfold in the imagination: "'tis a quiet spirit-healing nook! [...]. My God! It is a melancholy thing/For such a man, who would full fain preserve/His soul in calmness." The lines are from Coleridge's poem *Fears in Solitude* (1798), which was written in the context of the impending invasion of the Napoleonic troops. In the same way, the poem "I Wandered Lonely as a Cloud" (1804) by his friend William Wordsworth presented an image of nature engendered "upon that inward eye" as an inner "flash" and which evokes "the bliss of solitude", the wonderful impression of a meadow full of daffodils in bloom. Around 1820, however, it was also the heyday of the Gothic novel in England. The uncanny was reflected in the poems of Emily Brontë, as, for example, in the poem about the final sunset (1838), "It will not shine again." The conclusion speaks of "the cold, bright sun". With its spectral apparitions on an Alpine peak, Lord Byron's dramatic poem *Manfred* (1817), the inspiration for multiple musical compositions (e.g. Schumann, Tschaikovsky), belongs to the genre of Gothic fiction, but as well as a depiction of horror it is also a tender rendition of a desolate nature morte.

In France, romantic thought emerged at the beginning of the nineteenth century. Weary of the revolutionary turmoil and the Napoleonic wars, many artists turned to nature as a longed-for refuge of absolute solitude, which in its profusion of life was at the same time overwhelming. Francois-René Chateaubriand, a royalist who was temporarily forced to emigrate, depicted absolute solitude in these terms in his story *René* (1802), describing the palpable *Weltschmerz*, a feeling of melancholy and world-weariness, as the *mal du siècle*. Chateaubriand took as his model the reveries of Rousseau's *Promenades*. Other points of reference came about with the publication of Germaine de Staël's book *Germany*. Published in Paris in 1810, it was banned by the censors and reprinted in England in 1814. This coincided with the publication of an English translation which was in turn taken up by an American publisher. For Madame de Staël, who revelled in the atmosphere of the French salons, Germany represented the epitome of

94   FROM THE ABYSS OF LONELINESS TO THE BLISS OF SOLITUDE

solitude, for it was her view that communication there took place in writing only. She believed furthermore that (1814, I, p. 141):

> What is called study in Germany is truly admirable: fifteen hours a day of solitude and labor, for several years in succession, appear to them a natural mode of existence; the very ennui of society gives animation to a life of retirement.

Whether this reasoning stands up to historical reality may be doubted. In the third volume, Madame de Staël wrote very knowledgeably about German philosophy. She described Fichte and Schelling as the most important philosophers after Kant, and was especially impressed by Schelling (1800, vol. III, p. 117). She talked about his adoption of pantheist ideas:

> But what distinguishes him is, the astonishing sagacity with which he has managed to connect his doctrine with the arts and sciences; […] the depth of his mind is particularly surprising when he does not pretend to apply it to the secret of the universe …

However, she rejected Schelling's doctrine of universal animation because it contradicted her belief in the supremacy of man.

It was only from 1835 onwards, in the circle that gathered around Abbé Bautain, that pantheist teachings began to be discussed in a theological context in France, which viewed itself as the land of rationality. Prior to this, however, Victor Cousin, the most important French philosopher of the nineteenth century, had learned of pantheism on his trip to Germany through personal meetings with philosophers like Georg Wilhelm Friedrich Hegel and Schelling in the late 1820s. Cousin and Schelling carried on a lengthy correspondence (Fedi, 2018). Schelling's natural philosophy in particular made a strong impression on Cousin. But Cousin did not adopt Schelling's concept of intellectual intuition, for example, the identity of conceptually comprehending reason and intuitive sensuality that can only be attained in art. For Cousin, the basis of all human knowledge is an act of the consciousness. A reference to Descartes? He reasoned psychologically that the absolute could only be given an ontological and metaphysical foundation through the cognisant consciousness. In *On True, on Beautiful, and on Virtuous*, revised repeatedly between 1818 and 1853, he developed an aesthetic that he explicitly wanted to be understood as sensualistic, but which he considered spiritualistic as well. He indicated in the preface of the 1853 edition that with the exception of Kant, he was leaving German philosophy behind. And yet Schelling's idea of nature as God's first poem seems to hover over Cousin's conception of nature. As an expression of the absolute (*absolute being, God*) it reveals an ideal beauty that serves the genius as a model. Cousin draws here on Chateaubriand. But the latter's concept of nature is less congruent with Cousin's than are the ideas of later artists.

Chateaubriand was still on a quest for self-knowledge in the solitude of nature, as in former times—one might think here of Gryphius or Purcell. To the following generation, however, nature itself seemed to be animate. In 1823, Alphonse de Lamartine described a walk in the

Jura Mountains in his *New Meditations with Commentaries*, noting (in translation): "All poets call forth solitude in their souls, the better to listen to God." And: "Nature occupies the space between our eye and God." Victor Hugo describes himself in *To the Trees*—published only in 1856 in the anthology of poems spanning twenty-five years—under the trees in the great forests: "Alone in your depths, [...] Attentive towards your sounds which all speak somehow, Trees, you have seen me flee man and seek God!" In his diary, Hugo noted: "How sad to think that nature speaks and mankind doesn't listen." The widespread pantheist thought among artists in the nineteenth century coupled a possible revelation of absolute being with the solitude of man in nature. Ultimately, however, the poets did not believe that being revealed itself in existence, for speaking nature would disclose only *that* it is, but not *what* it is. Alone in nature, the existential condition can be felt, but cannot be expressed in words.

Natural philosophy: loneliness/solitude and music

Schelling's natural philosophy had parallels in the German Romantic art song, especially in Robert Schumann's *Song Cycle*, op. 39 (1840, revised 1850) based on twelve poems by Joseph von Eichendorff. The secret, wondrous language of nature can be heard in these songs; nightingales sing, the lonely woods murmur, or the phantasmagorical night speaks confusedly in dreams. Joseph von Eichendorff was familiar with Schelling's work, and he believed that Schelling's idea of the animation of nature was the basis of Romanticism. Schumann himself, though well-lettered, was not familiar with Schelling's natural philosophy. But he did know the poems of Friedrich Schlegel, who was for a time a close friend of Schelling's and who had expressed their shared belief in the aphorism "spirit is natural philosophy". Robert Schumann prefaced his Fantasie in C Major, op. 17 with the final lines from Schlegel's poem "The Thicket" (1802): "Resounding through all the notes/In the earth's colourful dream/There sounds a faint long-drawn note/For the one who listens in secret."

Solitude in nature is the prototypical situation of the lyrical persona, often portrayed as homeless, in Schumann's settings of Eichendorff's poems. Noises and sounds are of great significance. "In a Foreign Land" is the title of the opening song of the *Song Cycle*. Melodically tight in composition, a melody concealed in the piano accompaniment briefly sounds, accentuated two times, above the highest note of the singer, at the expectation of imminent death. It descends at the thought of the "lonely woods" to the susurration of an arpeggio. The "sweet murmur of lonely woods" has a mysterious air because it audibly moves away from the home key of F sharp minor. By means of its relative major as a diminished seventh chord (modulating to B minor) we touch on a foreign realm, which returns with a suspiratio motif to the lyrical persona's memory of being in a foreign land. Song No. 8, "I Hear the Brooklets Murmuring", likewise carries the heading "In a Foreign Land". The lyrical persona, cast out and alone, experiences the forest as a place of solitude and desolation, because it is completely unknown: "I do not know where I am." The nightingales are singing. But here, too, what they want to say, though they say it chorally, in unison, leads in terms of harmony somewhere strange and unknown. Thus, in all the songs of the Eichendorff cycle, something uncanny is in the air.

Horror and dread become the central theme in No. 10, the "Twilight" of dusk. The question the poem poses, "What can this dusk and dread imply?", refers to the experience of the uncanny, which, as something dark and obscure, cannot be discerned or known. The fact that nature does not reveal unknowable being, disclosing only that it is, is expressed in Eichendorff's work through the experience of the uncanny dread as a threat. Schumann's setting of "Twilight" differs from the context of the other songs in its use of counterpoint: "Voices wander to and fro." The extended prelude features multiple diminished seventh chords, the immediately dissonant effect of which already had a historical dimension for some listeners in Schumann's time. This chord, with its unclear harmonic references, appears again shortly before the end and culminates in an interrupted cadence. The following staccato, lightly accented sounds, leading to the regular cadence "Be wary, watchful, on your guard!" seem like a warning. Of what?

The "Moonlit Night" (No. 5) is the most famous song of Schumann's Eichendorff settings. So much has already been written about it that just one aspect shall be mentioned here, the subjunctive of the ending, the experience of the lyrical persona in the moonlight of a clear starlit night (in translation): "And my soul spread her wings out wide, flew across the silent land, as though flying home." Does the narrator's soul really fly home? The singing voice, considered in isolation, ends stably on the root note of the main key, E major. But this root note is harmonically reinterpreted by the piano accompaniment to a dominant seventh chord that leads away to the subdominant, which then creates a weak plagal cadence because the note that leads to the root note is missing. The result is an expression of uncertainty. This harmonic configuration can best be explained if we consider that this kind of plagal cadence is often set to the text "Amen", for which reason it is also known as the amen cadence. The hope of the amen is only in the subjunctive: so be it. Schumann had already composed the subjunctive at the beginning of the song. The prelude, harmonically open, does not clarify whether it is four or six bars long. It leads into the song: "It was as though Heaven had softly kissed the Earth." From a musical point of view, this kiss is not clearly defined. It is left open and unresolved on the dominant. The subjunctive "as though ..." is even expressed with a discordant dissonance that is difficult to sing (with the note E in the piano accompaniment and an E sharp for the singer). Jean Paul, a poet Schumann loved beyond measure, had described the *Zwielicht* (twilight or gloaming) of a moonlit night as a *Zweifellicht*, a light of misgivings or doubt. This is precisely what Schumann composed.

His cycle *A Poet's Love* op. 48, likewise composed in 1840, is based on sixteen poems from Heinrich Heine's *Lyrical Intermezzo, Book of Songs* of 1827. Heine was a confirmed Hegelian. In his extensive essay *On the History of Religion and Philosophy in Germany* he speaks ironically, in contradistinction to his naming of other authors, always only of "Mr" Schelling. Heine considered Hegel the apex and culmination of all philosophy. But Schumann did not go along with the irony with which Heine treats the idea of animate nature in his poems as well. The concept of nature remained in his work comparable to the one expressed in the *Song Cycle*. In No. 12 of *A Poet's Love*, "One Bright Summer Morning", Heine has the flowers speak; though their request is only meaningless and banal, they ask the silent, unfortunate man for forgiveness as he wanders through the garden, full of longing and desire for his loved one. Schumann deviated from the triviality of the language of the flowers. Instead, nature as it blooms and unfurls is portrayed in his setting as foreign, with the greatest and clearly audible distance from the home key (minor second step). An almost inaudible melody runs through this and other songs, because in the piano accompaniment, the first note of each run of semiquavers is additionally notated as a crotchet with the stem pointing up. These notes, held for longer, resonate in the sequence of semiquavers with a distinct timbre. The same technique is found in the *Song Cycle*. Here Schumann often composed the impression of an inner voice almost inaudibly, merely as an appeal to the imagination, though as an event to be heard and not only read, as in the "Humoreske", op. 20. For at times, for a brief moment, this inner voice can lead to a melodic unfolding. In the song "One Bright Summer Morning", this voice can in fact be heard throughout the whole piece. It is followed by a long piano postlude that is really an additional stanza. In it, this inner voice is developed melodically—and in fact taken much further than the singing voice that preceded it. This closing section is repeated at the end of the entire Heine cycle.

The topos of solitude continued with a subsequent generation of musicians. Franz Liszt created a monument to nature in its many forms in his *Years of Pilgrimage* (1855). He set Heinrich Heine's poem "A Pine Is Standing Lonely" (1848) to music. Liszt prefaced his "The Blessing of God in Solitude" as well as two other pieces from the piano cycle *Poetic and Religious Harmonies* (1853) each with a poem by Alphonse de Lamartine. Nature loomed large in the work of Richard Wagner as well. The Rhine gold had been snatched away from her in *The Ring of the Nibelung* (1848–1874). The murmuring of the forest in the midst of which *Siegfried* listens in solitude to the bird draws on the Romantic idea of speaking nature. The prelude to *The Rhinegold* with its harmonic stasis lasting several minutes in a rumbling E flat major, slowly transitioning to a brighter realm, has become the prototypical example for all musical nature scenes (Stephan, 1970, p. 316). Bedřich Smetana used the same method in his opera *The Kiss* (1876) for the representation of the dawn. The impression of a summer's morning at the lake in Arnold Schönberg's third movement of the *Five Pieces for Orchestra*, op. 16 (1909) still recalls this technique with its tone colours repeatedly running gently into one another at the beginning. The same is true of the third movement of the *Suite bergamasque* (1890), *Clair de lune*, by Claude Debussy, and of *Nuages* from the orchestral work *Trois Nocturnes* (1889), which flow gently by in interwoven sequences without cadential caesuras. With their blurred structure, the clouds in György Ligeti's work for orchestra (and female voice) *Clocks and Clouds* (1973), inspired as always by a book of the same name by Karl Raimund Popper, contain references to previous musical images of nature, not least the aforementioned *Nuages*.

Claude Debussy was influenced by symbolism and thus by a point of view that often evoked loneliness and lost-ness in fine art and poetry. This is also true of the opera *Pelléas et Mélisande* (1902, libretto: Maurice Maeterlinck) with its characters ineluctably enmeshed in loneliness and isolation. Though Debussy is not counted among the Romanticists, he still dreamed of a kind of music performed outdoors, in which "… the tall peaceful trees would be like the pipes of a great organ." Several of his works, such as the orchestral work *La Mer*, are devoted to impressions of nature such as these. Rather than suggesting the language of nature, however, they are intended to have the effect of enigmatically sensorial sensations.

Nature as a mirror of hopeless despair: the *Winterreise*

The expression of loneliness in the twenty-four songs of the *Winter Journey*, op. 89 (1827, D 911), which, like no other work, inspired twentieth-century composers to create arrangements in search of orientation, can scarcely be surpassed. Schubert composed the songs in two parts, as he had not come across all of Wilhelm Müller's poems at once. Winter, bitter cold, darkness, terror, rocky chasms, cawing ravens, cold winds, and ultimately a hostile nature surround the lonesome wanderer. Here nature confronts man only in the form of the uncanny, instilling fear. The first verses of No. 5, "The Linden Tree", are an exception—a memory of a dreamer that became a popular ballad. In the arrangement by Friedrich Silcher, four verses can be sung to the melody of the first. This simplification does at least give an intimation in the rustling of the branches that the wanderer may yet find his eternal rest under the linden tree. Schubert, however, had already harked back to the previous song in the prelude, to a "Numbness" in ice and snow, and again in the fifth stanza of "The Linden Tree": "The cold wind blew straight into my face [...], I did not turn back" with fading, monotone repetitions of the notes. At the end, the piano accompaniment drops chromatically into the depths. The renewed recollection of the rustling of the tree in the sixth verse is now merely a vain hope, and even the closing section recalls again the numbness. Song No. 12, which concludes the first part, is titled "Loneliness". Here, too, a memory is called to mind, but this time it is of the raging storms. The wanderer now goes on his way through "bright, joyful life" as one excluded from it. He thinks back to how "When storms were still raging I was not so wretched." The calm of the "bright" world is counterpointed by the extreme agitation of the tremolo of a diminished seventh chord, repeated four times, in the piano accompaniment. The "Hurdy-Gurdy Player", which concludes the *Winterreise*, "lets everything go on as it will"; he turns his instrument on a pedal point of the empty fifths: "his little plate remains forever empty". Should the wanderer join him in this utter hopelessness? The song is melodically austere; there is no longer any harmonic development. Scarcely anywhere else in the history of music has such resignation been composed. For, though the aria of King Philip ("She never loved me!") expresses desperate loneliness in the nocturnal scene in Giuseppe Verdi's opera *Don Carlos* (Act II, scene 2), the dark grief, sung in a monotone, erupts into frantic anguish. Gustav Mahler's setting (1901) of Friedrich Rückert's poem "I Am Lost to the World" likewise invests the music with heightened emotion. The second verse is to be sung *poco animando, espressivo*, becoming more lively and more expressive. The third verse returns to an enraptured state: "I live alone in my heaven, in my love, in my song!" A distinction must be made between this and other examples, and the expression of the song of the "Hurdy-Gurdy Player". Schubert composed an inner torpor, an utter emotional numbness. It is therefore too simple to interpret the hurdy-gurdy player as death, as has been done so often, and to answer the lyrical persona's question as to whether he should go with him accordingly. The following bar, just the piano, after this question, with a brief *forte* and a brief crescendo, gives no answer. It is, with a tiny rhythmic deviation, a literal repetition (of bar 27), where a small crescendo was likewise intended; the accompanying passage is: "his little plate remains forever empty". There is no resolution from this void, neither in Schubert's cycle nor in Wilhelm Müller's poem. In the numerous composed interpretations of the *Winter Journey*, including by composers of new music, political interpretations had already been suggested before they began to be considered in academic discourse.

Wilhelm Müller was a politically engaged author. Like Eichendorff, he had participated in the war against Napoleon in 1813. He became known for his poems in support of the liberation of Greece. His biography *Lord Byron* (1822), whom he revered not only as a poet but also for his liberal values, was banned by the censors. And Schubert had drawn the first part of the *Winter Journey* from the journal *Urania*, which was banned in Austria. He also had contact with opposition groups and was once taken into police custody. The *Winter Journey* packaged night, terror, numbness, dashed hopes in the guise of an unhappy love story so as to avoid being banned.

Solitude as political hopelessness

Longing, solitude, and loneliness had never been such central themes for artists as they were in the nineteenth century. Many saw dreams as the only means of escape. But the developments in the different countries were only partially comparable, as the Napoleonic wars had not raged as violently everywhere as they had in Germany. The 1815 Congress of Vienna was convened to restore the old systems of rule. This restoration, which in Germany continued almost until the end of the nineteenth century, was accompanied by prohibitions and censorship. For many intellectuals, the so-called "persecution of demagogues" resulted in prison sentences. The attempt at a parliamentary constitution in 1848 failed in 1849. Following the failed revolution of 1848, many German artists withdrew inwards to a kind of romanticised, folkloric idyll—including, for example, Robert Schumann, who was after all also the composer of a German Freedom Song. But there were power struggles taking place in all the European countries, because hopes for freedom had been destroyed by a temporary return to aristocracy. The Restoration in France ended after the additional revolutions of 1830 and 1848. England, where already the "Glorious Revolution" had taken place in the seventeenth century, was affected by internal upheavals, because the earlier onset of the Industrial Revolution had brought about the impoverishment of sections of the population, leading to labour disputes. Many individuals saw no hope of finding a place in these societies.

This also applies to Dimitri Shostakovich. His work is a testimony to the isolation of a composer in a social system, even when political conditions had improved for him in the 1960s. His Eighth String Quartet, op. 110, in C minor, to which he added the dedication "to the victims of fascism and war" only later, is a reflection on his own identity (Feuchtner, 1968). It is, as Shostakovich noted in a letter, a requiem to himself, interspersed with numerous referencing quotations. Such from *Winter Journey*, however, are not to be found among them. Nevertheless, the string quartet expresses a comparable hopeless loneliness in places. It opens with a fugato over the motif d-es-c-h (English: d- e flat- c-b) formed from Shostakovich's initials as spelled in German (D.Sch.). This motif pervades the entire piece. It appears with different expressive valeurs: resistant, dogged, melancholy. In the fourth movement, a Largo, it seems powerless, as if on the verge of self-sacrifice. This is underlined by the quotation of an older song attributed

Social interaction of the individual and society

The wise Madame de Staël had already sought to demonstrate that social conditions are crucial for artistic production. Georg Simmel (1908, p. 77) had addressed the problem of solitude and loneliness specifically in the light of this "sociation". Unlike other sociologists, he did not work on the premise of the group as the smallest social unit, but of the individual and his or her possibility of belonging to a society. For Simmel, solitude is not defined merely by absence from society, but by its "negated existence", which he did, however, explain as an effect of reciprocity: "Solitude receives its unambiguously positive meaning as a distant effect of society." This can lead to happiness or bitterness, both of which he attributed to different kinds of reactions to social influences.

The forms of solitude, or loneliness, described here demonstrate a relationship to society in line with Simmel's characterisation. A positive view of solitude in the midst of society was conveyed by the likes of Meister Eckhart, Montaigne, and Hildegard of Bingen. In the songs of the minnesingers and the music of Dowland, on the other hand, loneliness manifested as a state of exclusion. In Romanticism, a "distant effect" of society determined the relationship to nature, which was cast by solitude's companion, longing, in the light of a paradisiacal place of comfort and solace. Loneliness and solitude are relational concepts. This also applies to artistic representations, both of a positive state of solitude as well as of the dismay of being forsaken (*St. Matthew Passion*) or irretrievably lost (*Don Giovanni*).

Simmel was an important precursor of the theory of the social interaction of the individual and society. He was very influential on American sociology. An examination of David Riesman's unpublished writings also suggests that he was familiar with Simmel's theory. In their book *The Lonely Crowd*, Riesman et al. (1950) described the conformist, other-directed character of the modern person, driven by an anxious, gregarious need for the approval of others, regardless of the loss of his or her own autonomy: "One prime psychological level of the other-directed person is a diffuse anxiety," Riesman and colleagues wrote (p. 26).

Solitude as happiness, which Simmel also spoke about, would appear to be rarely experienced in modern society. When empirical psychological research began to be conducted in the 1960s, loneliness was demonstrated to be a complex experience through a multidimensional structure of experiencing life, which could be differentiated in terms of two overarching aspects: social and emotional loneliness. In surveys of the terminally ill, however, another form of loneliness could be distinguished, namely one that was of an existential nature. It concerned self-identity and the question of the meaning of life. Musically, however, solitude was reflected primarily in the form of the first two factors mentioned above. The forsaken women in Arnold Schönberg's *Expectation* and Francis Poulenc's *The Human Voice* expressed this, as did Paul Hindemith's pallid landscape of the "Nocturne" in the *Suite 1922* and Helmut Lachenmann's music theatre piece *The Little Match Girl*. There are certainly still religious works, *Requiem* or *Stabat Mater* (György Ligeti, Wolfgang Rihm), that follow in the tradition of comfort and solace. Despite modern tonal means, the *St. Luke Passion* by Krzystof Penderecki makes a reference to Johann Sebastian Bach with the motif: German "h-b-a-c" (English: b-b-flat-a-c) in the opening movement.

But solitude/loneliness is not a central theme of new music. On the other hand, loneliness has been taken up many times in popular music, as the experience of thwarted love, of desolation, and of longing. This may have to do with the fact that young adults are processing similar negative emotions by listening to music in order to feel less alone. Delia Decroupet kindly pointed me to an overview of popular *Songs about Loneliness* (*Spinditty*, 2016).

This chapter provides an overview of the historically changing conceptions of loneliness and solitude in various artistic forms of expression, among which music is considered to be of special importance, not only because of its expressive content, but also because of the comforting nature of some music. It becomes clear that the theme of loneliness preoccupied almost every important composer and, thus, great creativity was required to find new ways to express it.

References

Assmann, J. (2000). Literatur und Einsamkeit im alten Ägypten. In: A. Assman & J. Assman (Eds.), *Einsamkeit* (pp. 97–111). Munich, Germany: Fink.

Benjamin, W. (1928). *Ursprung des deutschen Trauerspiels*. Berlin: Rowohlt.

Borowski, M. (2006). *Die Glaubens- und Gewissensfreiheit*. Tübingen, Germany: Mohr Siebeck.

Burton, R. (1621). *The Anatomy of Melancholy, Vol. 3*. Oxford: Cripps.

Burwick, F. (1990). Coleridge and Schelling on mimesis. In: R. Gravil & M. Lefebure (Eds.), *The Coleridge Connections* (pp. 178–199). London: Palgrave Macmillan.

Cooper, A. A., 3rd Earl of Shaftesbury (1711). *Characteristics of Men, Manners, Opinions, Times, Vol. 3*. London: John Darby.

Cousin, M. V. (1818). *Du Vrai, Du Beau et Du Bien*. Paris: Didier, 1853.

Fedi, F. (2018). Schelling en France au xixe siècle. *Les Cahiers philosophiques de Strasbourg, 43*: 13–80.

Feuchtner, B. (1968). *"Und Kunst geknebelt von grober Macht"—Dimitri Schostakowitsch. Künstlerischer Identität und staatliche Repression*. Frankfurt am Main, Germany: Sendler.

Freud, S. (1914b). The Moses of Michelangelo. *S. E., 13*: 209–238. London: Hogarth.

Freud, S. (1917e). Mourning and melancholia. *S. E., 14*: 237–258. London: Hogarth.

Freud, S. (1919h). The "uncanny". *S. E., 17*: 217–256. London: Hogarth.

Gray, T. (1751). *"Elegy Written in a Country Church Yard"*. London: Thomas Dodsley.

Heine, H. (1823), Lyrisches Intemezzo. In: *Tragödien nebst einem lyrischen Intermezzo* (pp. 69–126). Berlin: Dümler.

Hildegard, S. (1151). Scivias. In: M. Böckeler (Ed. & Trans.), *Wisse die Wege. Scivias*. Salzburg, Austria: Müller, 1954.

Hoffmann, E. T. A. (1810). Ludwig van Beethoven, 5. Sinfonie. In: F. Schnapp (Ed.), *E. T. A. Hoffmann. Schriften zur Musik* (pp. 34–51). Munich, Germany: Winkler, 1963.

Hugo, V. (1856). *Les Contemplations. Aux Arbres*. Paris: Hachette.

Küpper, J. (2002). *Petrarca: Das Schweigen der Veritas und die Worte des Dichters*. Berlin: de Gruyter.

Lamartine, A. de (1823). *Nouvelles Méditations Poétiques*. Paris: Urbain Canel.

Lavater, J. C. (1776). *Physiognomische Fragmente, zur Beförderung der Menschkenntnis und Menschenliebe, Vol. 2*. Leipzig, Germany: Weidemanns Erben.

Meister Eckhart (1300). Von der Abgeschiedenheit. In: J. Quint (Ed. & Trans.), *Meister Eckhart: Die deutschen Werke (Vol. 5, treatise 3)*. Stuttgart, Germany: Kohlhammer, 1963.

Meister Eckhart (1300). The German Works. In: L. Sturlese & M. Vinzent (Eds.), *Meister Eckhart: The German Works*. Leuven, Belgium: Peeters, 2019.

Müller, U. (Ed.) (1986). *Minne ist ein swaerez Spil. Neue Untersuchungen zum Minnesang und zur Geschichte der Liebe im Mittelalter*. Göppingen, Germany: Kümmerle.

Petrarch, F. (1346). De vita solitaria. In: J. Zeitlin (Trans.), *The Life of Solitude*. Urbana, IL: University of Illinois Press, 1924 [reprinted Urbana, IL: University of Illinois Press, 1978].

Riesman, D., Glazer, N., Denney, R., & Gitlin, T. (1950). *The Lonely Crowd: A Study of the Changing American Character*. New Haven, CT: Yale University Press.

Rousseau, J. J. (1782). Les rêveries du promeneur solitaire. In: *Collection complète des Oeuvres, Vol. 10* (pp. 369–517). Geneva, Switzerland: Deleatur. Available at https://rousseauonline.ch/pdf/rousseauonline-0077.pdf (last accessed 7 October 2021).

Schelling, F. W. J. (1800). System des transzendentalen Idealismus. In: K. F. A. Schelling (Ed.), *Sämmtliche Werke 1799–1800, Vol. III* (pp. 327–634). Stuttgart-Augsburg, Germany: Cotta, 1858.

Simmel, G. (1908). *Untersuchungen über die Formen der Vergesellschaftung*. Leipzig, Germany: Duncker & Humblot.

Spinditty. (2016). Flourish Anyway. 112 Songs about Loneliness and Feelings of Isolation. *Spinditty*. https://spinditty.com/playlists/Pop-Rock-Country-Songs-About-Loneliness (last accessed 14 January 2021).

Staël, A. L. G. (1814). *Germany, Vol. 3*. London: John Murray.

Stephan, R. (1970). Sichtbare Musik. In: R. Damm & A. Traub (Eds.), *Vom musikalischen Denken* (pp. 300–308). Mainz, Germany: Schott, 1985.

Sulzer, J. G. (1771, 1774). *Allgemeine Theorie der schönen Künste*. 2 Vols. Leipzig: Weidmann & Reich.

Timofte, A. (2014). Einsamkeit (ver-)schreiben. Umwertungen im anthropologischen Diskurs des 18. Jahrhunderts. *Recherches Germaniques*, 4: 27–49.

Voltaire, F. (1764). *Dictionnaire philosophique, portatif*. Geneva, Switzerland: Grasset.

Wolff, C. (1721). *Vernünfftige Gedancken von dem gesellschaftlichen Leben der Menschen*. Halle, Germany: Renger.

Zimmermann, J. G. (1784–85). *Über die Einsamkeit, Vol. 4*. Leipzig, Germany: Weidemann & Reich.

Zimmermann, J. G. (1788). *La solitude considerée relativement à l'esprit et au coeur*. Paris: Leroy.

Zimmermann, J. G. (1799, 1800). *Solitude or The Effect of Occasional Retirement, 2 Vols*. London: Vernon & Hood.

CHAPTER 6

Myth of the solitary artist

Aleksandar Dimitrijević

Wir sind die Bienen des Unsichtbaren. Nous butinons éperdument le miel du visible, pour l'accumuler dans le grande ruche d'or de l'invisible.

We are the bees of the invisible. We frantically collect the honey of the visible for the grand, golden hive of the invisible.[1]

—Rilke, Letter to Witold von Hulewicz, November 13, 1925

Wo ich bin, ist Deutschland. Ich trage meine deutsche Kultur in mir.

Where I am, there is Germany. I carry my German culture in me.

—Thomas Mann in *The New York Times*, February 22, 1938

Loneliness is, being a ubiquitous human phenomenon, frequently portrayed in artworks, where we might be tempted to see it as autobiographical. The most famous examples include Hamlet, Papageno, many of Kafka's characters, Smeagol (Gollum), Violeta Valery who describes herself as "povera donna sola, abbandonata, in questo popoloso deserto che appellano Parigi", Shostakovich in his "musical self-portraits", or John Merrick of *The Elephant Man*. Both the solitude and loneliness of artists are also frequently discussed topics in psychoanalytic literature and beyond. The source of this is supposed to be twofold: artists are claimed to seek

---

[1] The most probable reason for Rilke to switch to French in a letter to his Polish translator is the verb "butinon" for which in German he would need several words. It is also worth noting that the adverb "éperdument" is a derivative of the verb "perdu"—meaning "lost". It could, therefore, also be translated as "selflessly" ("Je t'aime éperdument" means "I love you madly" or "I'm crazy in love with you", which implies loving someone to the level of losing one's mind, to the state of selflessness). I refrained from using this interpretive option, anxious that I might be overstating similarities between Rilke's and Winnicott's thinking.

solitude more than persons in other professions (i.e. "Artistic creation is a solitary vocation"—Knafo, 2012a, p. 54), and other people's attitude towards them can make them isolated, misunderstood, considered deviant.

In this chapter, I will contest these notions and try to show that the situation is far more nuanced and largely depends on the phase of the creative process (inspiration, execution, having finished, or being in the grips of a creative block). My argument will claim, first, that artists can bear aloneness because they tend to be absorbed in the artwork, and, second, that artists can create and endure aloneness only thanks to a dialogue they keep inside themselves with whole cultural traditions. Because contrary to the widespread belief, creativity is the precondition for being able to bear solitude as much as solitude is a necessity for creative work.

Creativity and solitude

The loneliness of creators has been noticed and discussed long ago. They are claimed to very often feel frustrated due to the lack of close relationships, understanding, love, sympathy. Indeed, many artists and scientists put their work ahead of any social relationship or commitment, and consequently they live alone, their marriages often fail, their children get neglected. One should only think of Eugene O'Neill's children's horrible destiny (Dimitrijević, 2005), or Picasso's marriages. Here is a summary of just one such history, by now very well documented:

> Biographers describe Beethoven's life as mostly spent in isolation, especially after he had moved away from his family in Bonn. He was unable to build a single longstanding reciprocated romantic bond, and had no family and children of his own. His deafness, which he thought would destroy him as a musician, led to suicidal plans and writing a testament when he was thirty-two, and to further social isolation because visitors had to write in his notebooks. At the age of forty, he wrote "I haven't a single friend; I must live alone." (to Bettina von Arnim, quoted by the recipient in her letter to Goethe, May 28, 1810)
>
> Closely connected to this are his failed attempts to adopt his nephew Karl. After his brother Kaspar Anton Karl's death, Beethoven raised several lawsuits against the widow, stating that she was not capable of raising a child. Sadly, even when the boy was under Beethoven's custody, he lived with him only briefly, he lied, stole from his uncle and ran away, and no real bond was ever established between the two of them.
>
> Beethoven wrote: "Friendship and similar sentiments bring only wounds to me. Well, so be it; for you, poor Beethoven, there is no outward happiness; you must create it within you—only in the world of ideality shall you find friends" (to Gleichenstein, about 1808). The only option left for Beethoven was to turn to music altogether (Dimitrijević, 2020). Desperate with the loneliness of his ultimate disappointment in humankind and

his kin, Beethoven focused on the composition of his Ninth Symphony, wherein the Fourth movement contains Schiller's verse with the "All people will be brothers" motif, and the final set of string quartets, which, in his own words, are his conversations with the "spirit". Loneliness that haunted him in his family life, the genius could overcome only through creation.

Another layer of this is that some artists claim that they crave solitude or consider it a necessary precondition for the development of their creativity (see Bion in Caldwell, this volume; Knafo, 2012a, 2012b, 2012c). Indeed, uninterrupted concentration on a creative problem is a sine qua non for many artists and scientists (or chess players). However, this tendency is also often treated in a romanticised and idealised way. Popular opinion considers Rainer Maria Rilke the epitome of this tendency towards solitude, who, indeed, himself wrote this repeatedly. In the famous "Letters to a young poet", first published in 1927, this is his frequent advice to Kappus, his correspondent:

> Works of art are of an infinite loneliness (p. 29). There is but one solitude, and that is great, and not easy to bear, and to almost everybody come hours when they would gladly exchange it for any sort of intercourse, however banal and cheap, for the semblance of some slight accord with the first comer, with the unworthiest … But perhaps those are the very hours when solitude grows; for its growing is painful as the growing of boys and sad as the beginning of springtimes. But that must not mislead you. The necessary thing is after all but this: solitude, great inner solitude. Going-into oneself and for hours meeting no one—this one must be able to attain. (pp. 45–46)

Rilke's biography and his only novel are in accord with this. He spent the last years of his life alone in a village high in the Swiss Alps, where he finished the *Elegies*, wrote the *Sonnets*, and turned to writing poetry in French. And where he died in late 1926, without having established a single reliable long-term bond with anyone. *Malte*, published in 1910, is focused on the "intransient love", the suffering of the loved ones, and the absence of the prodigal son that lasts until even dogs forget him.

This, however, is not the whole story, and a careful study of biographies, works, and psychological processes will help us discover many nuances, ambivalences, and contradictions. Hopefully, our understanding of the human experience of aloneness, both in its positive and negative aspects, will be enriched in this way as well.

When do artists feel that aloneness is painful?

In all human activities, the most sensitive parts are the transitions: beginnings, shifting, and endings. In our everyday lives, we see this in meeting and parting, births and deaths, growing close and separating. In psychoanalytic sessions, it is obvious when we observe beginnings and endings of sessions, or preparations for vacations or terminations. Great artists know that transitions are their biggest challenges and pay special attention to them. Leonardo's sfumato or Mozart's harmonies make transitions breathtakingly smooth. Contrary to this, the Cubists' forms or Stravinsky's rhythms accentuate every transition to the level of pain. Beyond the artworks, studying transitions in the creative process can teach us a lot about creativity and about loneliness.

Discovering one's voice

For various reasons, some children may have a problem communicating emotions to adults and/or peers.[2] If the child has difficulties speaking or recognising emotions, and/or if parents are not sensitive enough, or they are preoccupied with themselves, depressed, or addicted, a child will not have enough opportunities to practise and develop the skills necessary for adequate emotional exchange. The child may demand something too strongly, too loudly, in an aggressive manner, or shyly, cautiously, or not at all.

Where this is the case, artistic talent, if present, can be of much help. If a child can draw, or sing, or dance beautifully, that can become her way of reaching others and having proof that she has managed to provoke an emotional reaction in them. It is very important to note that the "message" and reactions will not be what the child initially wanted to share and receive feedback for, but the pain of loneliness at a young age can be so fierce that a child would take anything she can find, even punishment or abuse, and especially praise.

Over time, particularly if reinforced by success, the child can find solace in creativity and make it her primary way of communicating emotions with others. Art, thus, becomes precious, for many, necessary, because it is their way out of loneliness. One can even hypothesise that a child may neglect a talent unless it is necessary for her to be able to reach the significant others in that way.

For many such children, growing up does not change things substantially, and their loneliness and their talent keep going hand in hand. The only novelty might be that they start believing they have something special to say in their chosen domain of arts, science, or crafts. Some search for this "voice", be it their message, question, finding, technique, for years or even decades. The point is, however, elsewhere. The proverbial pursuit of one's voice as an author can ignite passion only in persons who feel that they cannot express their emotions, thoughts, opinions, or experiences in their everyday social life, that their interactions are stifled, inhibited, inarticulate. They may believe that there is something important that they have to say; the truth is, however, that it is the manner of expression that they did not acquire as children and need to discover now, when it is already quite, if not even too late.

---

[2] More about this process in Chapter 10 of this volume, "Loneliness and insecure attachment".

Inspiration

If we focus on how the creative process starts, we face the ever-mysterious issue of inspiration. Historically believed to be connected to divine influence, inspiration is today more often related to neurophysiological specificities or the capacity to harness the fruits of unconscious processes (Rothenberg, 1994). Some people cherish these special moments and do whatever they can to develop them to their full potential, while others enjoy them carelessly and after a brief play abandon them.

> In December 1911, tormented by the inability to write since the publication of his novel, Rilke walked outside the Duino castle and heard a voice telling him what will become the first line of his most important collection of poems. Princess Thurn und Taxis, whose guest he was at Duino, described it like this:
>
> > It seemed that in the roar of the wind a voice had called out to him: "If I cried out, who would hear me up there among the angels' orders?"
> > He stood still, listening. "What is that?" he whispered. "What is coming?"
> > He took out the notebook that he always carried with him and wrote down the words, and right afterward a few lines that formed without any effort on his part. He knew that the god had spoken. (Quoted in Leppmann, 1984, p. 288)
>
> Almost a decade later, both cycles of *Sonnets to Orpheus* and the largest part of *Duino Elegies* were written between 2 and 26 February, 1922 (Louth, 2020, pp. 358–359). Rilke described this creative process as an "ouragan de coeur et d'esprit" (letter to Baladine Klossowska, 9 February, 1922) or "taking dictation within" (letter to Jean Strohl, 7 February, 1922).

Among many less consequential attempts, in the history of psychoanalysis there were two dominant theories that aimed at explaining inspiration, both developed during the 1950s, and both fundamentally albeit implicitly connected to solitude. One, most famously espoused by Ernst Kris (1939, 1952), was focused on the issue of the ego strength, the other, Winnicott's, on the undifferentiated states of being.

Although he initially wrote about classical psychoanalytic understanding of creativity, like "pre-genital and genital experiences" (1939, p. 389), Kris developed an original idea that he termed "regression in the service of the Ego". Being one of the central proponents of the school of ego psychology, he dealt with issues like the relevance of the ego, and not the drives, for the creative process. How much control can the ego muster over the production (discipline, work habits, concentration as the most demanding mental function) without interfering with the spontaneity of the creative process? Can the impulses rising from the id and the controls descending from the superego be automatically integrated into the creative production coordinated by the ego? In his opinion (Kris, 1952), inspiration is a passive experience, a projection of certain unconscious wishes and impulses, which are subsequently passively received from the external world. The creative person can have an experience that the inspiration comes from the outside, while it is only an internalisation of previously projected impulses.[3]

Kris's creator is, thus, solitary in two ways. On the one hand, he or she might be completely consumed by these processes, so much so that there is no energy left for social life or family. On the other hand, he or she is not in real contact with their environment but sees only their projections. Still, this was not a major concern for Kris.

For better or worse, Winnicott's interpretation of the creative process is almost directly, although most probably unintentionally, opposite to Kris's. For Winnicott (1971, p. 64), playfulness, and consequently creativity, are opposite not only to drive impulses but also to the state of integration and come from the state of "unintegrated personality". In order to play and/or create, one must be capable of tolerating the feelings of uncertainty, lack of control and censorship, rules or results. But whoever is capable of that will have the privilege to experience the moments of losing oneself in play or other favourite activity, moments of selflessness and absorption.

The best Rilke interpreter among psychoanalysts wrote:

> For Rilke, the creative process leading to the achievement of great work places the artist "in danger" because he must be open to his "personal madness" and must go all the way through an experience which that "madness" makes increasingly "private," "personal," "singular," and lonely. The unsupported isolation of his strivings is necessary because discussing one's "personal madness" with someone else would deflate its energy and force. (Kleinbard, 1993, p. 43)

Hence his reluctance to begin a psychoanalytic treatment, which he described would correct him with "red ink like a child's exercise in school" (letter to Lou, January 24, 1912), despite the belief that "there is nothing real about me; and I divide again and again and flow apart" (letter to Lou, August 8, 1903) and many other complaints and worries.

What Winnicott describes is definitely not a process or product of disintegration, or a sign of pathological processes. Play is, however, "always liable to become frightening" (1971, p. 50). It can easily happen that a child or a creative adult becomes afraid that unintegration could turn into disintegration. A resolution of this problem, or its prevention in the first place, requires protection, and an invisible one at that. This is the task of what Winnicott termed the "environment mother"—the role of the same mother who a moment ago did the feeding, cleaning, changing, but whose task it is now to recognise that she is not in focus anymore. A child still depends on her fundamentally, just not for the satisfaction of drive wishes as much as for the safety of the context in

---

[3] The same approach is present in the so-called reader-response theory, where it is considered that the reader/spectator/listener finds in the work of art only what she or he projects from her or his interiority.

which playing will be possible. The child must be able to develop trust that the mother is available and will react immediately to each sign of her needs. And until then, she better remain invisible.[4]

A parent flexible and skilful in switching between these two roles will help the child build a solid representation of her capacities in her- or himself. Slowly but steadily, the child will learn ("internalize the capacity") to trust herself and depend on her mother less. The mother will not be needed in the room because she will live continually in the child's mind (Winnicott, 1958). And the smoother the operating of this function in the child's mind is, the more she will be capable of enjoying solitude, playing, creating, and challenging the status quo.[5]

Inspiration, thus, in Winnicott's interpretation, even if it happens in solitude, is made possible by the invisible presence of a trustworthy caregiver.

Creative block

A particular problem that plagues many artists is that of creative block: a period of incapacity to create due mostly to internal reasons and not external circumstances. An artist can feel depleted, exhausted, incapable of saying anything new for protracted periods of time, although she or he had previously managed to obtain the usual or even perfect work conditions. Possibly the most humorous illustration of creative block is the plot of the first part of *Shakespeare in Love*, and many have suffered from it in reality as well.

> Rilke repeatedly feared losing sanity, and most often in between large writing projects. Possibly the worst one came after he had finished his only novel, *The Notebooks of Malte Laurids Brigge*, in 1910. He complained of "this long drought … reducing my soul to famine" (letter to Princess Thurn und Taxis, May 1911). He approached Lou Salomé, after several years of silence, and their correspondence from this period is almost all focused on the creative block and his interest in her opinion as to whether he would benefit from psychoanalysis. And when he was able to bring the Elegies to fruition, he wrote of the block as "a mutilation of my heart that the elegies weren't there" (letter to Salomé, February 11, 1921).

This phenomenon was repeatedly discussed by psychoanalysts (see for instance Akhtar, 2003; Amado, 2021; Milner, 1950), and was actually for the first time described by a psychoanalyst (Bergler, 1950), albeit under the name "writer's block". It is considered curable, and various

---

[4] Indeed, the microanalysis of mother–infant interaction shows that mothers who cannot recognise the non-verbal signals of "I need a break" (stopping the eye contact, head movement back and to the right, lifting both hands in front of the face) or who cannot tolerate being alone until the child shows signs of interest again, but protrude their faces through the baby's hands, as a rule, have insecurely attached children (Beebe et al., 2016).

[5] This line of thinking can also shed some light on possible reasons for gender differences in creativity. It is not the issue of anyone's superiority related to psychological capacities or competencies. It is (partly) that the state of unintegration is not something one can afford oneself as a mother who has to hold an infant or child naturally prone to disintegration.

explanations of its origin have been offered, ranging from oral masochism to lack of adequate mirroring in development and fear of emptiness. Akhtar (2003, p. 43) provides the following list: non-specific, overwhelmed state of the ego; inability to create the self-holding function; excessive guilt over the replacement of the object mother by one's own self; "anxiety over the separation from a tradition that has become unconsciously equated with the symbiotic mother"; "anxiety over desires to please an imaginary audience and fears of one's critics, especially if these two parties come to represent the parental couple in the unconscious".

I will here focus only on one aspect, and that is how creative block can make feelings of loneliness acute. The incapacity to express oneself creatively, even if temporarily, leads to considerable frustration and dissatisfaction. It can be plausibly assumed that a significant part of these emotions comes from the fear, most probably unconscious, that without artistic expression, no expression whatsoever is possible. If someone gets stuck as an artist, he or she can quickly feel stuck as a person, stuck utterly. Like there is nothing else relevant inside, and the person is worthless without the artistic side. The root of this feeling is in the lifelong use of art to overcome isolation and the lack of confidence that this is possible to achieve otherwise.[6]

Heinz Kohut, given his general interest in the topic, discussed artists' narcissistic cathexes. He claimed that, contrary to popular opinion, artists do not have a narcissistic relationship with their audiences, but with their works (Kohut, 1977, 1978a, 1978b). This means, in the framework of Kohut's conception of narcissism, that artists experience their poems or compositions not as external, separate objects, distinct from them as persons, but as parts, as extensions of their personalities. In other words, emotions which babies and mothers feel for one another are what artists feel about their work, Kohut believed. Their work never entirely becomes just a physical object; criticising it feels like criticising artists as persons, while praising it can feel like personal appreciation. Consequently, not being able to create may make one isolate and try to hide a believed purposelessness, emptiness, and unworthiness of others' attention. Also, this can haunt one to such an extent that all social issues become irrelevant and seem trifling.

Kohut's interpretation also explains the pain of separation from the artwork and an unwillingness to share, publish, or sell it once it is finished.

Ending the creative process

Narcissistic issues sometimes play a major role in the ending of a creative process as well. The transitional phase that starts once the creative work is over can be experienced as painful. Some authors compare it to depression and can feel depleted, exhausted, and purposeless. At these moments, loneliness can turn into a devastating problem, even leading to suicide attempts.

---

[6] There are various excuses for artists to use alcohol and drugs. The need for those is possibly most acute in periods of creative blocks: because allegedly they should provide the lacking inspiration, because of rebellion against social norms, or in order to belong to a (sub)group. Genuine reasons are much closer to the pain of loneliness, not belonging, futility, emptiness.

Ending a significant creative process is challenging in two different ways. Insecurity brought about by the fear of depletion and consequent creative block, discussed in the previous section, is only one of them. The other is the pain of separation from the creative product.

Once the work is finished, it is, almost as a rule, shared with others: published, performed, exhibited. With notable exceptions, some artists can experience this as exhibiting the most private parts of their personality to complete strangers (and the bigger the success, the more numerous the strangers!). The feelings caused by this can oscillate between feverish expectation, jubilation, and despair. Enthusiastic artists present elements of their personalities, sometimes the sublimated images of their innermost lives, to (potentially) large masses of people. Therefore, the reaction from the audience can hurt or sustain a profound and sensitive part of the artist's personality, the part decisive in feeling accepted or abandoned as an individual. It can bring acceptance or rejection that are both experienced personally much more than professionally. For this reason, if the product cannot be multiplied (unlike scientific papers or literary works, which can), as in the case of performances or sculptures and paintings, the artist might refuse to give such a work away and lose contact with it, as it could feel like losing a part of the self.

Another special form of this problem is that both artists and scientists feel and actually are socially isolated when they encounter critical attitudes. The desperation of unrecognised artists comes from the unconscious conviction that with the rejection of their work they are rejected as persons. Many people mistake absorption into creative work with deviant behaviour, overlooking (or not being able to see) that this is one of the basic features of self-actualisation (Maslow, 1962). On another level, Heinz Kohut advocated the notion of the "anticipatory function of the arts" (see Kohut 1977, pp. 285–290; 1978a, p. 253; 1978b, p. 330), which he, unfortunately, never came to elaborate sufficiently. According to his conception, the arts anticipate changes in the psychological status of an epoch by a generation. In other words, a phenomenon recognised, described, and explained by scientists must have been described and intuitively grasped by artists several decades earlier. If correct, this might be another explanation for the loneliness of artists: some of them are misunderstood and abandoned because their environment cannot keep pace with their vision.

Kohut does not consider the unusual position of performing artists, those who must identify with someone else's creation and express it so that it will strike a chord in the audience. Especially in the case of actors, be it in theatre, opera, or film, a feeling can appear that they are accepted only when they represent someone else and forgotten when they want to be who they are, to use their own words. That can exacerbate the feeling of loneliness immediately after or in between performances.

Loneliness, alas, must be present even after a particularly positive reception from the audience. After a short period of huge narcissistic gratification, like a standing ovation at the end of a performance or after an aria, during which a performer might feel seen, recognised, embraced, a more extended period of isolation, especially in empty hotel rooms on tours, may follow, with equal amplitude.

When is solitude sustaining?

Despite the previously discussed instances of painful loneliness—and often exactly because of them—many creative persons seek isolation from others, even their beloved ones. They find these moments sustaining of their creativity and sometimes personal development, which is why these moments lead to solitude and not loneliness. As Rilke wrote to Kappus, "the young poet": "But your solitude will be a hold and home for you even amid very unfamiliar conditions and from there you will find all your ways" (1927, p. 40). There seem to be two specific instances when this is possible.

Absorption

Hours, days, weeks, and even years on end—as long as and whatever it takes to come up with a perfect solution. Newton allegedly did not have time to eat, Michelangelo and Beethoven did not waste time on personal hygiene, Kafka wrote at night and did not sleep, Cezanne did not attend his mother's funeral as that would "take away a whole work day". Examples are countless.

> Once I worked for about two years with a young man who had diverse talents. His choice was to pursue the career of an artist. He was moderately successful, had several international exhibitions and some good feedback from colleagues and curators. An expat, who hardly knew anyone in Berlin and spoke no German, he came to psychotherapy with problems related to falling asleep and intense anxiety about his health issues. He has already been taking antidepressants, and more than one psychiatrist suspected that he suffered from the Bipolar Affective Disorder.
>
> After several sessions, I started asking him questions about his daily routine (not a usual thing for me to do, but this time I felt something was strange). This is what I learned: usually, he woke up around 10am, went to the studio, worked on his art for ten to twelve, sometimes for sixteen hours straight. He then returned to the apartment, had a brief meal, and then wrote a catalogue of his artwork for another couple of hours. He went to bed around 5am. He lived without social life, sexual life, exercise, cooking, and claimed that he would often forget to eat. A couple of times he felt intense thirst during sessions and could not remember the last time he had drunk water. He had neither time for nor interest in any of these activities. He moved houses frequently, and sometimes lived in studios, where there was no real separation between his work and private times/spaces.
>
> In the weeks to come, he tried to describe what fulfilment the feeling of total absorption had been bringing him for years already. He valued above all else the moments— actually, possibly hours—when he lost all sense of time and worked until physical exhaustion. He was creating something, and that "thing", by forcing him to re-evaluate everything he knew and has already created, created him, in return, he felt. Everything else he had ever experienced was inferior to that.

He was aware that, like all other living creatures, he also needed the recharge of energy. Providing it for himself, however, was a nuisance, a waste of time, losing the flow. He would work until his organism collapsed from exhaustion, hunger, lack of sleep. Then anxiety that he could be deadly ill dominated his mind, he was unable to work, and got afraid that he will never be able to reach the flow again.

The concept of absorption became prominent in humanistic psychology. Most notably, Abraham Maslow (1962) believed that what he called peak-experiences, among which he included the moments of creativity, included fascination, total absorption, and the totality of attention on a single object. This referred to enjoying both external sources of beauty, like landscapes, art, or wine, and the internal ones, like fantasies, imagination, ideas, or emotions. The experience is precious because these are the moments of heightened openness, when whatever comes from inside or outside is received as the only important impression, so much so that the boundaries are at least slightly blurred, and the subject and objects to a certain extent become one. Empirical research has connected the operationalisations of this phenomenon with creativity, hypnotisability, and the flow (Manmiller et al., 2005).

In *Malte*, Rilke described only interiority: "I don't know why it is, but everything enters me more deeply and doesn't stop where it once used to. I have an interior that I never knew of. Everything passes into it now. I don't know what happens there" (p. 5).

Several years later, however, he introduced one of his most important concepts— *Weltinnenraum*, which can roughly be translated in English as world-inside-space. He used this term only once, in a poem written in 1914 (untitled, first line "All things summon us to feel"), to designate the space of the poem, coining a word that entails the unity of the external world, personal interiority, and space.

> Durch alle Wesen reicht der eine Raum:
> Weltinnenraum. Die Vögel fliegen still
> durch uns hindurch. O, der ich wachsen will,
> ich sehe hinaus, und *in* mir wächst der Baum.

> (Through all beings the *one* space reaches:
> world-inside-space. The birds fly quiet
> throughout us. Oh, I who growth desire,
> I look out, and *in* me the tree grows.)

In the poem "To music", this phenomenon will be renamed *Herzraum*, the "heart space" (see Louth, 2020, p. 338), but its meaning will remain the same: the dissolution of personality boundaries (which we too often misunderstand as "psychotic") so that the "infinity passed into him from all sides in so familiar a manner that he could believe he felt within him the gentle presence of the stars which had now appeared" (Rilke, 1978, p. 91).

Absorption seems to be one of the capacities that decide whether an artist will feel that a moment of aloneness leads to loneliness or to solitude. As long as absorption by an internal or external object is present, loneliness is not a danger. It also seems plausible to expect that being absorbed in creative work is intentionally creating something beautiful, is even more profound and intense compared to being exposed to objects and passively enjoying their beauty. Some people experience this feeling as more rewarding than any other experience they could have, and, although alone, never feel lonely while it lasts. One could even say that they feel less lonely while absorbed in the creative work than when surrounded by people or at any other moment of their lives.

Yet, being merged with the object of beauty and particularly being selfless in the moments of creation can be both psychologically necessary and socially debilitating. Once the flow is gone, an artist can feel deep loneliness and anxiety that the inspiration is gone forever, coupled with a horrifying realisation that the skills necessary for establishing close, and especially long-term, relationships have withered, if they were ever actually developed. And so, the abyss of personal loneliness can alternate with the bliss of creative solitude, producing, among other things, the motivation to create.

Creative dialogue with one's tradition

The other instance when one can remain in aloneness and not experience it as painful is when the inner (and not so much the "social") dialogue is not broken. Although they might declare they strive towards solitude, creative artists, philosophers, or scientists need the presence of others in at least two different senses.

First, there must be a person who will play the above-mentioned role of "environment mother": invisible, reliable, devoted, always ready to jump in and provide support in any way necessary, and not demanding anything for herself, or indeed himself. Once the capacity for solitude (i.e. creative work) is spent, one needs an empathetic and nurturing other to overcome the exhaustion of the organism and the (hopefully, temporary) loss of confidence and meaning of life. In many cases, however, what one needs nurtured is not the relationship in and of itself but only the capacity to create, which can often be very disappointing for the partner.

> Rilke was long preoccupied with the theme of invisibleness, his ideal form of love and relation to the world in general in which both someone's presence and our internalisation of them should be performed using the smallest possible modicum. In the novel, this is mostly applied to family bonds, and it ends with the parable about the prodigal son; in the Elegies, it is about the Earth becoming invisible in us. When it came to his personal life, Rilke proclaimed that "love and friendship are there for the purpose of continually providing the opportunity for solitude" (letter to Paula Modersohn-Becker, February 12, 1902) and that "a good marriage is that in which each appoints the other guardian of his solitude, and shows him this confidence, the greatest in his power to bestow" (letter to Emanuel von Bodman, August 17, 1901). Later, he wrote to Lou

Andreas-Salomé (letter of December 28, 1911): "I had a ceaseless longing to bring my solitude under shelter with someone, to put it in someone's protection." His dependence on her stands in stark opposition to this. She had a role of "an unofficial, informal, geographically distant mother-therapist" (Kleinbard, 1993, p. 106), practising psychoanalysis on Rilke "at their every encounter and throughout their correspondence" (Binion, 1968, p. 450; see also Freedman, 1998, p. 380).[7] There were several other women, most notably the one he called Benvenuta (Hattingberg, 1949), usually much younger than him, playing this role of devoted intimate, though not always sexual, companions, who were supposed to defend his solitude and at the same time defend him from loneliness.

Gustav Mahler explicated this in his "ultimatum letter" to his wife-to-be, Alma Schindler, in December 1901: "You must become 'what I need' if we are to be happy together. Would it mean the destruction of your existence if you were to give up your music entirely in order to possess and also to be mine instead? (…) You, however, have only *one* profession from now on: *to make me happy*! (…) You must give yourself to me *unconditionally*, shape your future life, in every detail, entirely in accordance with my needs and desire nothing in return save my *love*!" And when ten years later Mahler learned about Alma's affair with the young Walther Gropius, he felt devastated, showed dependence on her that at moments was almost infantile, consulted Freud, wrote the painful nine-tone chord for the adagio of his last symphony, and died mere nine months later (Dimitrijević, 2007).[8]

On the other side of this are the unfortunate cases of artists who do not have this kind of support, who can usually endure only at the price of great suffering, addiction, depression, or even suicide.

The second and more intriguing level of this is the support that comes from the dialogue with a creator's tradition.[9] It is only now, I believe, that we come to the essential precondition to creativity. Artistic or scientific work is possible only when one has one's whole tradition safely internalised and available at any moment. One can create, with or without a "mother substitute", if and only if one can be in incessant dialogue with the predecessors, supporters, or critics.

Whether in Paris, Duino, or Muzot, Rilke is almost always physically alone. Nevertheless, his creative process is always a dialogue with his predecessors and contemporaries. Rodin, to whom Rilke served as a secretary, is always present in his mind as an ideal artist. His only novel is full of these dialogues: Rilke wrote some of the most beautiful sentences about Beethoven (Rilke, 1910,

---

[7] When Rilke underwent a brief analysis with Paul Federn after the First World War, he kept it secret from her (Binion, 1968, p. 450; Kleinbard, 1993, p. 106).

[8] Psychoanalysts could easily be reminded of Freud's relationships with Fliess, Jung, Ferenczi, or Rank.

[9] Psychoanalysts usually focus on inner objects as understood in the various forms of object relations theory (see Knafo, 2012b, p. 89, 2012c, p. 24), but all too often neglect a wider social and diachronic dimensions.

pp. 129–131),[10] described his meeting with Tolstoy, and referred to his favorite Danish author, Jakobsen. Very similar with his poetry: Duino elegies, his most intimate works, are full of Islamic theology, the Fifth is a reaction to a Picasso painting, while the Third and the Fourth are full of psychoanalytic topics (some critics call the Third a "Freudian Elegy", although it is full of solutions ahead of psychoanalysis of that age).[11]

This process can be found almost everywhere, and it forms the basis of creativity throughout the time of Western civilisation. Before Romanticism, it was taken for granted that artists were immersed in this dialogue. Ancient tragedians were not allowed to present new plots to their audiences, but only what everyone already knew well. Shakespeare invented only one plot, for *The Tempest*, his last play, and even in that one work we can discern the influence of the famous Bermuda shipwreck that took place two years previously. More importantly, an artist is cognizant of his technical tradition, and, given that aesthetic categories, like sonnet or still life, do not exist in nature, he must find original expression through established forms. Shakespeare did not borrow stories and heroes only, but he also used Marlowe's blank verse for his invention of dramatic soliloquies. This sometimes traverses cultural boundaries, as in the case of Bach, the cornerstone of German classical music, whose rhythms are all too often appropriated from French dances: gigue, sarabande, minuet, gavotte, bourée, courante. Sometimes the purpose of this dialogue is the identification with another author—as when Kafka writes that Kierkegaard supports him like a true friend (diary entry of August 21, 1913) or a literary character.[12] It can also be a direct illustration of an author's belief that he has surpassed a competitor or a hero of his youth.[13]

---

[10] For instance, "You mighty spring, you would have poured forth, unheard, giving back to the universe what only the universe can endure. The Bedouins would have hastened by, keeping a superstitious distance; but the merchants would have cast themselves down on the ground, out on the edges of your music, as if you were a tempest. Only a few lone lions would have prowled around you at night, alarmed at what was within themselves, threatened by their own troubled blood."

Also, the "clearly struck hammers of the heart" ("den klargeschlagenen Hämmern des Herzens") from the Tenth Elegy are considered a reference to the Hammerklavier sonata (see Louth, 2020, p. 434). Although, to the best of my knowledge, unconfirmed, this idea is particularly beautiful because it could indicate that the hammers of the heart are identified with the hammers of the piano, and give the reader the poetic images of Beethoven's heart with the size of a piano and of his piano with the sensitivity of a heart.

[11] Rilke not only learned from Andreas-Salomé about psychoanalysis, but she tried to help him herself and introduced him to Freud, whom he saw twice, but only briefly and without forming a lasting bond.

[12] Interestingly, Kohut also wrote about "cultural selfobjects", by which he meant that we sometimes experience the artwork or even biographical details of historical figures we will never actually be able to meet, as sustaining parts of our personalities. These works resonate in us deeply and make us believe that someone has already felt what we are feeling, suffered from the loneliness we are suffering. Thus the product of the loneliness of one person can be a consolation for the loneliness of another/others.

[13] This could easily be the case of Beethoven's 4th Piano Concerto, which was so obviously modelled on Mozart's No. 17 and opens in the same tonality—G major. This time, however, with the solo piano, for the first time not

Theorists call this process intertextuality, and it became ever more prominent in the twentieth century, as in Joyce's use of Homer and Shakespeare in *Ulysses*, Mahler's constant quotations from nineteenth-century composers or natural sounds, or Thomas Mann's capacity to not only bring the whole German cultural tradition with him in his exile in California but also to write (with the generous help of Adorno) a novel that largely revolves around Beethoven's last piano sonata and around Wagner's *Lohengrin*. Jorge Luis Borges famously made this process the central topic of much of his oeuvre, starting with the brilliant *Pierre Menard, Author of the Quixote*, inventing, along the way, what in France was to become fashionable under the name postmodernism.

When it comes to science, everyone deals with the findings and limitations of giants on whose shoulders we are standing. Even revolutions, like Einstein's, would be impossible without a fundamental insight into Newton's understanding of gravity. After some time, the periodic table, calculus, or Latin declensions become so automatised, internalised, that we may temporarily forget that they are not our nature but inherited from our cultural forefathers. Not only does one, during the educational process, learn about the principles and possibilities, but one learns how to ask questions, which questions are still unanswered, what would have been the alternative approaches, etc. This is what we teach our students when it comes to explicating rationale for their research: learn everything about the topic so that you will be able to define gaps in knowledge.

An art historian would undoubtedly be able to list hundreds of examples like these.[14] However, the point of this discussion is that this process is necessary not only in finding a solution to a creative problem, but it helps the author overcome the risk of loneliness through profound and constant dialogue with the creative giants of the past. Therefore, it is not only that solitude is a condition for creation; creation through a dialogue is a condition for solitude. This is precisely why artists can feel so lonely before the creative process starts and once it is over.

Conclusion

We can see clearly that an artist at work seeks solitude because he can become absorbed and "contains multitudes" of his predecessors and is internally never alone; moreover, this process provides to many artists the most profound connection with their social environments; finally, artists' loss of creativity shows us how much fear of loneliness is hidden behind creativity.

Despite a widespread belief, it seems that creativity and solitude stem from the same root, and you cannot be in solitude except creatively, or be creative without temporary solitude.

---

the orchestra. Does Beethoven want to proclaim that he has surpassed even Mozart and won the right to introduce new rules of composing?

[14] All my examples come from the European classical tradition. I believe the process is universal and creators who belong to other cultures absorb and transcend their traditions. The best example of this can be the way Keith Jarrett plays various jazz standards.

Yet, there is more. Creativity (where there is talent, of course) may also be connected to not only the fear and remembrance of fundamental loneliness, but also to the lack of skills that would lead to real connectedness with another person as a subject in his or her own right, or indeed a genuine interest in them. Solitude, thus, is possibly a more precious relief, loneliness a deeper pain than in most people's lives.

References

Akhtar, S. (2003). Writer's block. In: *New Clinical Realms: Pushing the Envelope of Theory and Technique* (pp. 25–44). Northvale, NJ: Jason Aronson.

Amado, N. (2021). Psychoanalytic views of "writer's block": Artistic creation and its discontents. *International Forum of Psychoanalysis* (pp. 1–8).

Beebe, B., Cohen, P., & Lachmann, F. (2016). *The Mother–Infant Interaction Picture Book: Origins of Attachment*. New York: W. W. Norton.

Bergler, E. (1950). Does "writer's block" exist? *American Imago, 7*(1): 43–54.

Binion, R. (1968). *Frau Lou*. Princeton, NJ: Princeton University Press.

Dimitrijević, A. (2005). An attempt at unmasking Eugene O'Neill. *Journal of the American Academy of Psychoanalysis and Dynamic Psychiatry, 33*(1): 163–175.

Dimitrijević, A. (2007). "Gustav Mahler. A Life in Crisis" by Stuart Feder. *American Imago, 64*(1): 109–119.

Dimitrijević, A. (2020). Incapacity to experience jealousy. In: M. K. O'Neil & S. Akhtar (Eds.), *Jealousy* (pp. 79–95). London: Karnac.

Freedman, R. (1998). *Life of a Poet: Rainer Maria Rilke*. Evanston, IL: Northwestern University Press.

Hattingberg, M. (1949). *Rilke and Benvenuta: A Book of Thanks*. New York: W. W. Norton.

Kleinbard, D. (1993). *The Beginning of Terror: A Psychological Study of Rainer Maria Rilke's Life and Work*. New York: New York University Press.

Knafo, D. (2012a). Alone together: Solitude and the creative encounter in art and psychoanalysis. *Psychoanalytic Dialogues, 22*(1): 54–71.

Knafo, D. (2012b). Solitude and relatedness: A wily and complex twinship. Reply to commentaries. *Psychoanalytic Dialogues, 22*(1): 83–92.

Knafo, D. (2012c). Artists' solitude and the creative process. In: A. K. Richards, L. Spira, & A. A. Lynch (Eds.), *Encounters with Loneliness: Only the Lonely* (pp. 15–36). Astoria, NY: I P Books.

Kohut, H. (1977). *The Restoration of the Self*. Madison, CT: International Universities Press.

Kohut, H. (1978a). Self psychology and the sciences of man. In: P. H. Ornstein (Ed.), *The Search for the Self: Selected Writings of Heinz Kohut, 1978-1981* (pp. 235–260). Madison, CT: International Universities Press, 1991.

Kohut, H. (1978b). Reflections on advances in self psychology. In: P. H. Ornstein (Ed.), *The Search for the Self: Selected Writings of Heinz Kohut, 1978-1981* (pp. 261–358). Madison, CT: International Universities Press, 1991.

Kris, E. (1939). On inspiration—preliminary notes on emotional conditions in creative states. *International Journal of Psycho-Analysis*, *20*: 377–389.

Kris, E. (1952). *Psychoanalytic Explorations in Art*. New York: International Universities Press.

Leppmann, W. (1984). *Rilke: A Life*. New York: Fromm International.

Louth, C. (2020). *Rilke: The Life of the Work*. Oxford: Oxford University Press.

Manmiller, J. L., Kumar, V. K., & Pekala, R. J. (2005). Hypnotizability, creative capacity, creativity styles, absorption, and phenomenological experience during hypnosis. *Creativity Research Journal*, *17*(1): 9–24.

Maslow, A. H. (1962). *Toward a Psychology of Being*. 2nd edn. Princeton, NJ: Van Nostrand, 1968.

Milner, M. (1950). *On Not Being Able to Paint*. New York: International Universities Press.

Rilke, R. M. (1910). *The Notebooks of Malte Laurids Brigge*. M. D. Herter Norton (Trans.). New York: W. W. Norton, 1992.

Rilke, R. M. (1927). *Letters to a Young Poet: With the Letters to Rilke from the "Young Poet"*. D. Searles (Ed.). New York: Liveright, 2020.

Rilke, R. M. (1978). *Where Silence Reigns*. New York: New Directions.

Rothenberg, A. (1994). *Creativity and Madness: New Findings and Old Stereotypes*. Baltimore, MD: Johns Hopkins University Press.

Winnicott, D. W. (1958). The capacity to be alone. *International Journal of Psycho-Analysis*, *39*: 417–420.

Winnicott, D. W. (1971). *Playing and Reality*. London: Pelican.

CHAPTER 7

Places of loneliness

Karin Dannecker

When the Beatles featured their song about *Eleanor Rigby* in 1966, it became one of the band's most celebrated songs. Beginning with the line "Ah, look at all the lonely people", it introduces the story of a lonesome scullery maid, dreaming through her life, and when she died at the age of forty-four, nobody except Father McKenzie came to her funeral. Unanswered linger the questions in the song's refrain:

> All the lonely people
> Where do they all come from?
> All the lonely people
> Where do they all belong?

The sad outcome of a lifetime—nobody being at your funeral—portrays a situation most people do not want to envision. We can speculate that the song's unwavering success is related to the listeners' unconscious identification with a deeply feared state of being alone when life is coming to its end.

In 2020, the first year of the pandemic of the coronavirus, the world was repeatedly confronted with reports about places with countless coffins containing victims of the deadly disease. Many of them had been alone when their life ended and many of their loved ones remained in desperate loneliness not even having been able to say goodbye. Millions of people were forced to spend time in isolation, due to government-imposed lockdowns. Quarantine rules ordered them to remain home from work, from school; they restricted contacts with other people. Physical distancing was expected to help stop spreading the virus. The impact of this social distancing on people's well-being was aggravating.

In recent history, this has not happened for the first time. During the SARS epidemic in 2002–04, similar restrictions to social and personal life produced increased anxiety, depression, and other mental health problems. But "the number one emotion that people are dealing with is loneliness" (Antoniades, 2020). During the pandemic the question about *all the lonely people* has become scarily universal.

In this chapter I will approach the subject of loneliness from several angles, aiming to examine various places where indeed it occurs. Researching the localisation of the actual physical detention when one feels lonely will point to some evidence for therapeutically and creatively helpful interventions—assuming that there are inseparable links between places of loneliness and their symbolic meanings.

Loneliness is a common human experience we all know from various times in life. Periods of being alone have a range of functions and meanings in the human life cycle (Larson, 1990). It may be that times alone are enjoyed, as by the hiker in the forest, the exhausted mother taking a wellness weekend, the child browsing through a picture book: often needed to recover from too many social demands. This kind of solitude is beneficial and voluntarily sought after. As Long and Averill (2003) define, it is denoting times of privacy, referring to the ability to control the degree to which other people and institutions intrude upon one's life.

Thus, being alone does not automatically mean feeling lonely. Most people want both—intimate relationships and pauses from being with anybody in a community. The philosopher Svendsen explains (2019, p. 22):

> We all carry a certain antagonism or dualism inside, which means that we are attracted to others, because we have a need to be with them, but we have as well a desire to withdraw from them, because we long for distance, in order just to be by ourselves.

The purpose and meaning of this kind of aloneness is to provide opportunities for greater self-understanding and authenticity. In the same sense, the psychiatrist Storr (1988) describes that removing oneself voluntarily from one's habitual environment promotes self-understanding and contact with those inner depths of being which elude one in the hurly-burly of day-to-day life. This kind of willing and purposeful retreat encompasses a certain life-enriching state.

However, being lonely can be rather aversive and distressing with highly negative impacts on physical as well as mental health. Fromm-Reichmann (1990) differentiates between "real loneliness … the deep threat of the uncommunicable, private emotional experience of severe loneliness" and the type of "creative loneliness" which is culturally determined and defines creativity.

In the following, the distinction will be elaborated between the positive state of being alone, mostly termed *solitude*, related to creativity and spirituality, a prerequisite for individual growth and expanding capacities in life, and the negative *loneliness* which is enforced and involuntary, causing immense suffering, massively influencing the well-being of someone.

The negative consequences of loneliness are depicted in a growing body of research. Results clearly indicate that loneliness matters for physical health and mortality (see Özçürümez Bilgili,

Chapter 12, this volume). Hawkley and Cacioppo (2010) posited that it can be regarded as the social equivalent of physical pain, hunger, and thirst. If left untended, loneliness has serious consequences for cognition, emotion, behaviour, and physical and mental health. Core mental symptoms such as poor concentration, distress, tension, disturbed sleep, and disengagement, along with depression and general dissatisfaction, greater neuroticism, lower self-esteem, and higher potential for suicide have been observed and documented in numerous studies (DiTommaso & Spinner, 1997, p. 481). Physical symptoms, such as heart disease, strokes, and Alzheimer's disease are also considered to be related to loneliness. It increases the risk of dying three times earlier compared to persons who have many and satisfying social contacts (Spitzer, 2019), and its symptoms become equivalent to someone smoking fifteen cigarettes a day. Loneliness even has the power to influence the DNA-transcription in our immune system (Cacioppo & Patrick, 2011).

Years before the actual pandemic, loneliness was considered the greatest public health challenge. In 1978, researchers at the University of California, in Los Angeles, released a scale containing twenty questions to measure a person's level of loneliness. The scale was revised several times, yet it is still widely used today. This and other surveys revealed that nearly 50 per cent of Americans and 34 per cent of Europeans report that they sometimes or often feel alone, rarely interact with others, and refer to the television or a pet as the main source of company (Howe, 2019). In 2018, the British Prime Minister Theresa May put loneliness on the Government's agenda, implementing strategies to "social prescribing" of doctors' and community workers' tailored support to help people alleviate their suffering. It was found that up to a fifth of all UK adults feel lonely most or all the time (Gov.UK, 2020).

In December 2020, the same ministry announced funding projects targeting relief to those most at risk of loneliness during the coronavirus pandemic with £7.5 million. Among the support sectors are the arts, presuming that they bring communities together and reduce social isolation. The therapeutic benefits of making art to combat social isolation has been researched in several studies. Hawkley and Cacioppo (2010) reported that patients participating in art activities had reduced their feelings of loneliness and enhanced their sense of social connectedness. Art therapy can combat depression during self-isolation for many people like the elderly, prisoners (Amsen, 2020), and people with mental health problems (Mann et al., 2017).

The double power of art, to communicate loneliness as well as a medium to overcome it, can be illuminated by two related comprehensive theoretical frameworks: the interpersonal tradition of psychoanalysis and the psychodynamics of the creative process. Reviewing approaches from both perspectives—scientific researchers and artists themselves—will reveal that being alone can be, under certain circumstances, a beneficial experience and making art an intervention to lower loneliness, a crucial aim in art therapy.

The arts provide numerous examples where loneliness is reflected in paintings, drawings, and sculptures as well as in literature, dance, and musical and theatrical pieces. Some films make loneliness an issue. A fairly humorous example is Zemecki's *Castaway*, a kind of Robinsonade, where Chuck, played by Tom Hanks, the only survivor of an aeroplane crash, stranded on an island in the South Sea, has to live there for four years. A volleyball he found on the beach helped him to overcome his existential longing for companionship. After hurting himself he used his own blood to paint a face on it and further personified him by calling him "Wilson", the label of the sporting goods company. Talking to him, asking him for his advice, Wilson became his steady, quiet company.

In Martin Scorsese's film *Taxi Driver*, the protagonist Travis Bickle confesses in desperation: "Loneliness has followed me my whole life. Everywhere. In bars, in cars, sidewalks, stores, everywhere. There's no escape. I'm God's lonely man." We see the driver in his car, in an almost pressing close-up through the window; outside on the streets of the city couples and people in groups obviously enjoy each other's company. The discrepancy between social life outside and isolation inside the cab is tangibly obvious. This sequence, shown on YouTube, lasts one minute and has over 250,000 comments, most viewers deeply sympathising with Travis, admitting their own suffering through loneliness.

Likewise, the filmmaker Aki Kaurismäki believes that all artists are connected through their loneliness, knowing that there is nobody out there who helps (Kaurismäki, 2011).

Similarly, and often referred to, are the letters Rilke wrote to the young poet Kappus, who is anxiously doubting his abilities to become a good writer, comparing himself to others. Rilke suggested: "You are looking outside, and that is what you should most avoid right now. No one can advise or help you, no one (…) Go into yourself." Finally, he is pleading: "Therefore love your solitude and try to sing out with the pain it causes you, for those who are near you are far away, you write, and this shows that the space around you is beginning to grow vast" (Rilke, 1903).

For Wordsworth, another poet, it was the retreat on his sofa, bolstering the lyrics to emerge as he wrote in his poem, "I Wandered Lonely as a Cloud":

> For oft, when on my couch I lie
> In vacant or in pensive mood,
> They flash upon that inward eye
> Which is the bliss of solitude …

—Wordsworth (1807)

Noteworthy here is the equivalence of the psychoanalytic couch situation intended to support a patient's regression to freely associate about his fantasy life.

Hence, being successful requires the artist to withdraw from the demands and influences of the outside world. This move into a solitary state is an undoubted condition of the creative process, sometimes appearing almost cliché-like, as can be observed in Rembrandt's *The Artist in his Studio*, or Spitzweg's *The Poor Poet*.

Withdrawing into a kind of voluntarily sought solitude has been the basis for many beneficial outcomes for humankind. Charismatic figures in history, religion, mysticism, culture, and philosophy have sought seclusion to receive revelation and spiritual insight, often practised in celibate forms of life. Spiritual leaders, philosophers, and artists have shared what they have discovered in solitude and thereby exerted great influence on society and individuals. Thus, solitude is inherently social as it relies on the human capacity to reflect upon and interpret one's own experiences. This ability to consider our own thoughts arises from our development of the ability to represent the thoughts of others. Long and Averill (2003) summarise that the paradigm experience of solitude is a state characterised by disengagement from the immediate demands of other people—a state of reduced social inhibition and increased freedom to select one's mental or physical activities.

To make creative use of solitude requires states of positively being with oneself. In this respect, Rilke again convincingly conveys: "The necessary thing is after all but this: solitude, great inner solitude. Going into oneself for hours meeting no one—this one must be able to attain" (Rilke, 1903).

In her famous paper about loneliness, Fromm-Reichmann (1990) names this type of state yielding towards creative productivity *constructive* aloneness, claiming that only the creative person who is not afraid of constructive aloneness will have free command over his or her creativity. She indicates, as well as Rilke, that someone who wants to make use of his or her creative potential must be endowed with certain psychological strengths.

In his essay on being alone with oneself, the cultural scientist and philosopher Macho (2000) writes that this state of solitude must be attained like any cultural technique, and one must develop strategies to initiate and cultivate self-perception aiming at incitation of the inner dialogue. He emphasises that this requires a certain amount of discipline and mastery. Randomly unleashing the inner dialogue without applying certain techniques leads to the dangers and perils of obsessions and passions. The experience of freely encountering the inner world needs "ego strength" to prevent unwanted uncontrollable uproar. The techniques of solitude require certain places—places of solitude, as Macho goes on approaching conditions of beneficial aloneness. In the history of solitude techniques, these places are characterised as where people usually do not live or want to live: caves, deserts, wilderness, and distant mountains. Such "no man's lands" foster freedom for the faculty of imagination and create the danger of the "big other"—the competitive demons, inclined to appear when the environment is perceived as monotonous, and no cultural technique is available.

Cultural history provides the impressive example of St Anthony. Menacing demons afflicted the saint in Athanasius's biography *The Life of St. Anthony*. A major influence on his experience was played by the places he purposefully chose for retreat. The saint secluded himself in the desert to live an ascetic life. When his search for solitude initially failed, having not been able to cut himself off from his friends and followers, he ultimately climbed a mountain. This, as Barasch (2000) describes, became the climax of the hermit's seclusion. He points to what Athanasius has told the reader is "the interior of the mountain": an enclosed space where the saint lived from now on and dwelled in a grave. Whereas the desert is a projection of the hermit's inner experience functioning as a reification of his inner life, the grave and the cave forcefully convey the idea of loneliness and isolation. These are the places of total detachment from human society and where the ascetic encounters the demons. The author concludes that

Anthony's story reveals the emergence and violence of the demons as a revelation of the concealed and repressed conflicts of the hermit's inner world. Solitude is the condition for the unveiling of these conflicts. The experience of solitude is not only unutterable, but it also carries the connotation of the demons (Barasch, 2000).

The inherent danger of the loss of relatedness ultimately may lead to delusional states, prevailing when the environment does not function as a safe holding space anymore. Fromm-Reichmann focuses on this non-constructive disintegrative kind of loneliness, which renders people emotionally paralysed to the development of psychotic states, and here she quotes Sullivan: "the exceedingly unpleasant and driving experience connected with an inadequate discharge of the need for human intimacy, for interpersonal intimacy" (1990, p. 309). According to Frie (2012, pp. 34–35), it is the development of states when patients communicate with extra-terrestrial beings, when their language becomes private and with no understandable syntax: "The loss of relatedness menaces one's survival and the psychotic is able to return from a state of delusion only through the repair of his or her relations with other people and the world."

A decrease in immediate social interaction may lead to the disengagement from the concern for others and foster chronic social withdrawal (Long & Averill, 2003). This often correlates with certain character traits which make attachment with others difficult. As Cacioppo and Patrick (2011, p. 189) describe, the lonely person tends to evaluate his environment negatively, sensing dangers and devaluation in social areas. He or she develops a defensive attitude towards others expecting rejection, constantly ready for self-defence. Thus, sustained loneliness impairs the capacity for self-regulation combined with a distorted social cognition and inability to perceive the perception and intentions, mental states, of others. Such behaviour often leads to what is feared most—the withdrawing and turndown of the others. Like a vicious circle, consequently, loneliness tends to function self-reinforcingly. As Svendsen states, the pain of social isolation and the longing for overcoming physical and mental distance to somebody beloved simultaneously are necessary part of loneliness (2019, p. 24).

Psychoanalytic concepts

To understand the difference of what is called *positive aloneness* and "the painful, frightening experience that people will do practically everything to avoid it" (Fromm-Reichmann, 1990, p. 306), it is useful to recapitulate relevant psychoanalytic theories.

Mostly, they relate the capacity to cope with being alone to the quality of one's internal objects—the mental representation of relationships with external objects. From this aspect, the experience of aloneness begins with birth; this is an existential human fact. In her paper, "On the Sense of Loneliness", Melanie Klein (1963) disputes that ultimately it is the earliest relation with mother and the always remaining unsatisfied longing for an understanding without words that contributes to the sense of loneliness. The yearning for an unattainable perfect internal state is experienced to some extent by everyone.

The importance of the bond between mother and child, Bowlby elaborated in his attachment theory. The role of mother in the early attachment relationship requires her empathic attunement to and modulation of her baby's emotional states. Normal affect development does not occur, when she is unable to recognise the emotional cues and moderate them. Bowlby described this state as secure attachment, when a child can peacefully be by itself, not having to be afraid of her irregular and unexpected absence. A disruptive breaking of the affectional ties evokes a sense of abandonment and feelings of emptiness and isolation that are associated with loneliness (Bowlby, 1977).

The mother serving as container/contained for the infant's unregulated emotions is captured by Bion (quoted in Taylor, 2012). Her containing function influences the affect development as well as the quality of the nature of the individual's internal object world and the capacity to be alone (Taylor, 2012). Positive experiences with reliable, trustworthy attachment figures form the basis for the development of feelings of safety, continuity, and trust. Only a child with good internalised objects can rely upon them, when in outer reality they are not present. By the same premise creativity presumes a state of inner security and confidence.

In his seminal paper on "The Capacity to be Alone", Winnicott suggests that the capacity to be alone in adult life basically originates in the infant's or small child's experience to be alone in the presence of the mother (Winnicott, 1958). He calls it a paradox since the capacity to be alone needs someone else to be present. Being alone in life can take place when the ego immaturity is naturally balanced by ego support from the mother. It is the internalised good object in the psychic reality which makes the individual confident about the present and future.

Winnicott goes on to describe that the significance of ego relatedness allows impulses from within the id sphere which can be accepted and integrated.

> The infant is able to become unintegrated, to flounder, to be in a state in which there is not orientation, to be able to exist for a time without being either a reactor to an external impingement or an active person with a direction of interest or movement. The stage is set for an id experience. In the course of time there arrives a sensation or an impulse. In this setting the sensation or impulse will feel real and be truly a personal experience … The capacity to be alone is a highly sophisticated phenomenon. It is closely related to emotional maturity. (Winnicott, 1958, p. 418)

Here Winnicott sets parallels to the psychodynamic aspects of the creative process. Psychologically seen, an artist possesses a rather strong ego in order to enter a "stage of id experience". Several psychoanalytic authors, including Freud, have theoretically highlighted the artist's capacity to overcome the censorship of external boundaries to intentionally get in touch with his inner world. Kris talks about the artist's special ability for regression in the service of the ego, denoting that an artist allows himself to get in touch with unconscious primary processes in his inner fantasy life, from where he gets his material to create. The artist's rather strong and intact ego allows him to evolve out of the regressive id state, applying its functions, memories, thinking, and motor abilities to shape his material into form (Kris, 1952). These are inner conditions, originating in early positive experiences with a motherly figure.

Yet another prerequisite for a successful creative process is external: a physical space where the artist is not distracted by outer stimuli, where she or he feels safe and does not need to worry about demands from his environment. Usually this is his studio, workspace, or another kind of refuge.

Sometimes it may even be only the sheet of paper that becomes a much longed-for place just for oneself. When he was a prisoner in a Nazi concentration camp Frederick Terns secretly made drawings. In a documentary film he later described the preciousness of the experience, that he could feel "moments of total privacy in front of that piece of paper. Then the world of the Nazis or the Gestapo did not really exist, I was the total master of that little paper, I was my own boss" (in R. E. Frye's 1996 film, *The Journey of the Butterfly*). Although his life was ultimately threatened, in the drawing process Terns activated his capacity to relate to inner experiences of feeling safe and alive. It was probably the blank paper which helped him to emotionally carry on, through connecting to earlier emotionally holding environments.

In a similar place, the ghetto of Theresienstadt, children received art lessons from the Bauhaus artist Friedl Dicker-Brandeis. Many of them eventually were murdered, and only a few survived. Some of the children's drawings are preserved. Although some show depictions of the hard and troublesome life in the camp, there are others where the children drew images of their past unthreatened world. It is remarkable that there are many self-portraits, signed by the children repeatedly with variations of their names. Not a single self-portrait carried the camp number, although daily life in the camp was determined by all kinds of numbers and stamps. Makarova assumes that these portraits provided them with a sense of self, of which they had been forcefully deprived (Makarova, 1999). Again, these art works helped to bridge inner and outer worlds, while the outer one only remained bearable on the illusionary place of the drawing. As with Frederick Terns these children must have had access to a source of inner relatedness from which they got their strength to resist the threatening environment.

In his earlier paper on the "Transitional Objects and Transitional Phenomena" Winnicott (1953) had already described the importance of the mother as a good enough external object as a prerequisite for her infant to develop an internal object that is alive and real. The core idea in the paper is that with the infant's growing ability to account for failure of mother's adaptation (e.g. her breast is there when the baby is hungry) and to tolerate the results of frustration, he is able give up the former illusion that what he creates really exists. The result of this disillusion process is that he is now able to use an external transitional object to maintain continuity (in time) of the external emotional environment, helping the process of weaning (Winnicott, 1953). The transitional object relates inner and outer reality, providing an intermediate area of experience. This intermediate area of the infant's experience is retained in the intense experiencing that belongs to the arts and to religion and to imaginative living, and to creative scientific work.

If a mother is unable to adapt to her child's needs, her child cannot use an external object for comforting in her absence. The sense of hopeless void determinates his feelings. He cannot develop the capacity to creatively fill moments of aloneness. This is what Sartre meant when he said: "If you're lonely when you're alone, you're in bad company." Balint described the "horrid empty spaces" when the encounter with oneself is so terrifying (1955, p. 225), as can be seen in the behaviour of people clinging to their objects, intending to avoid frustrating loneliness (Willock, 2012, p. 298).

Consequently, an empty white sheet of paper is not perceived as a place of creative wish fulfilling, as in the above examples, but it can cause feelings of abandonment, un-relatedness, and fear. Some artists express signs of panic or depression when unable to start working. This can be observed even more so with patients in art therapy.

The freedom and joy of curiously entering the inner world of fantasies by leaving a first trace with a pencil on a white paper or a brush stroke on the canvas, seems to be inhibited, and more so, impossible. This missing trust in the positive outcome of the creative endeavour may be traced to early childhood, when the primary relational object was unduly absent and the child was forced to concentrate all his psychic energy to overcome his feelings of abandonment and loneliness. Instead of playfully building an inner treasure of creative experiences lasting into adulthood, the inside world remained empty, and phantasy was replaced by fear. The result is a *horror vacui*—a place of a deep lonely void (Dannecker, 1999). The cause might not always be a mothering figure; there also could have been insensitive teachers in the course of development, disqualifying the student's attempts for creative endeavours in school with excessive criticism, bad grades, or exposing the student to embarrassing situations in front of the class. The loneliness of a child having lost face in front of peers can be long-lasting, in the worst case causing the child to cease making any artistic effort in life, often hidden in the belief of not being talented.

The psychoanalyst Phyllis Greenacre has treated many artists as well as studied biographies of known artists. She emphasises how the creative person's autonomous gifts and maturational phases create special problems and give a specific cast to his conflicts in his relational environment. The gifted artist has an inborn heightened sensitive perceptiveness of the outer world, an unusual capacity for intensified and precocious awareness of form and rhythm. Therefore, she says,

> The child of potential genius is inevitably a lonely child, no matter how many people surround him. For he is a child who senses his own difference, feels isolated and inferior thereby: or, if he becomes aware of his gift, is still isolated, finding the greater sustenance in fantasy until his ability begins to be realised in some definite expression. I believe that this realisation of ability is often a great relief to extremely talented people, not so much because of the narcissistic gratification of recognition and not because of balance and harmony, but because of the temporary interruption of essential loneliness. (Greenacre, 1958, pp. 531–532)

The creative child reacts to the external world by investing his libidinal attachment to what other children invest in the direction of the object relationship. Greenacre refers to this increased range of outer objects as "collective alternates"—"alternates because they may on occasion substitute for the warmer personal human objects, if for any reason these latter are temporarily unavailable" (Greenacre, 1958, p. 539). Creative people thus are protected from the expectable pathogenic effects of childhood traumata because they are already engaged at the times of these vicissitudes in what Greenacre called a "love affair with the world". Gedo comments and continues:

> The implication of this notion is that such children are less vulnerable to inadequate nurture than we might predict because of the result of early involvement with some aspect of the external world that they experience with admiration or even awe, they are already relatively independent of their parents. (Gedo, 1996)

He attributes the protective function of creativity to the enormous boost in self-esteem provided by any sense of unusual competence. At this point he disagrees with Greenacre, in that the love affair is not with some aspect of the external world but with the child's own talents; the creative potential protects the individual from injuries to self-esteem (Gedo, 1996).

We may conclude: the artistic process itself is a space of lessening feelings of alienation and isolation; making a painting or sculpture is to bring a vis-à-vis object into being (Dannecker, 2002). The rhythmic exchange of applying the material and making the form is a reciprocal process, in which artists often perceive their work as a counterpart on which they can exert influence and which they can shape. Hence, the art process entails a kind of feedback system, where artist and art work continuously transform each other (Dannecker, 2021).

The artist communicates in two directions—with himself and with the potential audience. His art bridges the gap of his own and the external world, a place where the inevitable human experience of existential separateness can be alleviated. It is the intermediate area of experiencing, as Winnicott stated, "a resting-place for the individual engaged in the perpetual human task of keeping inner and outer reality separate yet inter-related" (Winnicott, 1971, p. 3).

Lonely at home

In the next part I will investigate the actual physical ambiance where loneliness most often occurs. As we have already noted, in the case of the artist it often is the studio or atelier. The scientist goes into his laboratory or office, the hermit retreats into a distant dwelling—all are physical settings conducive to solitude, facilitating creativity, inventions, and self-examination.

Voluntariness seems to be the single most important factor distinguishing between positive and negative aloneness. Long and Averill (2003) refer to studies which found that many people seeking positive solitude prefer the natural environment outdoors, whereas generally most episodes of loneliness occur at home. It is at home where loneliness literarily most often takes place, comprising 75 per cent of the time of any experience of loneliness. Solitude in the wilderness usually is associated with freedom, while spending time alone at home often is perceived as resulting from no choice and being beyond the individual's control (Long & Averill, 2003).

In this sense, *home* is likely to evoke a range of feelings from positive to negative dimensions. Home can be felt as the place of family and intimate social life, of safety and trust, as well as social disconnectedness, alienation, confinement, and isolation, ultimately experienced as loneliness.

Most recently, *home* has received unexpected attention: during the pandemic of the COVID-19 crisis people had been under government regulation to stay at home, involuntarily disconnecting from the physical world outside. The repeated implementation of a lockdown caused everything from that moment on happening at home: home office, home schooling, home shopping. Despite the internet and social media providing digital access to the world at most people's disposal, the subjective experiences of social isolation, disconnectedness, and depression undoubtedly induced and magnified loneliness as a parallel pandemic. From one day to the next, the meaning of being at *home* had changed for many people.

The following brief study of the range of what *home* means may reveal insights about the impact of the place where we spend a large part of our lifetime. It will examine the symbolic aspects of the house epitomised in psychological evaluations, in the arts, mainly the visual arts, referencing three known artists and depictions of houses from patients in art therapy. It aims to understand the significance of the house as a symbolic representation of profound universal human experiences regarding the self and the relationship with others.

It is the house with doors, walls, roof, basement, windows, and all kinds of additional attributes—the features of the physical architecture and its function as a dwelling place which are causing countless associations and fantasies, feelings, and forms of behaviour. The house is an object so universal and familiar that it is used as a device in a personality test, the House-Tree-Person (HTP) projective drawing technique, developed in 1958 by Emanuel Hammer, published in the book *The Clinical Application of Projective Drawings*. The task to draw a house, a partial segment of the complete test, is easily accepted because everybody has a certain affinity for or identification with it. It qualifies as a projective technique where the stimulus is either so unstructured or so ambiguous that its meaning for the subject must come, in part, from within himself. The depiction of a house is symbolically fertile in terms of unconscious significance (Hammer, 1958, p. 169). The test asks for an achromatic (pencil) and a chromatic (crayon) house to be drawn on a 7 × 8½ inch sheet of paper, assuming that the chromatic house cuts through defences and taps into deeper levels of personality (Hammer, 1958).

A thirty-four-year-old woman was amazed about the expression of the houses she had drawn in the HTP-test and began to talk about her own loneliness.

The pencil house (Figure 1) is presented as a frontal façade, three empty unprotected windows and five black ones blocking the view from the inside as well as preventing the look inside, simultaneously entrapping and exposing, a half-visible figure in the doorway, undecided if he or she is leaving or hiding. In the attic, there is another black window, actually meant to allow occupiers to look far away, but here it is completely closed down. The pathway is wide, an invitation for visitors to come by. The pencil ductus of the house's environment appears to be fiercely and angrily putting pressure on the building. There are ambivalences regarding contact wishes in many parts. The colour crayon drawing (Figure 2) conveys the impression

Figure 1. Mrs A, *House*, Pencil, 21 × 29.7 cm © K. Dannecker

Figure 2. Mrs A, *House*, Crayon, 21 × 29.7 cm © K. Dannecker

of a sad black house, lonely as it stands on a faraway hill, shrunk in its size, but longing to be approached: a wide bright yellow path leading straight to the illuminated door. Once the visitor has passed three dark rooms inside, where the windows are shut, she or he will get to illuminated rooms of the house. There seems hope for overcoming the state of be alone, also seen in the more relaxed ductus of the blue and green lines of the background.

As a dwelling place the house has been found to arouse associations concerning home life, family and spousal relationships, and the domestic situation in general. Symbolically, its basic form carries the character of a human body; essential features function like physical bodily parts, captured by sayings like "eyes are windows to the soul", "there is something wrong upstairs", a reference to the roof as the location of fantasy life and thinking, "the skeletons in the closet" for repressed areas of consciousness. The house's vertical structure is likely to bring to mind the psychic apparatus of an upper part as the superego, with the usually dark basement of the id and in the middle of the ego. Details of a house, like window shutters, doors, stairways, fences reflect the drawer's issues around social connectedness and boundaries. One detail most frequently symbolically addressed during the pandemic is the *lock*; when it is *down* on the door, it is beyond the control of moving freely in or out of the house. The forced isolation is pre-programmed in the term.

Further aspects must be taken into consideration regarding the drawer's personality: the line quality entails messages about the strength of the parts—the self, faintly sketched walls; a missing bottom line may raise apprehensions about a psychic breakdown.

> Whoever has no house now, will never have one.
> Whoever is alone will stay alone …
>
> —Rilke, *Autumn Day* (1920)

Rilke's words encompass the house as a primary source for relatedness. In his musing *On the Longing for Home*, Seiden (2012) suggests that the ever-present yearning for home is essential to the human condition and an inevitable aspect of loneliness. Development and home are closely intertwined: from the beginning we must live with the consequence of growing up and eventually having to leave home. Seiden's narratives relate to literature, history, clinical work with patients. Home, he says, is a concept, not a place. It is a state of mind, where self-definition starts and where one first learns to separate. It remains in the mind as the place where reunion, if it ever were to occur, would happen (Seiden, 2012). In growing up, every child gets to know the compelling power of home and its threatened loss. Seiden reports of Bowlby, the great theorist of attachment and loss, that his interests began at the age of seven when sent to a boarding school—a traumatic life-shaping experience of mourning.

The longing for home contrasts with the "twinned opposite", the separation motive, referring to Freud's notion of *the uncanny*, in German *das Unheimliche*, the un-homely, frightening aspects of family life, signalled in repressions of unconscious motives affecting feelings towards familiar "objects". The longing for home, to a painful extent, is literally homesickness and can turn into depression. Psychoanalysts assume that it is a focus on a lost object, mothers in particular, perhaps even mother's breast (Seiden, 2012). The house as a symbol for the female, especially mother's body, is easy to convey; ideally it functions as a place for emotional security, a prenatal container. This is even found in the image of a church, often described as Mother Church (Mater Ecclesia), meaning that she will give birth to many children of God and nurture their beliefs (Hirsch, 2011).

All these aspects of maternal and parental solitude lead to the basic ambivalent conflict between autonomy and dependency, aimed at having to leave the house eventually in adulthood. The developmental need for separation and individuation needs rapprochement. According to Seiden, the only solution is to find a new home. He notes that nostalgia (originally meaning the pain of longing for home from Ancient Greek *algos*, pain, and *nostos*, the voyage home) is different from homesickness, an affective-cognitive experience, involving memories in one's past with an affective coloration as "bittersweet". Nostalgia is a substitute for mourning, as an attempted mastery through idealisation (Seiden, 2012, p. 273). In this spirit, numerous songs, folk tales, poems, and sayings are about home, often intertwined with themes of love of a significant other, the loss of each and both, and longing for return.

Andrew Wyeth

A moving visual example about longing for belonging is *Christina's World*, a painting by Andrew Wyeth (Figure 3). When the American artist showed it for the first time in 1948, it received little public reception and critics commented on it as "kitschy nostalgia" (!) at the period of American abstract expressionism. However, in the ensuing decades it has become one of the most iconic and admired works of the Museum of Modern Art in New York City. It depicts a scene situated in Cushing, Maine, in which a woman is crawling across a dry barren field, looking longingly up towards a far-off farmhouse. She appears to be about thirty years old, wearing a pink dress. Her limbs are slim. Only on a closer inspection does one detect that they are crippled. Her face is invisible, we only see her back. This makes the viewer automatically follow the direction of her gaze towards the old sinister-looking timber house. The effects of the meticulous brushstrokes of the black hair and the grass on the vast ground, the grey building achieved through the tempera paint and the use of perspective, made Wyeth praised as the master of magic realism with haunting effects on the viewers.

Wyeth was inspired by the sight of his befriended neighbour Christina Olsen, who is looking from that distance at her parents' old farmhouse. At the time when Wyeth made the painting, she was in her mid-fifties, having suffered from a degenerative muscular disorder, supposedly polio, since the age of three. Her whole life, Christina refused to use a wheelchair. As is known, in this painting Wyeth did not intend it to be a portrait of her as a person. His model was his own wife Betsy; from Christina he borrowed the hair with the braid and the depiction of the pitiful limbs. This is most irritating, as the writer Sulzer admits, even more than the haunting house in the elevated background. The irritation is augmented through the non-existent

Figure 3. Andrew Wyeth, *Christina's World*, 1948. Egg tempera on gessoed panel. 32 1/4 in × 47 3/4 in (81.9 cm × 121.3 cm), Museum of Modern Art, New York. © VG Bildkunst Bonn

face, indicating that the subject disappears behind the rickety creature and the viewer never will know if the longing, forward crawling over the unsurmountable distance brought her to her destination (Sulzer, 2011). Wyeth surrendered the act of looking to the windows of the house, as "they are the eyes, indeed part of the soul itself. For me each window is another part of Christina's life" (quoted in Sulzer, 2011, p. 3). Asked about the meaning of the painting for himself, the artist responded that he intended to convey his own emotional world: "I felt the loneliness of that figure—perhaps the same loneliness as I felt myself as a kid" (quoted in Potter, 2006, p. 878). His own affinity with suffering from loneliness is traced to his childhood when he had been a weak and ill child, taken out of school by his parents, tutoring him at home, being alienated from his friends: "I played alone and wandered a great deal over the hills, painting watercolors that literally exploded" (quoted in Potter, 2006, p. 879). Wyeth's art became his sublime substitute for social connectedness; with *Christina's World* he rendered his own and her yearning for a house promising a sense of belonging, connectedness, containment, and alleviation of pain. Looking at his work most probably leaves nobody untouched—it's almost impossible to diverge from its universal messages of the threat of loss of the significant other and the longing for return.

Patients longing for home

Longing for an unattainable object has an extensive history in Western culture, as already notable in Ancient Greek and Roman writings: *paraklousthyros* means literally "laments before closed doors". Psychoanalysts assume it has to do with the infantile wish to possess the mother as a sexual object, a paradise lost, and a "prelude to loneliness" (Goldin, 2013, p. 273). Closed doors or other insurmountable obstacles inhibiting access to a beloved person, children get to know early in fairy tales such as *Rapunzel* and *Sleeping Beauty*. In each, the main character finds his fortune through overcoming bricked towers, overgrown castles—stories which help the child to deal symbolically with the separation-individuation function of a house. Interestingly, it is the low viewpoint applied to express longing in the pictorial representations: Rapunzel on the highest point of the tower hanging out her golden hair, a castle far away for Sleeping Beauty, or an old shack on top of the hill for Christina Olson. To overcome longing, one must make a huge, sometimes inconceivable effort like Christina in her world.

A drawing from a patient in art therapy shows similar features with a likewise sad story. The thirty-two-year-old man suffered from schizophrenia. He lived alone in a big city. Artistically talented, he wanted to become a musical performer, but had failed to pursue a career because

Figure 4. Mr S, *Island*, Watercolour, Pencil, 24 × 32 cm © K. Dannecker

of his inhibitions and frequent depressive states, causing him to be in and out of psychiatric wards. He sometimes talked about the tiny island in the North Sea where he came from, saying that he was homesick and that he wanted to see his mother there. Although she had announced her visit to him in the hospital several times, she never came. In the watercolour (Figure 4) he wanted to show his island, the place where he grew up. We see two hills, each with a building. On the top of the left one there is a church, not very stable, almost sliding down; there is a path leading to a street. On the other hill stands a house, it looks like it is deteriorating, walls and roof are not connected; the front has an anthropomorphic expression, the eye as one window peering longingly to the church building. There is no path which connects the two—the unsurmountable separation and yearning are utterly visible. Again, as in the drawing of the houses of the HTP and in *Christina's World*, the hills and a long pathway emphasise the distance as well as the wish for overcoming it. The church, most probably an unconscious, symbolic representation of mother, is unstable itself, unable to provide connectedness to the neighbouring, sad, fragile, and lonely house.

Anthropomorphic-looking houses are the result of projecting human features to non-living objects—seemingly a useful tactic to overcome loneliness (Cacioppo & Patrick, 2011, p. 326).

Figure 5. Ms B, *House*, Watercolour, Charcoal, 29.7 × 42 cm © K. Dannecker

Schizophrenic patients often create such face-houses. They can be understood as desperate attempts to defeat the horror of feeling disconnected, often combined with persecutory fantasies with staring-looking windows, doors turning into a shouting mouth, as we see in the following example.

The image of a young woman with a psychotic breakdown portrays, on a fluid watercolour background, a charcoal house with an infantile and fearful expression (Figure 5). There is no holding and protecting boundary line between the bottom and the environment. Inside the house, underneath the roof, there seems to be a lot of accumulated heat—smoke rises from the chimney. The nearby trees seem like people approaching overwhelmingly, a strange creature watching from above. The house seems in a desperate state of having to defend itself against evil outer influences—reflecting the patient's hypervigilance for social threat. However, a path and an accentuated letterbox are perhaps waiting for good connecting news. The use of a frame line suggests an attempt to hold things together as well as directing the viewer's gaze to the story of the image. It is a picture of the patient's fragmented floundering, suffering self in psychosis.

Edward Hopper

The most prominent painter of American scenes, who made solitude his life's work, was Edward Hopper (1882–1967). His art is often described as evoking feelings of isolation and loneliness. All his life he was an introverted man, devoted principally to his art (Schmied, 1995, p. 15), concentrating on depicting the alienation in the world. Quite up to date, during the COVID-19 pandemic, Hopper's paintings are referred to as representations of the crisis of loneliness with the catastrophic loss of direct human contact: "We are all Edward Hopper paintings now," an unknown sender of a WhatsApp message confessed (Jones, 2020).

Hopper was interested in capturing the reality of the "American Scene" of his time, rural America as well as city life, including street scenes, a movie theatre, interiors of buildings. The figures Hopper depicted are often alone in a place, appearing anonymous, self-contained, and lonely. The viewer looks into a private scene, in a hotel room, a café, an office, a train carriage— and becomes a voyeur of loneliness and alienation. Even when there are several figures in a painting, they seem to be disconnected and non-communicating.

Characteristically, all of Hopper's scenes are immersed in strong contrasts in the use of colours, intending to emphasise the structure of reality as he saw it. He treated the light in his paintings impinging harshly on objects, highlighting portions of them, and plunging others into deep shadow. Schmied described the light in Hopper's paintings as gliding off the objects in his paintings as if it could not take hold of them. These sharply discriminating formal elements of light and shadow and the detached views contribute to the creation of feelings of isolation and stillness in his work (1995, p. 36).

While Hopper generally was not prone to talking about his own work, he provided background information about one of his most famous paintings—*Nighthawks*, a night scene in a bar: "It was suggested by a restaurant on Greenwich Avenue where two streets meet. I simplified the scene a great deal and made the restaurant bigger. Unconsciously I was painting

Figure 6. Edward Hopper, *People in the Sun*, 1960, Oil on Canvas, 40 3/8 × 60 3/8 in (102.6 × 153.4 cm), National Museum of American Art, Smithsonian Institution, Washington DC. © VG Bildkunst Bonn

the loneliness of a large city" (quoted in Schmied, 1995, p. 56). The tension of visibility in a city of glass and the proliferating disconnection make *Nighthawks* an eerie, powerful, and often reproduced painting. Laing (2017) commented on Hopper's urban scenes as replicating the central experiences of being lonely in a city: the way of feeling separation, of being walled off or penned in, combined with a sense of unbearable exposure. But Hopper also was aware that he was depicting his own experiences: "The man's the work. Something does not come out of nothing" (quoted in Kuh, 1960, p. 131).

He knew that spaces could unleash feelings—titling one of his earliest etchings *The Lonely House*. Noteworthy here is his attribution of human features to an object—a house which cannot have feelings itself, but, as we have seen, it is a receptive object for the projection of human feelings. The etching depicts the three lowest floors of a house, standing isolated in a landscape. Two tiny-appearing children on the gable end play on the barren wall. The lonely house has the quality of a mothering role not well fulfilled—the children seem lost at the bland huge flat wall.

People in the Sun is a remarkable painting because it suggests a way to overcome experiences of alienation (Figure 6). Five people, hotel guests, are sitting parallel to each other on folding chairs, their shadow on a sunlit patio sharply sketched on the floor. Four of them are staring into the landscape—a wheatfield, confined on one side by a grey path, on the other by a distant, dark, even mountain range, reflecting stiffness and limitation. The four figures' facial expressions appear shallow, unfocused—not perceiving impulses from either outside or inside. They seem to be freezing—all are dressed up with warm elegant clothes. The bright patio looks like a stage, exhibiting the empty silence and solidification of the people in the front row. The partially obscured house emphasises the closedness of the space.

But there is one person making a difference: a man is sitting behind them, relaxed in his body posture, he is reading a book. His concentration is absorbed by what he reads, he appears self-forgotten. In contrast to the other guests, he is participating in another world, sharing with the author what he had offered to the reader.

In his book *The Invention of Solitude* (1982), the author Paul Auster has beautifully portrayed what exists between writer and reader:

> In reading, an isolated individual becomes absorbed in something beyond his own preoccupations and communes with another mind ... It is possible to be alone and not alone at the same time. Reading literature creates a kind of companionship that preserves the solitariness of reading and writing. (Quoted in Knafo, 2013, p. 25)

In this painting, Hopper has exemplified that immersing in art—here it is reading the work of a writer—is a path out of the painful emotional distance and solitude of the four people in the sun.

Rachel Whiteread

Materialising nothingness and filling voids encompass the main concern of the contemporary British sculpture artist Rachel Whiteread (born in 1968). Rather than producing a mould to make a replica from a regular, pre-existing item by pouring a liquid such as plaster, concrete, fibreglass, or resin, she creates a cast from the negative space around the object. For these reversal processes she uses domestic human artefacts with architectural references like entire large-scale buildings, staircases, windows, doors, closets, the space underneath chairs, beneath a table, a bed, and other everyday small objects such as hot water bottles. It is the unseen space that remains after the outer shell is peeled away, causing a process of visual estrangement translating negative space into solid form. In recording surfaces absence becomes presence. As Wong (2016) put it: the result is an enquiry about the value or meaning of everyday things through recontextualised form. Whiteread refers to autobiographical moments in her work. About one of her first sculptures, *Closet* (1988), whose interior plaster volume is covered with black felt, she says that it was her comforting place in childhood where she liked to hide. Inside this wardrobe she was in complete solitude. In her interviews she leaves open whether her retreat into the completely black space was an escape from unpleasant occurrences outside or because of the pleasure of complete reduction of stimuli in solitude.

She generally aims at "embalming lives, embalming the air, mummifying the space inside the room" (Cork, 2017). The intended effect is comparable to the plaster casts made of those who died at Pompeii. Her casts often are associated with death masks or a tomb, like *Ghost*, a full-scale reversed fireplace of a Victorian terraced house, as Whiteread said "a mausoleum for a certain social class, a certain way of life" (quoted in Farago, 2018). The story of *Walden* by Henry David Thoreau, who chose to live two years in a hermitage in the woods to write his book *Civil Disobedience*, inspired her to a reverse cast of a lonely and detached cabin on Governor's Island, an isolated place across from Lower Manhattan.

Recently she made a series of windows, focusing on new textures, light, and reflection, reporting that since she was a child she liked looking into windows being nosy and out of curiosity about the reflections from light inside (Whiteread, 2020). The central theme for Whiteread is, as she repeatedly says in interviews, "to fossilise and record surfaces". From a psychodynamic aspect, it might be the symbolic expression of wanting to fill spaces, which are felt empty and meaningless, with durable material—sculptural material which is creating a tangible presence. Removing the original surface of an object presumably is an act full of tension and hope that the inside negative cast is weightier, more reliable, and more meaningful, carrying messages otherwise unseen.

Figure 7. Rachel Whiteread, *House*, at Grove Road, London E3, 1993. © Rachel Whiteread. Photo by Sue Omerod. Courtesy of the artist and Gagosian

Whiteread's most iconic early work is *House* (1993), for which she won the renowned Turner Prize. The artist knew it would be only temporary, since the government had plans to tear it down as the last of a group of dilapidated dwellings in East London. The owner had been evicted, having lost a years-long fight to keep his home. The artist cast the walls inside with concrete and then removed the exterior of the house, leaving not the façade but a memorial of the intimate and private interior visible for every passer-by (Figure 7).

In this work, all elemental functions of a house are suspended: the massive volume of the sculpture contains a door with no function, the windows are impenetrable, there is no escape and no access. Ultimately the house has absolutely no space for anybody. The passer-by's unavoidable gaze at the private interior induces uneasy impressions of involuntary voyeurism. One is confronted with hurtful feelings of loneliness and memories of loss.

Whiteread applied the same principles in much of her later work, especially in her memorial of the victims of the Holocaust (2000) at the Judenplatz in Vienna. Scaled like the bourgeois apartments of the houses around, she constructed a library where the walls of full bookshelves are cast as negative and face outward, memorialising the former readers and their wordless faith. This sculpture is one of the most powerful three-dimensional works of art entailing the loss of humanness leaving behind painful emptiness.

Aloneness, solitude, detachment, and memories of losses are core issues in the art of the three discussed artists—Wyeth, Hopper, and Whiteread. All of them focused on spaces in- and outside houses; their interest was sparked by these places because symbolically they conveyed their own feelings. Even so, at different times their art works attained enormous success—the audiences appreciating their capacity to represent the universal experience of loneliness.

From a psychodynamic point of view, we may think that, according to Greenacre (1958), these artists experienced not the narcissistic gratification of recognition, but the temporary interruption of essential loneliness. We may assume that their creative potential made them less vulnerable and protected them from injuries to self-esteem (Gedo, 1996).

The role of the audience is essential for any artistic working person. It effectuates communication and reactions—stepping out of the solitary artistic retreat. The situation parallels aspects of the early developmental stage, where understanding, attunement, mirroring in the mother–child dyad prepare the ground for the capacity to be positively alone.

Conclusion

The last place of loneliness we visit in this chapter is a painting (Figure 8) created in art therapy by Mrs M, a thirty-eight-year-old patient, who suffered from panic attacks and hypochondriacal disorders. She participated for many hours in art therapy, using material from the hospital's supplies, usually not talking much about her artwork. In this session, she described the scene she had created as the stairway to the basement of her family's house, where she had spent her childhood summers. Mrs M made it with strips of adhesive sticking plaster, carefully painting them with watercolour, cutting and applying it as collage material. The only additional

Figure 8. Mrs M, *Stairway to Basement*, Watercolour, adhesive sticking plaster (21 × 29.5 cm)

comment she made was about the light of yellow on the steps, remarking that physically it is not correct because on the bottom steps it is actually wider than it should be, but that her intention was to direct the viewer's eye to the bottom floor.

A fellow patient replied that the carpet on the floor looked like shards of broken glass. Upon this remark, Mrs M silently nodded. Without verbal interpretation, I and the group of fellow patients sensed a painful story she just had shared with us in her art. Whatever had happened in that basement of her childhood house was destructive, leaving the child abandoned and extremely lonely. Knowing that the art therapy group would be an audience open for what in psychotherapy is called "joint attention", she was able to communicate her frightening experience, based on her feelings of now being in a safe and holding environment (Dannecker, 2021).

Loneliness, isolation, and solitude happen in many places, at various times, and in different intensities in life. The external form, symptom, or symbol in which these feeling states assume a form, relates to inner and outer experiences—shaped by the quality of relationships from the beginning. As I wanted to demonstrate, art has the capacity to transform loneliness from a negative to a positive place.

References

Amsen, E. (2020, March 30). Can art therapy combat depression during self-isolation and social distancing? *Forbes*. https://forbes.com/sites/evaamsen/2020/03/30/can-art-therapy-combat-depression-during-self-isolation-and-social-distancing/?sh=50f1db6034eb (last accessed May 5, 2021).

Antoniades, K. (2020, July 16). Loneliness and the pandemic. We need to talk about loneliness amid this pandemic. *Health*. https://self.com/story/coronavirus-emotional-helpline-what-its-like (last accessed January 2, 2021).

Balint, M. (1955). Friendly expanses—horrid empty spaces. *The International Journal of Psychoanalysis*, *36*: 225–241.

Barasch, M. (2000). The hermit in the desert. In: A. Assmann & J. Assmann (Eds.), *Einsamkeit* (pp. 153–172). Munich, Germany: Wilhelm Fink.

Bowlby, J. (1977). The making and breaking of affectional bonds. I. Aetiology and psychopathology in the light of attachment theory. *British Journal of Psychiatry*, *130*: 201–210.

Cacioppo, J. T., & Patrick, W. (2011). *Einsamkeit. Woher sie kommt, was sie bewirkt, wie man ihr entrinnt*. Heidelberg, Germany: Spektrum akademischer Verlag.

Castaway (2000). Directed by Robert Zemeckis. Twentieth Century Fox.

Cork, R. (2017, September 13). "Rachel Whiteread" review: poetic sculptor of emptiness. Absence becomes presence in her poignant casts. *Wall Street Journal*.

Dannecker, K. (1999). Horror in der Kunst—Horror Vacui? Angst in der Kunst von Kindern und Jugendlichen. In: R. Hampe, D. Ritschl, & G. Waser (Eds.), *Kunst, Gestaltung und Therapie mit Kindern und Jugendlichen* (pp. 206–222). Universität Bremen: Universität Bremen.

Dannecker, K. (2002). Die Fähigkeit zum Gegenüber. *Kunst & Therapie, Zeitschrift für künstlerische Therapien*, *1*: 27–30.

Dannecker, K. (2021). *Psyche und Ästhetik* (4th edn.). Berlin: Medizinisch Wissenschaftliche Verlagsgesellschaft.

DiTommaso, E., & Spinner, E. (1997). Social and emotional loneliness: a reexamination of Wiess' typology of loneliness. *Personality and Individual Differences*, *22* (3): 417–427.

Farago, J. (2018, October 4). Ghosts of the past, embalmed in plaster. *The New York Times*.

Frie, R. (2012). The lived experience of loneliness. In: B. Willock, L. C. Bohm, & R. C. Curtis (Eds.), *Loneliness and Longing: Conscious and Unconscious Aspects* (pp. 29–37). London: Routledge.

Fromm-Reichmann, F. (1990). Loneliness. *Contemporary Psychoanalysis*, *26*: 305–329.

Gedo, J. (1996). *The Artist and the Emotional World*. New York: Columbia University Press.

Goldin, D. (2013). Review of "Loneliness and Longing: Conscious and Unconscious Aspects," edited by Brent Willock, Lori C. Bohm, and Rebecca Coleman Curtis. *International Journal of Psychoanalytic Self Psychology*, *8*: 231–242.

Gov.UK (2020, May 22). Government launches plan to tackle loneliness during coronavirus lockdown. https://gov.uk/government/news/government-launches-plan-to-tackle-loneliness-during-coronavirus-lockdown.

Greenacre, P. (1958). The family romance of the artist. In: *Emotional Growth: Psychoanalytic Studies of the Gifted and a Great Variety of Other Individuals, Vol II* (pp. 505–532). New York: International Universities Press, 1971.

Hammer, E. F. (1958). *The Clinical Application of Projective Drawings*. Springfield, IL: Charles Thomas, 1980.

Hawkley, L. C., & Cacioppo, J. T. (2010). Loneliness matters: a theoretical and empirical review of consequences and mechanisms. *Annals of Behavioral Medicine, 40*: 218–227.

Hirsch, M. (2011). *Das Haus. Symbol für Leben und Tod, Freiheit und Abhängigkeit*. Giessen, Germany: Psychosozial Verlag.

Howe, N. (2019, May 3). Millenials and the loneliness epidemic. *Forbes*. https://forbes.com/sites/neil-howe/2019/05/03/millennials-and-the-loneliness-epidemic/ (last accessed April 4, 2021).

Jones, J. (2020, March 27). "We are all Edward Hopper paintings now": is he the artist of the coronavirus age? *The Guardian*. https://theguardian.com/artanddesign/2020/mar/27/we-are-all-edward-hopper-paintings-now-artist-coronavirus-age (last accessed March 3, 2021).

Kaurismäki, A. (2011, August 21). Künstler sind einsame Menschen. *Rheinische Post Online*. https://rp-online.de/panorama/leute/kuenstler-sind-einsame-menschen_aid-13201867 (last accessed June 1, 2021).

Klein, M. (1963). On the sense of loneliness. In: *Envy and Gratitude and Other Works 1946–1963* (pp. 299–313). London: Hogarth.

Knafo, D. (2013). Artists' solitude and the creative process. In: A. Kramer Richards, L. Spira, & A. A. Lynch (Eds.), *Encounters with Loneliness: Only the Lonely* (pp. 15–36). New York: International Psychoanalytic Books.

Kris, E. (1952). *Psychoanalytic Explorations in Art*. New York: International Universities Press.

Kuh, K. (1960). *The Artist's Voice: Talks with Seventeen Artists*. New York: Harper & Row.

Laing, O. (2017). *The Lonely City: Adventures in the Art of Being Alone*. Edinburgh, UK: Canongate.

Larson, R. W. (1990). The solitary side of life: an examination of the time people spend alone from childhood to old age. *Developmental Review, 10*: 155–183.

Long, C. R., & Averill, J. R. (2003). Solitude: an exploration of benefits of being alone. *Journal for the Theory of Social Behaviour, 33*(1): 21–44.

Macho, T. (2000). Mit sich allein. Einsamkeit als Kulturtechnik. In: A. Assmannn & J. Assmann (Eds.), *Einsamkeit* (pp. 27–44). Munich, Germany: Wilhelm Fink.

Makarova, E. (1999). *Friedl Dicker-Brandeis—Ein Leben für die Kunst und Lehre*. Vienna: Brandstätter.

Mann, F., Bone, J. K., Brynmor, L.-E., Frerichs, J., Ruimin, P., Wang, M. J., & Johnson, S. (2017). A life less lonely: the state of the art in interventions to reduce loneliness in people with mental health problems. *Social Psychiatry and Psychiatric Epidemiology, 52*: 627–638. doi: 10.1007/s00127-017-1392-y.

Potter, P. (2006). On the threshold of illness and emotional isolation. *Emerging Infectious Diseases, 12*(5): 878–879. doi: 10.3201/eid1205.AC1205.

Rilke, R. M. (1903/2018). *Letters to a Young Poet*. Berlin: Insel No. 1450.

Rilke, R. M. (1920). *Autumn Day*. In: R. M. Rilke, *The Book of Images*. New York: North Point Press.

Schmied, W. (1995). *Edward Hopper: Portraits of America*. Munich, Germany: Prestel.

Seiden, H. M. (2012). On the longing for home. In: B. Willock, L. C. Bohm, & R. C. Curtis (Eds.), *Loneliness and Longing: Conscious and Unconscious Aspects* (pp. 267–279). London: Routledge.

Spitzer, M. (2019). *Einsamkeit. Die unerkannte Krankheit*. Munich, Germany: Droemer.

Storr, A. (1988). *Solitude*. Glasgow, UK: Flamingo Fontana Paperbacks.

Sulzer, A. C. (2011, December 12). Das Einzige, was zählt. *Neue Züricher Zeitung*.

Svendsen L. (2019). *Philosophie der Einsamkeit*. Wiesbaden, Germany: Wiesbaden University Press.

Taxi Driver (1976). Directed by Martin Scorsese. Columbia Pictures.

Taylor, G. J. (2012). Loneliness in the disaffected (alexithymic) patient. In: B. Willock, L. C. Bohm, & R. C. Curtis (Eds.), *Loneliness and Longing: Conscious and Unconscious Aspects* (pp. 148–158). London: Routledge.

The Journey of the Butterfly (1996). Directed by R. E. Frye. Bolthead Communications Group.

Whiteread, R. (2020, October 14). Rachel Whiteread and Ann Gallagher in conversation. *Gagosian Quarterly*. https://gagosian.com/quarterly/2020/10/14/video-in-conversation-rachel-whiteread-and ann-gallagher/ (last accessed April 3, 2021).

Willock, B. (2012). Loneliness, longing, and limiting theoretical frameworks. In: B. Willock, L. C. Bohm, & R. C. Curtis (Eds.), *Loneliness and Longing: Conscious and Unconscious Aaspects* (pp. 293–314). London: Routledge.

Winnicott, D. W. (1953). Transitional objects and transitional phenomena—a study of the first not-me possession. *International Journal of Psycho-Analysis*, *34*: 89–97.

Winnicott, D. W. (1958). The capacity to be alone. *International Journal of Psycho-Analysis*, *39*: 416–420.

Winnicott, D. W. (1971). *Playing and Reality*. London: Routledge.

Wong, T. (2016). Casting Call: Spatial Impressions in the Work of Rachel Whiteread. *The Plan Journal*, *0*(0): 97–110. doi: 10.15274/TPJ-2016-10008.

Wordsworth, W. (1807). "I wandered lonely as a cloud". *British Library Images Online*. https://en.wikipedia.org/wiki/I_Wandered_Lonely_as_a_Cloud (last accessed June 15, 2021).

CHAPTER 8

Seven kinds of loneliness: mental pain, language, and interaction in David Rabe's play *Hurlyburly*

Dominic Angeloch

David Rabe's play *Hurlyburly*, premiered in New York and Chicago in 1984, was brought to Broadway in the same year and was made into a movie with a star cast by Anthony Drazan in 1998 based on a script also written by David Rabe. The multiple award-winning play—set "a little while ago" (Rabe, 1995, p. 165) in the mid-1980s, the film accordingly in the late 1990s—often is characterised as "dark comedy". Actually, however, it is more of a "dark drama"—if this play offers "comedy", then it is the kind that lets your laughter stick in your throat. The seven characters, all of them from the sphere of low- to mid-level Hollywood show business, are constantly on the move, only without knowing where they are going, and talk incessantly, only barely with each other, either as if or actually on drugs. "There is no need to race, but there is little room for pauses" (p. 167), says a stage direction right at the beginning of the play—characteristic not only of the characters' way of talking, but also of their lives, a sequence of failed and ever more failing relationships. Their talk seems like the realisation of the postmodern nightmare of a chain of signifiers without any reference to that which can never be signified, because it must never be signified. Here everyone is talking for their lives, but in the end all they do is talk themselves manically into severe inner and outer trouble.

What this is about never becomes apparent. But it can be felt, at least by the viewer, very clearly: the play negotiates its—existential—themes with an extremely high discursive turnover and yet in secret, hidden away under the polished, shining surfaces.

On the basis of a close reading of the play, the "circles of interaction" (Lorenzer, 1981, pp. 23–47) in which the characters move, their "forms of interaction" (Lorenzer, 1977, pp. 75–101), and the language used to circle around what may be spoken out but must never be felt, this chapter traces the depiction of overwhelming and therefore isolating "mental pain" (Bion, 1963, pp. 60–63), and the result of this "practical solipsism" (Wittgenstein, 1963), for example, the absolute loneliness in the midst of roaring company. Each of the characters is lonely in their own way. In looking at their interactions—by recourse to Wilfred Bion's (1959) description of what happens in "attacks on linking" as well as to the narratological distinction between "told self" and "performative self" and the "positioning" of the characters via their speech (Deppermann, 2015)—both the causes of their loneliness and the way they *produce* it— in themselves and in others—come into view, as well as why it is impossible for each of them to overcome it. The lives of the characters, the society from which they emerge, as well as the play itself, thus become recognisable as networks of intricate interweavings of unbearable mental pain and insurmountable solitude, an alignment of manifold kinds of loneliness that reflect into each other to infinity like mirrors in mirrors.

Hurlyburly: play, film adaptation, and the role of language

First performed in 1984, *Hurlyburly* soon was transferred to Broadway, where it played 343 times, with a top-class cast including Christopher Walken, Sigourney Weaver, and Harvey Keitel. In 2005, the play, directed by Scott Elliott and cast with, among others, Ethan Hawke, was revived off-Broadway and again received critical acclaim (Fisher, 2011, p. 378).

In 1998, the film version, with the same name, was released, directed by Anthony Kazan, with again a stellar cast: Sean Penn and Kevin Spacey give a breathtaking performance in their parts as Eddie and Mickey—each extraordinarily difficult to play for very different reasons; Chazz Palminteri, Robin Wright Penn, Anna Paquin, Meg Ryan, and Garry Shandling are no less brilliant in the smaller roles.

The text of the screenplay, also written by David Rabe, is not significantly different from the text of the stage play: here, too, the fundamental dramatic function lies less in the plot, which in itself is thin to barely existent, than in what is negotiated in the dialogues, which follow one another at breakneck speed. Whereas in other dramas language is a vehicle of action and serves essentially to illustrate plot elements, what happens in *Hurlyburly* happens so directly and almost exclusively in language that one can state: here, language *is* plot. While the film version of, for example, *A Streetcar Named Desire*

> takes great pains to emphasise the film's origins in the theatre, *Hurlyburly*'s basic lack of narrative structure renders such questions of plot irrelevant. It does not matter whether what we see is a play or a film; the text is its own expression. (Raw, 2013, p. 234)

For this reason, I will not pursue the differences between the stage and film versions here.

The dramatis personae and their forms of interaction

The play, divided into three acts, takes place in a house "crowded into one of the canyons between Sunset Boulevard and Mulholland Drive in the Hollywood Hills". It is, as the stage directions specify, "completely surrounded by wild vegetation [...] bleeding into the interior of the house" (Rabe, 1995, pp. 165 f.). This description points to the conditions of life of its inhabitants: only those who have succeeded in the "dream factory" of Hollywood can afford such an estate; but even those who have reached the top are not free of all constraints, here symbolised by the vegetation growing into the house.

Eddie and Mickey, the residents, work as casting agents. Together they run a permanent open house for their friends in the movie business and habitually consume massive amounts of cocaine, uppers and downers, alcohol, and joints.

Mickey tries to keep his life under control and to keep himself distant by means of coolness and cynicism—so distant that one could get the idea nothing was of interest to him: "You're just too laid back for human tolerance sometimes, Mickey. A person wonders if you really care," Eddie tells him (p. 287).

The control Mickey clings to, on the other hand, is slipping further and further from Eddie's grasp. "Last time I saw you, you were a relatively standard alcoholic Yahoo, Eddie," Mickey tells him in the very first scene of the first act. "Now all I can find for breakfast is densely compressed chemicals and you're sniffin' around the living room like a warthog" (p. 182).

Both have failed marriages behind them (p. 190); now they trade women among them like things. This includes Darlene, a fashion photojournalist. Eddie wants a "meaningful relationship" (p. 260) with her, and the beginnings of it are there, but it keeps falling apart—it just doesn't work out, without either of them having any idea why: "DARLENE: I'm just—I mean, I don't—Weird, weird, weird" (p. 220).

As we shall see further on in more detail, it is worth taking this utterance at face value. One tends to perceive it as a conglomerate of interrupted, unconnected, and non-connectable ellipses. In the context of the whole play, however, such an understanding would be at least inaccurate. From a conversation-analytical point of view, the half-sentences that appear here as elliptical-incomplete are actually complete statements, since the "personal" dimension of Darlene's loneliness in fact finds a precise expression in this syntactical structure. The sentence "I'm just …" can only be completed by a pause. Starting with "I mean" cannot catch the connections with a symbolic dimension. These apparently incomplete expressions are the *form* of unconsciously presenting both solitudes.

At the beginning of the play, Darlene has something going on with Mickey, too. Right after Mickey points out to Eddie that his drug use has become problematic, Eddie, without any context, blurts it out:

EDDIE: […] But there are not a lot of dynamite ladies around anywhere you look, Mickey, as we both know, and I am the one who met Darlene first. I am the one who brought her by, and it was obvious right from the get-go that Darlene was a dynamite lady, this was a very special lady.

MICKEY: We hit it off, Eddie, you know. I asked you.

EDDIE: Absolutely. Look, I'm not claiming any reprehensible behavior on anybody's part, but don't ask me not to have my feelings hurt, okay. I mean, we are all sophisticated people, and Darlene and I most certainly had no exclusive commitment of any kind whatsoever to each other, blah-blah-blah.

MICKEY: That's exactly what I'm saying. Rapateta.
EDDIE: There's no confusion here, Mickey, but have a little empathy for crissake.
(Mickey *nods, for "empathy" is certainly something he can afford to give.*) (p. 190)

This dialogue continues for a quite considerable while—six pages in the book, several scene changes in the movie—but its basic structure, the dynamic that fuels it, can already be discerned from this short passage. Eddie wants to express something: here it is his attraction to Darlene and his reproach to Mickey that he, as his friend, has nevertheless gone to bed with her—*perhaps* it is that, for Eddie himself does not know so clearly whether it is that which he wants to express, or something else entirely, and we, the viewers, do not learn it, but can at most guess. And the more Eddie talks, the more he surrenders to the over-intellectualised psychologising "blah-blah-blah" fed to him by his drug-accelerated, continuously firing synapses, the more unclear it becomes what it is actually about.

Mickey answers from the distance of an uninvolved person—which he hardly is, of course, as a friend and roommate of Eddie's—and with his ostentatious coolness, alleged transparency, and rationality he thus contributes his part to the tightening of the dialogue knot: by evading communication through communicative refusal to communicate.

Thus, this interaction, as every other interaction in the play, begins in contradictions and ends in further contradictions—or rather does not come to an end at all. "It is worth noting", we learn in the stage directions at the beginning of the play,

> that in the characters' speeches, phrases such as "watchamacallit", "thingamajig", "blah-blah-blah" and "rapateta" abound. These are phrases used by the characters to keep themselves talking. [...] There is [...] little room for pauses. (pp. 166 f.)

The other four characters in the play also work in the Hollywood film industry milieu.

Phil is trying to eke out a living as a failing character actor. His marriage to Susie, long in crisis, is falling apart. Phil has a criminal past that the play only hints at. Rabe explores this back story, along with the back story of Phil and Susie's relationship, in a post-*Hurlyburly* companion piece set before the events which come about in *Hurlyburly* take place: *Those the River Keeps* (1991; Rabe, 1995, pp. 1–154). In the preface to this play, Rabe describes Phil as:

> someone capable of one of those anomalous and inexplicable outbursts, funded and detonated by the unacknowledged elements of a denied and festering past of which he is no longer consciously aware. (p. ix)

In Phil's own words about himself after, once again, knocking someone down for no reason:

> You wanna tell me how come I have all the necessary realizations that any normal human being might have—only by the time I have them, nothin' but blind luck has saved me from

doin' a lifetime in the can, and they can serve no possible purpose but to torment me with the realization that I am a totally out-of-control prick!? (p. 252)

Highly volatile, Phil poses a constant danger to all around him. *Hurlyburly* opens when Phil arrives to inform Eddie that he happens to have knocked out Susie's tooth in an argument and that she has—once again—broken up with him. In response to Eddie's question as to how this came about, one of those dialogues unfolds which, instead of coming to an end, spins faster and faster on itself:

PHIL: It was just this disgusting cloud like fucking with me and I went crazy.
EDDIE: Right. Whata you mean?
PHIL: You know, this fog, and I was in it and it was talking to me with her face on it. Right in front of me was like this cloud with her face on it, but it wasn't just her, but this cloud saying all these mean things about my ideas and everything about me, so I was like shit and this cloud knew it. That was when it happened.
EDDIE: You whacked her.
PHIL: Yeah. (p. 176)

Eddie is fascinated by Phil and maintains a friendship with him, treating him like a somewhat retarded protégé with a hidden talent: "Underneath all this bullshit, you have a real instinctive thing [...]. It's like this wide-open intuition [...] you could channel it" (p. 265). For the others, though, Phil is kind of a savage pet—dangerous and entertaining at the same time, an absurdity like the entire artificial world of show business in which they have all been moving for so long that they take it for reality. That Phil could also have a somewhat different function for Eddie than he himself realises, Mickey tries to suggest to him in the second act with the following words, carefully moderated by the trick of purporting to reflect not his but Artie's view of Eddie's relationship to Phil:

MICKEY: I think what he was trying to get at is that he, you know, considers your investment in Phil, which is in his mind sort of disproportionate and maybe even— and mind you, this is Artie's thought, not mine—but maybe even fraudulent and secretly self-serving on your part. So you know, blah-blah-blah, rapateta—that this investment is based on the fact that Phil is very safe because no matter how far you manage to fall, Phil will be lower. You end up crawling along the sidewalk, Phil's gonna be on his belly in the gutter looking up in wide-eyed admiration. [...]
EDDIE: This is what Artie thinks? (p. 285)

Artie, "a mix of toughness and arrogance, a cunning desperation" according to the stage directions (p. 196), is an apparently quite successful screenwriter. About ten years older than Mickey

152   FROM THE ABYSS OF LONELINESS TO THE BLISS OF SOLITUDE

and Eddie, he, unlike them, pursues a certain work ethic that makes him the target of cynical comments: "Artie's an obnoxious, anal-obsessive pain in the ass who could make his best friend hire crazed, unhappy people with criminal tendencies to cut off his legs, which we have both personally threatened to do" (p. 171), Eddie says at the beginning, shortly before Artie's arrival (to the failing Phil, which of course somewhat relativises this statement). And to Artie himself: "What I want you to understand, Artie, is the absurdity of this business, and the fact that you're a success in it is a measure of the goddamn absurdity of this business [...] to which we are all desperate to belong as a bunch of dogs" (pp. 256f.).

Artie brings Donna, a sixteen-year-old hitchhiker from the Midwest whom he "found" in the elevator of his hotel, where she was hiding from her boyfriend, who—unclear why—wants to kill her. As a "CARE package," he offers her to Eddie and Mickey's pleasure:

ARTIE: [...] I figured, I don't need her, you know, like you guys need her. You guys are a bunch of desperate guys. You're very desperate guys, right? You can use her. So I figured on my way to the studio, I'd drop her by, you can keep her. Like a CARE package, you know. So you can't say I never gave you nothing. (p. 198)

Bonnie enters the play in the course of the second act. Her marriage has also failed, and she is the single mother of a baby girl. Like Chrissy, the protagonist from Rabe's earlier play *In the Boom Boom Room* (Rabe, 1975), she ekes out a living as a stripper and convinces herself that her performances have artistic merit:

EDDIE: [...] This is a bitch who dances artistically in this club. That's her trip.
MICKEY: With a balloon.
(*Now they break apart.*)
EDDIE: That's what makes it artistic. Without the balloon, what is she?
ARTIE: A naked bitch. (p. 267)

Like Chrissy, she secretly hopes to find love by selling herself for sex, but like Chrissy, this only makes her more exploitable:

EDDIE: You would wanna fuck her, though.
ARTIE: Anybody would.
EDDIE: She's a good bitch, though, you know what I mean? She's got a heart of gold.
MICKEY: What's artistic about her is her blow jobs. [...]
MICKEY: She's critically acclaimed.
EDDIE: (*dialing*) And the best part about her is that she's up for anything. (p. 267)

Eddie invites her to the house in order to set her up with Phil and thus distract him from his misery. He seems to ignore or amuse himself with the danger he is exposing her to. Of course, things go wrong: Phil becomes paranoid and throws her out of her own moving car. Injured, she limps back to Eddie, hoping to receive an apology, a ride home, any sign of affection or remorse from him at all, but Eddie, confronted, defends himself by attacking Bonnie and insinuating that she must have provoked Phil. Her following monologue is among the most significant and saddest in *Hurlyburly* because she seems to be the only one in the play aware of her situation and able to voice her conflicts. Unlike Chrissy from *In the Boom Boom Room*, who is, in the words of a critic, "the butt of a joke which she never understands" (Bigsby, 2000, pp. 272 f.), Bonnie knows exactly where she stands and who put her there:

Oh. Okay. [...] You consider desperation you and your friend's own, private, so-called thingamajig. Who would have thought other? I mean, I can even understand that due to the attitude I know you hold me in, which is of course mainly down. [...] "Wrong", is what I'm saying. See, because I am a form of human being just like any other, get it! [...] I am a person whose entire life with a child to support depends on her tits and this balloon and the capabilities of her physical grace and imaginary inventiveness with which I can appear to express something of interest in the air by my movement and places in the air I put the balloon along with my body, which some other dumb bitch would be unable to imagine or would fall down in the process of attempting to perform in front of crowds of totally incomprehensible and terrifying bunch of audience members. And without my work what am I but an unemployed scrunt on the meat market of the streets? Because this town is nothin' but mean in spite of the palm trees. [...] So that's my point about desperation, and I can give you references, just in case you never thought of it, you know; and I just thought I was over here—some mindless twat over here with blonde hair and blue eyes. (pp. 297 f.)

Her monologue shows Bonnie as what no one would have her to be: compassionate, reflective, aware of herself and her situation. The sole purpose of her monologue is to ask for recognition, or at least to be seen. It is bound to hit a void, because Eddie has long since lost himself in drug-induced paranoia and wounded self-righteousness. "You're just some bitch who thinks it matters that you run around with balloons and your tits out" (p. 299), he says, again referring to her as what she has just proven she clearly is not. With this, he shows that he is unable to establish any other connection with her than that of attack.

Seven characters: seven kinds of loneliness.

Minus phenomena: "Attacks on linking" as sole way of relating

In *Hurlyburly*, relationships are emptied of any meaning, any significance: "interpersonal fuck up[s]", as Eddie puts it to Bonnie (p. 299). They appear as mere shallow, bad entertainment, background noise like the chatter from TV, where even the puny remnant of sense and meaning is talked away in an endless stream of news that are none, until only a vague echo of what used to be life is left: "We're all just background in one another's life. Cardboard cutouts bumping around in this vague, you know, *hurlyburly*, this spin-off of what was once prime time life" (p. 299; emphasis added).

As the dramatis personae in *Hurlyburly* neither feel nor define the relationships in which they navigate—neither on the outside, in the other person, nor in their own interior—they constantly try to ensure themselves of them (i.e. by categorisation: "We are all just background", "You are just some bitch"). This constant reassurance, however, has a shape that is characteristic of almost all the characters; in Eddy, it emerges most clearly. Except for Bonnie and Donna, all the characters in *Hurlyburly* show an aggressive, destructive form of "attacks on linking" (Bion, 1963) in their attempts to take in, to hold, to save, and even to enquire about the current situation in their relationships. In the context of psychoanalytic practice, "attacks on linking" are "destructive attacks [...] which the patient undertakes on anything which he feels serves to connect one object with another" (Bion, 1959, p. 105). Although these attacks are subtle, they pervade everything. Artie complains to Eddie thus:

EDDIE: Artie, first of all, I don't consider your statement that I dump on you accurate, so why should I defend against it?

ARTIE: It's subtle. Hey, you think that means I'm gonna miss it? It's an ongoing, totally pervasive attitude with which you dump on me subtly so that it colors almost every remark, every gesture. And I'm sick of it. (p. 267)

Whoever cannot endure relations—for example, because he cannot endure himself in it—must attack them. At the same time, attacks on linking are always attempts to reassure oneself of the relationship: in the attack, the relationship is tested for its nature or its carrying capacity, or, even more elementarily, for its presence and existence. The reason for this paradoxical form of relating through attacks on linking is that "the splitting processes are extended to the links within the thought processes themselves. [...] Consequently, the formation of symbols [...] becomes difficult" (Bion, 1957, p. 50). As a result, first the consciousness of inner and outer reality breaks down, then the distinction between them.

Sigmund Freud and Melanie Klein understood love and hate as the elements by which inner and outer objects relate to and among each other. Wilfred Bion explicitly adds a third element: Knowledge, which for him is the most important because it is through this element that the mental apparatus is nourished. For Bion (1962a), all internal and external objects are linked through Love, Hate, and Knowledge. Each of these links, indeed even emotions themselves, can be subject to destructive attacks: "In this state of mind emotion is hated; it is felt to be too powerful to be contained by the immature psyche, it is felt to link objects and it gives reality to objects which are not self" (Bion, 1959, p. 108). These attacks on the links then result in minus phenomena (Bion, 1963, pp. 51*f.*): non-emotion—understood as the destruction of an emotion, leaving a kind of black hole into which other emotions and thoughts are sucked—or non-knowledge, understood as the destruction of all curiosity, for example, the wanting to know, the precondition of all learning and the search for truth that nourishes the mental apparatus.

The attacks on links and their subsequent destruction lead to non-emotion, non-knowledge, or misrepresentations, because neither the relationship nor the thinking apparatus are still available as "containers" for affects, emotions, and thoughts. Experiences can no longer be integrated or made, learning can no longer take place, development and growth henceforth are impossible. Emotions "fulfil a similar function for the psyche to that of the senses in relation to objects in space and time" (Bion, 1962b, p. 119). With the destruction of one's emotions, attacks on linking also result in the destruction of the ability to think and thus in mental pain: "The patient appears to have no appreciation of causation and will complain of painful states of mind while persisting in courses of action calculated to produce them" (Bion, 1959, p. 108). Although the aggressor suffers from his or her own work of destruction, indications to this work of destruction are useless because it takes place unconsciously: "the patient [...] has no interest in why he feels as he does" (Bion, 1959, p. 108).

What remains are only the unstable, (seemingly) rational, "crazy" (pseudo-)links that have been stripped of all emotion: "These attacks on the linking function of emotion lead to an overprominence in the psychotic part of the personality of links which appear to be logical, almost mathematical, but never emotionally reasonable. Consequently, the links surviving are perverse, cruel, and sterile" (Bion, 1959, pp. 108 *f.*).

This is what Darlene is talking about when she tells Eddie in the first act: "Your thoughts are a goddamn caravan trekking the desert, and then they finally arrive and they are these senseless beasts of burden" (Rabe, 1995, p. 216).

No longer horizontally connected to each other and no longer connectable, non-"contained" emotional experiences lead not only to our inability to recognise these experiences as such, but also to the attempt to destroy the links between associations: creating islands of knowledge isolated from each other, not connected in thoughts or sentences, and no longer able to be connected. Attacks on linking are an attack on those interconnections between thoughts that make knowledge and cognition possible in the first place. What is left is confusion, paranoia, and distress, "thoughts without a thinker", as Bion describes it (1997, p. 27). "Dark thoughts", Phil calls them in the following dialogue with Eddie, which impressively sums up both the process of attacking links and its consequence:

EDDIE: I don't know what you're talking about.

PHIL: [...] Dark thoughts. Your dark thoughts, Eddie. This is not uncommon for people to have them. ... But please—this, now—dark thoughts and everything included, this is our friendship. Pay attention to it, it's slipping by.

EDDIE: I wanna! YEAH, but I'm gettin' confused here, Phil. I tol' you—I don't feel good.

PHIL: [...] It's chaotic is why you're confused, Eddie. That's why you're confused. Think nothin' of it. I'm confused. [...] The goddamn situation is like this masked fucking robber come to steal the goods, but we don't even know is he, or isn't he. [...] I mean, we got these dark thoughts, I see 'em in you, you don't think you're thinkin' 'em, so we can't even nail that down, how we going to get beyond it? They are the results of your

156   FROM THE ABYSS OF LONELINESS TO THE BLISS OF SOLITUDE

unnoticed inner goings-on or my gigantic paranoia, both of which exist, so the god-damn thing in its entirety is on the basis of what has got to be called a coin toss. [...]

EDDIE: I can figure it. You know I can, that's why you came to me. But I feel like you're drillin' little hunks a cottage cheese into my brain. Next thing, you're sayin', it's a goddamn coin toss—it's not a goddamn coin toss! (pp. 240 f.)

What cannot be brought to language, and why: loneliness and pain as results of loss of the self and the other

A person who attacks links because he or she experiences them as ruinous and destructive is left with an extremely limited and distorted ability to experience emotions. Eddie cannot understand himself because he has destroyed the links between thoughts and emotions; he thus cannot feel the love of Darlene that he so longs for. At the end of the second act, Eddie spells it out to Bonnie, who, unlike the others, really listens to him:

> You ever have that experience where your thoughts are like these totally separate, totally self-sustaining phone booths in this vast uninhabited shopping mall in your head? You ever have that experience? [...] My inner monologue has taken on certain disquieting characteristics, I mean, I don't feel loved. Even if she loves me, I don't feel it. I don't feel loved, and I'm sick of it, you know what I mean? (p. 309)

Darlene is confused about her own inner world—"Weird, weird, weird" (p. 220)—because the links between her emotions are destroyed, so she, in consequence, has lost access to her affects and thoughts. Therefore, both Eddie and Darlene are unable to understand each other because they are unable to understand themselves, and, on that basis, cannot make each other understand. "I evidently have to break through this goddamn cloud in which you are obviously enveloped in which everything is just this blur totally devoid of the most rudimentary sort of distinction" (p. 328), Eddie yells at Darlene at the beginning of the third act, when they talk in turn about a previous pregnancy that Darlene aborted, because the child could have been by two men, both of whom she claims to like equally, and then about a visit to either a Chinese or a French restaurant, both of which she also claims to like equally—to Eddie's despair, since he suspects that Darlene is also unable to distinguish between him and Mickey, which he obviously is unable to communicate to Darlene, who, in turn, is both unable to feel her feelings as well as to understand what the whole thing Eddie is trying to express really is about:

DARLENE: [...] Take my word for it, you're acting a little nuts.

EDDIE: Oh, I'm supposed to trust your judgement of my mental stability? [...] I'm supposed to trust your evaluation of the nuances of my sanity? You can't even tell the difference between a French and a Chinese restaurant!

DARLENE:	I like them both. [...]
EDDIE:	But they're different! One is French, and the other is Chinese. THEY'RE TOTALLY FUCKING DIFFERENT!
DARLENE:	NOT IN MY INNER EMOTIONAL SUBJECTIVE EXPERIENCE OF THEM!
EDDIE:	[...] The tastes, the decors, the waiters, the accents. The fucking accents. The little phrases the waiters say. And they yell at each other in these whole totally different languages, does none of this make an impression on you!?
DARLENE:	It impresses me that I like them both.
EDDIE:	Your total inner emotional subjective experience must be THIS FUCKING EPIC FOG! I mean, what are you on, some sort of dualistic trip and everything is in twos and you just can't tell which is which so you're just pulled taut between them on this goddamn high wire between people who might like to have some kind of definitive reaction from you in order to know! (pp. 328 f.)

And finally, Darlene herself puts it out there: "I can't stand this goddamn semantic insanity anymore, Eddie—I can't be that specific about my feelings—I can't" (p. 333).

When the connections to one's emotions, and thus to one's ability to think, are severed, all that finally remains is a "nameless dread" (Bion, 1962b, p. 116), which threatens to inundate and sweep away the entire personality, despair, emptiness, and loneliness. Archaic fears and diffuse states of tension also must be projected and absorbed by the other person; if not absorbed and pre-digested by the counterpart, a fear of annihilation is reintrojected as nameless dread. The world then appears as a disturbing and frightening place where nothing is in its place because nothing has a place. It appears as empty as the interior emptied of emotions and therefore dominated by minus phenomena:

EDDIE:	Who'm I'm going to complain to? [...] Who's listenin'? And even if they are, what can they do about it?
BONNIE:	I'm listenin'.
EDDIE:	She doesn't love me. [...]
BONNIE:	Who?
EDDIE:	My girlfriend?
BONNIE:	Whata you mean?
EDDIE:	Whata you mean, whata I mean? She doesn't love me. Is that some sort of arcane, totally off-the-wall, otherworldly sentiment that I am some oddity to find distressing so that nobody to whom I mention it has any personal reference by which they can understand me? What is going on here? My girlfriend doesn't love me. (p. 308)

But it is the links formed, based on emotions, which give life its vitality. Attacks on linking are, in the last consequence, attacks on life itself: "It is a short step from hatred of the emotions to hatred of life itself," writes Bion (1959, p. 107).

What began in (inner) disintegration must end in (outer) destruction, in *Hurlyburly*, too. At the end of the play, Phil takes his own life by crashing his car into the abyss on the Mulholland Drive mountainside. He leaves Eddie a mysterious message: "The guy who dies in an accident understands the nature of destiny" (Rabe, 1995, p. 337). Mickey strongly advises Eddie not to involve himself with it: "You're gonna die a this shit, Eddie. Does it not cross your mind?" (p. 346). But Eddie, desperate for an explanation—any explanation—consults the dictionary, calculates the numerical value of words, tries to find meaning where there is none.

To understand others, one must turn to them, and to understand oneself, one must be able to see oneself reflected in others—both of which are impossible for everyone in this play. With the destruction of links, reference, not only to the others but also to oneself, is lost. Language establishes community and connects the speakers with each other; in dialogue, if it succeeds, a common narrative can emerge about what is the case here and now, between the persons or within them, also about what was the case in the past and now may have an effect on the present interaction. Not so in *Hurlyburly*: just the opposite, language here is the means by which the connections inside and outside are destroyed. In a (literally) dramatic way, it becomes apparent here that language is always, as Daniel Stern (1995) puts it, "a double-edged sword":

> It also makes some parts of our experience less shareable with ourselves and with others. It drives a wedge between two simultaneous forms of interpersonal experience: as it is lived and as it is verbally represented. Experience in the domains of emergent, core- and intersubjective relatedness, can be embraced only very partially in the domain of verbal relatedness. And to the extent that events in the domain of verbal relatedness are held to be what has really happened, experiences in these other domains suffer an alienation. (They can become the nether domains of experience.) Language, then, causes a split in the experience of the self. It also moves relatedness onto the impersonal, abstract level intrinsic to language and away from the personal, immediate level intrinsic to the other domains of relatedness. (pp. 162 *f.*)

The dramatis personae of *Hurlyburly* suffer loneliness, but at the same time they *actively produce* it, in others and in themselves.[1]

This becomes particularly clear when the "performative acts" that constitute the characters' "speech acts" are considered against the background of the narratological distinction between "told self" and "telling self". In all interactions of the characters of *Hurlyburly*, the interrelation between "told self" and "telling self" is disproportional and disrupted, a disruption that entails systematic and characteristic "a narrative distortions" (Habermas, 2006). In a narrative, a "told self" is presented, while in telling the narrative, a "performative self" must organise the listeners' attention and understanding. The "told self" narrates "vertically" something of a

---

[1] For invaluable comments and advice which led to the formulation of the following two paragraphs, the author sincerely thanks Michael B. Buchholz.

more or less recent past; the "performative self" acts in the interactional, horizontal dimension. The "told self" creates links to one's history and experience, the "performative self" creates links to listeners who are attentive to the "positioning" (Deppermann, 2015). Losing access to one's history makes one existentially lonely from one's past; one loses the sense for what kind of a person one is. Losing links with others makes one unable to use language and talk in order to connect with others, and one loses the sense for what kind of relationship one has with others.

While language, dialogue, interaction in general, can serve to narrativise the "performative self"—when, for example, the self that shapes the current interaction with the listener is unconscious, and therefore provides access to the unconscious scene—so that it can be brought into the speaking community (Deppermann et al., 2020), the characters in *Hurlyburly* systematically and compulsively smother their "told self"—for example, the self of which the narrative is about—under their performative self. The performance in and of the dialogues overtakes, spills over, overrides any narrative meaning—and so it (whatever "it" may be) goes on forever. The "told self" thus disappears not only from the dialogue but also from the self-relation—memory becomes impossible, and every word immediately turns to "blah-blah-blah, rapateta", mere words referring only to themselves, mirroring themselves in one another instead of referring, pointing to something essential. This creates a "chase-and-dodge pattern" (Beebe, 2014, pp. 11ff.).[2]

Shared history can neither be created nor continued, thoughts can no longer be thought, and communication not only becomes impossible, but even a means to distort and destroy reality: "If the lived past and the narrated past are very discrepant [...] story making can establish and perpetuate distortions of reality—distortions that contribute significantly to mental disturbance" (Stern, 1992, pp. 136f.). The inevitable result is loss of agency; loss of one's own history, in fact, of every history, and thus the establishment of an eternal present: loss of the self and self-reference, and thus the senselessness of every thought and every communication worthy of this name.

Pain and language: "If you do not bring forth what is within you, what you do not bring forth will destroy you"

Because no one understands oneself, no one understands the other, and while they talk, they don't even know what they mean. In the closing dialogue between Eddie and Mickey, it is finally made explicit:

MICKEY: You don't know what you're saying. You don't. [...]
EDDIE: I do.

---

[2] In infant research this pattern describes how mother and three-month-old baby play and observe each other joyfully, eye to eye. However, there are mothers who for fractions of a second dodge a glance and the joyful chase is interrupted. Beebe (2014) was able to show that such a videotaped interaction can predict an insecure attachment pattern when the baby is one year.

MICKEY: [...] I know what you think you're saying, but you're not saying it.
EDDIE: I do. I do. I know what I'm saying. I don't know what I mean, but I know what I'm saying. Is that what you mean?
MICKEY: Yeah. [...]
EDDIE: Right. But who knows what anything means, though, huh? It's not like anybody knows that, so at least I know I don't know, which is more than most people. They probably think they know what they mean, not just what they think they mean. (pp. 346 f.)

That it was possible to express that nothing can be expressed, because no one knows what he or she means, and also not what the other means, here, has death as a prerequisite: Phil's death, and with it also the memory of one's own, which will inevitably come. But death cannot be explained, never. If Phil's message has any meaning, it is this: only death has the power to reveal, in retrospect, the logic that led to it—but when the logic is revealed, you cannot think it because you are dead. A paradox that, much like Mickey warns Eddie, one can indeed despair of.

No drug can make the reality of death and its inexplicability disappear, no words, no "goddamn ultra-modern, post-hip, comprehensive, totally fucking cost-efficient explanation of everything by which you uncover the preceding events which determined the following events", as Mickey puts it, confronting Eddie (p. 348). In the frenzied chatter of *Hurlyburly*, only the final reality of death allows an exit from the endlessly processing empty *parole* along the chain of *signifiants* without reference to any *signifié* to become conceivable. And thus, an encounter with oneself:

EDDIE: You feel that, Mickey, huh? (*As Mickey turns on the TV, Eddie does a line of coke off the coffee table.*) About death, that when it comes, you're just going along in this goddamn ongoing inner rapateta, rapateta, blah-blah-blah, in which you understand this or that, and tell yourself about it, and then you ricochet on, and then it just cuts out mid-something. Mid-realization. "Oh, now I under—" Blam! You're gone. Wham! Comatose. Dead. You think that's how it is? (p. 347)

Until that fails too:

MICKEY: I'm going to bed. (*Turning off the TV.*) And you should, too. Go to bed. You're a mess. [...]
EDDIE: You lie to yourself, Mickey.
MICKEY: Who better? (pp. 347 f.)

What is it that the dramatis personae of *Hurlyburly* lie to each other about? What is it that their dialogues, which fail into ever more dialogues, are circling around? What cannot or must not be addressed in them?

The longing of all the characters is directed towards the happiness of real relationships. Nonetheless, in every constellation the characters always encounter only their own problems, their own inadequacies, the "minus" they themselves have produced: "Everyone [...] has his own problem, to which he is thrown back again and again in the midst of society, which thus separates him from his fellow human beings" (Szondi, 1956, p. 33; transl. D.A.). To be without encounters, without ties, without relationships, however, is to be lonely and isolated even in the midst of the most effervescent company. The time in which these characters live is the ultimate present, marked by absence and lack, an eternal interim of a never-ending state of exposure to what can never be understood, or even felt, that also spills over into the past and the future. Instead of a true dialogue, in which there would be understanding and orientation, in *Hurlyburly*, there is only a talking past each other. The law of dialogues here is the systematic failure of everything by everyone with everyone. Intertwining and knotting together, words become a minus process, an ever faster swirling maelstrom dragging all feelings and thoughts into its abyss.

This abyss, this crater that pulls everything into itself, bears a name: pain. While it forms the background of everything said, shines through all dialogues, it must not be named, because its reasons must remain unconscious. And because this pain must not be called by name, cannot be spoken, it must always and incessantly be circled, in cascades upon cascades of words that lack the reference to what they are actually about.

That—also—lies in the nature of pain. While language is directed outwards, always addressed, pain goes inwards. It intrinsically has no object and no outside, and is, in this respect, self-referential. Pain forces the sufferer to focus attention entirely on the pain—but what the sufferer finds when exposed to pain is amorphous, it cannot be ignored or denied, but is at the same time difficult to grasp and can hardly be described, at most indirectly, or not at all. Pain thus immediately leads to the edges of language or even destroys language altogether (Scarry, 1985, p. 4). It isolates in an inside without an outside, a timeless, eternally present now; it is absolutely unintegratable and makes one lonely. This is what William Styron called "aching solitude" in *Darkness Visible*, an account of his descent into a crippling, all-encompassing depression that brought him to the brink of suicide (Styron, 1990, pp. 3–20).

But while pain eludes language and takes it instantly to its edges, language also offers a way to escape pain: "Pain is made real by the ways in which we name, frame, and treat it" (Buchbinder, 2015, p. 12). If the communication of pain is successful, the escape from isolation and loneliness also becomes possible: "Language offers the possibility of escape. If somehow, we could communicate how we feel, we can reverse the isolation" (Biro, 2013, p. 16). Language is thus "a bridge that can lead us directly back to the communal world" (Biro, 2010, p. 15).

The same pain that renders speechless is what drives to language. That which cannot be expressed is at the same time that which needs expression: that which must be expressed so that it does not crush us, strangle us, eat us up from within. Logion 70 of the apocryphal Gospel of Thomas can also be understood in this sense: "If you bring forth what is within you, what you bring forth will save you. If you do not bring forth what is within you, what you do not bring forth will destroy you."

What must remain unsaid: "a grief that, though there are tears, is beyond them"

That Phil will not be able to achieve this is clear from the beginning of the play. Because he is already lost and suspects it, he is, paradoxically, also the only one who succeeds in expressing his misery. Thus, already in the first act, he says to Eddie: "I can't stand it. The loneliness. And some form of totally unusual and unpredictable insanity is creeping up on me about to do I don't know WHAT—God forbid I find out" (Rabe, 1995, p. 234). By the end of the play, it's clear what it is, what it's driving him towards: self-destruction.

That is the direction in which Eddie is heading, too. Eddie has lost every object, every emotion has been destroyed, and with it, his ability to think, even to locate himself in space and time. Thus, he remains "timelessly suspended in a no-man's land where there is neither imagination nor reality, neither forgetting nor remembering, neither sleeping nor waking up" (Ogden, 2003, p. 23). When Mickey has left to go to bed, the unbearable loneliness collapses on Eddie: "All right. All right. I'm on my own" (Rabe, 1995, p. 351). He tries to overcome it by talking to the talk show host on TV: "You think that's funny? Bullshit! Funny is your friends disappearing down roads and behind closed doors. We got a skull in our skin, John, and we got ghosts. That's funny" (p. 351). But what happens on TV has nothing to do with what Eddie is feeling without being able to feel it: "My own sense of discrimination has taken quite a blast. I've been humbled, John. [...] I've been blasted. [...] Right, John? You're not listening to me. [...] You never listen to me. You never listen to me" (p. 352).

Eddie brings the gun he found in the pocket of Phil's jacket to his temple. At this moment, Donna enters, who had fled the house in the second act and now returns unexpectedly after hitchhiking the East Coast. She addresses Eddie directly, and her simple questions and candid answers help Eddie, in the midst of his murderous confusion, to come to his senses and become aware of where he actually is:

DONNA: [...] How you been?
EDDIE: I'm a wreck.
DONNA: [...] You look a wreck, actually, but I didn't want to be impolite and mention it.
EDDIE: I don't know what I'm doing, you know what I mean? (*He is like a lost child.*)
DONNA: You're watchin' TV.
EDDIE: [...] Right. (*He looks at the TV.*) (p. 353)

His despair is total: "I don't know what of everything going on pertains to me and what is no account at all. [...] So how'm I supposed to feel about it? See that's what I don't know" (p. 354). "And I can't find out. How'm I supposed to find out?" (p. 356).

This final dialogue of the play between Eddie and Donna is crucial. Instead of also lapsing into confusion and upset like Darlene, reacting with hatred and aggression like Phil, ironically twisting statements like Artie, or evading communication through distancing and cynicism

SEVEN KINDS OF LONELINESS 163

like Mickey, Donna remains calm yet compassionate in the face of Eddie's overwhelming pain, confusion, and despair. In doing so, she provides a "container" for all the free-floating projections, unfelt emotions, and unthought "thoughts without thinkers". And suddenly he can articulate what it's really all about:

> (EDDIE *stares at her.*)
> EDDIE: Did you know Phil is dead? [...]
> DONNA Wow. So that's why you're such a wreck, Eddie. No wonder. (*Moving to him, she*
> (*she drops kneels on the floor beside him.*) You were at the funeral.
> *the paper,*
> *looks at him*):
> EDDIE: Yeah.
> DONNA: That'd wreck anybody.
> EDDIE: Yeah. (pp. 357 f.)

Donna asks: "Was it sad?" (p. 358). At that, she takes his hand, as we learn from the stage directions. Eddie begins to talk about the funeral, abstractly at first, then more and more concretely. "Was it sad?" Donna asks again, squeezing Eddie's hand. And finally, the grief Eddie feels, without being able to feel it, can take hold: "*Somewhere here it hits him*," says the stage direction, "*a grief that, though there are tears, is beyond them: It is in his body, which heaves and wracks him*" (p. 358).

The emotions were destroyed and yet are still there, only without being able to be felt. With their return, one can be reconnected with the other, contact with inner and outer reality can be re-established. Eddie's drug-fuelled, murderous confusion and nameless dread, in his interaction with Donna, gives way to an emerging sense of space and time. The "contact barrier" (Freud, 1950a; Bion, 1962a, p. 17) between dream and reality is re-established, the hallucinations of the psychotic dream in which timelessness reigns give way to emotions that provide the connections by which what is inside and what is outside can be thought again. Not only Eddie, but also Donna, now, via the shared relationship, succeed in reinscribing themselves in the space–time coordinates, which never exist in isolated, solitary island worlds, but always only as shared ones:

> DONNA You know somethin', Eddie. I didn't really go to all these places on my clothes.
> (*she pats him*):
> EDDIE: No.
> DONNA: I thought about them all though and bought the souvenirs at a local souvenir
> place, and I dreamed these big elaborate dreams, but actually I went out of
> here north toward San Francisco, but I got no farther than Oxnard.
> EDDIE (*sitting up, trying to get himself under control*): I know where Oxnard is.
> DONNA (*with immense enthusiasm, incredible happiness*): Great!

EDDIE What's so great about me knowing where Oxnard is?
(*laughing a little*):
DONNA: It's great when people know what each other are talking about, right, isn't that what we been talking about? (p. 359).

In *Hurlyburly*, for an entire play, no one knew what the other was talking about. But in order to locate ourselves in our space–time coordinates, we must find ourselves by way of intermediation of the other. Here, at the end of the play, we get a glimpse that this was what they were all talking about all along.

References

Beebe, B. (2014). My journey in infant research and psychoanalysis: microanalysis, a social microscope. *Psychoanalytic Psychology, 31*(1): 4–25. doi: 10.1037/a0035575.

Bigsby, C. (2000). *Contemporary American Playwrights*. Cambridge: Cambridge University Press.

Bion, W. R. (1957). The differentiation of the psychotic from the non-psychotic personalities. *International Journal of Psycho-Analysis, 38*: 266–275. [Reprinted in *Second Thoughts* (pp. 43–64). London: Karnac, 2007].

Bion, W. R. (1959). Attacks on linking. *International Journal of Psychoanalysis, 40*: 308–315. [Reprinted in *Second Thoughts* (pp. 93–109). London: Karnac, 2007.]

Bion, W. R. (1962a). *Learning from Experience*. London: Karnac.

Bion, W. R. (1962b). A theory of thinking. *International Journal of Psychoanalysis, 43*: 306–310. [Reprinted in *Second Thoughts* (pp. 110–119). London: Karnac, 2007.]

Bion, W. R. (1963). *Elements of Psychoanalysis*. London: William Heinemann. [Reprinted London: Karnac, 2005.]

Bion, W. R. (1997). *Taming Wild Thoughts*. London: Karnac.

Biro, D. (2010). *The Language of Pain: Finding Words, Compassion, and Relief*. New York: W. W. Norton.

Biro, D. (2013). When language runs dry: Pain, the imagination, and metaphor. In: L. Folkmarson Käll (Ed.), *Dimensions of Pain: Humanities and Social Science Perspectives* (pp. 13–26). London: Routledge.

Buchbinder, M. (2015). *All in Your Head: Making Sense of Pediatric Pain*. Oakland, CA: University of California Press.

Deppermann, A. (2015). Positioning. In: A. de Fina & A. Georgakopoulou (Eds.), *Blackwell Handbooks in Linguistics: The Handbook of Narrative Analysis* (pp. 369–386). Chichester, UK: Wiley Blackwell.

Deppermann, A., Scheidt, C. E., & Stukenbrock, A. (2020). Positioning shifts. From told self to performative self in psychotherapy. *Frontiers in Psychology, 11*: 2632. https://doi.org/10.3389/fpsyg.2020.572436.

Fisher, J. (2011). *Historical Dictionary of Contemporary American Theater 1930–2010*. Lanham, MD: Scarecrow.

Freud, S. (1950a). Project for a scientific psychology. *S. E., 1*: 281–391. London: Hogarth.

Habermas, T. (2006). Who speaks? Who looks? "Who feels"? Point of view in autobiographical narratives. *International Journal of Psychoanalysis, 87*: 497–518.

Lorenzer, A. (1977). *Sprachspiel und Interaktionsformen. Vorträge und Aufsätze zu Psychoanalyse, Sprache und Praxis.* Frankfurt, Germany: Suhrkamp.

Lorenzer, A. (1981). Zum Beispiel "Der Malteser Falke". Analyse der psychoanalytischen Untersuchung literarischer Texte. In: B. Urban & W. Kudszus (Eds.), *Psychoanalytische und psychopathologische Literaturinterpretation* (pp. 23–46). Darmstadt, Germany: Wissenschaftliche Buchgesellschaft.

Ogden, T. (2003). On not being able to dream. *International Journal of Psychoanalysis, 84*: 17–30.

Rabe, D. (1975). *In the Boom Boom Room.* New York: Grove, 1994.

Rabe, D. (1995). *Hurlyburly and Those the River Keeps: Two Plays.* New York: Grove.

Raw, L. (2013). Actor, image, action: Anthony Drazan's "Hurlyburly" (1998). In: W. R. Bray & R. Barton Palmer (Eds.), *Modern American Drama on Screen* (pp. 220–237). New York: Cambridge University Press.

Scarry, E. (1985). *The Body in Pain: The Making and Unmaking of the World.* New York: Oxford University Press.

Stern, D. N. (1992). *Diary of a Baby: What Your Child Sees, Feels, and Experiences.* London: Basic Books.

Stern, D. N. (1995). *The Interpersonal World of the Infant: A View from Psychoanalysis and Developmental Psychology.* London: Karnac, 1998.

Styron, W. (1990). *Darkness Visible: A Memoir of Madness.* New York: Vintage.

Szondi, P. (1956). *Theorie des modernen Dramas (1880–1950).* Frankfurt, Germany: Suhrkamp, 2011.

Wittgenstein, L. (1963). *Tractatus logico-philosophicus. Logisch-philosophische Abhandlung.* Frankfurt, Germany: Suhrkamp.

Part III

Developmental psychology and health

Introduction to Part III

Michael B. Buchholz

This section confronts us with some disturbing facts. Talking and thinking about loneliness in everyday discourse is rapidly guided by the silent assumption shared by most participants that loneliness is a state to be avoided as quickly as possible. Everyone must have somebody to talk to, "communication" is the magic formula. Couples who quarrel are advised to talk to each other more, children playing alone are pitied and consoled. Others see beginning symptoms of serious developmental disorders when children play by themselves. Alarm cries follow. However, if so advised, couples begin to talk more to each other, things often get worse; and if children absorbed in a game get interrupted by well-meaning helpers, they often start crying. Experienced clinicians confirm, this is not a symptom of a beginning autism disorder.

In her contribution, Inge Seiffge-Krenke starts with this ambivalence of loneliness as a resource *and* as an obstacle. Little babies often return into a "dreamy state" with half-closed eyes, and if mothers offer play and try to attract their babies' attention, they begin to cry. Something in dreamy seclusion requires respect. But children of school age cope better with mobbing than the lonely ones. Seiffge-Krenke singles out a special solution some children use to overcome loneliness. They invent an imaginary companion. Surveying the small amount of existing literature, the kinds of aid an imaginary companion delivers and the developmental contexts are carefully described. Arriving at an older age, the personal diary shows up as a trustful companion for many as a support to process and differentiate forms of experience. Sometimes promoting creativity and social skills, sometimes warning signs for better adjustment can be described and considered as helpful. The capacity to be alone, as described in psychoanalysis, obviously is an achievement of self-development and here one finds clinical hints and scientific overview of relevant studies related to it.

Aleksandar Dimitrijević's contribution follows with delving into the strands of attachment theory, which is one of the empirically best-studied theories of early development and its influences into adulthood, partner choice, self-regulation, and friendships. He starts with a seemingly droll question: "Why is sex so pleasurable?" and responds with a wide excursion into evolutionary theory and the experience of human interactions and relationships. Freud's answer to the question was that sex was necessary for the survival of the species. But new obstacles arise. There is long parenthood to endure—and again a rich overview of empirical studies shows further answers. One of them is named "evolutionary bribe". Human neonates survive by attracting their parents' affection and attention by sweetness, smiles, and cute utterances. Thus, parents are sensitised to their children's needs and the baby's attention is attracted to who the parents are. A circle of mutual monitoring establishes itself as the base for relating and socialising. The parents and child develop a deep emotional bond, which makes cultural learning possible. When human babies are born, they are so far back in development compared to their nearest companions in evolution, chimpanzees for example, that they would never survive—if not for the fundamental bond that supports the survival of parent–child units. Here cultural and social learning takes place in a quickly evolving manner, so rich that babies after several years of growing up in parental attachment possess skills one would not have expected. And they possess them in a degree exceeding everything our nearest ancestors could achieve. Attachment, as a fundamental bond, has proved to be the launching pad from earliest helplessness to highest technical skills, to abstract reasoning and rich variations of human smiles, to influencing next generations and communicating with forerunners of earlier generations (e.g. thanks to reading). The brain is a "social organ" is Dimitrijević's compelling conclusion; but this does not mean that it requires permanent attentiveness by others. What is needed is illustrated by three case presentations, followed by critical considerations about what kind of clinical support and social help lonesome adolescents need—and what not. The risk of stigmatisation lurks everywhere. Dimitrijević convincingly concludes that to understand aloneness also in individual cases requires an extension of clinical theory to a social perspective.

That such loneliness was not only an "inner" state of single individuals but a social matter was acknowledged in 2018 when in the UK a minister for loneliness was installed. Nevertheless, Eva M. Klein, Mareike Ernst, Manfred E. Beutel, and Elmar Brähler define loneliness as a psychological condition resulting from a mismatch between attachment needs and the experienced state of affairs with other people. Loneliness is the "dependent variable" created by many independent social variables. It is advisable to follow these authors' distinction between objective-structural and subjective-emotional aspects of loneliness, for both of which they review empirical studies. Just to mention one surprising result: many people expect the elderly to be the most lonesome group in individualistic modern societies. However, young men are at the highest risk of going through serious states of loneliness (in adolescence) and they feel lonelier than young women do. One hypothesis to understand this counter-stereotypic empirical result might be that adolescents realise that they have to master two complex life tasks: to find a companion and a profession. But how can you take a path and not even know where you want to go yourself? Shyness would be the expectable attitude—and its defensive countering by all variants of counter-phobic attitudes. The elderly, on the other hand, have often acquired more social competencies to deal with loneliness. Thus, well conducted empirical research contrasts our stereotypes. This leads to valuable clinical conclusions. However, not only in one direction! Further social-political conclusions can be drawn from the discovery that loneliness has a regional distribution. Do you have neighbours to meet? Opportunities for sports? Amateur theatre or other active groups? And how far are the distances to travel in order to meet these? Such factors co-determine the distribution of loneliness in a population. Many valuable results from empirical studies are brought together in this chapter. Psychological disorders, such as depression, can strongly contribute to the feeling of loneliness. The causal influence goes in both directions.

The complex relationships between loneliness and health are addressed in the following two contributions by Gamze Öcürümez Bilgili. She starts with a reference to the World Health Organization declaring that social disconnection is a risk not only for mental health, but for higher morbidity and mortality. This makes it suddenly clear how strongly the COVID-19 pandemic with higher demands for isolation has increased the risks of loneliness for many people. Loneliness has a tendency to become a chronic state as lonely people feel insecure and shy and easily feel threatened by social life; they do not feel comfortable with others but hold themselves in a state of alertness, which hinders experiencing joy in social company. An overwhelming list of studies is summarised and they all document such relationships and the circular consequences of loneliness. One path leads from loneliness to depression, to enhanced bodily discomfort with increased risks of heart conditions or other serious bodily disorders with a higher risk of early mortality, and this reflects back as the subjective perception of one's own state resulting in increasing loneliness via subjective self-perception as a disabled person.

In her second contribution, this author goes deeper into these complex relationships. She builds on Dimitrijević's formula of the "social brain", as she documents the brain's contribution to the processing of social stimuli and self-reflective activity to new relationships and continuation of social learning. The brain mediates what has been termed "social homeostasis". Steps of brain development are described, and these descriptions illustrated by quotations from poets. Being competently guided through this field gives one a profound feeling that there is something that connects clinical experience, and brain studies in humans and even in mice, with studies on child maltreatment or even abuse, and with a profound understanding articulated by poets. This "something common" in so divergent fields of professional experience, careful empirical studies, and poetic articulation is a valuable lecture in the service of studying loneliness. It connects.

CHAPTER 9

Loneliness and imaginary friends in childhood and adolescence

Inge Seiffge-Krenke

Loneliness can be considered both as a developmental resource and as an obstacle. This chapter focuses on resources in dealing with loneliness. It outlines the development of loneliness in children and adolescents, clarifies the developmental context in which loneliness may develop, and presents the creative coping styles of children and adolescents suffering from loneliness. Different developmental functions of loneliness are discussed in particular: as an important tool for the development of self and identity, but also as a method for regulating relationships. This dual character is already obvious in early development in babies and toddlers but is particularly evident in adolescence. From the beginning, it is important that the parents allow and support this dual function. However, changes in parental rearing styles in recent years, in which parents use the child as self-object and employ psychological control and manipulative strategies, are very harmful and do not promote a healthy development of self in relationships.

Reasons for loneliness in babies, children, and adolescents

The disastrous effects of loneliness have been documented since Spitz's early studies in 1945. He described children in an orphanage who were raised almost without human contact—even the bottle was handed to them on a pillow—and called the serious consequences of this deprivation anaclitic depression. Decades later, numerous studies demonstrated the consequences of parental deprivation and a reduced contact with caregivers having serious effects on psychological, emotional, and social development, resulting in a high percentage of insecure attachment patterns (Lionettia et al., 2015). Depression in lonely children has often been described as a clinical phenomenon. International studies show that parents of clinically referred children and adolescents were extremely concerned about the lack of friends of their children (Rescorla et al., 2007). Shy and withdrawn children and adolescents are more likely to suffer from bullying and then withdraw even more. Although peer victimisation generally decreases with age, a small group of the young are chronically victimised across primary and secondary school (Oncioiu et al., 2020). The meta-analysis by Modecki and colleagues (2014) indicates that children and adolescents who have at least one close friend usually cope better with victimisation than those who are friendless.

Lifespan studies have revealed that adolescents report high rates of loneliness (Luhmann & Hawkley, 2016), probably because of the accelerated development of autonomy and the importance and specific quality of friendship relations in this age group. As part of their identity development, adolescents may experience that they are different from their peers, and that too can increasingly lead to withdrawal and loneliness. Not feeling comfortable in their body, the confrontation with core gender identity triggered by physical maturity, and the question of acceptance of one's own body and gender can also lead to retreat and loneliness in adolescents (Diamond, 2006; De Vries & Cohen-Kettenis, 2012).

Loneliness is defined as the negative feeling that children and adolescents experience when they perceive their social relationships as deficient, either in a quantitative or a qualitative way. Similar to research on adults (cf. Klein et al., in this book), it is often difficult to distinguish loneliness in children and adolescents from other constructs. Depression and social anxiety are among the most prevalent internalising problems in children and adolescents (Klein et al., 2018) and are both highly co-morbid with loneliness in cross-sectional studies. The longitudinal study of Danneel and co-workers (2020) indicates that the three internalising problems are distinct from one another longitudinally, but co-develop across adolescence. Further, there is a conceptual overlap with withdrawal, a form of avoidant coping. In particular, rejection by parents and peers was related to withdrawal, and an avoidant coping style (Meesters & Muris, 2004). Cross-cultural studies have suggested an overall adaptive way of coping with relationship stress in adolescents in all countries, but also a fairly rigid use of withdrawal in a small subgroup in each country (Persike & Seiffge-Krenke, 2015). All forms of withdrawal, whether stable or not, were linked with high levels of depressive symptoms even two years later (Seiffge-Krenke & Klessinger, 2000).

Loneliness undoubtedly has an impact on the physical health and emotional, psychological, and cognitive development of children and adolescents. In this chapter we want to shed light on the productive way children and adolescents deal with loneliness. We want to show how they deal with the loss of relationships creatively and, further, illustrate the important function of self-chosen loneliness (Winnicott's *capacity to be alone*), which serves the autonomy from the parents. Again, the evidence is most impressive in adolescents, but many examples can be found in younger children as well. We will also take a closer look at the developmental context in which loneliness arises and analyse the strategies used to cope with loneliness.

Helpful fantasy to overcome loneliness: the imaginary companion

Imaginary companions, that is, "invisible, named persons who have psychic reality for the designer over a longer period of time and to which he or she refers in everyday communication" (Svendsen, 1934, p. 985), are fantasy productions that occur quite frequently in childhood and adolescence. Such a phenomenon was described for the first time in developmental psychology as early as 1895 by Vostrovsky; subsequently sporadic empirical studies were carried out.

Taylor and colleagues (2004) reported that between 18 and 30 per cent—the percentages vary depending on the study—of all children and adolescents seem to have an imaginary friend for some time. Thus, a substantial proportion of children apparently go through a phase in which they play with an imaginary companion who has a defined name and a characteristic appearance and who only exists in their imagination. Imaginary companions often go undetected by parents. Some authors name the age from three to six years (Piaget, 1951), others have found high frequencies in the ages of seven to ten (Taylor et al., 2004), and still others have substantiated that the imaginary companion occurs just as often in adolescents (Seiffge-Krenke, 2000a). As far as gender is concerned, the results are much more consistent and show that imaginary companions were found most frequently in female children and adolescents. This is explained by the greater dependency of girls on relationships in terms of identity and autonomy development (Seiffge-Krenke, 2017).

Important functions of imaginary companions

As mentioned earlier, loneliness can be caused by relationship deficits, feelings of inadequacy, and being different from peers. It can be triggered by a shamefully experienced personality, low self-worth, and an unacceptable physical maturity. Accordingly, coping with loneliness, for example, through imaginary companions, has a multitude of functions that are related to the causes of loneliness and dependent on the developmental context.

Imaginary companions as an aid to experiences of loss and loneliness

The fact that some children and adolescents develop imaginary friends when they feel alone is a particularly important function. A study by Majorie Taylor and colleagues (2004) revealed that 73 per cent of the five- and six-year-olds who had developed fantasy friends were first-borns or only children. The studies she carried out on preschool children, school children, and adolescents also show that children who have experienced a loss or deficit in their close relationships are particularly prone to constructing an imaginary companion (Taylor, 1999). Imaginary companions in children appear when the mother is pregnant with another child or a sibling is born, during the absence of a parent due to frequent hospital stays, or when the mother, father, or other caregiver dies, when parents divorce, or a friend is lost.

> A ten year old suffered from severe loneliness in her childhood. Her mother was hospitalised for severe depression from the time the girl was eight years old. Since then, she had often been alone and left to herself. In this situation, she invented a fantasy brother who was completely dependent on her, whom she took care of motherly (as she would probably like to be taken care of herself). She often lay on her bed for days, deep in conversation with her invisible brother. When the mother returned home, the fantasy brother disappeared from one day to the next.

Apparently, children and adolescents can sometimes compensate for feelings of loneliness, loss, or rejection with an imaginary companion. He or she offers the child a relationship independent of external circumstances, in which the child experiences love and support, but also company. This "very special friend" can thus be developed to compensate for relationship deficits (such as the loss or separation of parents or friends). As a consequence, he or she disappears when the child actually makes real friends or is better able to cope with the circumstances that have brought loss and isolation with them.

Furthermore, the extensive collection of psychoanalytic case studies by Nagera (1969) illustrate that feelings of loneliness, loss, abandonment, or rejection induce the construction of an imaginary companion in a child. However, in no single case was this construction the cause of hospitalisation or psychotherapy. Through the self-created imaginary relationship, the child experiences love and support in the face of the burden of being alone and abandoned, for example, through a fantasised twin, a sibling, or a playmate of the same age (Lax, 1990). Consequently, and as mentioned earlier, this construction disappears when the child has no real need for it anymore.

Imaginary companions as an aid for impulse control and the development of autonomy

Other functions of fantasy friends as a means of impulse control or as a defence against narcissistic insults have been described, especially in younger children. Often the imaginary friend is allowed to do everything that is forbidden to the child. Obviously, many younger children use the imaginary companion as an intermediate step between external control (in the form of parental supervision) and their own maturely developed morality. It should be noted that the imaginary companion appears at a point in time of rapid development in the cognitive functions, so that he or she also represents a way of expressing affects and impulses that the child knows that the parents will not tolerate.

Further, the imaginary companion can represent a projection of the child's feelings of omnipotence in a situation of painful dependency. According to Piaget (1951), this phenomenon is associated with ego development. An imaginary companion, from his point of view, offers emotional support in the service of individuation and differentiation, regardless of the parents.

The developmental context in which helpful fantasies arise for coping with loneliness

It is noteworthy that the beginning of a developed fantasy of the imaginary companion with its helpful function of comforting loneliness is reported at the earliest from the age of three. One must consider that essential learning processes of self-object differentiation must be completed and that a stable inner image of the parents must be acquired which makes separations tolerable over a certain period of time. A study by Harris (2000) shows that from the age of three separations between real and fantasised people are possible; even if the separation of fantasy and reality is not as robust as it is in older children.

Fantasies, the use of symbols, and creativity are subject to development-related changes. Even in preschool children, illusion and fiction games emerge, in which an object is playfully constructed from just a few features. Further developmental changes affect the quality of the description of the self and important others. Knowledge of one's own person is essentially relational; for example, it mainly arises from the processing of relationship experiences, which become more and more important with age (Seiffge-Krenke, 2020a). There is also a more mature understanding of privacy. Small children do not yet differentiate between private and public information. Privacy is only understood from the age of around ten, and a little later information about oneself and important information about partners is deliberately kept secret, changed, and manipulated. Significant advances in developing empathy favour this development. Real friendships and imaginary companions change accordingly. At around the age of twelve, it becomes very important to talk to friends about problems (Seiffge-Krenke, 2000b). A breach of trust is the most common reason for ending a friendship. According to empirical results, adolescents expect a good friend to tell them confidential information and to be available as a recipient for their own revelations, with girls emphasising mutual trust and the disclosure of intimate experiences as a genuine characteristic of friendships more than boys (Bauminger et al., 2008). It is only from adolescence on that friendships are based on a close emotional exchange with increasing exclusivity, while younger children still play with everyone at random. These development-related changes lead to a gradual narrowing of the circle of friends to a few close friends with whom an intimate, reciprocal exchange is maintained.

Comforter in loneliness and helper in constructing identity: the imaginary friend in the diary

The increased need of adolescents for a trusted companion explains why lonely teenagers often develop imaginary companions—at least for a short time—to comfort themselves and not feel so alone. On the basis of the developmental changes described earlier, it becomes clear why especially young people who are lonely have particularly good prerequisites for briefly developing such a fantasy construction. It is also important that they have complete control over the contact. In my own research on adolescents, I have found that they often write diaries and speak or write to an imaginary friend in these diaries (Seiffge-Krenke, 2000a). In the content analysis of the diaries, a continued dialogue became apparent. They talk to him or her, explain their experiences in more detail ("of course you can't know …", "I forgot to tell …") and say goodbye again. This applies to a third of male and 60 per cent of female diary writers ("I speak in it like to a friend"). All writers introduced questions or comments after describing certain events or experiences and invited him or her to take over, criticise, or evaluate the writer's position. The way in which they asked these questions and invited comments shows that they obviously had very precise ideas about their imaginary companions. It is interesting that boys as well as girls are more likely to choose females as illusory companions (75 per cent of boys and 61 per cent of girls). Boys choose an almost perfect female variant of their person (they are similar in appearance and age and the essential psychological characteristics), while girls have fantasy companions who can be similar to them, but also very different from them.

The imaginary companion then seems to lose its personal definition in the course of adolescence—this presumably coincides with the impending end of the diary—and is finally hardly mentioned by older adolescents. Incidentally, we asked the diary writers again a few years later, and it was noticeably few who could still remember a fantasy friend (Seiffge-Krenke, 2020a). Apparently, when the function of the fantasy friend is fulfilled, he or she is given up and forgotten, just as the keeping of a diary is only very rarely practised by adults.

Signs of pathology or of maturity, social skills, and creativity?

Although research on this specific population has been sporadic over the last century, the results of several studies suggest that having an imaginary companion confers a developmental advantage in a number of important socio-cognitive areas. As a rule, an imaginary companion is not viewed as an expression of pathology. All imaginary companions examined in psychology so far are the production of normal children and adolescents. The vividness of this fantasy and the fact that it can be sustained over a long period of time often irritates parents, teachers, and therapists. However, because the designers are always aware of their creations, imaginary companions can be clearly distinguished from pathological processes such as psychoses: the child or adolescent never feels at the mercy of this imaginary companion; on the contrary, this "very special friend" can be designed, changed, and manipulated as desired. The designer and the imaginary companion are therefore clearly separated from each other. The structuring and development of this fantasy is evidently up to the child, who also determines the duration of the imaginary friendship. Thus, in contrast to the relationship with parents, the relationship with an imaginary friend can be regulated much more freely.

This assumption of good psychological adaptation in children and adolescents who construct imaginary companions has been confirmed in studies, in which, above all, the creativity and social skills of these children were examined. Preschoolers with an imaginary companion showed a greater percentage of self-initiated and creative play and more actively participated in family and friendship activities. School children with an imaginary companion were much more positive in their affective expression, and they showed more cooperation and empathy towards playmates than children without imaginary companions (Roby & Kidd, 2008).

A very similar result was found when analysing the characteristics of diary writers who addressed their diary as an imaginary friend and entered into an ongoing dialogue. The young people who did address their diary as an imaginary friend showed higher levels of creativity and social skills than those without such a special companion. Above all, high values for empathy were found in adolescents with imaginary companions, compared with a comparison group without imaginary companions (Seiffge-Krenke, 2000a). The hypothesis of good psychological adjustment and high creativity certainly also applies to Anne Frank, who, at a time of severe isolation and loneliness, invented an imaginary companion, "Kitty", in her diary, with whom she exchanged ideas. This production was not Anne Frank's only creative achievement. In addition to several poems, parts of a novel were also found in her estate.

Different developmental prerequisites: attachment, loss, and the transitional object

While having an imaginary companion confers a developmental advantage in a number of important socio-cognitive areas, it is less clear which developmental prerequisites are favourable for good coping capacities with loneliness. Two opposing theories are noted, suggesting that either secure attachment or, in contrast, loss, serve as a prerequisite. While studying the development of severely mentally disturbed children and adolescents, Bowlby (1969) repeatedly encountered extreme early childhood traumatisation in these children and recognised that the effects on the development of creativity and imagination were very significant. Some attachment researchers (e.g. Cassidy & Shaver, 1999) explicitly assume that only children with a secure attachment can be creative and imaginative, that the exploration can only ever take place "from a secure base" (Bowlby, 1988).

In contrast, there is also evidence that children and adolescents who have experienced numerous events of loss are particularly creative and able to fantasise as a means of coping with loneliness. In her work *Separation and Creativity*, Mannoni (1999) gives various examples of artists, especially writers, who have come to terms with severe losses in life by the creation of a meaningful work. However, this is only possible for a few children who have had traumatic experiences, as the classic study by Leonore Terr (1979) on "The Children of Chowchilla" shows. Studies on imaginative play actually suggest that play behaviour decreases when the physical and psychological needs of these children are impaired. This can be seen particularly dramatically in the limited imagination and play of neglected and abused children (Finkelhor, 1995).

In 1908, Freud described that every child, in play, works like a creative writer or artist by creating their own world. Winnicott (1971) later created the "potential space" that stands between psychological and external reality. This gap between fantasy and reality is filled by a loving relationship with the mother. According to Winnicott (1983), "good enough mothering" is necessary. Only a child with such a transitional space is able to cope with loss and separation. With his concept of the *transitional object*, Winnicott (1983) gives another indication of how loneliness can be processed. He observed that children in situations in which they had to separate from their mother took objects, such as cuddly toys or favourite blankets, and clung to them. He explains this behaviour by saying that these preferred objects symbolically represent the absent mother as transitional objects. This enables the child to process the separation intrapsychically and to bridge the transition from being with the mother to being separated through symbolisation.

Loneliness and the "capacity to be alone": development of autonomy and changing parenting styles

The capacity to be alone is a further important developmental advance described by Winnicott (1983). Compared to children, teenagers drastically reduce the time spent with parents in favour of time with friends and alone, which they spend secluded in their room. From a developmental perspective, it has been proven that during adolescence daydreaming is particularly frequent (Singer, 2014). Further, retreating into one's own room is consciously chosen in order to distance oneself from the parents and to have time for oneself and one's daydreams, but also to have friendship relationships both offline and online. This large volume of time spent alone occurs primarily at home and emerges in early adolescence; pre-adolescents spend much less time alone (Larson, 1997). Although being alone appears to be a negative experience in childhood, studies suggest that in adolescence moderate solitude has a positive relation to psychological adjustment.

In addition to the construction of fantasy friends, adolescence is characterised by an unusually high rate of daydreams, and we must assume that both play an important role in the process of separation and the new conceptualisation of identity. Besides the frequency, we don't know much about the daydreams of young people. Even so, it can be assumed that they are concerned with anticipating the future, dealing with friends and romantic partners, and developing various facets of their own identity. In adolescence we not only find enormous increases in daydream rates and in diary writing, the private, non-public character is also important. The imaginary companions in the diary are a very individual and creative form of symbolisation that sets adolescents apart from their parents. The secret mode of the diary and the hiding or encrypting of the diary has created a private space of autonomy that parents should respect. The imaginary companion as a fantasised conversation partner represents a constructive possibility of self-exploration in a self-determined framework, and it seems reasonable to assume that daydreaming fulfils a similar function.

It is important to what extent parents or adults generally allow this space for autonomous exploration and imagination. This includes, for example, that parents reduce their support in order to allow the child to gain competence and to develop an independent identity. However, findings in recent years have shown that too much parental support delays identity development and autonomy and also affects the mental health of adolescents. There are clear cultural differences in how much parental support is experienced as appropriate during adolescence (Seiffge-Krenke, 2020b). For most Western industrialised countries, however, too much support over a long period of time is associated with negative consequences for the health of "children" and leads to higher rates of depression and anxiety (Lemoyne & Buchanan, 2011).

In recent years, children in general have become very important for their parents' self-esteem, and especially among adolescents and young adults there is a noticeably high level of parental support. Many studies that demonstrate impaired development of autonomy and identity focus on dysfunctional parental styles of upbringing such as psychological control and intrusive behaviour (Barber, 2002), but also anxious monitoring (Affrunti & Woodruff-Borden, 2017). These dysfunctional parental behaviours are frequently based on parental fear of separation (Kins et al., 2011) and lead to increased monitoring and control of the offspring. The "circling over the children" with the willingness to step in at any time, helping when problems arise, is a combination of warmth and strong control with little autonomy support (Seiffge-Krenke, 2020b). Too much support, psychological control, and anxious monitoring are also consistently associated in international studies with delayed identity development or identity diffusion in adolescents (Weitkamp & Seiffge-Krenke, 2019). Such parenting behaviour was even found with adult children, which underlines that currently an over-involvement ("helicopter parents", Darlow et al., 2017) has become relatively common.

Parenting behaviour has thus changed, overall, in the direction of more fearful control and high, sometimes intrusive support. It is obvious that the mechanisms of targeted withdrawal, described in this article, such as being alone or continued conversation with a fantasy friend of about the same age, are helpful in order to achieve autonomy and an independent identity in a situation of great, oppressive dependency.

Final comment

The importance of fantasies in coping with loneliness is a clinically relevant topic, which, however, has rarely been conceptualised and dealt with in terms of its practical significance in psychotherapy with children and adolescents. This chapter highlights theoretical concepts and empirical findings on the fantasy activity of children and adolescents, explores the underestimated potential for fantasies in lonely children and adolescents, and encourages increased use of these data in psychotherapy and counselling. It shows the enormous self-healing powers of children and adolescents who cope with loneliness and loss independently, through the development of specific fantasies without becoming clinically conspicuous, but also clarifies the limits for those patients who were severely traumatised. A special construction was presented that children and adolescents create themselves: the imaginary companion. It can fulfil very different functions, which we have to describe predominantly as protective and resource oriented.

These fantasies are not only important for narcissistic self-regulation, when one is disappointed in one's parents and feels left alone, but also serve to regulate relationships by keeping the objects at a distance. The specific design of this "very special friend" depends on the level of development, and in addition to coping with loneliness, there are also age-dependent functions, for example, impulse control and identity construction. The fact that the imaginary companion is not only constructed independently, but also—when he or she has fulfilled its function—is given up again, underlines its positive, development-promoting function.

The fantasies presented in this chapter, often hidden from our eyes, correct our parent- or therapist-centredness. In the creative fantasies that are communicated, or occur in our presence in the therapeutic session, one should provide the transitional space that is filled with a good therapeutic relationship. It should be remembered that the patient's creativity can very easily be "stolen" by the therapist if the therapist intervenes too early or knows "too much" (Winnicott, 1971).

Future studies should systematically deal with the developmental requirements of fantasies as means of coping in cases of loneliness and clarify the question of attachment *vs.* loss. We also need to know more about the possibilities of helping traumatised children to overcome their loneliness. So far, there is hardly any research on cross-cultural aspects. Cultural scripts of connectedness and individuality could play a role, which we should urgently examine in view of the increasing cultural diversity in all Western industrial nations. This diversity is also reflected in the inpatient and outpatient setting and it would be therapeutically helpful to know more here.

References

Affrunti, N. W., & Woodruff-Borden, J. (2017). The roles of anxious rearing, Negative affect, and effortful control in a model of risk for child perfectionism. *Journal of Child and Family Studies, 26*(9): 2547–2555. https://doi.org/10.1007/s10826-017-0767-8.

Barber, B. K. (2002). *Intrusive Parenting: How Psychological Control Affects Children and Adolescents.* Washington, DC: American Psychological Association.

Bauminger, N., Finzi-Dottan, K., Chason, S., & Har-Even, S. (2008). Intimacy in adolescent friendship: The roles of attachment coherence, and self-disclosure. *Journal of Social and Personal Relationships, 25*(3): 409–428. doi: 10.1177/0265407508090866.

Bowlby, J. (1969). *Attachment and Loss.* New York: Basic Books.

Bowlby, J. (1988). *A Secure Base: Clinical Applications of Attachment Theory.* London: Routledge.

Cassidy, J., & Shaver, P. R. (Eds.) (1999). *Handbook of Attachment: Theory, Research, and Clinical Applications.* New York: Guilford.

Danneel, S., Geukens, F., Maes, M., Bastin, M., Bijttebier, P., Colpin, H., Verschueren, K., & Goossens, L. (2020). Loneliness, social anxiety symptoms, and depressive symptoms in adolescence: Longitudinal distinctiveness and correlated change. *Journal of Youth and Adolescence, 49*(11): 2246–2264.

Darlow, V., Norviltis, J. M., & Schuetze, P. (2017). The relationship between helicopter parenting and adjustment to college. *Journal of Child and Family Studies, 26*: 2291–2298.

De Vries, A. L., & Cohen-Kettenis, P. T. (2012). Clinical management of gender dysphoria in children and adolescents: the Dutch approach. *Journal of Homosexuality, 59*(3): 301–320.

Diamond, M. (2006). Atypical gender development: a review. Gender Identity Research and Education Society (GIRES). *International Journal of Transgenderism, 9*(1): 29–44.

Finkelhor, D. (1995). The victimization of children. *American Journal of Orthopsychiatry, 65*(2): 177–193.

Freud, S. (1908e). Creative writers and day-dreaming. *S. E., 9*: 143–153. London: Hogarth.

Harris, P. L. (2000). *Understanding Children's Worlds: The Work of the Imagination*. New York: Blackwell.

Kins, E., Soenens, B., & Beyers, W. (2011). "Why do they have to grow up so fast?" Parental separation anxiety and emerging adults' pathology of separation-individuation. *Journal of Clinical Psychology, 67*(7): 647–664.

Klein, A. M., de Voogd, L., Wiers, R. W., & Salemink, E. (2018). Biases in attention and interpretation in adolescents with varying levels of anxiety and depression. *Cognition and Emotion, 32*(7): 1478–1486. https://doi.org/10.1080/02699931.2017.1304359.

Larson, R. W. (1997). The emergence of solitude as a constructive domain of experience in early adolescence. *Child Development, 68*: 80–93.

Lax, R. F. (1990). An imaginary brother: His role in the formation of a girl's self image and ego ideal. *Psychoanalytic Study of the Child, 45*(1): 257–272.

Lemoyne, T., & Buchanan, T. (2011). Does "hovering" matter? Helicopter parenting and its effect on wellbeing. *Sociological Spectrum, 31*(4): 399–418.

Lionettia, F., Pastoreb, M., & Barone, L. (2015). Attachment in institutionalized children: A review and meta-analysis. *Child Abuse & Neglect, 42*: 135–145.

Luhmann, M., & Hawkley, L. C. (2016). Age differences in loneliness from late adolescence to oldest old age. *Developmental Psychology, 52*(6): 943–959. https://doi.org/10.1037/dev0000117.supp.

Mannoni, M. (1999). *Separation and Creativity*. New York: Other Press.

Meesters, C., & Muris, P. (2004). Perceived parental rearing behaviors and coping in young adolescents. *Personality and Individual Differences, 37*(3): 513–522.

Modecki, K. L., Minchin, J., Harbaugh, A. G., Guerra, N. G., & Runions, K. C. (2014). Bullying prevalence across contexts: a meta-analysis measuring cyber and traditional bullying. *Journal of Adolescent Health, 55*(5): 602–611.

Nagera, H. (1969). The imaginary companion. Its significance for ego development and conflict solution. *Psychoanalytic Study of the Child, 24*(1): 165–196.

Oncioiu, S. I., Orri, M., Boivin, M., Geoffroy, M. C., Arseneault, L., Brendgen, M., Vitarom, F., Navarro, M. C., Galéra, C., Tremblay, R. E., & Côté, S. M. (2020). Early childhood factors associated with peer victimization trajectories from 6 to 17 years of age. Pediatrics, *14*(5). https://doi.org/10.1542/peds.2019-2654.

Persike, M., & Seiffge-Krenke, I. (2015). Stress with parents and peers: How adolescents from 18 nations cope with relationship stress. *Anxiety, Stress, & Coping, 29*(1): 38–59.

Piaget, J. (1951). *Play, Dreams, and Imitation in Childhood*. New York: W. W. Norton.

Rescorla, L., Achenbach, T. M., Ivanova, M. Y., Dumenci, L., Almqvist, F., Bilenberg, N., & Erol, N. (2007). Epidemiological comparisons of problems and positive qualities reported by adolescents in 24 countries. *Journal of Consulting and Clinical Psychology, 75*(2): 351–369.

Roby, A., & Kidd, E. (2008). The "referential" communication skills of children with imaginary companions. *Developmental Science, 11*(4): 531–540. doi: 10.1111/j.1467-7687.2008.00699.

Seiffge-Krenke, I. (2000a). Ein sehr spezieller Freund: Der imaginäre Gefährte. *Praxis der Kinderpsychologie und Kinderpsychiatrie, 49*: 689–702.

Seiffge-Krenke, I. (2000b). "Liebe Kitty, du hast mich gefragt ...": Phantasiegefährten und reale Freundschaftsbeziehungen im Jugendalter. *Praxis der Kinderpsychologie und Kinderpsychiatrie, 49*: 620–631.

Seiffge-Krenke, I. (2017). *Psychoanalyse des Mädchens*. Stuttgart, Germany: Klett-Cotta.

Seiffge-Krenke, I. (2020a). *Auf der Suche nach dem neuen Ich: Identitätsentwicklung im Jugendalter*. Stuttgart, Germany: Kohlhammer.

Seiffge-Krenke, I. (2020b). Parenting adolescents in an increasingly diverse world: links to adolescents' psychopathology. *Psychology, 11*(6): 874–887. doi: 10.4236/psych.2020.116057.

Seiffge-Krenke, I., & Klessinger, N. (2000). Long-term effects of avoidant coping on adolescents' depressive symptoms. *Journal of Youth and Adolescence, 29*(6): 617–630.

Singer, J. L. (2014). *Daydreaming and Phantasy*. London: Routledge.

Svendsen, M. (1934). Children's imaginary companions. *Archives of Neurology and Psychiatry, 2*(5): 985–999.

Taylor, M. (1999). *Imaginary Companions and the Children Who Create Them*. New York: Oxford University Press.

Taylor, M., Carlson, S. M., Maring, B. L., Gerow, L., & Charley, C. M. (2004). The characteristics and correlates of fantasy in school age children: imaginary companions, impersonation, and social understanding. *Developmental Psychology, 40*(6): 1173–1187.

Terr, L. (1979). The children of Chowchilla. *Psychoanalytic Study of the Child, 34*(1): 547–623.

Vostrovsky, C. (1895). A study of imaginary companions. *Education, 15*: 383–398.

Weitkamp, K., & Seiffge-Krenke, I. (2019). The association between parental rearing dimensions and adolescent psychopathology: a cross-cultural study. *Journal of Youth and Adolescence, 48*(3): 469–483.

Winnicott, D. W. (1983). *Transitional Objects and Transitional Phenomena: A Study of the First Not-Me Possession*. New York: Basic Books.

Winnicott, D. W. (1971). *Playing and Reality*. London: Penguin.

CHAPTER 10

Loneliness and insecure attachment

Aleksandar Dimitrijević

Attachment theory has grown to be extremely popular in developmental and clinical psychology, psychotherapy research, studying romantic relationships, parenthood, religious feelings, and much else. It seems, however, not completely clear that it is actually a fundamentally psychoanalytic theory or that it is a theory about the evolutionary importance of loneliness. This chapter will be focused on elucidating the latter of the two neglected notions.

Why is sex so pleasurable?

The approaches to mental life developed by Sigmund Freud and by John Bowlby may look like inverted images of one another. Bowlby emphasised that attachment is a more fundamental need than sexuality and rooted his psychoanalytic thinking in the evolutionary theory of Charles Darwin:[1] "Not a single feature of a species' morphology, physiology, or behaviour can be understood or even discussed intelligently except in relation to that species' environment of evolutionary adaptedness" (Bowlby, 1969, p. 64). It might turn out, however, that both

---

[1] Freud, and several other early psychoanalysts, were interested in the idea of evolution. Unfortunately, they were not able to realise the revolutionary nature of Darwin's theory, and remained loyal to some older approaches that are now considered to have no scientific value. The most obvious is the influence of Lamarck on both Freud's idea of the death drive and Ferenczi's Thalassa.

Freud sees the libido "coinciding with the Eros of poets and philosophers, which holds all living things together" (e.g. 1920g, p. 54; he repeats this in his discussion of Weismann's protoplasm theory, not in the letters to Fliess but also in the "Project"). Elsewhere he sees the "extended sexuality of psychoanalysis" as close to the "Eros of the divine Plato" (1905d, p. 32). The most detailed discussion of this aspect of Freud's theory can be found in Sulloway (1992).

186   FROM THE ABYSS OF LONELINESS TO THE BLISS OF SOLITUDE

approaches are necessary for a better understanding of us as a species and individuals, and for the understanding of these two theoretical systems.

Today, most people are aware that sex is intensely pleasurable. Not only are we willing to sacrifice almost anything in order to obtain sexual pleasure, but also most Western civilisations and religions are extremely prohibitive of sexuality, thus confirming their awareness of its power as a motivational force. Ultimately, sensual pleasure, overall excitement, and emotional happiness included in sexual acts can hardly be surpassed by any other human activities either in their raw intensity or in their unique quality. The reason for this is inextricably connected to the phenomenon of attachment.

Indeed, why is sex so pleasurable? During our evolution, several processes of "bribing" were developed. Some actions bring much pleasure, and they are all, save one,[2] necessary for survival. We proved too unreliable, too distractable, to be delegated the responsibility of, say, timing water intake. Wherever there is an intense, universal pleasure, it only means we were too childish about something crucially important, and a "bribe" had to be introduced so that we would want to repeat that activity. Evolution in this domain is like a desperate teacher who offers enormous rewards for any, even the minimal, homework done.

The power of sexuality is another "evolutionary bribe". Whatever is necessary for survival is accompanied by intense pleasure, so we will not forget to obtain and/or provide it. That sex is a more potent source of pleasure than any other testifies that our distant predecessors needed reminder and reward to procreate.

That sexuality is such a powerful "bribe" must be connected to it a) being the activity most important for the survival of the species, and b) leading to some painful or at least frustrating consequences we would be happy to avoid. Both of these refer, obviously, to pregnancy, childbirth, and parenting.

Exhausting and long parenthood

No species on earth has ever faced such a complicated, exhausting, and long-lasting parenthood as humans do. It puts so much pressure on parents that it makes sense to wonder why exactly it is that we protect our offspring, once our powerful urges have led to sexual activity, conception, and childbirth.

An empirical study made evident the way evolution manipulated us into parenthood (Bartels & Zeki, 2004). By scanning the brains of twenty young mothers, the researchers could discern a unique neurophysiological reaction to the photograph of their own baby smiling (compared to crying and neutral, as well as unknown babies). This reaction, in a nutshell, can be described as 1) the activation of the ventral tegmental area, which leads to the production of dopamine, and consequently to experiencing happiness, and 2) the activation of the nucleus accumbens, which

---

[2] A major mystery here is music, incredibly stimulating for the brain and liked in all cultures and all epochs, yet without any evolutionary purpose in humans.

is related to addictions. What does this mean? The authors do not go deep into possible interpretations, but I believe that this tells us a lot about the "evolutionary bribe" necessary for the survival of the species. If you only think about parenthood 20,000 or 200,000 years ago—without antibiotics, obstetricians and paediatricians, kindergartens, nappies, warm water, and so much else—you would not be happy to be a parent either. Children must have died frequently and in so many cases from abandonment. In harsh winters, frequently hungry, constantly haunted by predators, let us face it, we would often leave the kids behind and run faster too. Unless ... Well, it seems plausible to speculate that only those youngsters survived who, when feeling content and cared for, smiled in such a seductive way that their parents felt happy about it and wanted that to repeat. So they took good care of the child, then the child smiled again, then they experienced a "happy and want more" reaction. And this, over time, led to a bond strong enough that parents would not abandon the child at any cost and ensured the survival of the species. It is a de-idealising fact, yet a fact nonetheless, that good parenting is based on the activation of this "reward system", as it is known—the exact same mechanism that addictions activate.[3]

The curse of upright walking

None of this bothers any of the primates, our closest relatives in nature. Not to mention mammals or, say, lizards, who can move, eat, or swim basically the minute they hatch, often without the presence of parents, much less any instruction, while we can barely breathe. At the age of eighteen months, chimpanzees are acrobats; we can hopefully walk but still cannot dream of running or jumping. To them, aloneness is not an issue; to us, it is our demise.

Human babies lag so far behind the babies of other species of the same age because, ironically, we are born prematurely, and we start developing, especially when it comes to our brain maturation, much later than others do. We need much more than forty-two weeks of pregnancy, yet we cannot afford that.

To make things even more interesting, this did not bother us in earlier times either. We used to be "normal" primates, and for a long time had adequately long pregnancies and babies that were more independent. Everything changed with the acquisition of upright walking. Of course, it brought us enormous advantages. First, with the ascent of distant senses, mostly vision, we became capable of noticing either predators or prey much earlier than when we were relying on smell and touch only. This made it possible to prepare for a fight, call for help, set a trap, or run away, and we started becoming the dominant species we are today. Second, arms and hands were suddenly free and could be used for tasks more sophisticated than mere walking. Holding babies, collecting fruit, punching someone in the nose may have come first, but using tools and weapons, or growing opposable thumbs may have been crucial in our evolving into civilised beings, *Homo sapiens*.

---

[3] At the same time, breastfeeding helps the release of oxytocin, which contributes to the development of mothers' bonding with their infants.

This change, however, brought about a fundamental problem (besides having to grow and endlessly exercise the muscles that keep the spine and neck upright). Over time, walking changed the shape and functionality of our pelvic bones, making them too fragile to carry foetuses, and birth canals turned out to become too narrow for their large heads.[4] Therefore, human babies are being born when they become too large and heavy to be held any longer, which makes them more helpless and dependent than any other living creature on earth.

Helplessness of man cubs

To be alone in nature must have been extremely dangerous, and especially so at the times when our forefathers lived in caves, forests, or homes that many predators were able to smash in the blink of an (anxious) eye. Humans are not tough enough to defend themselves without weapons (which did not always exist) or without other members of their group, as we are not equipped with sharp teeth, or claws, or hundreds of kilos of muscles. But this is incomparably worse for youngsters, who would not even be able to use the weapons or even run away. The aloneness of a child in nature very easily equals death even today. And this is exactly where the story of attachment as we know it in humans begins.

Bowlby thought that the basic function of attachment was in the protection from predators, in the environment of evolutionary adaptations, similar to the living environment of the other primates of today. He recognised several natural clues to an increased risk of danger—unfamiliarity, sudden change, rapid approach, height, and being alone. We crave company because that is our basic way to survive. But being the only available means of survival, the social nature we develop is in our core and not developing or losing it is a burden if not a curse. He learned from ethologists that the phenomenon of imprinting shows the importance of contact with the protective parent even in birds. Ethologists also considered that the behavioural systems used by a young monkey to establish and maintain attachment to its mother were instinctual.

This is obvious and easily observable in human ontogeny as well:

1. Babies are born with a capacity for clinging,[5] and, thanks to Moro and Darwin reflexes, can briefly hang without outside support.
2. Social contact is pleasurable regardless of previous experience or learning. The brain of a newborn "produces" happiness whenever another person comes close to her face, looks her in the eyes, and talks softly, and this reaction will last into adulthood unless traumatically severed.
3. At the age of about eight weeks, "social smiling" appears. Babies distinguish between physical objects of round shape, drawings of a human face with scrambled features, and a real

---

[4] Because of this detail the whole theory was named "obstetrics dilemma".

[5] This was first described by Imre Herrmann, a psychoanalyst and polymath from Budapest, whose influence Bowlby always acknowledged (see Kächele, 2009).

human face, and it is only the last of these that can cause smiling, especially at the moment of eye contact. Attention and direct response of the adult make the reaction of the baby stronger regardless of the possible gratification of physiological needs.

This inborn focus on others easily overpowers interests in physical objects, like food or toys, which testifies to the importance of avoiding loneliness. Another way to look at this is by the now accumulated evidence that nothing makes children suffer more than parental neglect, that any attention, even traumatic, is better than no attention at all.

To signal that attachment is needed (which basically means that anxiety is on the rise), children can use different forms of behaviour: crying, smiling, and calling, as well as clinging, following, and non-nutritive sucking.[6] These behaviours are most often followed by most intense emotional reactions, to underline the urgency of the need for another person's support or company.

Possibly exactly because the need is so urgent, newborns are not capable of establishing and maintaining attachment to one particular person. In the long period up to the age of four to eight months, almost every benevolent person can calm down a crying child or engage her in play. When loneliness equals death, one cannot be picky but "grabs" any support available. This pertains to direct causes of fear as well as to the indirect ones (like darkness, noise, being left alone or startled).

All of this led to Bowlby's conclusion that "There is clear evidence that babies are equipped to readily react to social stimuli and quickly get involved in social interaction" (1969, p. 265). The work of Daniel Stern, and even more so of his former doctoral student and now a leading researcher in the field, Beatrice Beebe, with the use of frame-by-frame analysis of the interaction between mothers and four-month-old infants, has confirmed Bowlby's ideas. This "social microscope" has provided clear evidence that babies are indeed capable of initiating, maintaining, and interrupting social interaction, even at that very tender age (Beebe et al., 2016).

> Another perspective that taught us a lot about this is the focus on social deprivation and separation anxiety. The work, mostly started in the 1940s, by Spitz, Bowlby, Harlow, and several other researchers (see Van der Horst & Van der Veer, 2008), showed that: "… what is crucial is the availability of the figure. It is when a figure is perceived as having become inaccessible and unresponsive, that separation distress occurs, and the anticipation of the possible occurrence of such a situation arouses anxiety (Ainsworth et al., 1978, p. 21).

The lack of early social interaction leads to illnesses, slower development, and mental disorders, which provides another proof of its vital importance.

---

[6] All these components exist in rhesus monkeys as well, except for the smile, which exists in chimpanzees (Suomi, 1999).

Brain is a social organ

But what is this capacity that makes seducers of us all?

Our brain development cannot be finalised in only the nine months of pregnancy. Human infants are thus born entirely dependent on a benevolent caregiver for everything necessary for survival: food, water, safety, acquisition of walking, and speech. This lasts for at least twelve months, during which many things develop at nearly the same speed as in the womb, so much so that these two periods can almost be seen as one.

Because we are so dependent, we have to come with an inborn capacity to make adults want to take care of us. Again, something so crucial cannot be left to depend on our readiness or capacity, it must be an ingrained part of our "hardware". It is almost as if many aspects of development are halted for the whole first year of life so that near-perfect conditions for the continuation of brain development can be provided out of the womb.

Because our brains develop more slowly, they are more open to learning than is the case with any other animal species. Our brain at birth is largely "empty", and there is plenty of space for "uploading new software" in it. The brain of a chimpanzee is "delivered", three quarters full, so it starts with a substantial advantage but soon reaches the limits of its capacity for acquiring new skills and knowledge. Our brains are "full" with "software" only up to a quarter of their capacity, so we start behind but can write symphonies and send vehicles to Mars.

If we are born with the minimum of software necessary for survival, it is safe to presume that whatever is there must be the core of who we are as a species and as individuals, and whatever is not there is less urgently needed and can be lived without or abandoned if necessary. This core consists of:

- Reflexes that are basic like breathing, swallowing, Babinsky, etc.
- Reflexes that will soon disappear, like sucking, Moro, grasping, all necessary for survival
- The capacity to recognise your mother almost from the first moment—by the smell of her milk from as early as three days after birth (Macfarlane, 1975).[7] Paying attention to drawings of a human face in the first minutes of life
- A strong preference for the mother's voice.

Human infants are also uniquely capable of imitating movements and facial expressions, which contributes strongly to the feeling of belonging and to social learning (for details see Meltzoff et al., 1999; Meltzoff & Prinz, 2002): they can imitate adults as early as twenty minutes after birth, but only with their intentional gestures, not, for instance, sneezing; the extraordinary plasticity of the brain develops synapses and neural pathways with unbelievable speed when human babies

---

[7] It also helps if babies are not washed immediately after birth, because they learn most by smelling. Experiments show that newborns move towards the mother's breast that is not washed and still has amniotic fluid on it (Music, 2010, pp. 24–28).

are exposed to intense and diverse physical stimulation; the central importance of mutuality is reflected in an even more extraordinary plasticity and perceptiveness for social interaction. This became even more obvious after the incidental discovery at the University of Parma of the so-called mirror neurons, a large section of our motor cortex that fires like we are performing some action when we are merely observing someone performing it. This discovery provided empirical evidence for much of the psychoanalytic theorising coming from the interpersonal tradition.

There is now solid empirical evidence for the aforementioned capacity of human infants to regulate social interaction: initiate it through establishing eye contact, smiling, crying, or approaching; maintain it through smiling, moving towards, raising arms; and terminate it through turning the head away, breaking the eye contact, raising hands in front of the face (Beebe et al., 2016).

The same is true of the capacity termed implicit relational knowing (Stern et al., 1988): despite the inborn preparedness of the human brain to process social interaction in a superior way, the details of it must be negotiated in each individual dyad. For instance, how loud should the baby cry for the mother to wake up and take her in the arms or how loud should the mother sing a lullaby so that the baby will fall asleep. This will hypothetically form the basis of all the adult social skills.

The brain has evolved under the enormous influence of environmental and societal changes, and it is still our most receptive organ. All of that was made possible by (early) social interactions as much as the brain makes interacting possible. Considering the human brain a "biological basis" of behaviour or disorders is the saddest of all reductionist fallacies.[8]

> The brain is formed by mental life … it is not a creator, but a relational organ: it is embedded in the meaningful interactions of a living being with its environment. It mediates and enables these interactive processes, but it is in turn also continuously formed and restructured by them. (Fuchs, 2011, pp. 197–198)

Natural collaborators

What humans have and other species do not is the capacity to collaborate via joint attention and "intention reading":

> The infant is attending not only to the adult's attention to the object, but also to the adult's attention to her attention to the object, and to the adult's attention to her attention to the adult's attention to the object, and so on. It is not that the infant engages in this kind of recursive thinking explicitly, but that the underlying structure of joint attention means that they both know together that they are both attending to the same thing. They are sharing experience. (Tomasello, 2019, p. 56; see also Tomasello & Farrar, 1986)

---

[8] Like believing that babies are born full of hatred is the saddest of all psychoanalytic misconceptions.

Our core nature is that we are animals capable of collaborating (Tomasello, 2009); our consciousness a mere fetishised by-product of this capability.[9] We can plan together, organise, make traps, join forces, brainstorm thanks to the capacity for "intention reading". That is not only the feature that makes us more human than our primate relatives, and that has enabled us to conquer this planet (and possibly destroy much of the life on it) but is also what we developed to fight against the death threats in the form of tigers, ice, or electricity.

This is why we are too fragile to survive unable to observe others. The ideas of primary narcissism or primary autism, developed by Freud, Klein, Winnicott, or Mahler, have been refuted by recent empirical research. The situation is more accurately described as sensory separation with moments of emotional merger (Mitchell, 2014): infants can observe others as separate entities but whenever anxiety gets intense crave comfort that comes from becoming one unit with the mother emotionally.

Such is the importance of uninterrupted exchange with others, especially in the sensitive developmental periods, that mothers respond to their infants' social interaction signals in one sixth of a second (Beebe et al., 1977).

Internal working models

The core of the more psychoanalytic side of the attachment theory is Bowlby's idea about internal working models (IWMs). In his efforts to develop a more scientific form of object relations theory, Bowlby focused on observation as his primary research method, and described the secure base—a social object, an actual person and not an unconscious fantasy, capable of providing to the infant the feeling of security and the encouragement to explore. When anxious, hungry, hurt, a child will signal that she needs comfort. When comforted, she will be happy to return to exploration, alone or with other children.

The psychoanalytic part comes in when Bowlby introduces the idea that the secure base is gradually internalised and transformed into IWMs. The feeling of security will become the inner sense of personal value and likeability, which he termed the IWM of the self, and boldness to explore will turn into the inner sense of trust in and respect for others, or the IWM of the other. These two are, by definition, the sets of expectations about how all future relationships are going to develop. If my caregivers exaggerated in any direction, due to personally or culturally preferred parental practices, I might expect everyone will choose friends and partners or raise my children in accordance with this.

This narrative can also be seen as centred on loneliness. Thus, positive IWMs and secure attachment are related to confidence that loneliness is not a destiny, that in the Strange Situation the mother will return, and the stranger is not dangerous. That, proverbially, even if I am alone, I am not in bad company.

---

[9] One could also advocate that psychoanalysis would find its research agenda much better if it focused on studying this capacity for collaboration and the unconscious as one of its aspects.

LONELINESS AND INSECURE ATTACHMENT 193

Insecure attachment, on the other hand, is not only related to one's current experience of loneliness but also to the lack of hope that loneliness will be overcome ultimately. It is very often a reaction to being left alone too often, for too long, and/or too early.

Once I had a client who worked from the apartment where she lived alone, left mostly for some solitary activities, while her couple of close friends lived on other continents, and romantic relationships ended before she would manage to understand that she had developed any feelings.

Quite some time into the therapy, and we were meeting two or three times per week, she mentioned a specific childhood game. At probably four years of age, she would leave the house and hide in a large garden. (I have no idea whether it was objectively large, or it looked so to a little girl.) At least in later iterations, this was well planned, and she would bring bread, peanut butter, and cutlery. She then waited to be discovered by her parents and siblings, probably hoping the hide-and-seek would turn into a happy family picnic. Every time, however, she would be sorely disappointed, as no one ever showed up. Worse still, once she gave up and returned inside, it was obvious no one had even noticed her absence. She would then silently go to her room and entertain herself, luckily, most often by reading. Until she gave up.

Loneliness can also be a consequence of low parental attunement, which leads to feelings of abandonment and despair, and can motivate a young person to repeat the most painful blows.

Martin used to be the joy of his family, class, and every party he was invited to. Cute, extraordinarily witty, and with an exceptional sense of humour, he could not have been more popular.

Unfortunately for me, this had all disappeared at least fifteen years before I first met him. The person I saw was tense, without concentration, with problems keeping a steady job, effeminate, promiscuous, a passionate member of the Berlin nightclub scene, where he would sometimes spend sixty hours at a time, with the help of substances that reset the brain quite heavily.

He liked his way of living, but needed help focusing, especially when it came to work. Also, it happened, maybe once or twice a month, that he could not fall asleep for hours. Nothing happened; nothing was of help. Already in bed and with lights off, he would "see" his room burn with flames that he could not do anything against. That was all.

He did not like talking about his past. He reluctantly told me that his family relationships were terrible, which was an additional reason to move to Berlin. Expectedly, it turned out they were the source of pain and anger that burned like a consuming fire.

By the age of fourteen, Martin had no doubts that he was gay. He also felt it was natural to be candid about it with his parents. Coming out to his mother, however, was a disaster. She got furious, then desperate. The father told him something like "In this house, we do not accept gay", decided to punish him, probably thinking it was a childish whim. The boy found no other options but to avoid the parents and all social events that involved family and/or family friends. He spent workdays in his room surfing or chatting. Every Friday after school, which he could not care less about, he would take a bus from Brno to Vienna and return early on Monday mornings, full of alcohol and drugs, and having spent nights with significantly older boyfriends.

I felt he had been homeless in what he described as a large, comfortable house. The worst thing was that no one ever asked where he was and what he did over the weekends. And, to put it simply, he only looked for protection of affectionate older persons, although they, alas, probably did not see in him anything but the trait his parents refused to recognise—that he was a gay boy.

A set of unfortunate circumstances can, of course, also be internalised and shape our emotional lives in a powerful way.

A young woman contacted me when she needed help with overcoming a painful breakup. She could not understand why things like that happened when she was very devoted, loyal, and observant of the partner's needs and wishes.

It soon turned out that she had many friends and behaved similarly towards them. Since she did not have regular work time, she was always available to provide a helping hand, listen, and advise. She was happy that some of her friends had told her she would be an excellent psychologist.

We then discovered that the relationships were devoid of reciprocity: she never spoke about herself and never asked to be heard.

She listed various possible reasons for this: insecurity, low self-esteem, seductiveness, guilt that she lived comfortably. I did not think any of these could explain this form of chronic loneliness (an altruist's loneliness?).

Telling me about her worries related to her cognitive capacities, she mentioned that some doctors had found her autistic as a small child. This sounded utterly wrong! She explained it away with another detail from her medical history: due to an unrecognised ear condition, she barely heard anything until the age of three. And now, she not only enjoyed listening, but she learned how to use it to prevent rejection and labelling.

Learning how to collaborate in the world full of others

Pervasive, existential aloneness can thus be seen as a consequence of failure in understanding social interaction signals that the other persons sometimes send in a split second and replying to them with accuracy and matching speed. This is inevitable even in the best synchronised mother–infant dyads, given that their exchange is extremely urgent and communication channels fragile. The idea of IWMs may help us understand various aspects of the relationship between unconscious expectations we have of other people and the experience of aloneness:

- Disorganised attachment, the most problematic pattern, may be a reaction to the complete lack of predictability in the together-alone dynamic, so that the child faced with aloneness does everything at the same moment or nothing at all.
- Child abuse, be it physical, verbal, or sexual, can be described as an overwhelming malignant togetherness, where the victim is sometimes even forever haunted by the presence of the perpetrator in her mind.
- Neglect, on the other hand, leads to an overwhelming aloneness, which one may lose hope will ever be overcome.
- When it comes to parental strategies, secure attachment includes gradual, often undeliberate, preparation for solitude, in terms of encouraging children to be autonomous and independent. Opposite to this, "helicopter parenting" makes preparations for solitude impossible.

All these considerations are, however, limited to dyadic processes, to the relationship a child has with one of her caregivers, and the context of development is certainly not limited to that.

Every child, very early in his or her development, must look for an, as it were, entrance ticket to the social worlds of adults and that of her peers (this can be the same "ticket", but sometimes two or more are needed). One child will be recognised as humorous and will repeatedly be invited to share new jokes. Others can sing well, be smart, pretty, sporty. Whatever the specific trait, the child will rely on it when recognition, acceptance, or narcissistic gratifications are needed: for instance, in the case of frustration, failure, jealousy, or abandonment.

In large families, younger children will discover that "some tickets are already sold", and, wishing to escape the shadow(s) of the older one(s), they will develop traits not already prominent in their elder siblings. Of course, the more siblings one has, the tighter the space for his or her self-expression gets. For this reason, say, a fifth child can become a rebel, and draw the attention of adults in that way. The same could be the case with aggressive behaviour, low school achievement, and being a "problematic child" in general. In many families, unfortunately, children are not able to find any other outlet but chronic illness. Because they develop a medical condition, they receive the attention of their parents and other adults, who talk to them in a concerned way, seriously, in a soft, caring tone.

All these strategies are precious, because they defend from loneliness and isolation. They are a child's way to acquire feelings, on one level, of being accepted, protected, belonging, instead of neglected or ridiculed, and on the other level, in favourable cases, of being appreciated, seen as promising, respected.

Some children, however, cannot find this clue and never receive continuous and predictable recognition from adults and peers, for one or more of the numerous possible reasons:

- They do not understand social signals because their intelligence is limited.
- As infants and toddlers they have very "difficult" temperaments that adults struggle to contain.
- Caregivers may give social cues that are so unpredictable that children cannot learn, for instance, the connection between a mental state, behaviour, and punishment or reward.
- Abuse, trauma, and neglect are, unfortunately, quite widespread and lead to severe problems in emotional development (Dimitrijević, 2015; Perry & Szalavitz, 2006).
- They may have been born after an elder sibling had died, and they get the role of a replacement child (Anisfeld & Richards, 2000), who does not get the opportunity to develop his or her own identity.[10]

In each of the listed cases, the child will not have the opportunity to regularly practise emotional expression and recognition, or initiating, moderating, and terminating social interactions. And, as was mentioned previously, these sets of social skills, also called implicit relational knowing, can only be acquired through constant practice, for years, dozens of times each day.

We now know that fundamental childhood loneliness is predictive of later aggressive behaviour, substance abuse, delinquency, criminal behaviour, or mental disorders. We have ample research evidence of its connections with intelligence, language acquisition, theory of mind, mental health, and much more (Banjac et al., 2013; Dimitrijević et al., 2013).

Although the discourses of neurophysiological malfunctions and malignant psychological experiences may be more frequently heard, mental disorders and their outcomes are obviously connected to social causes. Sociology of mental disorders is a very well-established research discipline, with scientific journals or university departments fully focused on it (see Cockerham, 2010). We often do not pay enough attention to its achievements, but it has located and analysed various factors that connect loneliness and mental disorders,[11] where both are sometimes causes and at other times consequences. The most prominent among them are:

- Stigmatisation, which isolates a person with a mental disorder from the rest of the community, thus quite possibly making the problem still worse (Clay, 2005; Timimi, 2014). It is worth noting that the mentally ill are the only group stigmatised in every known community and historical period. The gravest outcomes are related to auto-stigmatisation, which can completely destroy self-respect (Link & Phelan, 1999).
- It is very well known, at least since Goffman's book on asylums (1961) that old-fashioned mental healthcare institutions, totalitarian in their nature yet still present in most European countries, do not help their inmates but only force them to adapt to a new set of social rules that strips them of their personal identities.

---

[10] This was the case with several famous artists, like Rainer Maria Rilke and Salvador Dalí.

[11] Of course, there are many other social factors connected to mental disorders, like poverty, illiteracy, immigration, social class, etc.

- Iatrogenic (Hadley & Strupp, 1976) or re-traumatising (Dimitrijević, 2021) effects of psychotherapy.
- Consequences of the incapacity to understand residual, unwritten rules as a potential cause of mental disorders (Scheff, 1999).

Social isolation for its part only deepens one's incapacity to understand oneself, so that the inner loneliness becomes more obvious and threatening. As discussed in the classic paper by Frieda Fromm-Reichmann (see Hornstein, Chapter 15, this volume), this inescapable loneliness is at least connected to various mental disorders and may even be at their core:

- As many as 91 per cent of heroin addicts in one clinical sample were classified as insecurely attached (Grubač et al., 2011), making it obvious that no one chooses a substance when there are persons available and accessible.
- Patients with somatoform and psychosomatic disorders, compared to a control group, show significantly less developed capacities for understanding the emotional processes of themselves and others as well as significantly higher negative IWMs of self, so they tend to be less involved in social relationships and to experience more problems with controlling their impulses (Božović et al., 2013).
- Juvenile offenders, especially boys, have lower scores on the measures of empathy and reflective functioning (Milojević, & Dimitrijević, 2014; Protić et al., 2020).
- Veterans of wars in the former Yugoslavia develop PTSD significantly more rarely, compared to a control group, if they are insecurely attached (Berleković & Dimitrijević, 2018).

In accord with this are also the basics of the treatment for all of these conditions. Even when someone is willing to listen, it would take the lonely much time to believe that there is hope they could reach others, and then even more time to learn how to understand and express themselves, without which this gap cannot be bridged.

Conclusion

Emotional reactions to aloneness must be put into a wider, social perspective, beyond what psychoanalysis and psychology are usually ready to take into consideration. Nothing more natural than to rely, first, on the evolutionary theory, the "backbone" of all life sciences. Loneliness, seen in this way, is the by-product of the dangers life in nature is full of. We have had to learn how to prevent and avoid it, so much so that the results of this learning are the social skills—and this is the second wider perspective—now so deeply ingrained that we are born with them and they are the core of our nature. And when, for one reason or the other, we do not develop them or lose them along the way, this causes such profound pain that we may begin to feel not fully human.

References

Ainsworth, M. D., Blehar, M., Waters, E., & Wall, S. (1978). *Patterns of Attachment: Assessed in Strange Situations*. Hillsdale, NJ: Lawrence Erlbaum.

Anisfeld, L., & Richards, A. D. (2000). The replacement child: variations on a theme in history and psychoanalysis. *Psychoanalytic Study of the Child, 55*: 301–318.

Banjac, S., Altaras Dimitrijević, A., & Dimitrijević, A. (2013). Attachment, mentalization and intelligence in adolescence. *Psihološka istraživanja, 16*(2): 175–190.

Bartels, A., & Zeki, S. (2004). The neural correlates of maternal and romantic love. *Neuroimage, 21*(3): 1155–1166.

Beebe, B., Cohen, P., Lachmann, F., & Yothers, D. I. (2016). *The Mother–Infant Interaction Picture Book: Origins of Attachment*. New York: W. W. Norton.

Beebe, B., Lachmann, F., & Jaffe, J. (1997). Mother–infant interaction structures and presymbolic self- and object representations. *Psychoanalytic Dialogues, 7*(2): 133–182.

Berleković, V., & Dimitrijević, A. (2018). Attachment patterns differentiate between war veterans with and without PTSD. In: A. Hamburger (Ed.), *Trauma, Trust, Memory: Psychoanalytic Approaches to Social Trauma*. London: Karnac.

Bowlby, J. (1969). *Attachment and Loss, Vol. 1*. London: Penguin.

Božović, M., Dimitrijević, A., & Milojević, S. (2013, July 28–August 1). Attachment and mentalization in persons with psychosomatic and somatoform disorders [conference presentation]. International Psychoanalytical Association Conference, Prague, Czech Republic.

Clay, S. (Ed.) (2005). *On Our Own, Together: Peer Programs for People with Mental Illness*. Nashville, TN: Vanderbilt University Press.

Cockerham, W. C. (2010). *Sociology of Mental Disorder*. London: Routledge.

Dimitrijević, A. (2015). Trauma as neglected factor in the etiology of mental disorders. *Sociologija, 57*(2): 286–299.

Dimitrijević, A. (2021). Silence and silencing of the traumatised. In: A. Dimitrijevic & M. B. Buchholz (Eds.), *Silence and Silencing in Psychoanalysis: Cultural, Clinical and Research Perspectives*. London: Routledge.

Dimitrijević, A., Altaras Dimitrijević, A., & Jolić Marjanović, Z. (2013). An examination of the relationship between intelligence and attachment in adulthood. *InPACT, 2013*: 21–25.

Freud, S. (1905d). *Three Essays on the Theory of Sexuality*. S. E., 7: 123–246. London: Hogarth.

Freud, S. (1920g). *Beyond The Pleasure Principle*. S. E., 18: 1–64. London: Hogarth.

Fuchs, T. (2011). The brain—a mediating organ. *Journal of Consciousness Studies, 18*(7–8): 196–221.

Goffman, E. (1961). *Asylums: Essays on the Social Situation of Mental Patients and Other Inmates*. Chicago, IL: Aldine Transaction, 1968.

Grubač, K., Dimitrijević, A., & Hanak, N. (2011, August 19–21). Attachment and heroin addiction [conference presentation], "Attachment—the importance of intimate relationships from the cradle to the grave". Oslo, Norway.

Hadley, S. W., & Strupp, H. H. (1976). Contemporary views of negative effects in psychotherapy: an integrated account. *Archives of General Psychiatry, 33*(11): 1291–1302.

Kächele, H. (2009). A Hungarian precursor of attachment theory: Ferenczi's successor, Imre Hermann. *American Imago, 66*(4): 419–426.

Link, B. G., & Phelan, J. C. (1999). The labeling theory of mental disorder (II): the consequences of labeling. In: A. V. Horwitz & T. L. Scheid (Eds.), *A Handbook for the Study of Mental Health: Social Contexts, Theories, and Systems* (pp. 361–376). Cambridge: Cambridge University Press.

Macfarlane, A. (1975). Olfaction in the development of social preferences in the human neonate. *Parent–Infant Interaction, 33*: 103–113.

Meltzoff, A. N., Gopnik, A., & Repacholi, B. M. (1999). Toddlers' understanding of intentions, desires and emotions: explorations of the dark ages. In: P. D. Zelazo, J. W. Astington, & D. R. Olson (Eds.), *Developing Theories of Intention: Social Understanding and Self- Control* (pp. 17–42). Mahwah, NJ: Lawrence Erlbaum.

Meltzoff, A. N., & Prinz, W. (2002). *The Imitative Mind: Development, Evolution, and Brain Bases.* Cambridge: Cambridge University Press.

Milojević, S., & Dimitrijević, A. (2014). Empathic capacity in convicted delinquent minors. *Psihologija, 47*(1): 65–79.

Mitchell, S. A. (2014). *Relationality: From Attachment to Intersubjectivity.* London: Routledge.

Music, G. (2010). *Nurturing Natures: Attachment and Children's Emotional, Sociocultural and Brain Development* (2nd edn.). London: Routledge, 2016.

Perry, B. D., & Szalavitz, M. (2006). *The Boy Who Was Raised as a Dog: And Other Stories from a Child Psychiatrist's Notebook—What Traumatized Children Can Teach Us about Loss, Love, and Healing.* New York: Basic Books.

Protić, S., Wittmann, L., Taubner, S., & Dimitrijević, A. (2020). Differences in attachment dimensions and reflective functioning between traumatized juvenile offenders and maltreated non-delinquent adolescents from care services. *Child Abuse and Neglect, 103*: 104420. https://doi.org/10.1016/j.chiabu.2020.104420.

Scheff, T. J. (1999). *Being Mentally Ill: A Sociological Theory*, 3rd edn. New York: Aldine de Gruyter.

Stern, D. N., Bruschweiler-Stern, N., Harrison, A. M., Lyons-Ruth, K., Morgan, A. C., Nahum, J. P., & Tronick, E. Z. (1998). The process of therapeutic change involving implicit knowledge: some implications of developmental observations for adult psychotherapy. *Infant Mental Health Journal: Official Publication of the World Association for Infant Mental Health, 19*(3): 300–308.

Sulloway, F. J. (1992). *Freud, Biologist of the Mind: Beyond the Psychoanalytic Legend.* Cambridge, MA: Harvard University Press.

Suomi, S. J. (1999). Developmental trajectories, early experiences, and community consequences: Lessons from studies with rhesus monkeys. In: D. P. Keating & C. Hertzman (Eds.), Developmental Health and the Wealth of Nations: Social, Biological, and Educational Dynamics (pp. 185–200). New York: Guilford.

Timimi, S. (2014). No more psychiatric labels: why formal psychiatric diagnostic systems should be abolished. *International Journal of Clinical and Health Psychology, 14*(3): 208–215.

Tomasello, M. (2009). *Why We Cooperate*. Cambridge, MA: MIT Press.

Tomasello, M. (2019). *Becoming Human*. Cambridge, MA: Harvard University Press.

Tomasello, M., & Farrar, M. J. (1986). Joint attention and early language. *Child Development, 57*(6): 1454–1463.

Van der Horst, F. C., & Van der Veer, R. (2008). Loneliness in infancy: Harry Harlow, John Bowlby and issues of separation. *Integrative Psychological and Behavioral Science, 42*(4): 325–335.

CHAPTER 11

Epidemiology of loneliness

Eva M. Klein*, Mareike Ernst*, Manfred E. Beutel, and Elmar Brähler

General introduction

In recent years, loneliness has come to the fore of (mental) health research. The recognition of loneliness as an important public health issue found expression in the appointment of the UK's first minister for loneliness (Cacioppo & Cacioppo, 2018). Over the last few years, across several countries increasing attention has been paid to the prevention and reduction of loneliness in the general population.

As a modifiable risk factor, loneliness could be targeted by prevention and intervention efforts in order to foster the individual's well-being and to diminish health care costs for society as a whole. Therefore, it is important to identify vulnerable populations, for example, through organised screening efforts or primary care providers' greater awareness of risk constellations.

In the following, we will briefly define loneliness and distinguish it from important, related constructs. An overview of epidemiological research exploring loneliness in the general population is provided, followed by a critical reflection of potential reporting biases and socialisation-related aspects shaping loneliness over the lifespan.

Definition of the term loneliness

Humans are inherently social beings who strive to feel close to others. While belonging to a social group was crucial for survival in our evolutionary past (e.g. Watt & Panksepp, 2009), we still live together in the form of families, communities, and other relationships today. Within

---

* Joint first authors.

these relationships, we depend on others—not just in order to master everyday challenges, but also to feel closeness and appreciation (Baumeister & Leary, 1995; Carver et al., 1989). However, short periods of being alone are a normal part of life and might even be perceived as invigorating (Long & Averill, 2003). This aspect characterises the experience of solitude which has been described as a pleasant state related to feelings of being free, spirituality, and the emergence of creativity. Loneliness, on the other hand, is defined as a subjective discrepancy between the social connections one desires and those that are currently available in the environment. This mismatch entails dysphoric emotional states (Mushtaq et al., 2014; Perlman & Peplau, 1984). Hence, being alone does not necessarily evoke feelings of loneliness, while being together with others does not always engender feelings of connectedness or emotional fulfilment. Thus, loneliness is a psychological condition rather than the mere lack of the physical presence of other people.

Differentiation from other (albeit closely related) concepts

Given the large amount of empirical research that has addressed the ramifications of loneliness in recent years, it is particularly important to distinguish the term from related constructs. For one, loneliness should not be conflated with (the absence of) *social support*. Social support has different facets: *structural* aspects of social support comprise objective indicators such as living situation (e.g. alone or in a shared household), marital and relationship status, and the size of a person's social network (e.g. the number of family members, co-workers, and friends one meets regularly). Indeed, such characteristics were associated with reports of loneliness in previous studies (see also below). For instance, loneliness occurred four times as often among those living alone (Beutel, Klein et al., 2017). However, one can certainly feel lonely even—or especially—in the company of others (Cacioppo et al., 2009). Hawkley and Cacioppo (2010) have pointed out that loneliness concerns the *quality* of relationship experiences rather than the *quantity*. Along these lines, previous research showed that the quality of a person's social network had stronger associations with loneliness than its size (Solmi et al., 2020).

Second, social support comprises *functional* features which relate to an individual's perceived or anticipated level of support by their environment. Thus, common assessment methods (such as, for example, the *Brief Social Support Scale* (Beutel, Brähler et al., 2017)) also give insight into a person's mental representations of their social environment, for example, whether others will be available for them. This subjective aspect represents a parallel to the complex subjective state that is loneliness; for example, the negative emotions co-occurring with the subjective evaluation that one's social needs are not being met.

This might also apply to individuals living in social isolation. Social isolation describes a living situation with little contact to other people. Like loneliness, it has also been construed as both a cause and a consequence of psychological morbidity. However, the term in itself does not directly refer to negative emotional states. Similar to social support, there are measurement approaches that distinguish objective and subjective aspects of the construct. The former focuses on living situations and numbers of social contacts, whereas the latter is also referred to as perceived social isolation (abbreviated as PSI) (Cacioppo & Cacioppo, 2014). Earliest investigations described it as "a chronic distress without redeeming features" (Weiss, 1973). Thus, it is used congruently with loneliness.

From a research standpoint, it appears sensible to study both objective-structural as well as subjective-emotional aspects; for example, living circumstances and loneliness and their interdependence (Beller & Wagner, 2018).

Loneliness in the general population: who reports to feel lonely?

Loneliness is a common phenomenon, albeit it is a transient experience for most people (Hawkley & Capitanio, 2010; Qualter et al., 2015). In the context of previous empirical studies that explored loneliness in the general population, 10–40 per cent reported some degrees of loneliness (Beutel, Klein et al., 2017) whereas the prevalence of chronic loneliness ranged from 15–30 per cent (Hawkley & Cacioppo, 2010). The literature has highlighted links between the degree of loneliness and structural and socio-demographic aspects, with the majority of research endeavours focusing on the association with gender and higher age. Growing evidence underscores the importance of acknowledging the intersectionality of age and gender in order to understand why people might feel lonely (Barreto et al., 2020; Klein et al., 2021). Additionally, several other socio-demographic and health related variables have been proposed as potential risk factors for loneliness. The following section presents a selection of these findings.

Gender and age

The association between gender and loneliness has been widely investigated, often without a theoretical hypothesis (Maes et al., 2019). The results of large-scale epidemiological studies were inconsistent: within representative samples, women were more likely than men to report loneliness (Beutel, Klein et al., 2017; Pinquart & Sörensen, 2001b). This observation mirrored previous results from the German Socio-Economic Panel (SOEP) (Luhmann & Hawkley, 2016), albeit the differences were small. In contrast, there were also reports of larger proportions of lonely men compared to women (Borys & Perlman, 1985; Nicolaisen & Thorsen, 2014). A recent cross-cultural study showed that young men living in individualistic cultures had the highest risk of experiencing loneliness (Barreto et al., 2020). Based on a meta-analysis, men felt slightly lonelier than women. However, due to the marginal effect size, the authors did not confirm statistically significant differences between women and men in their reported degree of loneliness (Maes et al., 2019).

According to common and persistent stereotypes, loneliness has been construed as a problem mainly affecting the elderly. However, research on loneliness over the lifespan counteracts this myth. Not only was loneliness reported by individuals of all ages; but an inverted u-shaped association between loneliness and age has been established (Pinquart & Sörensen,

2001a; Qualter et al., 2015). Loneliness peaked in adolescence, declined in middle adulthood, and increased again in late adulthood (Luhmann & Hawkley, 2016). The reasons for feeling lonely varied between age groups. For instance, social contacts and the desire for being acknowledged by peers becomes especially salient in puberty and adolescence, where a host of studies locate the first peak in the prevalence of loneliness (Hawkley & Capitanio, 2015). Explaining factors of loneliness in the elderly, however, are retirement, widowhood, loss of long-time social network and roles, as well as reduced physical health (Lee et al., 2020). Moreover, the elderly have developed greater coping skills to adjust adequately to solitude compared to adolescents (Mushtaq et al., 2014). While these factors generally co-occur within a specific life period, research has proposed a clear intersection between age and gender to explain the variance in loneliness. For instance, the often replicated finding that women in late adulthood reported higher levels of loneliness might be explained by the fact that women have on average a longer life expectancy and therefore a stronger probability to experience loneliness after the death of a spouse. By contrast, men showed a peak of loneliness in middle age (Klein et al., 2021). Higher divorce rates during this period of time may affect men's feelings of loneliness particularly strongly as they have a smaller social network outside their marriage than women (Kposowa, 2000). In addition, Luhmann and Hawkley (2016) identified work status, income, and relationship status as age-specific risk factors for loneliness in middle age. As economic success was found to be more important for men than women (Pinquart & Sörensen, 2001b), these factors might have a substantial impact on loneliness among middle-aged men. Whereas there undoubtedly are universal risk factors for loneliness over the entire lifespan, the existing body of research has recognised specific age-related factors which, in turn, are related to gender (Lasgaard et al., 2016; Luhmann & Hawkley, 2016; Qualter et al., 2015). Therefore, young adults who do not fulfil age-normative expectations, for example, having a partner, starting a family, gaining economic independence, and pursuing a professional career (Luhmann & Hawkley, 2016), might be particularly vulnerable to loneliness (Maes et al., 2019). However, beyond age-normative expectations, also a gender-normative perspective has to be taken into account to critically discuss and interpret different levels of loneliness across age and gender.

Relationship status and living arrangements

Not surprisingly, much research on loneliness has investigated characteristics and structural components of the person's social relationships and network as predictors of feeling lonely. Whereas a positive marital relationship was protective against loneliness (Hawkley et al., 2008), singles were vulnerable for high levels of loneliness (Buecker et al., 2020). Living alone was linked to loneliness in several studies (e.g. Beutel, Klein et al., 2017). However, there was no difference in loneliness among people living with their partner compared to those who had a partner but did not share a household (Buecker et al., 2020). Further, the relationship between loneliness, gender, and living alone seems to be complex as the effects of living without a partner were particularly strong for young women and middle-aged men (Beutel, Klein et al., 2017). Apart from relationship status, the quantity of social contact with friends and relatives decreased with a higher degree of loneliness (Buecker et al., 2020).

Other socio-demographic factors

Results of population-based samples have consistently shown that individuals with lower *socio-economic status* were more often affected by feelings of loneliness (Buecker et al., 2020). Income seemed to be a more important predictor of loneliness than educational attainment (Buecker et al., 2020). Regarding *employment status*, the higher vulnerability to loneliness among unemployed people has been replicated numerous times (Beutel, Klein et al., 2017; Buecker et al., 2020). Employment often provides social contacts and the feeling of being part of a (working) group. In line with this finding, the loss of employment in the past year predicted higher levels of loneliness five years later (Tibubos et al., under review). Moreover, *minority status* has been investigated in loneliness research with first-generation immigrants scoring higher on loneliness compared to the majority population (Eyerund & Orth, 2019). Experiences of discrimination and limited access to social participation, for example, due to language barriers, have been proposed as specific risk factors for loneliness among minority groups. Moreover, feelings of loneliness could be shaped by cultural differences between the country of origin and the country of residence. In fact, *cultures* differ with respect to the valuation of social relationships, including the conception of what kind and extent of social interaction is desirable or normal. While we can assume that the cultural surroundings influence personal ascertainment of loneliness, respective cross-cultural comparisons (e.g. between individualistic and collectivist countries) are difficult as they are confounded by countries' diverging age structures, languages, and economic situation (Barreto et al., 2020).

In a recent nationally representative German SOEP Study ($N = 17,602$), Buecker and colleagues (2020) went beyond the individual level by exploring the *regional distribution* of loneliness. Although individual-level characteristics had a stronger impact on the level of loneliness, the study revealed differences in loneliness across geographical regions. Characteristics of the region such as neighbourhood relations, longer walking distance to public parks, as well as the lack of sports and leisure facilities were associated with loneliness. The authors concluded that the place of residence also determined the degree of loneliness. Hence, not only risk populations with respect to personal characteristics, but also geographical areas with comparatively high rates of loneliness should be considered for public health strategies.

Health

Social relationships contribute enormously to general well-being. Over the last decade, research has studied the detrimental impact of loneliness on both physical and mental health.

Loneliness has been associated with an increased mortality rate (Holt-Lunstad et al., 2015), and the increased morbidity and mortality from chronic diseases (Friedler et al., 2015). Identifying risk groups, studies consistently showed higher prevalence rates of loneliness in participants suffering from mental disorders. A broad spectrum of symptoms has been linked to loneliness such as depression, anxiety, psychotic disorders, and personality disorders (e.g. Liebke et al., 2017; Sündermann et al., 2014). Moreover, population-based samples indicated a positive association between loneliness and suicidal ideation (Ernst et al., 2021b) which was characterised be a dose-response relation (Stickley & Koyanagi, 2016). For example, Beutel, Klein et al. (2017) found that more than half of the participants with severe loneliness reported depression symptoms compared to 5 per cent in the group of participants without loneliness. Suicidal ideation increased dramatically from 6 per cent to 42 per cent with a higher degree of loneliness. One longitudinal study of adults aged fifty years and older showed that loneliness was related to an increased risk for depression symptoms over a time period of twelve years, even after controlling for other social variables and genetic confounders (Lee et al., 2020). Researchers have suggested behavioural, physiological, and psychological mechanisms as three main pathways how loneliness may affect health (Valtorta et al., 2016): 1) health risk-behaviour like smoking and physical inactivity, 2) high blood pressure and defective immune functioning, and 3) psychological factors such as lower self-esteem and self-efficacy. For example, several studies found correlations between feeling lonely and health risk behaviour such as physical inactivity and smoking (Beutel, Klein et al., 2017; Solmi et al., 2020). However, studies which have explicitly studied these variables as causal mechanisms between loneliness and health are scarce.

The majority of research exploring the correlation of loneliness and mental health outcomes was cross-sectional and lacking any causal conclusion. Particularly the causal direction between depression and loneliness has been an issue of debate as both share common symptoms such as dysphoric states and feelings of helplessness (Mushtaq et al., 2014). Despite the overlap between loneliness and depression, they are distinct concepts (Lee et al., 2020). Based on a longitudinal study in 11,915 individuals, Tibubos and colleagues (under review) tested the direction between depression and loneliness over the course of five years. Results revealed that depression symptoms impacted the risk of feeling lonely more strongly than vice versa. Hence, there is a risk that mental disorders lead to loneliness, for instance, due to social withdrawal and lower participation in society. Other studies found bidirectional relationships (Nuyen et al., 2019) or that loneliness was predictive of subsequent changes of depression symptoms, but not vice versa (Cacioppo et al., 2010).

While discussing the detrimental impact of loneliness on mental and physical health, it is important to bear in mind that loneliness is not a clinical illness or disorder. McLennan and Ulijaszek (2018) criticised the medicalisation of loneliness as a social issue. The authors argued that holistic approaches rather than a solely medical view, which carries the risk of narrowing the perspective, are required to adequately address loneliness and potential negative ramifications.

Stressful life events

Research has also explored the role of critical life events for explaining the inter-individual variance in loneliness. Stronger feelings of loneliness were related to having experienced larger numbers of stressful life events (Stickley & Koyanagi, 2016). More precisely, life events which implied far-reaching changes or reduced access to one's social network caused loneliness—such as unemployment, change in residence, divorce, or separation from a partner (Tibubos et al., under review). Beyond that, potentially traumatic life events can make it more difficult for those who are affected to form close bonds with others or to relate to their reality of life (Palgi et al., 2012), aggravating perceived loneliness. This might particularly be the case if the development of attachments has been disrupted during formative periods of life such as childhood and puberty. For instance, previous research has shown that comparatively high proportions of survivors of paediatric cancer reported loneliness (Ernst et al., 2021a). Qualitative studies gave insight into their subjective experience: they sensed that the potentially traumatic experience, although they had survived it—by decades, even—had set them apart from their peers in some way (Howard et al., 2014).

Critical commentary and conclusion

Within the literature on loneliness, methodological, psychological, and socialisation-related aspects have been discussed in order to explain differences in loneliness across age groups and according to other differences such as gender, living situation, or (mental) health.

The mixed results have also revealed that the method of inquiry (e.g. the number of items of the survey instrument (Pinquart & Sörensen, 2001a)) plays a role in shaping the observed outcomes. Along these lines, there is a growing acknowledgement of measurement invariance of questionnaires as a basic prerequisite for comparisons across age/other groups of people (e.g. Mund et al., 2020). In short, measurement invariance denotes that the same values in different groups (e.g. men and women) mean the same, and only then are interpretations of differences (e.g. that one group experiences more loneliness than the other group) permissible.

What is more, in interpreting empirical results, we need to bear in mind that people differ with regard to their willingness to disclose distressing emotional states both to themselves and to others. For instance, masculine or feminine gender role socialisation, respectively, is implicated in gender-dependent differences with respect to both internalising symptoms and loneliness (Dahlberg et al., 2015). Stereotypical images of the abilities and demeanour of women and men in a society influence a person's self-image and their behaviour (Stockard, 2006; West & Zimmerman, 1987). In particular, internalised traditionally masculine gender norms that emphasise strength, agency, and stoicism can hinder introspection and the communication of suffering (Vogel et al., 2011). Correspondingly, research has shown that women find it easier to admit that they see themselves as lonely (Borys & Perlman, 1985). However, as described above, within large-scale epidemiological studies, gender differences in expressed levels of loneliness were inconsistent (Beutel, Klein et al., 2017; Luhmann & Hawkley, 2016; Nicolaisen & Thorsen, 2014; Pinquart & Sörensen, 2001b). The study of socialisation-based gender differences is complicated by the fact that upbringing and societal standards shift over time, that is, younger men might have had different male role models while growing up and might have not been exposed to as rigid gender-role concepts as today's senior citizens (Wienclaw, 2011). As a consequence, they might find it easier to report loneliness than their fathers or grandfathers.

On the other hand, such cohort effects (e.g. differences that arise due to membership of a particular birth cohort, such as the Baby Boomers, and associated socialisation) are difficult to disentangle from age effects, especially in cross-sectional investigations. Age effects refer to changes that can be attributed to developmental-psychological and other ageing processes including, for example, changes in psychobiology. Longitudinal studies are the most valuable to detect them. For example, as people grow older, they may realise that they only need few, but close, friendships to be content (whereas in younger years, the same person might have felt inadequate if they did not fulfil, for example, teenage conceptions of being part of a large circle of friends (Ayalon et al., 2016)). This example shows that the individual perception of loneliness is a result of a complex interplay of culturally predominant, age- and cohort-dependent normative expectations, one's own life experiences, and other individual differences.

Health care professionals such as general practitioners who play an important role in detecting distress in their patients (e.g. in the context of suicide prevention) should thus be mindful of these influences. In particular, they need to consider biases that obscure a person's mental health crisis. For instance, empirical studies have suggested that reports of loneliness might be a more grave warning sign in men as they were associated with worse (mental) health outcomes (Rico-Uribe et al., 2018). While circumstances such as a person's living situation have been established as risk factors, health care professionals should reflect their own normative framework and not transfer their own ideas of how a person should live to their patients. Instead, health care professionals should keep an open mind and should thoroughly explore the individual experience, her or his social environment and personal need of both autonomy and bonding. Otherwise, there is also the risk to pathologise transient feelings of loneliness.

Lastly, prevention and intervention efforts are not necessarily located within the medical domain. While loneliness is certainly a matter of the subjective experience of the individual person, it is dependent on their (social) surrounding—which is why measures that go beyond the individual level and address communities and other structures of living together within our society could be particularly helpful (Masi et al., 2011). Fully elucidating the phenomenology, causes, and consequences of loneliness requires interdisciplinary collaborations that include professions such as (social) psychology, medicine, psychotherapy, social work, and politics.

References

Ayalon, L., Palgi, Y., Avidor, S., & Bodner, E. (2016). Accelerated increase and decrease in subjective age as a function of changes in loneliness and objective social indicators over a four-year period: results from the health and retirement study. *Aging and Mental Health, 20*(7): 743–751. https://doi.org/10.1080/13607863.2015.1035696.

Barreto, M., Victor, C., Hammond, C., Eccles, A., Richins, M. T., & Qualter, P. (2020). Loneliness around the world: Age, gender, and cultural differences in loneliness. *Personality and Individual Differences, 169*(3): 110066. https://doi.org/10.1016/j.paid.2020.110066.

Baumeister, R. F., & Leary, M. R. (1995). The need to belong: desire for interpersonal attachments as a fundamental human motive. *Psychological Bulletin, 117*(3): 497–529. https://doi.org/10.1037/0033-2909.117.3.497.

Beller, J., & Wagner, A. (2018). Disentangling loneliness: differential effects of subjective loneliness, network quality, network size, and living alone on physical, mental, and cognitive health. *Journal of Aging and Health, 30*(4): 521–539. https://doi.org/10.1177/0898264316685843.

Beutel, M. E., Brähler, E., Wiltink, J., Michal, M., Klein, E. M., Jünger, C., Wild, P. S., Münzel, T., Blettner, M., Lackner, K., Nickels, S., & Tibubos, A. N. (2017). Emotional and tangible social support in a German population-based sample: development and validation of the Brief Social Support Scale (BS6). *PLoS One, 12*(10): e0186516. https://doi.org/10.1038/s41598-017-13510-0.

Beutel, M. E., Klein, E. M., Brahler, E., Reiner, I., Junger, C., Michal, M., Wiltink, J., Wild, P. S., Munzel, T., Lackner, K. J., & Tibubos, A. N. (2017). Loneliness in the general population: prevalence, determinants and relations to mental health. *BMC Psychiatry, 17*(1): 97. https://doi.org/10.1186/s12888-017-1262-x.

Borys, S., & Perlman, D. (1985). Gender differences in loneliness. *Personality and Social Psychology Bulletin, 11*(1): 63–74. https://doi.org/10.1177/0146167285111006.

Buecker, S., Ebert, T., Götz, F. M., Entringer, T. M., & Luhmann, M. (2020). In a lonely place: investigating regional differences in loneliness. *Social Psychological and Personality Science, 12*(2): 147–155. https://doi.org/10.1177/1948550620912881.

Cacioppo, J. T., & Cacioppo, S. (2014). Social relationships and health: the toxic effects of perceived social isolation. *Social and Personality Psychology Compass, 8*(2): 58–72. https://doi.org/10.1111/spc3.12087.

Cacioppo, J. T., & Cacioppo, S. (2018). The growing problem of loneliness. *The Lancet, 391*(10119): 426. https://doi.org/10.1016/S0140-6736(18)30142-9.

Cacioppo, J. T., Fowler, J. H., & Christakis, N. A. (2009). Alone in the crowd: the structure and spread of loneliness in a large social network. *Journal of Personality and Social Psychology, 97*(6): 977. https://doi.org/10.1037/a0016076.

Cacioppo, J. T., Hawkley, L. C., & Thisted, R. A. (2010). Perceived social isolation makes me sad: 5-year cross-lagged analyses of loneliness and depressive symptomatology in the Chicago Health, Aging, and Social Relations Study. *Psychology and Aging, 25*(2): 453–463. https://doi.org/10.1037/a0017216.

Carver, C. S., Scheier, M. F., & Weintraub, J. K. (1989). Assessing coping strategies: a theoretically based approach. *Journal of Personality and Social Psychology, 56*(2): 267–283. https://doi.org/10.1037/0022-3514.56.2.267.

Dahlberg, L., Andersson, L., McKee, K. J., & Lennartsson, C. (2015). Predictors of loneliness among older women and men in Sweden: a national longitudinal study. *Aging & Mental Health, 19*(5): 409–417. https://doi.org/10.1080/13607863.2014.944091.

Ernst, M., Brähler, E., Wild, P. S., Faber, J., Merzenich, H., & Beutel, M. E. (2021a). Loneliness predicts suicidal ideation and anxiety symptoms in long-term childhood cancer survivors. *International Journal of Clinical and Health Psychology, 21*(1): 1–8. https://doi.org/10.1016/j.ijchp.2020.10.001.

Ernst, M., Klein, E. M., Beutel, M. E., & Brähler, E. (2021b). Gender-specific associations of loneliness and suicidal ideation in a representative population sample: Young, lonely men are particularly at risk. *Journal of affective disorders, 294,* 63–70.

Eyerund, T., & Orth, A. K. (2019). *Einsamkeit in Deutschland: aktuelle Entwicklung und soziodemographische Zusammenhänge.* Cologne, Germany: Institut der deutschen Wirtschaft.

Friedler, B., Crapser, J., & McCullough, L. (2015). One is the deadliest number: the detrimental effects of social isolation on cerebrovascular diseases and cognition. *Acta Neuropathologica, 129*(4): 493–509. https://doi.org/10.1007/s00401-014-1377-9.

Hawkley, L. C., & Cacioppo, J. T. (2010). Loneliness matters: a theoretical and empirical review of consequences and mechanisms. *Annals of Behavioral Medicine, 40*(2): 218–227. https://doi.org/10.1007/s12160-010-9210-8.

Hawkley, L. C., & Capitanio, J. P. (2015). Perceived social isolation, evolutionary fitness and health outcomes: a lifespan approach. *Philosophical Transactions of the Royal Society of London. Series B, Biological Sciences, 370*(1669). https://doi.org/10.1098/rstb.2014.0114.

Hawkley, L. C., Hughes, M. E., Waite, L. J., Masi, C. M., Thisted, R. A., & Cacioppo, J. T. (2008). From social structural factors to perceptions of relationship quality and loneliness: the Chicago health, aging, and social relations study. *Journals of Gerontology Series B: Psychological Sciences and Social Sciences, 63*(6): 375–384. https://doi.org/10.1093/geronb/63.6.S375.

Holt-Lunstad, J., Smith, T. B., Baker, M., Harris, T., & Stephenson, D. (2015). Loneliness and social isolation as risk factors for mortality: a meta-analytic review. *Perspectives on Psychological Science, 10*(2): 227–237. https://doi.org/10.1177/1745691614568352.

Howard, A. F., Tan de Bibiana, J., Smillie, K., Goddard, K., Pritchard, S., Olson, R., & Kazanjian, A. (2014). Trajectories of social isolation in adult survivors of childhood cancer. *Journal of Cancer Survivorship, 8*(1): 80–93. https://doi.org/10.1007/s11764-013-0321-7.

Klein, E. M., Zenger, M., Tibubos, A. N., Ernst, M., Reiner, I., Schmalbach, B., Brähler, E., & Beutel, M. (2021). Loneliness and its relation to mental health in the general population: validation and norm values of a brief measure. *Journal of Affective Disorders Reports, 4,* 100–120.

Kposowa, A. J. (2000). Marital status and suicide in the National Longitudinal Mortality Study. *Journal of Epidemiology & Community Health, 54*(4): 254–261. https://doi.org/10.1136/jech.54.4.254.

Lasgaard, M., Friis, K., & Shevlin, M. (2016). "Where are all the lonely people?" A population-based study of high-risk groups across the life span. *Social Psychiatry and Psychiatric Epidemiology: The International Journal for Research in Social and Genetic Epidemiology and Mental Health Services, 51*(10): 1373–1384. https://doi.org/10.1007/s00127-016-1279-3.

Lee, S. L., Pearce, E., Ajnakina, O., Johnson, S., Lewis, G., Mann, F., Pitman, A., Solmi, F., Sommerlad, A., & Steptoe, A. (2020). The association between loneliness and depressive symptoms among adults aged 50 years and older: a 12-year population-based cohort study. *The Lancet Psychiatry, 8*(1): 48–57. https://doi.org/10.1016/S2215-0366(20)30383-7.

Liebke, L., Bungert, M., Thome, J., Hauschild, S., Gescher, D. M., Schmahl, C., Bohus, M., & Lis, S. (2017). Loneliness, social networks, and social functioning in borderline personality disorder. *Personality Disorders: Theory, Research, and Treatment, 8*(4): 349. https://doi.org/10.1037/per0000208.

Long, C. R., & Averill, J. R. (2003). Solitude: an exploration of benefits of being alone. *Journal for the Theory of Social Behaviour, 33*(1): 21–44. https://doi.org/10.1111/1468-5914.00204.

Luhmann, M., & Hawkley, L. C. (2016). Age differences in loneliness from late adolescence to oldest old age. *Developmental Psychology, 52*(6): 943–959. https://doi.org/10.1037/dev0000117.supp.

Maes, M., Qualter, P., Vanhalst, J., Van den Noortgate, W., Goossens, L., & Kandler, C. (2019). Gender differences in loneliness across the lifespan: a meta-analysis. *European Journal of Personality, 33*(6): 642–654. https://doi.org/10.1002/per.2220.

Masi, C. M., Chen, H. Y., Hawkley, L. C., & Cacioppo, J. T. (2011). A meta-analysis of interventions to reduce loneliness. *Personality and Social Psychology Review, 15*(3): 219–266. https://doi.org/10.1177/1088868310377394.

McLennan, A. K., & Ulijaszek, S. J. (2018). Beware the medicalisation of loneliness. *The Lancet, 391*(10129): 1480. https://doi.org/10.1016/S0140-6736(18)30577-4.

Mund, M., Ludtke, O., & Neyer, F. J. (2020). Owner of a lonely heart: the stability of loneliness across the life span. *Journal of Personality and Social Psychology, 119*(2): 497–516. https://doi.org/10.1037/pspp0000262.

Mushtaq, R., Shoib, S., Shah, T., & Mushtaq, S. (2014). Relationship between loneliness, psychiatric disorders and physical health? A review on the psychological aspects of loneliness. *Journal of Clinical and Diagnostic Research, 8*(9): WE01–WE04. https://doi.org/10.7860/JCDR/2014/10077.4828.

Nicolaisen, M., & Thorsen, K. (2014). Who are lonely? Loneliness in different age groups (18–81 years old), using two measures of loneliness. *International Journal of Aging and Human Development, 78*(3): 229–257. https://doi.org/10.2190/AG.78.3.b.

Nuyen, J., Tuithof, M., de Graaf, R., Van Dorsselaer, S., Kleinjan, M., & Have, M. T. (2020). The bidirectional relationship between loneliness and common mental disorders in adults: findings from a longitudinal population-based cohort study. *Social Psychiatry and Psychiatric Epidemiology, 55*(10): 1297–1310.

Palgi, Y., Shrira, A., Ben-Ezra, M., Shiovitz-Ezra, S., & Ayalon, L. (2012). Self- and other-oriented potential lifetime traumatic events as predictors of loneliness in the second half of life. *Aging and Mental Health, 16*(4): 423–430. https://doi.org/10.1080/13607863.2011.638903.

Perlman, D., & Peplau, L. A. (1984). Loneliness research: a survey of empirical findings. In: L. A. Peplau & S. E. Goldston (Eds.), *Preventing the Harmful Consequences of Severe and Persistent Loneliness* (pp. 13–46): Bethesda, MD: National Institute of Mental Health.

Pinquart, M., & Sörensen, S. (2001a). Influences on loneliness in older adults: a meta-analysis. *Basic and Applied Social Psychology, 23*(4): 245–266. https://doi.org/10.1207/153248301753225702.

Pinquart, M., & Sörensen, S. (2001b). Gender differences in self-concept and psychological well-being in old age: a meta-analysis. *Journals of Gerontology Series B: Psychological Sciences and Social Sciences, 56B*(4): P195–P213. https://doi.org/10.1093/geronb/56.4.P195.

Qualter, P., Vanhalst, J., Harris, R., Van Roekel, E., Lodder, G., Bangee, M., Maes, M., & Verhagen, M. (2015). Loneliness across the life span. *Perspectives on Psychological Science, 10*(2): 250–264. https://doi.org/10.1177/1745691615568999.

Rico-Uribe, L. A., Caballero, F. F., Martin-Maria, N., Cabello, M., Ayuso-Mateos, J. L., & Miret, M. (2018). Association of loneliness with all-cause mortality: a meta-analysis. *PLoS One, 13*(1): e0190033. https://doi.org/10.1371/journal.pone.0190033.

Solmi, M., Veronese, N., Galvano, D., Favaro, A., Ostinelli, E. G., Noventa, V., Favaretto, E., Tudor, F., Finessi, M., Shin, J. I., Smith, L., Koyanagi, A., Cester, A., Bolzetta, F., Cotroneo, A., Maggi, S., Demurtas, J., De Leo, D., & Trabucchi, M. (2020). Factors associated with loneliness: an umbrella review of observational studies. *Journal of Affective Disorders, 271*: 131–138. https://doi.org/10.1016/j.jad.2020.03.075.

Stickley, A., & Koyanagi, A. (2016). Loneliness, common mental disorders and suicidal behavior: findings from a general population survey. *Journal of Affective Disorders, 197*: 81–87. https://doi.org/10.1016/j.jad.2016.02.054.

Stockard, J. (2006). Gender socialization. In: J. S. Chafetz (Ed.), *Handbook of the Sociology of Gender* (pp. 215–227). New York: Springer.

Sündermann, O., Onwumere, J., Kane, F., Morgan, C., & Kuipers, E. (2014). Social networks and support in first-episode psychosis: exploring the role of loneliness and anxiety. *Social Psychiatry and Psychiatric Epidemiology, 49*(3): 359–366. https://doi.org/10.1007/s00127-013-0754-3.

Tibubos, A. N., Ernst, M., Klein, E. M., Reiner, I., Brähler, E., Marx, C., Schulz, A., Wild, P. S., Münzel, T., Lackner, K. J., Pfeiffer, N., Michal, M., Ghaemi, J., Wiltink, J., & Beutel, M. E. (under review). Bidirectional influences of loneliness and depressive symptoms—longitudinal results from the Gutenberg Health Study.

Valtorta, N. K., Kanaan, M., Gilbody, S., Ronzi, S., & Hanratty, B. (2016). Loneliness and social isolation as risk factors for coronary heart disease and stroke: systematic review and meta-analysis of longitudinal observational studies. *Heart (British Cardiac Society), 102*(13): 1009–1016. https://doi.org/10.1136/heartjnl-2015-308790.

Vogel, D. L., Heimerdinger-Edwards, S. R., Hammer, J. H., & Hubbard, A. (2011). "Boys don't cry": examination of the links between endorsement of masculine norms, self-stigma, and help-seeking attitudes for men from diverse backgrounds. *Journal of Counseling Psychology, 58*(3): 368–382. https://doi.org/10.1037/a0023688.

Watt, D. F., & Panksepp, J. (2009). Depression: an evolutionarily conserved mechanism to terminate separation distress? A review of aminergic, peptidergic, and neural network perspectives. *Neuropsychoanalysis, 11*(1): 7–51. https://doi.org/10.1080/15294145.2009.10773593.

Weiss, R. S. (1973). *Loneliness: The Experience of Emotional and Social Isolation*: Cambridge, MA: MIT Press.

West, C., & Zimmerman, D. H. (1987). Doing gender. *Gender and Society, 1*: 125–151. https://doi.org/10.1177/0891243287001002002.

Wienclaw, R. A. (2011). Gender roles. In: The Editors of Salem Press (Eds.), *Sociology Reference Guide: Gender Roles and Equality* (pp. 33–40). Pasadena, CA: Salem.

CHAPTER 12

Loneliness and health

Gamze Özçürümez Bilgili

Lying, thinking
Last night
How to find my soul a home
Where water is not thirsty
And bread loaf is not stone ...

—"Alone", Maya Angelou

The World Health Organization (WHO) declared social disconnection as a major public health crisis and there is growing concern that the lonely and socially isolated may face heightened morbidity and mortality risks including suicide (Courtet et al., 2020). On top of such a red flag, there occurred the COVID-19 pandemic. No doubt that social distancing and isolation are critical to prevent the transmission of this highly contagious virus; yet, these are acts that are intrinsically linked with various adverse psychological effects, including loneliness.

Although physical/objective social isolation can contribute to loneliness, individuals can feel lonely in a marriage, friendship, family, or congregation. It has been reported that the number and frequency of contacts with others is not as important a predictor of feeling isolated as the quality of the social relationships (Hawkley et al., 2008). For instance, introversion rarely emerges as a strong risk factor for individual outcomes such as broad-based morbidity or mortality; rather, the most toxic mental and physical health effects were found to be associated with perceived social isolation, that is, loneliness (Cacioppo, Hawkley, et al., 2006; Holwerda, Beekman, et al., 2012; Wilson et al., 2007). Whereas introversion refers to the preference for low levels of social involvement (Eysenck, 1947), loneliness refers to the perception that one's social relationships are inadequate in light of one's preferences for social involvement (Weiss, 1973).

Almost everyone feels the aches and pains of loneliness at certain moments. It can be brief and superficial, like not receiving a call on your birthday from your best friend, or it can be acute and severe, as in the suffering of loss of a loved one. Transient loneliness is so common, in fact, that we simply accept it as a part of life. Loneliness becomes an issue of serious concern only when it settles in long enough to create a persistent, self-reinforcing loop of negative emotions, thoughts, sensations, and behaviours (Cacioppo & Patrick, 2008, p. 5). Then, it is a debilitating psychological condition characterised by a deep sense of emptiness, worthlessness, lack of control, and personal threat. Chronic feelings of isolation can drive a cascade of physiological events that actually accelerates the ageing process: loneliness not only alters behaviour but shows up in measurements of stress hormones, immune function, and cardiovascular function.

John T. Cacioppo, the pioneer of the interdisciplinary field of social neuroscience, emphasises that, just as hunger prevents us from starving and pain causes us to retreat from physical danger, loneliness is a symptom of our basic need to connect (Cacioppo & Patrick, 2008, pp. 7–12). Functional magnetic resonance imaging (fMRI) shows that the emotional region of the brain which is activated when individuals experience social rejection is, in fact, the same region—the dorsal anterior cingulate—which registers emotional responses to physical pain (Eisenberger et al., 2003). To test the intuitive idea that unmet social needs evoke a motivation to seek social interaction, analogous to the way hunger motivates people to seek food, Tomova and colleagues (2020) used fMRI to measure neural responses in participants evoked by food and social cues after ten hours of mandated fasting or total social isolation. Dopaminergic midbrain regions (substantia nigra pars compacta and ventral tegmental area, SN/VTA) showed increased activation to food cues after fasting and to social cues after isolation; these responses were correlated with self-reported craving. Tomova et al. (2020) concluded that people who are forced to be isolated crave social interactions similarly to the way a hungry person craves food.

Findings from both studies strongly support the notion that the sensations associated with loneliness evolved because they contributed to our survival as a species. Social bonds serve for safety and for the successful replication of genes in the form of offspring. As a mammalian species, humans are born considerably immature, without the capacity to feed or fend for themselves and instead rely almost completely on a caregiver to provide care and nourishment. John Bowlby wrote:

> To be isolated from your band ... and especially when young, to be isolated from your particular caretaker, is fraught with the greatest danger. Can we wonder then that each animal is equipped with an instinctive disposition to avoid isolation and to maintain proximity? (2005, p. 47)

Feelings of loneliness generally succeed in motivating connection or reconnection with others following geographic relocation or bereavement, for instance, thereby diminishing or abolishing feelings of social isolation. But left untended, loneliness has serious consequences. There is increasing research and accumulating evidence that loneliness is a risk factor for broad-based morbidity and mortality. In the following, an overview of empirical research and meta-analyses exploring the manifold interactions between loneliness and health is provided.

Loneliness: morbidity and mortality

I lied a little. There are things I don't want to tell you.
How lonely I am today and sick at heart.

—Angel of Duluth, Madelon Sprengnether

The importance of social determinants of health, among which loneliness is included, has been gaining traction in the health care sector during the last decade (Magnan, 2017). Loneliness is a common experience; as many as 80 per cent of those under eighteen years of age and 40 per cent of adults over sixty-five years of age report being lonely at least sometimes, with levels of loneliness gradually diminishing through the middle adult years, and then increasing in old age (i.e. ≥70 years) (Hawkley & Cacioppo, 2010). Certain situational factors heighten the risk for increased loneliness. These include low socio-economic status, poor marital quality, infrequent contact with friends and family, few social roles, lack of participation in voluntary organisations, physical health symptoms, and physical limitations (Hawkley et al., 2008). For as many as 15–30 per cent of the general population, loneliness becomes a chronic state (Heinrich & Gullone, 2006). This chronicity occurs because isolation leads people to feel unsafe and screen their social surroundings for potential threats, being in a constant state of vigilance which leads to the deterioration of social connections and to specific physiological changes (Cacioppo & Patrick, 2008, pp. 15–16).

A growing body of longitudinal research indicates that loneliness predicts increased morbidity and mortality (Thurston & Kubzansky, 2009). Loneliness is associated with numerous adverse psychological and physiological consequences, including depression, anxiety, anger, poor cognition, low self-esteem, and cardiovascular risk. The effects of loneliness seem to accrue over time to accelerate physiological ageing. For instance, loneliness has been shown to exhibit a dose–response relationship with cardiovascular health (CVH) risk in young adulthood (Caspi et al., 2006). The greater the number of measurement occasions at which participants were lonely (i.e. childhood, adolescence, and at twenty-six years of age), the greater their number of CVH risks. This longitudinal analysis reveals that adults who were socially isolated as children are more likely to have risk factors for cardiovascular disease, including overweight, high blood pressure, high total cholesterol, low high-density lipoprotein (HDL) cholesterol, high glycated haemoglobin, and low maximum oxygen consumption.

The evidence base for an association with physical health conditions other than cardiovascular disease is less strong, with reviews identified for cancer, low back pain, diabetes, and chronic obstructive pulmonary disease (Leigh-Hunt et al., 2017). One systematic review, focusing on the risk of mortality in cancer patients, found that those with the largest social network size have a reduced relative risk of mortality (Pinquart & Duberstein, 2010). Penninx and colleagues (1997) showed that loneliness predicted all-cause mortality during a twenty-nine-month follow-up after controlling for age, sex, chronic diseases, alcohol use, smoking, self-rated health, and functional limitations. Loneliness accrual effects are also evident in a study of mortality in the Health and Retirement Study; all-cause mortality over a four-year follow-up was predicted by loneliness, and the effect was greater in chronically than situationally lonely adults (Shiovitz-Ezra & Ayalon, 2010). In short, there is robust evidence that social isolation and loneliness significantly increase risk for premature mortality, and the magnitude of the risk exceeds that of many leading health indicators. In a recent meta-analysis, it is reported that the negative impact of loneliness on mortality was consistent across thirty-five articles included in a systematic review, and this relationship is found across gender and age groups (Rico-Uribe et al., 2018).

For mental health, there is a moderately strong evidence base, with reviews identified for well-being, depression, anxiety, suicide, and dementia. One meta-analysis found an association between subjective mental well-being and social relationships, with the quality of relationships more important than the quantity of them (Pinquart & Sörensen, 2000). Two other systematic reviews suggested an association between social networks and depression, with large and diverse social networks with high-quality relationships protecting against depression (Santini et al., 2015; Schwarzbach et al., 2014). These findings were also true in relation to post-stroke depression, with diverse social networks of friends and family associated with a reduction in reported depression (Ouimet et al., 2001). In keeping with this, a systematic review of immigrant women in the perinatal period in Japan identified an association between social isolation and negative mental health outcomes after childbirth such as anxiety and stress (Kita et al., 2015).

It is widely acknowledged that loneliness and depression often go hand in hand, yet the exact temporal and causal relationship between the two states remains elusive. Behavioural changes often accompany depressive episodes. Most notably, patients show so-called sickness behaviours that include fatigue, reduced food and fluid intake, anhedonia, and social withdrawal. Despite this regular co-morbidity, studies show that depression and loneliness are statistically separable and functionally distinct (Cacioppo, Hughes, et al., 2006). Importantly, loneliness is found to put people at much higher risk of depression than social isolation, indicating that the subjective perception and evaluation of social relationships plays an important role in offsetting depressive episodes (Quadt et al., 2020).

Regarding findings on anxiety, a recent longitudinal study with over 1000 participants aged eighteen to eighty-seven measured loneliness over a period of six months and revealed that early state loneliness predicted later-state social anxiety, as well as paranoia and depression (Lim et al., 2016). The relationship between social anxiety and loneliness appears to be bi-directional, such that earlier state social anxiety also predicts later state loneliness. Despite the compelling evidence linking loneliness to social anxiety across various age groups, research on the relationship between loneliness and other forms of anxiety remains scarce (Quadt et al., 2020).

As loneliness is significantly associated with an increased risk of mortality, it is possible that suicidal behaviour plays an important role in this association. Similarly to loneliness, suicidal behaviour is called a worldwide epidemic that occurs in low- and high-income countries across all age groups (Naghavi, 2019). Systematic reviews covering suicide (ideation, behaviour, attempted, and completed) indicate a higher risk for loneliness (Quadt et al., 2020).

Loneliness is associated with more than twofold risk of dementia, in fact some authors signal it as prodromal stage of dementia (Holwerda, Deeg, et al., 2012). In loneliness, there is more rapid decline in global cognition, semantic memory, perceptual speed, and visuospatial ability. The basis of association of loneliness with Alzheimer's disease (AD) can be attributed to two possibilities. First possibility is that loneliness is a consequence of dementia, perhaps as a behavioural reaction to diminished cognition or as a direct result of the pathology contributing to dementia. Second possibility is that loneliness might somehow compromise neural systems underlying cognition and memory, thereby making lonely individuals more vulnerable to the deleterious effects of age-related neuropathology, and thereby decreasing neural reserves. Recently, Donovan and colleagues (2016) found that in a community-based sample of cognitively normal older people, higher in vivo cortical amyloid burden was associated with greater feelings of loneliness, suggesting that loneliness is a novel neuropsychiatric symptom in preclinical AD. In addition, the association of amyloid burden and loneliness was stronger in carriers of the AD genetic risk factor APOE.4 than in non-carriers, further strengthening the link between AD pathophysiology and loneliness. The results reveal that the distinct construct of loneliness may be a symptom of amyloid accumulation.

Loneliness and disability

Individuals living with disability are reported to be at higher risk for loneliness and its consequences at all times (Popa, 2021). Neurodivergent individuals with conditions including autism are now recognised as having greater vulnerability to the distress evoked by social isolation and to negative physical consequences associated with loneliness (Quadt et al., 2020). In adolescents and adults with autism spectrum disorder (ASD), social difficulties have been found to be associated with loneliness, anxiety, and depression (Hedley et al., 2018). Results highlight a possible contribution of loneliness to depression and thoughts of self-harm, suggesting that treatment options that target loneliness may prove beneficial in improving mental health outcomes in ASD. In an earlier study that examined the relations among loneliness, friendship, and emotional functioning in adults with ASD, number of friends provided unique independent effects in predicting self-esteem, depression, and anxiety above and beyond the effects of loneliness (Mazurek, 2013). The results indicated that loneliness was associated with increased depression and anxiety and decreased life satisfaction and self-esteem, even after controlling for symptoms of ASD.

Similar to ASD, social outcome remains poor for many individuals with schizophrenia. In many studies it has been demonstrated that cognition is significantly associated with social functioning (Green et al., 2004). Dysfunctions in social functioning emerge early in life in schizophrenia, years before the full onset of the disease. Indeed, large cohort studies showed that subjects who will be affected by schizophrenia showed higher preference for solitary playing as early as four and six years of age, lower social confidence at thirteen years, and higher social anxiety at fifteen years (Porcelli et al., 2019). It has been hypothesised that this early social withdrawal may trigger, in vulnerable individuals, the development of a full psychosis through social deprivation, resulting in a vicious circle (i.e. subtle social dysfunctions may cause early social withdrawal, which further exacerbate alterations in the social brain through deprivation, leading to more severe social withdrawal and facilitating the development/worsening of psychotic symptoms). Psychosis represents a symptom of several psychiatric, neurodevelopmental, and neurologic conditions, being the defining feature of schizophrenia spectrum disorders. Psychotic symptoms negatively impact an individual's ability to seek social interactions and to maintain close relationships, with both positive (i.e. hallucinations) and negative (i.e. anhedonia) symptoms reported to negatively influence social activities (Rabinowitz et al., 2013). Consequently, the percentage of individuals suffering from psychotic disorders reporting feeling lonely is high, and loneliness affects over 80 per cent of individuals with psychosis (Stain et al., 2012). Loneliness predicted symptoms of subjective thought disorder and anhedonia in individuals with a diagnosis of a psychotic disorder (including schizophrenia, schizoaffective disorder, depressive psychosis, and bipolar disorder with psychotic features), and poorer cognitive functions, indexed by lower digit symbol coding scores in individuals who reported feeling lonelier (Badcock et al., 2015).

Quantitative research has shown that the connection between loneliness and disability is not merely due to medical aspects, but because of structural barriers that prevent disabled individuals from accessing leisure activities outside the home, social interaction, or employment (Macdonald et al., 2018). Testimonies on how deaf individuals have been denied both social interaction and the communication of basic needs in institutional settings would be one example (Wong, 2020, pp. 59–63). Another example is the phenomenon of shrinking social circles not only for disabled individuals, but also for their family members or friends (Kafer, 2013, p. 8).

Causality

Loneliness has been associated with ill health in many studies, but determining causality is difficult (Leigh-Hunt et al., 2017). Lonely individuals may suffer more stress than others due to their lack of social networks and support. Stress responses as a result of loneliness can adversely precondition the neuroendocrine system, with genetic differences determining the degree to which this might occur (Immordino-Yang et al., 2009). To the extent that the brain is the central organ for evaluating interpersonal relationships, the neuroendocrine system becomes an important construct through which perceived social isolation may operate, at least in part, to affect morbidity and mortality (Cacioppo et al., 2015). Biological pathways have been suggested as an explanation for the effect of loneliness on health including reduced levels of protective hormones leading to adverse effects on heart rate, blood pressure, and the repair of blood vessel walls (Heffner et al., 2011); downregulation of the immune system and neuroendocrine dysregulation from a paucity or poor quality of sleep (Cacioppo et al., 2002); under-expression of genes bearing anti-inflammatory glucocorticoid response elements (GREs) and over-expression of genes bearing response elements for pro-inflammatory NF-κB/Rel transcription factors (Cole et al., 2007). Cole and colleagues (2015) also examined gene expressions in leukocytes that play key roles in the immune system's response to infection. They found that the leukocytes of lonely participants—both humans and rhesus macaques—showed an increased expression of genes involved in inflammation and a decreased expression of genes involved in antiviral responses. Simply put, people who feel lonely have less immunity and more inflammation than people who don't. Loneliness-related chronic stress can cause low-grade peripheral inflammation. The low-grade peripheral inflammation in turn has been linked to inflammatory diseases (Mushtaq et al., 2014), which include diabetes, autoimmune disorders like rheumatoid arthritis, lupus and cardiovascular diseases like coronary heart disease, and hypertension (Hawkley & Cacioppo, 2010).

Another possible cause of ill health associated with loneliness is health-compromising behaviour. Due to loneliness, there is an implicit vigilance for social threat which leads to diminished capacity for self-regulation. The ability to regulate one's thoughts, feelings, and behaviour is critical to accomplish personal goals or to comply with social norms. Of relevance for health is the capacity for self-regulation in the arena of lifestyle behaviours. Regulation of emotion can enhance the ability to regulate other self-control behaviours (Tice & Bratslavsky, 2000), as is evident from research showing that positive affect predicts increased physical activity (McAuley et al., 2007). In middle-aged and older adults, greater loneliness was associated with less effort applied to the maintenance and optimisation of positive emotions (Hawkley et al., 2009). Compromised regulation of emotion in lonely individuals explained their diminished likelihood of performing any physical activity, and loneliness also predicted a decrease in physical activity over time. Physical activity is a well-known protective factor for physical health, mental health, and cognitive functioning (Penedo & Dahn, 2005), suggesting that poorer self-regulation may contribute to the greater health risk associated with loneliness via diminished likelihood of engaging in health-promoting behaviours. A related literature shows that loneliness is also a risk factor for obesity (Lauder et al., 2006) and health-compromising behaviour, including a greater propensity to abuse alcohol (Mushtaq et al., 2014). Lonely individuals could also be more prone to hazardous health behaviours due to diminished capacity of self-regulation, such as smoking, drug abuse, or transient sexual encounters.

Loneliness and COVID-19

COVID-19 is proving to be a particularly cruel disease not just because of its pathophysiology but also due to its potentially devastating consequences for engendering loneliness (Miller, 2020). In order to contain and reduce the spread of COVID-19, many governments introduced nationwide lockdown measures which restricted time permitted outside, and all non-essential in-person contact. Those with certain high-risk medical conditions were advised to "shield" themselves (i.e. not leave the house for weeks, even months), and in most countries the elderly were advised to strictly adhere to the restrictions; even, in some countries, such as Turkey, not only those aged sixty-five and over were almost totally banned from leaving their houses, but also children and adolescents were subject to this particularly isolating measure.

Two cross-sectional studies have linked loneliness with decreased mental health and psychological distress, and a third indicated that people with low social support (a possible proxy for loneliness) had a more severe trajectory of depression during the pandemic (Frank et al., 2020; Frenkel-Yosef et al., 2020; Killgore et al., 2020). However, without data prior to 2020 it is impossible to evaluate fully the specific importance of these two factors. After accounting for pre-COVID-19 trends, Creese and colleagues (2020) reported that experiencing loneliness is a risk factor for worsening mental health during the pandemic.

Popa (2021) duly highlights the possible consequences of social isolation in the context of the public health response to COVID-19. She calls attention to the effects which are likely to be exacerbated for the older population and for individuals living with disability who were already more likely to struggle with loneliness before the pandemic (Courtin & Knapp, 2017). Among older adults in particular, loneliness is more likely to set in when an individual is dealing with functional limitations and has low family support (Hawkley & Kocherginsky, 2018). Popa (2021) describes the initial response to COVID-19 as overlooking the possibility of a more nuanced perspective regarding the psychological and social aspects of the pandemic, and loneliness, in particular, as potential trade-offs. Rumas and colleagues (2021) studied the predictors and consequences of loneliness during the COVID-19 pandemic, and stated that having two or more physical health diagnoses and two or more self-reported mental health diagnoses were each related to greater loneliness and lower quality of life, both cross-sectionally and longitudinally. This is consistent with findings of previous research that loneliness is associated with poorer mental and physical health (Heinrich & Gullone, 2006; Holt-Lunstad et al., 2015). On the other hand, contrary to popular perceptions, older age was associated with less loneliness. But Rumas and colleagues (2021) conducted their study in April of 2020, and the relevance of certain factors must be considered with respect to the situation surrounding the pandemic which is constantly evolving. This precaution is also valid for their finding that more virtual social contact was associated with more loneliness. It is unclear whether the specific type of virtual contact may play a role in the effect it has on loneliness, since previous research has found that active social contact in the form of having virtual conversations enhances well-being, while passive social contact through observing social media outlets does not (Burke & Kraut, 2016). Additionally, Shensa and colleagues (2020) have reported face-to-face emotional support to be more efficient in preventing depression than support via social media. Therefore, it may be prudent to be cautious in recommending virtual social contact exclusively, and further research on the effects of virtual social contact during the pandemic is needed.

Conclusion

Loneliness is a risk factor for a variety of mental and physical health conditions, ranging from depression and anxiety to Alzheimer's disease, cardiovascular disease, and cancer. It has been viewed as a marker of psychosocial stress with downstream effects on neural networks mediated by inflammatory processes. Although interventional studies show that improved social cognitive processing alleviates feelings of loneliness, the exact temporal and causal relationships between loneliness, and physical and mental health are yet to be determined. The detrimental effects of loneliness on health are likely complex and multifaceted, where chronic illness—mental and physical—can lead to social withdrawal, setting the vicious cycle in motion, or where extended social stress leads to chronic illness via social allostatic overload (Quadt et al., 2020).

Due to the increasing prevalence of loneliness and its detrimental effects in modern societies, many researchers have advocated the medical solution of loneliness as a public health problem (Holt-Lunstad et al., 2017; Cacioppo & Cacioppo, 2018). In this context, models that can be used to predict loneliness severity at the individual level may provide clinical utility in terms of diagnosis and prognosis in future.

Acknowledgement

I would like to thank Esra Emekli, MD, of Başkent University Department of Psychiatry, Ankara, Turkey, for her timely support and kind contribution in reorganising the references.

References

Badcock, J. C., Shah, S., Mackinnon, A., Stain, H. J., Galletly, C., Jablensky, A., & Morgan, V. A. (2015). Loneliness in psychotic disorders and its association with cognitive function and symptom profile. *Schizophrenia Research, 169*: 268–273.

Bowlby, J. (2005). *The Making and Breaking of Affectional Bonds*. New York: Routledge Classics.

Burke, M., & Kraut, R. E. (2016). The relationship between Facebook use and well-being depends on communication type and tie strength. *Journal of Computer-Mediated Communication, 21*(4): 265–281. https://doi.org/10.1111/jcc4.12162.

Cacioppo, J. T., & Cacioppo, S. (2018). Loneliness in the modern age: an evolutionary theory of loneliness (ETL). In: J. M. Olson (Ed.), *Advances in Experimental Social Psychology* (pp. 127–197). Cambridge, MA: Academic Press.

Cacioppo, J. T., Cacioppo, S., Capitanio, J. P., & Cole, S. W. (2015). The neuroendocrinology of social isolation. *Annual Review of Psychology, 66*: 733–767. doi: 10.1146/annurev-psych-010814-015240.

Cacioppo, J. T., Hawkley, L. C., Berntson, G. G., Ernst, J. M., Gibbs, A. C., Stickgold, R., & Hobson, J. A. (2002). Do lonely days invade the nights? Potential social modulation of sleep efficiency. *Psychological Science, 13*: 384–387.

Cacioppo, J. T., Hawkley, L. C., Ernst, J. M., Burleson, M., Berntson, G. G., Nouriani, B., & Spiegel, D. (2006). Loneliness within a nomological net: an evolutionary perspective. *Journal of Research in Personality, 40*: 1054–1085. https://doi:10.1016/j.jrp.2005.11.007.

Cacioppo, J. T., Hughes, M. E., Waite, L. J., Hawkley, L. C., & Thisted, R. A. (2006). Loneliness as a specific risk factor for depressive symptoms: cross-sectional and longitudinal analyses. *Psychology and Aging, 21*: 140–148.

Cacioppo, J. T., & Patrick, W. (2008). *Loneliness: Human Nature and the Need for Social Connection.* New York: W. W. Norton.

Caspi, A., Harrington, H., Moffitt, T. E., Milne, B. J., & Poulton, R. (2006). Socially isolated children 20 years later: risk of cardiovascular disease. *Archives of Pediatrics & Adolescent Medicine, 160*: 805–811.

Cole, S. W., Capitonio, J. P., Chun, K., Arevalo, M. G., Ma, J., & Cacioppo, J. T. (2015). Myeloid differentiation architecture of leukocyte transcriptome dynamics in perceived social isolation. *Proceedings of the National Academy of Sciences of the United States of America, 112*(49): 15142–15147. https://doi.org/10.1073/pnas.1514249112.

Cole, S. W., Hawkley, L. C., Arevalo, J. M., Sung, C. Y., Rose, R. M., & Cacioppo, J. T. (2007). Social regulation of gene expression in human leukocytes. *Genome Biology, 8*(9): 178–189. doi:10.1186/gb-2007-8-9-r189.

Courtet, P., Olié, E., Debien, C., & Vaiva, G. (2020). Keep socially (but not physically) connected and carry on: preventing suicide in the age of COVID-19. *Journal of Clinical Psychiatry, 81*(3): 1–3. doi: 10.4088/JCP.20com13370.

Courtin, E., & Knapp, M. (2017). Social isolation, loneliness and health in old age: a scoping review. *Health & Social Care in the Community, 25*(3): 799–812.

Creese, B., Khan, Z., Henley, W., Corbett, A., Da Silva, M. V., Mills, K., Wright, N., Testad, I., Aarsland, D., & Ballard, C. (2020). Loneliness, physical activity and mental health during Covid-19: a longitudinal analysis of depression and anxiety in adults over 50 between 2015 and 2020. *International Psychogeriatrics, 33*(5): 505–514. doi:10.1017/S1041610220004135.

Donovan, N. J., Okereke, O. I., Vannini, P., Amariglio, R. E., Rentz, D. M., Marshall, G. A., Johnson, K. A., & Sperling, R. A. (2016). Association of higher cortical amyloid burden with loneliness in cognitively normal older adults. *JAMA Psychiatry, 73*(12): 1230–1237. doi:10.1001/jamapsychiatry.2016.2657.

Eisenberger, N. I., Lieberman M., & Williams, K. D. (2003). Does rejection hurt? An fMRI study of social exclusion. *Science, 302*: 290–292. doi: 10.1126/science.1089134.

Eysenck, H. J. (1947). *Dimensions of Personality.* London: Kegan Paul, Trench, Trubner.

Frank, P., Iob, E., Steptoe, A., & Fancourt, D. (2020). Trajectories of depressive symptoms among vulnerable groups in the UK during the COVID-19 pandemic. *JAMA Network Open.* https://doi: 10.1001/jamanetworkopen.2020.26064.

Frenkel-Yosef, M., Maytles, R., & Shrira, A. (2020). Loneliness and its concomitants among older adults during the COVID-19 pandemic. *International Psychogeriatrics, 32*(10): 1257–1259. https://doi:10.1017/S1041610220003476.

Green, M. F., Kern, R. S., & Heaton, R. K. (2004). Longitudinal studies of cognition and functional outcome in schizophrenia: implications for MATRICS. *Schizophrenia Research, 72*: 41–51.

Hawkley, L. C., & Cacioppo, J. T. (2010). Loneliness matters: a theoretical and empirical review of consequences and mechanisms. *Annals of Behavioral Medicine*, 40(2): 218–227. https://doi.org/10.1007/s12160-010-9210-8.

Hawkley, L. C., Hughes, M. E., Waite, L. J., Masi, C. M., Thisted, R. A., & Cacioppo, J. T. (2008). From social structural factors to perceptions of relationship quality and loneliness: the Chicago Health, Aging, and Social Relations Study. *Journal of Gerontology*, 63: 375–384.

Hawkley, L. C., & Kocherginsky, M. (2018). Transitions in loneliness among older adults: a 5-year follow-up in the National Social Life, Health, and Aging Project. *Research on Aging*, 40(4): 365–387. doi: 10.1177/0164027517698965.

Hawkley, L. C., Thisted, R. A., & Cacioppo, J. T. (2009). Loneliness predicts reduced physical activity: Cross-sectional and longitudinal analyses. *Health Psychology*, 28: 354–363.

Hedley, D., Uljarevića, M., Wilmota, M., Richdale, A., & Dissanayake, S. (2018). Understanding depression and thoughts of self-harm in autism: a potential mechanism involving loneliness. *Research in Autism Spectrum Disorders*, 46: 1–7. https://doi.org/10.1016/j.rasd.2017.11.003.

Heffner, K. L., Waring, M. E., Roberts, M. B., Eaton, C. B., & Gramling, R. (2011). Social isolation, C-reactive protein, and coronary heart disease mortality among community dwelling adults. *Social Science & Medicine, 72*: 1482–1488. https://doi.org/10.1016/j.socscimed.2011.03.016.

Heinrich, L. M., & Gullone, E. (2006). The clinical significance of loneliness: a literature review. *Clinical Psychology Review*, 26: 695–718.

Holt-Lunstad, J., Robles, T. F., & Sbarra, D. A. (2017). Advancing social connection as a public health priority in the United States. *American Psychologist*, 72(6): 517–730.

Holt-Lunstad, J., Smith, T. B., Baker, M., Harris, T., & Stephenson, D. (2015). Loneliness and social isolation as risk factors for mortality: a meta-analytic review. *Perspectives on Psychological Science, 10*: 227–237. https://doi.org/10.1177/1745691614568352.

Holwerda, T. J., Beekman, A. T. F., Deeg, D. J. H., Stek, M. L., Van Tilburg, T. G., Visser, P. J., Schmand, B., Jonker, C., & Schoevers, R. A. (2012). Increased risk of mortality associated with social isolation in older men: only when feeling lonely? Results from the Amsterdam Study of the Elderly (AM-STEL). *Psychological Medicine, 42*: 843–853. doi: 10.1017/S00.33291711001772.

Holwerda, T. J., Deeg, J. H. D, Beekman, T. F. A., Van Tilburg, T. G., Stek, M. L., Jonker, C., & Schoevers, R. A. (2012). Feelings of loneliness, but not social isolation, predict dementia onset: results from the Amsterdam Study of the Elderly (AM-STEL). *Journal of Neurology, Neurosurgery, & Psychiatry, 85*(2): 135–142. doi: 10.1136/jnnp-2012-302755.

Immordino-Yang, M. H., McColl, A., Damasio, H., & Damasio, A. (2009). Neural correlates of admiration and compassion. *Proceedings of the National Academy of Sciences of the United States of America, 106*: 8021–8026. https://doi.org/10.1073/pnas.0810363106.

Kafer, A. (2013). *Feminist, Queer, Crip*. Bloomington, IN: Indiana University Press.

Killgore, W. D. S., Cloonan, S. A., Taylor, E. C., & Dailey, N. S. (2020). Loneliness: a signature mental health concern in the era of COVID-19. *Psychiatry Research, 290*: 113–117. https://doi.org/10.1016/j.psychres.2020.113117.

Kita, S., Minatani, M., Hikita, N., Matsuzaki, M., Shiraishi, M., & Haruna, M. (2015). A systematic review of the physical, mental, social, and economic problems of immigrant women in the perinatal period in Japan. *Journal of Immigrant and Minority Health, 17*: 1863–1881.

Lauder, W., Mummery, K., Jones, M., & Caperchione, C. (2006). A comparison of health behaviours in lonely and non-lonely populations. *Psychology, Health, and Medicine, 11*: 233–245.

Leigh-Hunt, N., Bagguley, D., Bash, K., Turner, V., Turnbull, S., Valtorta, C., & Caan, W. (2017). An overview of systematic reviews on the public health consequences of social isolation and loneliness. *Public Health, 152*: 157–171. http://dx.doi.org/10.1016/j.puhe.2017.07.035.

Lim, M. H., Rodebaugh, T. L., Zyphur, M. J., & Gleeson, J. F. M. (2016). Loneliness over time: the crucial role of social anxiety. *Journal of Abnormal Psychology, 125*: 620–630.

Macdonald, S. J., Deacon, L., Nixon, J., Akintola, A., Gillingham, A., Kent, J., Ellis, G., Mathews, D., Ismail, A., Sullivan, S., Dore, S., & Highmore, L. (2018). "The invisible enemy": disability, loneliness and isolation. *Disability & Society, 33*(7): 1138–1159.

Magnan, S. (2017). Social determinants of health 101 for health care: five plus five. *NAM Perspectives.* https://doi.org/10.31478/201710c.

Mazurek, M. O. (2013). Loneliness, friendship, and well-being in adults with autism spectrum disorders. *Autism, 18*(3): 223–232. https://doi.org/10.1177%2F1362361312474121.

McAuley, E., Morris, K. S., Motl, R. W., Hu, L., Konopack, J. F., & Elavsky, S. (2007). Long-term follow-up of physical activity behavior in older adults. *Health Psychology, 26*: 375–380.

Miller, E. D. (2020). Loneliness in the era of COVID-19. *Frontiers in Psychology, 11*: 2219–2225.

Mushtaq, R., Shoib, S., Shah, T., & Mushtaq, S. (2014). Relationship between loneliness, psychiatric disorders and physical health: a review on the psychological aspects of loneliness. *Journal of Clinical & Diagnostic Research, 8*(9): WE01–WE04.

Naghavi, M. (2019). Global, regional, and national burden of suicide mortality 1990 to 2016: systematic analysis for the Global Burden of Disease Study 2016. *British Medical Journal, 364*: 194–203.

Ouimet, M. A., Primeau, F., & Cole, M. G. (2001). Psychosocial risk factors in poststroke depression: a systematic review. *Canadian Journal of Psychiatry, 46*: 819–828.

Penedo, F. J., & Dahn, J. R. (2005). Exercise and well-being: a review of mental and physical health benefits associated with physical activity. *Current Opinion in Psychiatry, 18*: 189–193.

Penninx, B. W., van Tilburg, T., Kriegsman, D. M., Deeg, D. J., Boeke, A. J. P., & Can Eijk, J. T. M. (1997). Effects of social support and personal coping resources on mortality in older age: The Longitudinal Aging Study Amsterdam. *American Journal of Epidemiology, 146*: 510–519.

Pinquart, M., & Sörensen, S. (2000). Influences of socioeconomic status, social network, and competence on subjective wellbeing in later life: a meta-analysis. *Psychology and Aging, 15*: 187–224.

Pinquart, M., & Duberstein, P. R. (2010). Associations of social networks with cancer mortality: a meta-analysis. *Critical Reviews in Oncology/Hematology, 75*: 122–137.

Popa, E. (2021). Loneliness and negative effects on mental health as trade-offs of the policy response to COVID-19. *History and Philosophy of the Life Sciences, 43*: 15. https://doi.org/10.1007/s40656-021-00372-z.

Porcelli, S., Van Der Wee, N., van der Werff, S., Aghajani, M., Glennon J. C., van Heukelum, S., Mogavero, F., Lobo, A., Olivera, F. J., Lobo, E., Posadas, M., Dukart, J., Kozak, R., Arce, E., Afan, I.,

Vostman, J., Bilderbeck, A., Saris, I., Kas, M. J., & Seretti, A. (2019). Social brain, social dysfunction and social withdrawal. *Neuroscience and Behavioral Reviews*, 97: 10–33. https://doi.org/10.1016/j.neubiorev.2018.09.012.

Quadt, L., Esposito, G., Critchley, H. D., & Garfinkel, S. N. (2020). Brain-body interactions underlying the association of loneliness with mental and physical health. *Neuroscience and Biobehavioral Reviews*, 116: 283–300. https://doi.org/10.1016/j.neubiorev.2020.06.015.

Rabinowitz, J., Berardo, C. G., Bugarski-Kirola, D., & Marder, S. (2013). Association of prominent positive and prominent negative symptoms and functional health, well being, healthcare-related quality of life and family burden: a CATIE analysis. *Schizophrenia Research*, 150: 339–342.

Rico-Uribe, L. A., Caballero, F. F., Martín-María, N., Cabello, M., Ayuso-Mateos, J. L., & Miret, M. (2018). Association of loneliness with all-cause mortality: a meta analysis. *PLoS One*, 13(1): e0190033.

Rumas, R., Shamblaw, A. L., Jagtap, S., & Best, M. W. (2021). Predictors and consequences of loneliness during the COVID-19 pandemic. *Psychiatry Research*, 300: 113934. https://doi.org/10.1016/j.psychres.2021.113934.

Santini, Z. I., Koyanagi, A., Tyrovolas, S., Mason, C., & Haro, J. M. (2015). The association between social relationships and depression: a systematic review. *Journal of Affective Disorders*, 175: 53–65.

Schwarzbach, M., Luppa, M., Forstmeier, S., Konig, H.-H., & Riedel-Heller, S. G. (2014). Social relations and depression in late life—a systematic review. *International Journal of Geriatric Psychiatry*, 29: 1–21.

Shensa, A., Sidani, J. E., Escobar-Viera, C. G., Switzer, G. E., Primack, B. A., & Choukas-Bradley, S. (2020). Emotional support from social media and face-to-face relationships: associations with depression risk among young adults. *Journal of Affective Disorders*, 260: 38–44.

Shiovitz-Ezra, S., & Ayalon, L. (2010). Situational versus chronic loneliness as risk factors for all-cause mortality. *International Psychogeriatrics*, 22: 455–462.

Stain, H. J., Galletly, C. A., Clark, S., Wilson, J., Killen, E. A., Anthes, L., Campbell, L. E., Hanlon, M. C., & Harvey, C. (2012). Understanding the social costs of psychosis: the experience of adults affected by psychosis identified within the second Australian national survey of psychosis. *Australian & New Zealand Journal of Psychiatry*, 46: 879–889.

Thurston, R. C., & Kubzansky, L. D. (2009). Women, loneliness, and incident coronary heart disease. *Psychosomatic Medicine* 71(8): 836–842.

Tice, D. M., & Bratslavsky, E. (2000). Giving in to feel good: the place of emotion regulation in the context of general self-control. *Psychological Inquiry*, 11: 149–159.

Tomova, L., Wang, K., Thompson, T., Matthews, G., Takahashi, A., Tye, K., & Saxe, R. (2020). The need to connect: acute social isolation causes neural craving responses similar to hunger. *Nature Neuroscience*, 23: 1597–1605. https://doi.org/10.1038/s41593-020-00742-z.

Weiss, R. S. (1973). *Loneliness: The Experience of Emotional and Social Isolation*. Cambridge, MA: MIT Press.

Wilson, R. S., Krueger, K. R., Arnold, S. E., Schneider, J. A., Kelly, J. F., Barnes, L. L., Tang, Y., & Bennett, A. (2007). Loneliness and risk of Alzheimer disease. *Archives of General Psychiatry*, 64: 234–240. https://doi: 10.1001/archpsyc.64.2.234.

Wong, A. (2020). *Disability Visibility: First-person Stories from the Twenty-first Century*. New York: Vintage.

CHAPTER 13

Loneliness and the brain

Gamze Özçürümez Bilgili

Introduction

The complexity of the neural processes that underlie social living is enormous, including processes such as the detection and processing of social stimuli, mentalizing activity, bond/relationships formation, and social learning (Cacioppo et al., 2014). These processes are highly relevant in social species such as homo sapiens, to the point that some have suggested that complex social environments were the primary selective pressure for the human brain, being mediated by all the aspects of social problem solving (Dunbar & Shultz, 2007). As a consequence of this "social" evolutionary pressure, the human brain shows a high degree of specialisation for social stimuli processing, encompassing regulation from the neurotransmitter to the neural network level, resulting in a "social brain" (Dunbar, 2009). Economic processes underlie evolution, involved with adaptation of the structures and neurotransmitters, from their original general functions to the processing of social stimuli. Some structures (e.g. the Bed Nucleus of Stria Terminalis-BNST) and neurotransmitters (e.g. oxytocin-OXT), show a high degree of specialisation for the processing of social stimuli (Porcelli et al., 2019). Matthews and Tye (2019) introduce the idea that coordinated adaptations across discrete neural circuits function to maintain "social homeostasis". Beyond just constituting an unwelcome emotional side effect of social isolation, loneliness is theorised to represent an "adaptive predisposition", providing the motivational drive to maintain social contact and prevent the aversive consequences of isolation.

Unfortunately, such a high complexity may also be associated with a high susceptibility to several pathogenic interventions. In childhood and early adulthood, loneliness is associated, for example, with insecure attachment to parents (Akdoğan, 2017; Mund & Neyer, 2016). Hence, loneliness appears to be a stable construct that has been found to be present in individuals at every stage of life and has been shown to be associated with a range of psychological constructs implicated in poor mental health or maladjustment. In adults, loneliness correlates positively with shyness, depressive characteristics, social anxiety, and neuroticism (Schermer et al., 2020). Loneliness has also been found to correlate negatively with extraversion, self-esteem, self-confidence (Cheng & Furnham, 2002), acceptance of others, and mattering (Flett et al., 2016). Lonely people tend to engage in self-protective and social avoidant behaviour (Knowles et al., 2015) and have higher anxiety because of their perceptions about their social skills.

The high vulnerability of the social brain is confirmed by the clinical observation that social deficits can sometimes represent the first signs of several neuropsychiatric disorders, manifesting far before the full onset of the other symptoms (NICE, 2014). Social deficits could be broadly defined as impairments in the subject's capacity to integrate behavioural, cognitive, and affective skills to flexibly adapt to diverse social contexts and demands (Bierman & Welsh, 2000), resulting in behavioural outcomes which are judged as negative according to the standards of the specific social context (i.e. as impairments of the social competence) (Dirks et al., 2007). In the following, I will first try to outline the association between risk factors for the developing brain and loneliness, and then summarise the social neuroscience model for loneliness.

Loneliness and the developing brain

> From childhood's hour I have not been
> As others were—I have not seen
> As others saw—I could not bring
> My passions from a common spring—
> From the same source I have not taken
> My sorrow—I could not awaken
> My heart to joy at the same tone—
> And all I lov'd—I lov'd alone—
>
> —"Alone" by Edgar Allan Poe

The period from birth to adulthood is marked by progressive physical, behavioural, cognitive, and emotional development. Paralleling these stages are changes in brain maturation. Many factors can adversely impact neurodevelopment and lead to disruption in the processes that underlie social living; one of the end results might be chronic loneliness. Child neglect is the most prevalent, but least empirically studied, form of child maltreatment (De Bellis, 2005). Unmet childhood needs for intimacy and early attachment experiences have been thought to elicit feelings of loneliness. The social attachment between mother and infant is one of the most important experience-dependent developmental interactions in mammals. Frequent touching by the maternal caregiver is a biological necessity for physical and psychological growth.

Early studies have demonstrated that maternal deprivation is associated with dysregulation of developing biological stress response systems and abnormal infant behaviour (De Bellis, 2005). In relatively recent times, Romanian orphanages provided care similar to those of the early institutions, where children suffered from physical, emotional, and some forms of medical neglect. Romanian orphans lived with a low staff to child ratio (1 to 60) and lacked stimulation, appropriate medical care, and nutrition. A random sample of 200 orphaned Romanian children, living in these institutions, suffered from physical growth delays, including smaller body size and head circumference, poor social skills, and delays in cognitive and language development, when examined at three years of age (Macovei, 1986).

Primates subjected to prolonged periods of maternal and social deprivation have altered catecholamine and cortisol function and impaired immune function (De Bellis, 2005). Specifically, maltreated children have evidence of higher catecholamine and cortisol activity compared to non-maltreated children. In the developing brain, stress and elevated levels of stress chemicals may lead to: adverse brain development through the mechanisms of accelerated loss of neurons (Sapolsky, 2000), delays in myelination, abnormalities in developmentally appropriate pruning, inhibition of neurogenesis, or a stress-induced decrease in brain growth factors (i.e. brain-derived neurotrophic factor-BDNF). It is hypothesised that alterations of the development of a neglected child's major stress systems may contribute to adverse brain development and lead to psychopathology and compromised neuropsychological and psychosocial function. Even brief maternal separations during infancy have been shown to affect the functioning of the HPA-axis and glucocorticoid receptor gene expression in the hippocampus and frontal cortex in rats (Francis & Meaney, 1999).

Stress activates norepinephrine (NE), serotonin (5-HT), and dopamine (DA) neurons in the prefrontal cortex (PFC). The medial prefrontal cortex (mPFC) inhibits activation of the parts of the limbic system involved in anxiety (amygdala and related nuclei and circuitry) (LeDoux, 1998). The PFC subserves executive cognitive functions, such as planned behaviours, decision-making, working memory, and attention, and is activated during novel or dangerous situations. However, severe stress and its associated increased activation of catecholamines (especially NE and DA) can "turn off" this frontal inhibition of the limbic system. Thus, it is hypothesised that in neglected children, chronic amygdala activation impairs the development of the PFC leading to problems with the normal age-related acquisition of behavioural and emotional regulation including the inhibition of impulsive behaviours and social functioning (De Bellis, 2005).

The amygdala and its projections to the superior temporal gyrus, thalamus, and to the PFC are thought to compose the neural basis of our abilities to interpret others' behaviour in terms of mental states (i.e. thoughts, intentions, desires, beliefs). This process has been called theory of mind or social intelligence. In a human fMRI study, the amygdala, superior temporal gyrus, and PFC were activated during the performance of a social intelligence task in healthy volunteers (Baron-Cohen et al., 1999). Maltreated children with post-traumatic stress disorder (PTSD) demonstrated larger superior temporal gyrus volumes (De Bellis et al., 2002). Studies have found that childhood maltreatment can negatively affect social emotions (Maughan & Cicchetti, 2002), as well as the ability to assess, regulate, and appropriately use emotions, which may lead to a negative impact on emotional intelligence (Mattar, 2017). Emotional intelligence is the ability of people to monitor the emotions of themselves and other people, guiding their thoughts and behaviours by discriminating and using information about emotions. Studies have found that childhood maltreatment can lead to social withdrawal and behaviour issues and bad social interaction behaviours (Perroud, 2016). Findings have also shown that childhood maltreatment influences social support negatively through hampered emotional intelligence (Punamäki et al., 2005). In line with such findings, Schore (2001) summarised evidence for sensitised pathways that develop in the orbito-frontal cortex and long-lasting impairment in brain regions involved in regulation of the intensity of feelings. The expected consequences of these dysfunctions would include persistent orientation to threat and activation of the stress response, and affective dysregulation and impulsivity with poor anxiety tolerance and poor modulation of aggression.

"Social brain" includes brain regions that are generally responsible for mentalization and social cognitive processes. For the biological development of social interaction and interpretation capacity, engaging psychologically in sharing experiences, information, and affect is crucial (Bogdan, 1997, p. 94). As the dorsomedial prefrontal region has long been found to be involved in mentalization and other social processes, such as social perception and self-referential thoughts, it is possible that mentalization is critical in the feeling of loneliness (Wong et al., 2016). Indeed, mentalization and perspective taking are the building blocks for the processing of social information; they promote the development of a healthy and accurate perception of social connectedness. It is suggested that loneliness is particularly related to attention towards social information, to responsiveness to social threats and rewards, and to the mentalization ability through neural mechanisms. It is widely believed that these complex socio-cognitive processes are largely accommodated by two interrelated, yet distinct, neuro-cognitive network assemblies, commonly referred to as the mirroring and mentalizing networks (Porcelli et al., 2019).

The mirroring network comprises a selection of temporal, parietal, and sensory motor brain regions, which employ data on perceived motoric and biological movement (i.e. facial expressions and bodily gestures) for simulating and interpreting others' overt actions, as well as their basic emotions (Rizzolatti & Sinigaglia, 2016). Overall, this system allows basic understanding of others' actions and emotions, by mainly drawing on one's own sensory, motoric, and visceral representations of what is perceived. However, basic understanding of others' actions and emotions is not sufficient for higher-order inferences on causes and consequences of others' behavioural repertoires, and this is where the mentalizing network comes into play. The mentalizing network comprises a more wildly distributed collection of frontoparietal territories, which draw on past experiences and social knowledge for highly enriched and multimodal representation of socio-cognitive information (both internally and externally oriented). The original core of this network included the posterior superior temporal sulcus, the temporo-parietal junction, the anterior temporal poles, the mPFC, posterior cingulate/praecuneus, and inferior frontal gyrus (Porcelli et al., 2019).

Notably, the social brain regions that are postulated in the social neuroscience model of loneliness are still under maturation during adolescence (Wong et al., 2016). This may contribute to adolescents' increased and differential sensitivity to their social environment. Many behavioural studies have shown the significance of attachment security and social skills in adolescents' interactions with the social world. It is the adolescents' familial attachment that sets the baseline for neurobiological development. Therefore, the developing social brain regions involving mentalization could be highly relevant to heightened perceived loneliness during childhood and adolescence.

Mentalizing affords reflective, regulatory capacities and these seem dependent on the quality of the early environment and attachment experiences; specifically, the attachment figures' ability to respond with contingent and marked affective displays in response to the infant's subjective experience. Dysfunctional mentalization is one of the core features of borderline personality traits. Borderline personality disorder (BPD) patients are particularly likely to fall back on automatic mentalizing which is non-conscious, non-verbal, and unreflective at moments of intense emotional arousal; for example, in challenging interpersonal situations, feelings of shame, guilt, rage, or inadequacy (Fonagy et al., 2015). As a consequence, often there are severe impairments in social cognition. Typical symptoms such as sensations of chronic emptiness and fear of abandonment may specifically contribute to loneliness for those with BPD (Lieb et al., 2004). Although loneliness and an intolerance of aloneness (Matthies et al., 2018) are prevalent in those with BPD, in a maladaptive manner, it may actually lead to the avoidance of others (*vs.* affiliation with others). Hauschild and colleagues (2018) indicated that people with BPD tend to expect future relationships to be negative and therefore may avoid forming bonds with others. This process has been labelled as rejection sensitivity (Gao et al., 2017).

Studies investigating the relationship between borderline personality features and loneliness find a positive correlation between the two dimensions, that is, higher levels of borderline personality features are associated with feeling lonelier. Accordingly, Schermer and colleagues (2020) examined the relationship between borderline personality features and loneliness at the phenotypic, genetic, and environmental levels. The phenotypic correlation between loneliness and the total scale of BPD was 0.51. Their findings also suggest common aetiological factors in loneliness and borderline personality features. Specifically, loneliness was found to have a genetic correlation with the total BPD scale of 0.64 and a unique environmental correlation of 0.40. Just like BPD, the aetiology of loneliness is multifactorial. Studies document moderate (40 per cent) genetic contributions to BPD traits and symptoms (Amad et al., 2014). Loneliness is also heritable (Cacioppo et al., 2014), with genetic factors explaining between 35 and 48 per cent of the variance in loneliness in adults (Distel et al., 2010; Schermer & Martin, 2019). When it comes to environmental factors, in one of the studies, parent-reported childhood neglect predicted increased BPD severity ten years later, during early adulthood (Johnson et al., 2000). Unmet childhood needs for intimacy and early attachment experiences have also been thought to elicit feelings of loneliness. These recall Fonagy and Target's (2002) assertion that early attachment relationships matter because the mental mechanism, which moderates the expression of individual genotypes, is intrinsically linked to the quality of the early relationship with the primary caregiver.

Social neuroscience model for loneliness

And if the soul
is to know itself
it must look into a soul:
the stranger and enemy, we've seen him in the mirror.

—"Argonauts" by George Seferis

An emerging social neuroscience model posits that evolutionarily conserved neurophysiological mechanisms underlie the adaptive, short-term, self-preservation mode triggered by a lack of social connections/mutual protection (Cacioppo & Cacioppo, 2018). This model proposes that loneliness operates as an aversive signal designed to promote adaptation to the vulnerabilities of being alone and motivate reconnection (Cacioppo et al., 2014). Thus, the long-term disease states perpetuated by chronic loneliness may result from the prolonged engagement of neural systems that were intended for short-term preservation. This perspective on the origins of loneliness proposes that the vulnerabilities of isolation promote hypervigilance to guard against potential threats. Lonely individuals often show high levels of anxiety (Stednitz & Epkins, 2006), and hypervigilant responses to negative social stimuli, suggesting heightened recruitment of attentional and self-preservation mechanisms (Cacioppo et al., 2016). Among the range of neural and behavioural effects of perceived isolation documented in human adults other than increased implicit vigilance for social threats and anxiety are: hostility and social withdrawal; increased sleep fragmentation and daytime fatigue; decreased impulse control in favour of responses highest in the response hierarchy (i.e. prepotent responding); increased negativity and depressive symptomatology (Cacioppo & Hawkley, 2009). All these behavioural results support the social neuroscience model that perceived social isolation activates neural, neuroendocrine, and behavioural responses that promote short-term self-preservation.

In line with the above-defined model, when experiencing loneliness for a prolonged period, one's attempts at socialising are accompanied by defensiveness, which increases the likelihood of rejection, ultimately causing more loneliness (Cacioppo & Patrick, 2008, pp. 15–16). Consequently, growing evidence indicates that loneliness increases attention to negative social stimuli (i.e. social threats, rejection, exclusion). The effects of loneliness on attention to potential social threats appear to be largely implicit. In a modified emotional Stroop task, lonely participants relative to non-lonely participants show greater Stroop interference for negative social compared to negative non-social words (Cacioppo & Hawkley, 2009). Yamada and Decety (2009) investigated the effects of subliminal priming on the detection of painful facial expressions and found that lonely individuals are more sensitive to the presence of pain in dislikeable faces than are non-lonely individuals. Supporting data also comes from an fMRI study which indicates that loneliness is associated with greater activation of the visual cortex in response to negative social images in contrast to negative non-social images (Cacioppo et al., 2009). Eye-tracking research similarly shows that individuals high in loneliness are more likely to first fixate on and to spend a greater proportion of their initial viewing time looking at socially threatening stimuli in a social scene, whereas individuals low in loneliness are more likely to first fixate on and spend a greater proportion of their initial viewing time looking at positive stimuli in a social scene (Bangee et al., 2014).

Human and animal research on the effects of social isolation on the brain suggests the involvement of multiple, functionally distinct brain mechanisms including neural mechanisms involved in social threat surveillance and aversion (i.e. amygdala, anterior insula, anterior cingulate), social reward (i.e. ventral striatum), and attention to one's self-preservation in a social context (i.e. orbitofrontal cortex, mPFC, superior temporal sulcus, temporal parietal junction) (Bickart et al., 2014; Cacioppo et al., 2009; Eisenberger, 2012). Recent brain imaging studies on loneliness have demonstrated links between loneliness and changes in brain functions and structures important for affective, social, and cognitive processing. First, loneliness has been linked to attenuated ventral striatum responses to positive social information (Cacioppo et al., 2009; Inagaki et al., 2016), and enhanced insular responses to negative social information (Lindner et al., 2014), as well as aberrant fronto-limbic functional connectivity when processing negative stimuli (Wong et al., 2016). Second, loneliness is associated with altered structural morphometry and integrity in brain regions that are important for social perception, particularly the posterior superior temporal sulcus and temporoparietal junction (Kanai et al., 2012). Lastly, altered grey matter volume in the prefrontal system (i.e. dorsolateral prefrontal cortex) (Kong et al., 2015) as well as its within- and between-network organisations have been associated with diminished self-regulation in lonely people (Feng et al., 2019). Intriguingly, preliminary evidence has shown that associations between loneliness and altered brain functions and structures are mediated by neuroticism and extraversion (Kong et al., 2015).

Insight into how the brain represents subjective social connection may also come from close examination of the mPFC. While the mPFC is known to preferentially activate in response to thinking about the self, it exhibits similar activation when thinking about close others (Chen et al., 2013). Moreover, these activation levels persist after controlling for one's similarity to the close other (Krienen et al., 2010), and are elicited more strongly by deeper characteristics of the person (i.e. their personality) than by superficial characteristics (i.e. their appearance) (Moran et al., 2011). Collectively, these results suggest that the mPFC may play a key role in representing our personal connection to others. Consequently, Courtney and Meyer (2020) combined univariate and multivariate brain imaging analyses to assess whether and how the brain organises representations of others based on how connected they are to our own identity. Their findings confirmed that participants who were less socially connected (i.e. lonelier) showed altered self-other mapping in social brain regions. Most notably, in the mPFC, loneliness was associated with reduced representational similarity between the self and others. The social brain apparently maintains information about broad social categories as well as closeness to the self. Moreover, their results point to the possibility that feelings of chronic social disconnection may be mirrored by a "lonelier" neural self-representation.

Taken together, neuroimaging evidence indicates diverse manifestations of loneliness in multiple neuropsychological processes (Cacioppo & Hawkley, 2009; Cacioppo et al., 2014). The large body of available functional, anatomical, and neuropsychological data from rodents and primates on key regions, and more importantly, on circuitry involved in the social brain, delineate five large-scale brain networks: three partially distinct brain networks anchored in the amygdala (the so-called social perception network, social affiliation network, and social aversion network), and two other large-networks assemblies already extensively described, for example, the mirror network and the mentalizing network (Bickart et al., 2014; Porcelli et al., 2019). Deficits in any of these processes can result in personal difficulties and interpersonal problems, including perceived social isolation.

Conclusion

Loneliness is a negative emotional state induced by subjective perception of social isolation even when among other people. Susceptibility to loneliness is moderately heritable, stable across time, and varied across individuals. People high on loneliness experience gain less reward from daily social interactions, exhibit hypersensitivity to negative social information, show impaired social skills, and have poor self-regulation. Social dysfunction is influenced by basic domain deficits, in attention, working memory, and sensory processing. Alternatively, different neuropsychiatric disorders may share these impairments (at least partially), which in turn may determine social dysfunction and lead to loneliness. The deficits in social cognition related to the mental operations that underlie social interactions, including perceiving, interpreting, and generating responses to the intentions, dispositions, and behaviours of others are reinforced by social deprivation, maybe most significantly during childhood. Also, a growing amount of evidence suggests that social dysfunction is partially independent from other symptoms/deficits, as well as from cognitive and even from social cognitive impairments. Therefore, the observed social dysfunction likely reflects (at least partially) alterations in the social brain itself, which may be independent from other domains.

References

Akdoğan, R. (2017). A model proposal on the relationships between loneliness, insecure attachment, and inferiority feelings. *Personality and Individual Differences, 111*: 19–24.

Amad, A., Ramoz, N., Thomas, P., Jardri, R., & Gorwood, P. (2014). Genetics of borderline personality disorder: systematic review and proposal of an integrative model. *Neuroscience & Biobehavioral Reviews, 40*: 6–19.

Bangee, M., Harris, R. A., Bridges, N., Rotenberg, K. J., & Qualter, P. (2014). Loneliness and attention to social threat in young adults: findings from an eye tracker study. *Personality and Individual Differences, 63* :16–23.

Baron-Cohen, S., Ring, H. A., Wheelwright, S., Bullmore, E. T., Brammer, M. J., Simmons, A., & Williams, S. C. (1999). Social intelligence in the normal and autistic brain: An fMRI study. *European Journal of Neuroscience, 11*: 1891–1898.

Bickart, K. C., Dickerson, B. C., & Barrett, L. F. (2014). The amygdala as a hub in brain networks that support social life. *Neuropsychologia, 63*: 235–248.

Bierman, K. L., & Welsh, J. A. (2000). Assessing social dysfunction: the contributions of laboratory and performance-based measures. *Journal of Clinical Child & Adolescent Psychology, 29*: 526–539.

Bogdan, R. J. (1997). *Interpreting Minds.* Cambridge, MA: MIT Press.

Cacioppo, S., Bangee, M., Balogh, S., Cardenas-Iniguez, C., Qualter, P., & Cacioppo, J. T. (2016). Loneliness and implicit attention to social threat: a high-performance electrical neuroimaging study. *Cognitive Neuroscience, 7*(1–4): 138–159. doi: 10.1080/17588928.2015.1070136

Cacioppo, J. T., & Cacioppo, S. (2018). Loneliness in the modern age: an evolutionary theory of loneliness (ETL). In: J. M. Olson (Ed.), *Advances in Experimental Social Psychology* (pp. 127–196). New York: Academic Press.

Cacioppo, J. T., Cacioppo, S., & Boomsma, D. I. (2014). Evolutionary mechanisms for loneliness. *Cognition and Emotion, 28*: 3–21.

Cacioppo, J. T., & Hawkley, L. C. (2009). Perceived social isolation and cognition. *Trends in Cognitive Sciences, 13*: 447–454.

Cacioppo, J. T., Norris, C. J., Decety, J., Monteleone, G., & Nusbaum, H. (2009). In the eye of the beholder: individual differences in perceived social isolation predict regional brain activation to social stimuli. *Journal of Cognitive Neuroscience, 21*: 83–92.

Cacioppo, J. T., & Patrick, W. (2008). *Loneliness: Human Nature and the Need for Social Connection.* New York: W. W. Norton.

Chen, P. H., Wagner, D. D., Kelley, W. M., Powers, K. E., & Heatherton, T. F. (2013). Medial prefrontal cortex differentiates self from mother in Chinese: evidence from self-motivated immigrants. *Culture and Brain, 1*: 3–15.

Cheng, H., & Furnham, A. (2002). Personality, peer relations, and self-confidence as predictors of happiness and loneliness. *Journal of Adolescence, 25*: 327–339.

Courtney, A. L., & Meyer, M. L. (2020). Self-other representation in the social brain reflects social connection. *Journal of Neuroscience, 40*(29): 5616–5627.

De Bellis, M. D. (2005). The psychobiology of neglect. *Child Maltreatment. 10*(2): 150–172. doi: 10.1177/1077559505275116.

De Bellis, M. D., Keshavan, M., Frustaci, K., Shifflett, H., Iyengar, S., Beers, S. R., & Hall, J. (2002). Superior temporal gyrus volumes in maltreated children and adolescents with PTSD. *Biological Psychiatry, 51*: 544–552.

Dirks, M. A., Treat, T. A., & Weersing, V. R. (2007). Integrating theoretical, measurement, and intervention models of youth social competence. *Clinical Psychology Review, 27*: 327–347.

Distel, M. A., Rebollo-Mesa, I., Abdellaoui, A., Derom, C. A., Willemsen, G., Cacioppo, J. T., & Boomsma, D. I. (2010). Familial resemblance for loneliness. *Behavior Genetics*, *40*: 480–494.

Dunbar, R. I. (2009). The social brain hypothesis and its implications for social evolution. *Annals of Human Biology*, *36*: 562–572.

Dunbar, R. I., & Shultz, S. (2007). Evolution in the social brain. *Science*, *317*: 1344–1347.

Eisenberger, N. I. (2012). The pain of social disconnection: examining the shared neural underpinnings of physical and social pain. *Nature Reviews Neuroscience*, *13*: 421–434.

Feng, C., Wang, L., Li, T., & Xu, P. (2019). Connectome-based individualized prediction of loneliness. *Social Cognitive and Affective Neuroscience*, *14*(4): 353–365.

Flett, G. L., Goldstein, A. L., Pechenkov, I. G., Nepon, T., & Wekerle, C. (2016). Antecedents, correlates, and consequences of feeling like you don't matter: associations with maltreatment, loneliness, social anxiety, and the five factor model. *Personality and Individual Differences*, *92*: 52–56.

Fonagy, P., Luyten, P., & Bateman, A. (2015). Translation: mentalizing as treatment target in borderline personality disorder. *Personality Disorders: Theory, Research, and Treatment*, *6*(4): 380–392.

Fonagy, P., & Target, M. (2002). Early intervention and the development of self-regulation. *Psychoanalytic Inquiry*, *22*(3): 307–335.

Francis, D. D., & Meaney, M. J. (1999). Maternal care and the development of stress responses. *Current Opinion in Neurobiology*, *9*: 128–134.

Gao, S., Assink, M., Cipriani, A., & Lin, K. (2017). Associations between rejection sensitivity and mental health outcomes: a meta-analytic review. *Clinical Psychology Review*, *57*: 59–74.

Hauschild, S., Winter, D., Thome, J., Liebke, L., Schmahl, C., Bohus, M., & Lis, S. (2018). Behavioural mimicry and loneliness in personality disorder. *Comprehensive Psychiatry*, *82*: 30–36.

Inagaki, T. K., Muscatell, K. A., Moieni, M., Dutcher, J. M., Jevtic, I., Irwin, M. R., & Eisenberger, N. I. (2016). Yearning for connection? Loneliness is associated with increased ventral striatum activity to close others. *Social Cognitive and Affective Neuroscience*, *11*(7): 1096–1101.

Johnson, J. G., Smailes, E. M., Cohen, P., Brown, J., & Bernstein, D. P. (2000). Associations between four types of childhood neglect and personality disorder symptoms during adolescence and early adulthood: findings of a community-based longitudinal study. *Journal of Personality Disorders*, *14*: 171–187.

Kanai, R., Bahrami, B., Duchaine, B., Janik, A., Banissy, M. J., & Rees, G. (2012). Brain structure links loneliness to social perception. *Current Biology*, *22*(20): 1975–1979.

Knowles, M. L., Lucas, G. M., Baumeister, R. F., & Gardner, W. L. (2015). Choking under social pressure: social monitoring among the lonely. *Personality and Social Psychology Bulletin*, *41*: 805–821.

Kong, X., Wei, D., Li, W., Cun, L., Xue, S., Zhang, X., & Qui, J. (2015). Neuroticism and extraversion mediate the association between loneliness and the dorsolateral prefrontal cortex. *Experimental Brain Research*, *233*(1): 157–164.

Krienen, F. M., Tu, P. C., & Buckner, R. L. (2010). Clan mentality: evidence that the medial prefrontal cortex responds to close others. *Journal of Neuroscience*, *30*: 13906–13915.

LeDoux, J. (1998). Fear and the brain: where have we been, and where are we going? *Biological Psychiatry*, *44*: 1229–1238.

Lieb, K., Zanarini, M. C., Schmahl, C., Linehan, M. M., & Bohus, M. (2004). Borderline personality disorder. *Lancet, 364*: 453–461.

Lindner, C., Dannlowski, U., Walhöfer, K., Rödiger, M., Maisch, B., Bauer, J., Ohrmann, P., Lencer, R., Zwisterlood, P., Kersting, A., Heindel, W., Arolt, V., Kugel, H., & Suslow, T. (2014). Social alienation in schizophrenia patients: association with insula responsiveness to facial expressions of disgust. *PLoS One, 9*(1): e85014.

Macovei, O. (1986). *The Medical and Social Problems of the Handicapped in Children's Institutions in Iasi Bucharest, Romania*. Bucharest: Institutl de Igiena si Sanatate Publica.

Mattar, J. W. (2017). The difference in emotional intelligence in relation to levels of maltreatment of Jordanian secondary school students. *International Journal of Adolescence and Youth, 23*: 1–9. doi: 10.1080/02673843.2017.1292926.

Matthews, G. A., & Tye, K. M. (2019). Neural mechanisms of social homeostasis. *Annals of the New York Academy of Sciences, 1457*(1): 5–25. https://doi.org/10.1111/nyas.14016.

Matthies, S., Schiele, M. A., Koentges, C., Pini, S., Schmahl, C., & Domschke, K. (2018). Please don't leave me—separation anxiety and related traits in borderline personality disorder. *Current Psychiatry Reports, 20*(10): 83. doi: 10.1007/s11920-018-0951-6.

Maughan, A., & Cicchetti, D. (2002). Impact of child maltreatment and inter-adult violence on children's emotion regulation abilities and socioemotional adjustment. *Child Development, 73*: 1525–1542. doi: 10.1111/1467-8624.00488.

Moran, J. M., Lee, S. M., & Gabrieli, J. D. E. (2011). Dissociable neural systems supporting knowledge about human character and appearance in ourselves and others. *Journal of Cognitive Neuroscience, 23*: 2222–2230.

Mund, M., & Neyer, F. J. (2016). The winding paths of the lonesome cowboy: evidence for mutual influences between personality, subjective health, and loneliness. *Journal of Personality, 84*: 646–657.

NICE (2014). Psychosis and schizophrenia in adults: prevention and management. Clinical Guideline [CG178]. https://nice.org.uk/guidance/cg178 (last accessed September 2021).

Perroud, N. (2016). Childhood maltreatment. In: *Understanding Suicide* (pp. 361–370). Cham, Switzerland: Springer. doi: 10.1007/978-3-319-26282-6_29.

Porcelli, S., Van Der Wee, N., van der Werff, S., Aghajani, M., Glennon J. C., van Heukelum, S., Mogavero, F., Lobo, A., Olivera, F. J., Lobo, E., Posadas, M., Dukart, J., Kozak, R., Arce, E., Afan, I., Vostman, J., Bilderbeck, A., Saris, I., Kas, M. J., & Seretti, A. (2019). Social brain, social dysfunction and social withdrawal. *Neuroscience and Behavioral Reviews, 97*: 10–33. https://doi.org/10.1016/j.neubiorev.2018.09.012.

Punamäki, R. L., Komproe, I., Qouta, S., El-Masri, M., & de Jong, J. T. (2005). The deterioration and mobilization effects of trauma on social support: childhood maltreatment and adulthood military violence in a Palestinian community sample. *Child Abuse & Neglect, 29*: 351–373. https://doi.org/10.1016/j.chiabu.2004.10.011.

Rizzolatti, G., & Sinigaglia, C. (2016). The mirror mechanism: a basic principle of brain function. *Nature Reviews Neuroscience, 17*: 757–765.

Sapolsky, R. M. (2000). Glucocorticoids and hippocampal atrophy in neuropsychiatric disorders. *Archives of General Psychiatry, 57*: 925–935.

Schermer, J. A., Colodro-Conde, L., Grasby, K. L., Hickie, I. B., Burns, J., Ligthart, L., Willemsen, G., Trull, T. J., Martin, N. G., & Boomsma, D. I. (2020). Genetic and environmental causes of individual differences in borderline personality disorder features and loneliness are partially shared. *Twin Research and Human Genetics, 23*: 214–220. https://doi.org/10.1017/thg.2020.62.

Schermer, J. A., & Martin, N. G. (2019). A behavior genetic analysis of personality and loneliness. *Journal of Research in Personality, 78*: 133–137.

Schore, A. N. (2001). Contributions from the decade of the brain to infant mental health: an overview. *Infant Mental Health Journal, 22*: 1–6.

Stednitz, J. N., & Epkins, C. C. (2006). Girls' and mothers' social anxiety, social skills, and loneliness: associations after accounting for depressive symptoms. *Journal of Clinical Child & Adolescent Psychology, 35*: 148–154.

Wong, N. M., Yeung, P. P., & Lee, T. M. (2016). A developmental social neuroscience model for understanding loneliness in adolescence. *Social Neuroscience, 13*(1): 94–103. https://doi.org/10.1080/1747 0919.2016.1256832.

Yamada, M., & Decety, J. (2009). Unconscious affective processing and empathy: an investigation of subliminal priming on the detection of painful facial expressions. *Pain, 143*: 71–75.

Part IV

Psychoanalysis

Introduction to Part IV

Aleksandar Dimitrijević

Whatever shape and intensity loneliness can take in childhood, it will nowhere be as magnified and evident as in the transference during psychoanalytic treatments (even if you consider falling in love, poetry, or music). All details of the patient's need for closeness and understanding, like his or her pain of childhood loneliness and anger due to the separation at the end of the analytic hour, the coming of public holidays, the announcement of the analyst's vacations, will inevitably get into the focus before substantial improvement is possible. And our cast of distinguished psychoanalysts will share with us what they have learned from their patients.

In an absolute gem of a paper, Patrizia Arfelli donates to us four portraits of traumatically lonely persons—a newborn, a seven-year-old, and a fifteen-year-old, and a woman of thirty. She leads the reader through her unique empathetic capacity as well as the reflection on her therapeutic mistakes, which is all read with awe just as much as with anguish.

We feel very fortunate to have essays on all three classical psychoanalytic papers about loneliness and from the leading experts at that. Frieda Fromm-Reichmann's biographer and foremost scholar, Gail Hornstein, writes about Fromm-Reichmann's lifelong awareness of loneliness as the fundamental source of mental pain and her uncanny talent to reach even catatonic patients. Although her now famous paper, "Loneliness", was published only posthumously, it reflected her decades of thinking about this phenomenon, both from her own personal experiences as a refugee and as a central dynamic in the struggles of her patients.

The two pillars of British object relations theory have collaborated very closely, then parted ways, and finally reacted to one another's papers without personal communication but through "counter-papers". Lesley Caldwell, the co-editor of Winnicott's complete works, compares Winnicott's "Capacity to be alone" and Melanie Klein's "On the sense of loneliness" only to find (thanks also to Jane Milton's archival work) that the gap narrowed by Klein's implicit (and late) acceptance of actual social interaction.

A treasure trove of clinical wisdom, Jay Frankel's chapter explains what the role of a psychoanalyst should be in working with adults who grew up having narcissistic, self-absorbed parents. It opens with excerpts from a poignant novel and closes with three touching clinical presentations, yet what will make it most relevant is its "Therapeutic Implications" section, where a subtle balance of "intersubjective" and "abstinence" attitudes is succinctly presented.

Charles Ashbach deals with the consequences of trauma, especially in early development. He provides an insightful literature review, which synthesises everything a clinical psychoanalyst should read, as well as a presentation of long-term treatment and a detailed analysis of a dream. Among many concepts presented in this rich chapter, its implicit focus seems to be hope—its destruction under the influence of trauma and its resurrection in psychoanalytic treatments.

The keyword of Peter Shabad's contribution is—shame. That is, how we may remain encapsulated, chronically lonely because shame makes us think we are not good enough ever to be accepted by others. Standing on the shoulders of his psychoanalytic predecessors as much as on Kierkegaard's and Dostoyevsky's, Shabad is the next of our contributors who seems to excel in his sensitive clinical work, as his presentation shows.

The clinical section and the whole book both come to a close with another chapter by Michael B. Buchholz, who here introduces himself as an experienced empirical researcher and clinical psychoanalyst who can offer erudite theoretical discussion, clinical material, and the results of conversation analysis. Buchholz pleads for innovations that might move the whole field forward, like studying recorded sessions instead of anecdotal vignettes or changing the focus from unilateral psychotherapist interventions to a responsible form of psychoanalytic intersubjectivity—"doing We".

And as editors, we can only hope that we have managed to find a way for this "doing We" with our readers and that this book will help many to feel less lonely but inspired to creative solitude!

CHAPTER 14

The silent cry, the maze of pipes, the mice, and the cellar: the many voices of infantile loneliness

Patrizia Arfelli

A fertile current of thought—that originated with Sandor Ferenczi, runs across the thinking of the British Independents, and comes to the present day still fully relevant—concerns the effects that deficient primary relationships have on the development of the child's psyche.

The family environment can put in place affective transactions that, although not necessarily violent or abusive, can be a source of psychic disorder in the child, as well as in the adolescent and the adult she will one day become. Even an emotional climate characterised by neglect and inadequacy in terms of the child's needs can have a traumatic effect.

The emotional responses of children, resulting from the failure of their primary environment to understand and give sense to their needs, can translate to a great variety of symptoms. Here, I will focus on a specific defence mechanism, emphasising the sliding into a kind of loneliness that often means surrender. This withdrawal must be differentiated from solitude understood as a healthy capacity to be alone; on the contrary, it represents an insidious and invisible manifestation of deep suffering.

There are many ways in which loneliness unfolds improperly. It can have the features of hopeless resignation with a progressive surrender to psychic death, or it can be configured as an alternative world, which protects against disintegration and gives respite to psychic pain. It can assume the traits of a safe and unassailable fortress, where challenge and triumph dominate, as happens in some adolescents, or it can be the result of fragmentation, in which a part of the personality is segregated and left "alone", without any contact with the rest of the child's psyche.

* * *

The silent cry

"A person may be in solitary confinement, and yet not be able to be alone. How greatly he must suffer is beyond imagination": this statement of Winnicott (1957, p. 30) is, in my view, the most effective beginning in describing how an infant can fall into loneliness and fragmentation, easily risking withdrawal and psychic death, in spite of the presence of a mother who, although being containing and in contact, performs this function in an inconstant and discontinuous way.

The case I will illustrate does not refer to a strictly psychoanalytic situation, but more broadly to a clinical intervention. It is about a consultation I did when, many years ago, I worked as a doctor on a child neuropsychiatric ward and was a consultant to several other wards in the hospital, including pneumology.

Anna was born with an extremely severe congenital malformation that compromised her capacity to breathe autonomously and to survive. She was immediately hospitalised in the ICU and put on an automatic ventilator via tracheostomy. She could not see her mother. At that time, in the late 1990s, the presence of parents was considered a hindrance on the wards with at-risk children and visits were categorically forbidden. The parents could watch their children only through a window but were not allowed to enter the room and hold them, feed them, and take care of them. However, the babies in the ICU lived all together in a big room full of equipment where they were closely watched over and regularly monitored by the nursing staff, who were ready to intervene immediately at any anomalous "beep".

Anna lived on this ward for the first year and a half of her life. Even though her living conditions were characterised by heavy physical limitations (she was connected to a variety of medical devices that allowed her to survive, that is, tracheostomy to breathe, nasogastric feeding tube, intravenous fluids to correct the electrolyte imbalance ...), her psychic and relational development proceeded regularly enough. The ICU nurses described her as an attentive and present girl, lively and responsive, and especially capable of grasping with the eyes onto whoever passed by and of receiving in response some cuddling, some words, or a minute of precious time from her caregivers. She was hardly ever alone.

The progressive improvement of her physical condition over time led to her transfer to the pneumology ward, to have her oxygenation monitored and to free her, gradually, from the dependence on the automatic ventilator and the tracheostomy. Anna was eighteen months old when she finally met her mother and was moved to a single room with her. This change seemed to cause remarkable achievements and progress in the child: the proximity of her mother enhanced her relational and physical skills, and the child rapidly increased in weight, learning to walk (dragging the ventilator around, bulky yet still necessary for her survival), and to communicate effectively with gestures and facial expressions (the tracheostomy prevented Anna from making any kind of sound, but she knew how to make herself understood).

Everything seemed to be going for the better, but little by little the child started to "shut down". She became duller and less responsive to positive or negative inputs from the environment, and she spent more and more time in a state of anxious loneliness. She was often unresponsive to the calls of her mother and the hospital nurses, although she was not locked in an absent, autistic withdrawal. She rather seemed to be trapped in a state of distress that nobody could decode. Anna seemed to be really lonely now.

This was the reason I was consulted and came to know the girl. I went to the pneumology ward to carry out some observations. The child always appeared to be very capable of benefiting from the revitalising aspects of her mother's presence along with mine, but over the course of the day she would again become absent, anxious, unreachable.

In the numerous interviews I had with her mother—who was able to have an empathic connection and attunement with her daughter—her concern about Anna's evident suffering emerged. Going back in time, we confronted the terrible distress she had felt when her daughter's survival was still uncertain, the pain and helplessness of the time when she could only watch her through a window, her devastating fatigue after spending almost two years as a "sentinel", and finally the relief as her child began to improve physically and she could stay with her at least during the day.

We all had been so blind and unable to understand what was before our eyes, and only accidentally was I able to grasp the missing link. One afternoon I went to pneumology for an unplanned observation of that increasingly sad and lonely girl, and the scene before me was terrifying in its simplicity. Anna was alone in her room and was "crying" desperately; no sound came out of her throat, rendered useless by the tracheostomy, but I felt like I heard her mute scream rising from her wide-open mouth, her gaping eyes, her intensely red face, and the writhing of her entire body on the bed. When Anna lost the gaze of the nurses in the ICU and the constant relationship with them, she suddenly found herself alone. She was alone in a room the nurses rarely entered and alone with a mother who was certainly a "good enough" but also a very tired mother who increasingly needed to delegate the care of her daughter to the ward nurses so as to have a break, and some time to take a nap in her chair, to make a phone call, to get a coffee on the ground floor of the hospital.

The image of Anna screaming silently and failing to reach the other with her desperation, without any possibility of effect and transformation, lends itself to represent a state of loneliness (that can be assimilated to what Ferenczi called the *sideration* of the ego) and fragmentation, into which an infant can collapse when—for physical and/or more frequently psychic reasons—she is denied the possibility of meeting another subject who can give an affective meaning to what is happening in her body and her mind. Loneliness becomes not only an obvious consequence of a missing relational grasping, but also the result of a defensive withdrawal from an encounter which can create frustration and persecution that can annihilate the mind of the infant.

Understanding this dynamic drove the health care staff to accelerate her weaning from the automatic ventilator, a process that luckily went well without too many problems. Once the tube was removed from her trachea, the child had a chance to find her own voice, at first tenuous and then increasingly more powerful. And the ward resonated with her voice, her laughter, and her shouts—calls that were finally effective—until Anna, at the age of two, was finally able to go home.

The young plumber

Alex is a seven-year-old boy who has been diagnosed with Asperger's syndrome because he is very isolated and trapped in a world full of plumbing systems, especially pipes. He incessantly asks his parents to check the functioning of every water input and output system of the household appliances, and his school life and learning are compromised by this need for total control.

The narcissistic wound from having a child who is far from his parents' expectations, a challenging and demanding boy, has soon driven his parents—overtly devaluating and intrusive people—to emotionally distance themselves from Alex and to renounce any possibility of accepting and giving meaning to his evident anxieties—both skills that they don't particularly have. The child's dramatic response, which further increases his parents' distancing, is to escalate his compulsive requests and to isolate himself completely in long masturbatory activities, in a vain attempt to quell an anxiety he does not know how to limit.

When his parents take him to psychotherapy, surprisingly they do not ask to understand and work through the meaning of the boy's symptoms, but rather to replace it with something easier to manage. Behind their apparent acceptance of a diagnosis that they don't even question, there is much anger and shame, an evident and important lack of containment and acceptance of their son, who is so disturbing and alien to them, and a big affective disinvestment for the benefit of his younger brother who is a simpler and more "obedient" child. "If we could, we would change him," they tell me. But Alex, unlike the pipes, cannot be replaced …

The beginning of the treatment with Alex is disruptive: throughout the first year the boy enacts in each session what his parents have described to me with shame and desolation. He comes in, hardly greets me, runs into the bathroom to flush the toilet, tries to dismantle the ballcock, then comes into the therapy room, makes sure that the pipes are well fixed in the cabinet under the sink, goes back into the bathroom and checks the pipes of the bidet, flushes the toilet again, watches the mechanism for filling up the tank, and then everything starts over again. I follow him in each of his investigations, I assist him during these operations, I help him. Alex is astonished that I neither scold nor punish him. In the final part of every session, the child is so tired that he invariably lies down on the couch. There, he starts to masturbate vigorously and this activity leaves him so exhausted that he falls asleep, flushed and sweaty, until his mother arrives.

From the beginning, I am certain that Alex is not a child with Asperger's but is rather experiencing a *fundamental schizoid reaction* (Fairbairn, 1952). He is "possessed" by an anxiety that subsides only by checking pipes and masturbating, but he is not refractory in relating with me.

He just seems not to expect that the other can help him find a moment of peace. Me following and assisting him in his plumbing raids enables him to gradually discover me. He starts to ask me about the arrangement of some pipes, why a mechanism works in a certain way, and he especially asks for a guarantee of the watertightness of my plumbing system.

For a long time, my interventions are very concrete, aiming to give him containment and understanding, and I hardly make any classical interpretations. Alex keeps on checking the pipes, but gradually decreases his masturbatory activity, often resting by my side at the end of the session while we both quietly watch the running water.

After about a year of treatment, the child accepts my invitation to draw a plumbing system the way he imagines it, and his fantasies take an initial, embryonic form of representation that can be shared: for months he traces quick marks on countless pieces of paper that he immediately tears up. He designs intricate labyrinths of fine interwoven pipes that end in the void, at the edge of the paper. In his mazes Alex finds respite. I am reminded of the *psychic retreats* theorised by Steiner (1993)—psychic states defensively used to protect oneself against the pain, hiding places in which the patient finds relief from anxiety. The risk of Alex getting lost in the retreat and being trapped in the labyrinth is, however, very high.

One day I decide to draw a tub on his sheet of paper, at the end of one of the countless pipes, so that all the "water" running in them will not get dispersed and the whole system will not be in vain. My *ludic interpretation* (Rodrigué, 2015) opens up a two-handed production that becomes increasingly more accurate and developed: for many months, Alex is busy first drawing with me large hollow pipes that belong to sophisticated plumbing systems, and then constructing three-dimensional washing machines, sinks, and toilets out of paper, disinvesting at the same time in his need to explore actual pipes in our room and in his life.

A decline in his fragmentation/liquefaction anxieties and a parallel development of his capacity for representation that the treatment has rendered possible, along with his acquisition of symbolic activity that enables him to represent these anxieties instead of acting them out, lead to a remarkable clinical improvement in Alex, who rapidly invests in learning, makes friends at school, and gradually loses all interest in pipes.

The therapy is about to conclude and, in the last session, Alex, who is almost ten years old, asks me seriously: "Do you remember when I had to check all the pipes, here too? Do you know why I did it? Because pipes are important. You see, pipes contain and must not break … And if the external ones break, it is a disaster; but if our internal pipes break, we all flood and we can no longer live!"

The "rat boy"

John, like Anna, also met me when I worked at the hospital. At that time, we could offer psychotherapy to some young people who came to the outpatient clinic or the ward. John was one of them.

As Steiner (1993) says, an analyst who works with patients trapped in a *psychic retreat* will have to deal with huge technical problems. The technical issue on which I would like to focus here concerns the importance of *timing*. I aim to show how two years of patient listening and waiting on my part were nullified, in just one session, as a consequence of an interpretation that, although formally correct, was made too early with respect to the boy's capacity to accept and acknowledge it. My words turned out to be dramatically disruptive and provoked an immediate interruption of the treatment.

John's parents ask for help because their fifteen-year-old son had been found by the custodian of his former school as he was trying to break into it through a window. They describe him as a very lonely boy since childhood, unable to have long-lasting friendships because of his tendency to overwhelm the other. His favourite entertainment is catching insects and pulling off their legs or wings one by one. Also, in the relationship with his family, he alternates between long spells in which he is isolated and silent and sudden tantrums during which he shatters objects in the home.

So far, his parents have always denied his difficulty, and their attitude with him has been very placatory and compliant. Suffice it to say that, despite the perception of their son's potential harmfulness, they have given in to his request and have bought him a pellet gun, just to propitiate and appease him. Of course, we could discuss at length the pathogenic effects of collusive denials of those parents who cannot deal effectively with the suffering of their children, but the focus of this chapter is a different one and I shall concentrate on the boy.

John agrees reluctantly to meet, but his need to be listened to is so intense that he immediately "floods" the consultation sessions with accounts of his exploits, far more elaborate than those his parents know. The emerging picture is a *pathological organisation*, a cynical and contemptuous *retreat* (Steiner, 1993) in which the boy can renounce relationships with the others, even his peers, as he is satisfied by the cruel fantasies he cultivates covertly and acts out occasionally.

The sessions are a kind of show, broadcast once a week, with a constant regularity on his part: John, in two years of therapy, has never missed a session. Very soon, I understand that to access his retreat, I must for a long time just listen to his exploits, actual or imagined, without startling or confronting him as a superego with the actuality of his actions, mirroring without differentiating myself too much from him. In other words, every time John perceives that I am frightened or horrified by his actions, he withdraws and shelters in his fortress, mocking my despicable sensitivity and reaffirming his pleasure in being alone and inaccessible, in a place in his mind where he is omnipotent and there is no room for feelings or for the other.

For a long time, and with great countertransference pain, I am the only privileged spectator of the scenes coming to life in the sessions: John describes how he lurks down the road and fires his shots at stray cats and unsteady old women; he tells how he has finally managed to enter his former middle school and set a fire; not least, he brings his gun to a session and "shoots" me on a fresh, visible scar that I have on my forehead.

I think what helps me involve John in the treatment, in spite of his declarations of independence and refractoriness to the relationship, is his perceiving of my attitude and my rare words as some kind of respect for his extreme psychic suffering, with which he has lost all contact by splitting it onto the others in order to triumph over them.

I have often wondered what kind of a child he had been, how much uncontained pain he must have experienced, so as to structure such an archaic and despairing defence.

I never tried to determine whether his exploits were just imagined or actually acted out; I always took them as "true", because they were produced by his mind. Staying for a long time in the role of silent spectator of his sadistic fantasies—the only company that he would accept in his retreat—I was gradually able to offer myself as an object which not only listens but also mirrors and bears witness. My comments about his loneliness and the defensive function of his sadism, rather than causing his usual flight into his inaccessible place, finally found him listening and thinking.

It took two years for John to acknowledge our link which had been built with much effort; one session was enough to break it.

At that time, the boy was hardly mentioning his sadistic exploits and began to talk about the first "pet" that he could permit himself to have: a mouse. To the first mouse he soon added another one, because he felt that the first one was "too lonely". John kept them together in a cage and, to his great surprise, one day he found out that the second mouse was pregnant! We followed the progress of the pregnancy, and John even tolerated when I interpreted, in a light way, the fecundity not only of that link but also of ours, through which something new was being born.

Then the baby mice were born, and he spoke with tenderness of their small size and softness: "Next time, I'll bring them to the session," he said.

I felt touched and I could not refrain from saying: "Yes, sure, I'll gladly see them: I believe that now you feel you can bring these small and newborn parts of yourself here, without being afraid that they will get hurt."

John immediately recoiled and said: "You are insulting me. You are calling me a rat!" and then grew silent.

He cancelled the following session, refused to answer my phone calls and, despite my attempts to reconnect, he broke off the treatment without even a chance to say goodbye.

This "incontinence" of mine taught me a lot about the importance of timing: John allowed me to glimpse and even verbalise his painful psychic loneliness, but he was not yet ready to accept that the suffering child he had been could be recognised and named. I knew that I would have welcomed and respected him, but he had not yet come to this awareness, he had not yet structured enough of the trust in the "other" that allows a child to entrust the object with all his needs without fear of being mortified.

My over-hasty saturated interpretation caused John's immediate withdrawal into his psychic fortress, to which he denied me access forever, barring the door without any possibility for forgiveness.

The day the music died

I would like to enrich my thoughts about loneliness in the evolutive age with a final clinical vignette concerning the treatment of an adult patient; I will show how dissociated somatic memories of a traumatic event, experienced as a child and never worked-through, broke violently into the therapy room in a quest for "right of citizenship" that had been denied so far.

Nina is almost thirty years old when she consults me. She is the mother of a two-year-old boy. She is asking for help because she seems to need some support for her parental functions: her son annoys her with his vitality and exuberance. His requests for physical contact make her distance herself from him, and the feelings stirred in her are often characterised by rejection and repulsion, especially when it is time to change his nappy and clean his genitals.

Nina's marital relationship is good, but very poor sexually. She occasionally suffers from panic attacks that begin with a distressing feeling of being "attacked from behind" and then take the form of the conviction of being colonised from within by an untreatable, undiagnosed disease that will quickly kill her.

My intervention about parenthood very soon turns into psychoanalytic psychotherapy. Our work unfolds between the present and the past, between current events and remote memories, between her recent experiences as a mother and the emotional vicissitudes she experienced as a child. Nina has good capacity for insight but seems to have some "blind spots" that prevent her from working-through some particular issues in depth.

She does not talk much about her childhood, which she says was without meaningful events. She remembers herself as a serene and lively child, a cheerful girl who loved to sing, "always with music in the head". When she was about ten years old, her family moved to a different neighbourhood, and Nina dates the change in her character to that time; she became more isolated and silent, and hardly integrated into her new school and social environment. She spent many years in solitude, sadness, and desolation ("I no longer sang; music was dead in my head") until she began university, where she met her husband-to-be, a very containing young man. A few years later they got married.

Only after a year of psychotherapeutic work does Nina mention the courtyard of the house where she had lived until she was ten. It was a meeting place for all the children of the building and a safe playground, always under the watch of a parent from a balcony. But one day—Nina is not sure that it is a real memory, in fact she is almost certain that it is just a fantasy—the other children went home, and she was left alone in the courtyard ... she must have been about ten years old ... and she found herself in the cellar. She does not know how she ended up there. She seems to remember that a man came into the courtyard and, "attacking her from behind", dragged her into the cellar. But she has no memory, just a blurred impression ... it must have been an invention of hers, she says.

In the protected space of therapy, new details start emerging. They are no longer vague, and they make her account more and more plausible. Her mother went back into the apartment, nobody was on the balcony. She remembers a man holding her hand and taking her into the cellar, and then she wildly runs upstairs and enters her home upset; she remembers her mother's reaction, crushed by guilt because she had stopped watching her, and her father's violent rage.

At home nobody ever talked about that episode again, and Nina, in time, cultivated within the hypothesis that it was an imagined story, as if rejecting the event from her memory was an inevitable consequence of its total disavowal by her parents.

It was impossible for me not to think about abuse as Ferenczi meant it, as a result not only of the violent overlapping of the "language of passion" and that of "tenderness", but also of the denial by the family environment of the traumatic event and the ensuing despair, with dissociative outcomes on the child's psyche resulting in the well-known defensive mechanism of *autotomy* (Ferenczi, 1949).

The story now presses to be told, but the account always unfolds on a rational register, as if Nina is narrating a film; the emotional contact with the described horror is lacking, the pain is dissociated elsewhere. I feel that this suffering in part settles in my mind, but I am aware of having to keep it and wait before naming it, because the patient has not yet developed the tools to make this dramatic experience thinkable and representable.

Not only do her current symptoms (inhibited sexuality, panic attacks, presence of an internal persecutor) make sense in the light of what happened then, but also the sadness and quieting of the "inner music" that appeared after the family's move (probably a hasty flight from the house of the abusing experience), as well as the loneliness that stayed with Nina for more than ten years, assume new meaning in connection with the traumatic event that has not been worked-through. Her loneliness is not so much due to her distancing or frightened rejection of the other, but rather due to dissociating the most vital aspects of herself and due to the loss of contact with them, as an archaic defence against a pain impossible to bear by herself.

Recovering dissociated memories and emotions is far from painless and it happens during a dramatic session, three years into treatment.

Nina keeps on wondering about the silence and loneliness she was left in as a child, after the traumatic event, and she questions again the veracity of it, saying that she might have made it up, in an extreme attempt to avoid acknowledging the limits of her parents and the ensuing anger that their denial now stirs in her. "But it does not make any sense, perhaps it never happened … Why would that man ask me to show him where my cellar was and bring me there? There was nobody in the courtyard, what sense did it make to bring me down there?"

I reply, possibly too abruptly: "It was a trap to have you follow him, to hurt you without being seen …"

Nina bursts into tears and while sobbing she cries: "The smell of the cellar! Now I feel everything, I see the darkness, I smell the cellar …" It is an extremely intense moment for us both: Nina recovers contact with sensory mnestic traces of the trauma, dormant for many years in her mind, denied and apparently lost, and the pain she now feels is also connected with her rejoining and finding again a part of herself she had forgotten existed.

"Now I know that it happened," she says, and I feel with her the consolation of having helped that girl to leave the desolate loneliness of the cellar where she had been locked in for too many years.

* * *

I want to conclude with a final reflection about Anna, Alex, John, and Nina, whom—despite the different psychopathological meanings of their peculiar forms of loneliness—I have gathered through a common thread. I would like to briefly focus on some qualities that the analyst needs to display with those patients who, in order to protect themselves from the pain coming from a traumatic contact with reality (internal as well as external), have not been able to find a more vital alternative and have withdrawn into loneliness and isolation.

One of the first, indispensable qualities is the therapist's open-mindedness and freedom of thought. She needs to be able to observe and grasp hidden links, giving up on the "comfortable" known and theoretically reassuring stances, so as to explore scarcely lit scenarios, in which we often move uncomfortably and painfully.

Anna was trapped in a soundless universe, from which it was not so difficult to "extract" her. She has always reminded me of the children who are found alive under the ruins after an earthquake, annihilated by the darkness and the silence of the catastrophe but ready to cry when held in the arms that are able to grasp and rescue them. The usually traumatic experience in the ICU might paradoxically have given her a relational equipment that worked "as a shield", like the beams that protect against the debris, when the impact of an invisible loneliness actually risked fragmenting her. If it is true that my realisation about her mute cry triggered a thought and a project that brought her back to life, it is just as true that Anna, in spite of her progressive surrender, kept on giving a signal that luckily found a "sonar" capable of catching it.

Another essential and indispensable characteristic is respect: the analyst needs to be open to go where the patient is at that time, without asking him to "bend" to the analyst's theoretical and interpretive frameworks but instead respecting the patient's defences and reaching out on his terrain, no matter how uneven that is. This is particularly evident in child analyses.

Alex (superficially diagnosed with Asperger's) could not and did not want to let go of the obsessive control of the pipes that gave him a guarantee of containment, and for a long while I had to accompany him in that maze, to get lost with him, to experience isolation and the impossibility of finding a way out, and to feel his—and my—loneliness. To be accepted in such a forsaken world is the first step to being able to help the patient leave it.

However accessible the retreat might appear to be, very often we see its inviolability. Here our *negative capability* (Bion, 1970) comes into play, that is, the capacity to wait for the patient to be ready to emerge, even for a short time, from his loneliness, along with our openness to a contact in the brief moments of his "excursion". The respect I mentioned above is not only for suffering but also for the psychic time that the patient needs to be able to entrust us with his vulnerable aspects that he is tenaciously protecting in his isolation, in an effort not to attack us but to defend himself.

John's example illustrates dramatically, as we have seen, the traumatic impact of losing the attunement between the patient's and the analyst's needs. It is a common experience that a wild animal, however hungry it is, will not accept being fed directly from the hand of a human. It will need to be fed day by day with small bites of trust before it dares to approach a little, and then a little bit more … And any sudden movement on our part may make it go away forever, as happened with John.

A final, though not exhaustive, observation about the kind of emotional availability demanded of the analyst in treating this kind of patient is that we need to find the courage to reach children and adults who are annihilated by suffering, knowing that their psychic wounds need a delicate touch and that we will not remain "clean" and unscathed after contact with them.

In this respect, helping Nina leave the cellar was an extremely painful task for me as well; for a long time I had to respect her identification with her parents who could not see what had happened and, in so doing, denied it the right to be thought and told. I feared that the girl would remain "locked in down there" forever, unseen and forgotten, and I felt touched just like she was when, holding my hand, she came back into the light of the day.

References

Bion, W. R. (1970). *Attention and Interpretation*. London: Tavistock.

Fairbairn, W. R. D. (1952). *Psycho-Analytic Studies of the Personality*. London: Routledge.

Ferenczi, S. (1949). Confusion of the tongues between the adults and the child (the language of tenderness and of passion). *International Journal of Psycho-Analysis, 30*: 225–230.

Rodrigué, E. (2015). Ludic interpretation: an attitude towards play. In: N. Lisman-Pieczanski & A. Pieczanski (Eds.), *The Pioneers of Psychoanalysis in South America*. London: Routledge.

Steiner, J. (1993). *Psychic Retreats: Pathological Organisations in Psychotic, Neurotic and Borderline Patients*. London: Routledge.

Winnicott, D. W. (1957). The capacity to be alone. In: *The Maturational Processes and the Facilitating Environment*. London: Hogarth, 1965.

CHAPTER 15

Landscapes of loneliness: engaging with Frieda Fromm-Reichmann's pioneering work

Gail A. Hornstein

> You could never quite get used to loneliness—every time she thought she had, she sank further into it.
>
> —Brit Bennett, *The Vanishing Half*, 2020

At the start of her now classic paper on loneliness, Frieda Fromm-Reichmann wrote:

> I am not sure what inner forces have made me, during the last years, ponder about and struggle with the psychiatric problems of loneliness. I have found a strange fascination in thinking about it—and subsequently in attempting to break through the aloneness of thinking about loneliness by trying to communicate what I believe I have learned. (1959)

In this chapter, I explore Fromm-Reichmann's "strange fascination" with loneliness and her lifelong desire to "break through the aloneness", evident in that paper and more broadly in her work with patients, locked into states of what she called "non-communicative isolation". My focus on the links between Fromm-Reichmann's life and work—which have occupied my thinking since the 1990s, when I began the research for my biography, *To Redeem One Person Is to Redeem the World* (Hornstein, 2000)—seems especially apt for an inquiry into her writing on loneliness. She herself said that her insights into this topic emerged both from her work with patients "and from other experiences of my own".

Fromm-Reichmann confronted a paradox: the incommunicability of what she called "real loneliness" seemingly places the state beyond psychological investigation, since only experiences that can be put into words, however imperfectly, can be analysed phenomenologically. Illness may be another such state, as Virginia Woolf famously noted:

The merest schoolgirl, when she falls in love, has Shakespeare or Keats to speak her mind for her; but let a sufferer try to describe a pain in his head to a doctor and language at once runs dry. There is nothing ready made for him. He is forced to coin words himself, and, taking his pain in one hand, and a lump of pure sound in the other (as perhaps the people of Babel did in the beginning), so to crush them together that a brand new word in the end drops out. (1930, p. 7)

The philosopher Havi Carel (2016, p. 182) similarly remarks: "The kind of experiences illness affords are often difficult to make sense of ... perhaps certain extreme and unique experiences cannot be communicated in any direct, propositional manner ...." So why would Frieda Fromm-Reichmann—a busy, pragmatic, and focused clinician—spend years trying to analyse something that in her own view defied description?

Yet at some level, we might ask whether this is equally true of much of lived experience. We rarely have access to *any* experience directly, even in ourselves; transforming fragments of memory, feeling, thought, or image into narrative is a core challenge of human psychology (a phenomenon about which Spence, 1982 and Rogers, 2006 have written especially eloquently). Countless psychological works are based on the indirect accounts of people trying to articulate the contours of their own inchoate experiences, via psychotherapy or pastoral counselling, or in a less formal way, as in a diary. Indeed, for Fromm-Reichmann, that was the point of psychotherapy—to make it possible to put into words what has been too painful to articulate, even to oneself, and to make sense of such experiences in an atmosphere of compassion and understanding.

Since, by definition, truly incommunicable states can never be fully described, if we are to understand anything about them, we must rely on retrospective accounts by people who have been in such states but emerged sufficiently to be able to depict them (in words, artistic works, or in the case of one of Fromm-Reichmann's patients, with hand gestures). Such accounts enable at least some insight into what experiences of this kind are like, and Fromm-Reichmann relied heavily on them in analysing the phenomenology of what Rogers (2006) later called "the unsayable". Indeed, Fromm-Reichmann's use of, and respect for, first-person accounts of psychosis—either published or recounted by patients—inspired the use of such materials by later researchers (myself included, cf. Hornstein, 2011, 2017).

But if, as Fromm-Reichmann hypothesised, there is, at the core of every psychosis, a part that defies description, then the empathic response of another is precluded, leaving the patient utterly isolated. This "real loneliness", she concluded after years of study, is "an utterly painful and disintegrative experience", which people "can endure for only a limited period without becoming severely disturbed". She said it was an "unconstructive desolate state of aloneness", with a "specific character of paralysing hopelessness and unutterable futility". One of her Chestnut Lodge patients described it as "frozen in isolation into a block of ice".

Fromm-Reichmann emphasised that the intensity and destructive effects of this particular experience make it very different from other kinds of loneliness. For example, she noted a kind of "cultural loneliness" that can give people in Western societies—where individuality is valued above all else—a sense of isolation and lack of community connection which might be quite painful. There are also, she noted, the "states of seclusion voluntarily imposed to stimulate creativity", potentially causing a "creative loneliness" that comes from having to endure the struggles of solitude. "These states of self-induced loneliness (or should we rather say 'aloneness')", Fromm-Reichmann argued, "can be quite constructive", and she herself often sought them out for extended periods of writing. There is also, she noted, the "detachment" of "schizoid artistic personalities", which keeps them cut off from others and thus subject to constant loneliness. Finally, there are states of "temporary aloneness" (as imposed, for example, by illness), in which a person longs to be with others but cannot do so. But none of these, Fromm-Reichmann argued, is anything like the "essential loneliness" that was her focus.

Even the psychotic episodes that can occur "during solitary confinement (among prisoners, solitary sailors, or people stationed on isolated outposts)" are not as distressing as this "real loneliness", an experience she said is "beyond hope and despair" and "extremely uncanny, gruesome, painful and frightening". Years of careful comparison among these phenomenologically similar states led Fromm-Reichmann to define this extreme form of loneliness as

> a state of mind in which the fact that there were people in one's past life is more or less forgotten, and in which the hope that there may be interpersonal relationships in one's future life is out of the realm of expectation or imagination.

She wondered whether there might be other types of pathogenic loneliness as well, perhaps described under different names—for example, "catatonia", "loss of reality", or what Spitz called "anaclitic depression". Was "separation anxiety" essentially the same as "fear of loneliness"? Most importantly, she asked, given the complexity and importance of the topic, why does loneliness not even appear as an entry in psychiatric textbooks?

Fromm-Reichmann thought that part of the reason psychiatrists understood so little about this core experience of deeply distressed patients is that it is so "extremely frightening and gruesome" that those who manage to come out of it try to block any memory of the state or "even their fear of it". Without such first-hand descriptions, doctors have little to go on in understanding their patients' experiences. Unfortunately, Fromm-Reichmann noted, this has the effect of making such patients feel even worse, since "… it produces the sad conviction that nobody else has experienced, or ever will experience", what they had to endure.

The philosopher L. A. Paul's (2014) notion of "transformative experience" highlights the unique qualities of states that cannot be imagined or understood until or unless a person has actually entered them. Paul offers a range of examples, some real, some imagined: having a child, becoming a vampire, receiving a cochlear implant, enlisting in the military. But she does not talk at all about experiences as disturbing as the one that preoccupied Fromm-Reichmann, even though this "essential loneliness" seems to conform closely to Paul's definition of transformative experience—in particular, being a state that cannot be imagined without being in it. Attempting to communicate something which, by its very nature, cannot be fully articulated may have been a quixotic goal, but Fromm-Reichmann's persistence in uncovering some of its constituent parts has made her paper a classic, and we can learn from it still.

In it, she recognised the power of loneliness as experienced not only by the patient but also by the analyst, whose own feelings of estrangement and involuntary aloneness arise when her empathic efforts prove insufficient. Fromm-Reichmann did not seem to see this latter kind of loneliness—the one experienced by the analyst—as countertransference, that is, as the analyst's response to the *patient's* loneliness. Rather, she highlighted the analyst's direct experience of her *own* loneliness at failing to reach the patient sufficiently to create an empathic bond between them. Fromm-Reichmann could take even minimal efforts by a patient towards connection— moving aside on a bench to make room for her, communicating through gestures, etc.—as a signal of openness to relationship. But she found it deeply painful to experience the loneliness of reaching out and not being met by any response from the other. I believe it was her desire to come to grips with this profound sense of disappointment and isolation, both in herself and in her patients, that led Fromm-Reichmann to spend so many years drafting and redrafting a paper that—however classic it has become—was not something she herself thought conclusive enough to publish (and which came to be known only posthumously).

She was trying to get at a state much deeper than the temporary loneliness which psychologist Clark Moustakas (1961), for example, talks about, which can have positive effects or lead to a profound existential understanding of the human condition, as it did for him. In contrast, Fromm-Reichmann focused on a state so painful that the desire to escape it is paramount. Although she did not experience this state as intensely as her patients did, she clearly sensed its awfulness. Indeed, her lifelong effort to understand other people by empathically entering their experience and helping them to make sense of their own feelings—which began with her parents in childhood and continued throughout decades of work with withdrawn, sometimes deeply regressed patients—was key to Fromm-Reichmann's inspiring success as a psychotherapist.

But when she failed to find a way to reach the other person, thereby exposing the loneliness each of them felt, Fromm-Reichmann found it deeply distressing. Indeed, her choice to spend so much time trying to *understand* loneliness, to penetrate its secrets, could be seen as an attempt to avoid the anguish of actually *experiencing* it. Thinking analytically about an unendurable state is one way of trying to master it.

* * *

Reflecting on Fromm-Reichmann's work on loneliness in a paper presented shortly after her death, the psychoanalyst Henry von Witzleben (1958) suggested that while she was certainly influenced by Sullivan's focus on "interpersonal relationships", an earlier and much more powerful influence was her old friend Martin Buber's idea of "I and Thou", a connection far deeper than what Sullivan described. "I and Thou is not only a relationship, it is—and this is very important—the formation of something new: the *We*," von Witzleben (p. 42) noted. It was at this border, this edge, where Fromm-Reichmann sought to situate herself—the emotional space where the possibility of a new form of connection could begin to take shape. What made her such a brilliant therapist was her adept use of intuition to break through to even the most withdrawn patients, thereby creating at least the potential for the emergence of that "We". Fromm-Reichmann's greatest satisfaction was guiding people towards seeing their feelings—no matter how frightening or bewildering—as meaningful and as a potential bridge to empathy, towards the creation of that "something new" so fundamental to how she saw her role in life.

Fromm-Reichmann and Buber had first met in the 1920s, an intellectually fertile period for both of them. She was in the midst of creating a utopian psychiatric community in her home in Heidelberg that blended Judaism and psychoanalysis; he was working collaboratively in nearby Frankfurt with Franz Rosenzweig, Gershom Scholem, Erich Fromm, and others at the Freies Jüdisches Lehrhaus (Free Jewish Study House), the pioneering centre for adult education. Buber's *Ich und Du* (*I and Thou*), published in 1923, highlighted the central importance of authentic encounters characterised by mutuality and reciprocity, which each person enters as a true partner, never treating the other as an object to be acted upon. This epitomised Fromm-Reichmann's view of the psychotherapeutic relationship, even with severely distressed patients.

In her important paper "The Analyst's Experience of Loneliness", Sandra Buechler (1998, p. 95) argues that rather than seeing loneliness as "residing within the patient", it is more helpful to view it "as an occurrence in an interpersonal context that is a product of intrapsychic and interpersonal factors". This more interactional definition is closer to Fromm-Reichmann's, and highlights both the complexity of the experience and the opportunities offered to both therapist and patient to break free of its painful consequences.

Further, in her recent "Biography of Loneliness", the cultural historian Fay Bound Alberti (2019, p. 226) notes that the current view of loneliness—"an internalised sense of discomfort defined by lack"—only took on this specific meaning at the end of the eighteenth century. It arose as "a new way of talking about the negative emotional experiences of being alone" (p. 224). Prior to that time, Alberti notes, "... 'lonely' and 'oneliness' described the absence of another person, without any corresponding emotional lack". She sees this new experience of loneliness as linked to the challenges of a particular cultural context:

> In the absence of an all-knowing, benevolent Father and the persistent spread of a competitive individualism, a vacuum had emerged in which the self was alone, marooned and dependent on familial and social networks that were, by reason of these global changes, in a state of flux. (p. 229)

I find this argument a useful corrective to the widespread presumption that, as Alberti (p. 230) puts it, "[L]oneliness is universal and transhistorical ... a human condition and not a product of socio-political and economic choices". But Fromm-Reichmann was clearly talking about a much more profoundly distressing kind of experience, one so extreme it does seem beyond historicity. Being unable even to imagine the possibility of relationship is deeper than a "lack", which implies the possibility of its satisfaction.

Alberti calls loneliness an "emotional alienation", and says the state has no opposite. But Fromm-Reichmann saw the creation of that ontological "We" as a diametric contrast to loneliness itself. The times when she experienced the most anguish were when she had to face the loneliness that came from not being able to break through to the patient sufficiently to create that sense of "We-ness".

People who can assuage their own loneliness, even if acute—like the mourners Freud (1917e) wrote about, who cope with the loss of the loved one by fantasised reunion or identification—are not "the lonely ones" Fromm-Reichmann was concerned with. Indeed, even people who experience frequent voices or visions, often considered a sign of withdrawal from the world of external relationship, can, by extension, be considered less lonely than patients threatened by "the uncommunicable, private emotional experience of severe loneliness", which was her focus.

Fromm-Reichmann had first glimpsed the power of intuitive connection with psychotic patients while still in medical school (Hornstein, 2000). On one fateful day, sitting in the back row of a large amphitheatre with the handful of other women admitted for the first time to medical training at the University of Königsberg, she saw a patient being led down the aisle for that day's demonstration. (Turn-of-the-century medical education featured hapless patients forced to perform their symptoms on demand before hundreds of students.) As the man passed Fromm-Reichmann's seat, he blurted out excitedly to her: *Bertchen, Bertchen, hab ich dich endlich wieder!* ("Bertie, Bertie, at last I find you again!"). Fromm-Reichmann, who described herself at the time as being "extremely shy", was as astonished as everyone else by this outburst. Yet, as she told friends decades later, she turned to the patient without realising what she was doing and said: "Yes, that's fine, I'm very glad too, but you know now the professor wants to talk to you. I'll come and see you later". She recalled this experience as uncanny, as if she herself had not been speaking, but rather that the words had come from an external source: "'It' said out of me, not I said. I had no idea what to do", she recalled.

Other students had gasped and pointed at her; they were even more amazed when, at the end of the lecture, Fromm-Reichmann stood up and declared, "I must go and see that man, I have promised him". At the time, treating the outburst of a hallucinating patient as a meaningful communication was unheard of. "Who would say something to a crazy man, and then do it?" she mused, still stunned by her own iconoclasm. Later, in 1913, as an intern at the university hospital, when psychotherapy was not yet even on the curriculum of medical schools, she began sitting with the most disturbed patients, just listening to them. Sometimes she stayed all night. Although she couldn't understand what they were saying, she was absolutely convinced it meant something, despite the fact that Kraepelin, the most eminent psychiatrist in Europe, had insisted the opposite. He considered such patients untreatable; Fromm-Reichmann felt, for reasons she couldn't explicitly articulate, an intense desire to reach them.

She had been brought up with a deep respect for authority ("Who was I, as compared with a great teacher?" she told friends), but in these moments, Fromm-Reichmann was overwhelmed by an intense feeling, which seemed to come out of nowhere and was entirely discrepant with her conscious experience, that "said out of my mouth, 'This I could do better!'"

Colleagues often wondered why she chose to spend decades working with patients no one else thought treatable. Fellow psychoanalysts considered psychosis beyond the reach of their method, arguing that it prevented the development of an appropriate transference, the prerequisite for effective treatment. Most psychiatrists who worked in asylums and hospitals, as Fromm-Reichmann did, saw psychoses as brain diseases treatable only with somatic interventions like shock treatment, drugs, or surgery. But the fearless, daring side of Fromm-Reichmann—the part that declared on that fateful day in the amphitheatre, "I must see him, I have promised that man", in essence, declaring Kraepelin wrong—that side of her embraced the challenge of repeatedly attempting the high wire act that is intensive psychotherapy for psychosis.

Throughout her career, Fromm-Reichmann deliberately chose to work with patients who actively resisted all attempts to reach them. With some, she did eventually break through, creating enough of a connection to guide the patient out of extreme isolation. But with others, she did not, and it is illuminating to examine some examples of each, to see their similarities and differences, the lengths to which she was willing to go, and her (sometimes overly dogged) refusal ever to give up on anyone.

It's also revealing to pay attention to *how* Fromm-Reichmann recounted these cases. She never wrote long histories describing the whole course of treatment of a particular patient, in the style Freud favoured. Rather, she used brief vignettes, which often sounded like parables, in the tradition of the Hasidic legends that were a core part of her cultural heritage. She wrote about patients in precisely the style Buber (1956, p. ix) highlighted as characteristic of Jewish storytelling:

> The preponderance of the anecdote is primarily due to the general tendency of the Jewish Diaspora spirit to express the events of history and of the present in a pointed manner. Events are not merely seen and reported so as to signify something, but they are so cleanly hulled from the mass of the irrelevant and so arranged that the report culminates in a significant dictum.

This was also precisely the way Fromm-Reichmann told stories of her own life, especially those depicting key moments, like the one with the "Bertchen" patient.

In published works, Fromm-Reichmann often wrote about the same handful of cases, but here I have chosen instead to examine patients who received less attention, basing my account on the process notes, case conference transcripts, and tape recordings to which I was given access while researching my biography. (Fuller accounts of each case are provided there, Hornstein, 2000.)

Not surprisingly, the defining feature of the patients Fromm-Reichmann cited most frequently was their willingness to forge a bond with the therapist, no matter how frightened or cut off they may have been at the start of treatment. Even in highly distressed or extreme states, these patients responded in some way—however minimally—to Fromm-Reichmann's efforts to reach them. The ones I consider here were not like that, perhaps one reason Fromm-Reichmann rarely discussed them in her published works.

For example, there was Miss N, who spent decades on the disturbed wards of Chestnut Lodge and several other hospitals, cavorting in many extravagant ways—often unclothed—and frequently flushing her clothes down the toilet, thereby clogging the plumbing of the entire hospital for hours. She chattered incessantly in a singsong voice, urinated on the floor, frequently hit staff, and once bit a visiting psychiatrist. Miss N was also able to create a persona who could relate (often warmly) to Fromm-Reichmann, even as her *real* self remained forever cut off, from others as well as from herself. Miss N thought—for good reasons—that she was essentially an unaborted child who was meant not to exist; she therefore did everything possible to destroy her "real self", leaving it frozen in a lonely non-existence, unreachable by anyone, even Fromm-Reichmann. The persona she hid behind—a distinct benefit of her social class—allowed Miss N to have charming, at times witty and superficially warm, interactions with many people at Chestnut Lodge—even the plumber!—and to keep several talented therapists engaged for years in trying to try to reach "the real Miss N", as Fromm-Reichmann wistfully referred to her. Her case painfully illustrates how external relatedness (especially of the histrionic kind) can mask an intense inner state of loneliness.

Mr R was equally cut off and unreachable, but lacking this façade of friendliness, he suffered more openly. He also had a paranoid style—a huge difference from Miss N's exuberant hysteria—making even his hallucinatory relationships hostile and suspicious. Mr R's isolation and anger, overtly expressed in violence or passively aggressive, blocked all attempts to help him. He repeatedly tried to attack Fromm-Reichmann, masturbated in her presence, or refused to attend their sessions. What kept her going in the treatment were his occasionally thoughtful responses to an interpretation or his rare expressions of real feeling, especially his anger at a father who attempted to control every aspect of Mr R's life and at one point had hired detectives to monitor him. Throughout their years of work together, Fromm-Reichmann continued to believe that fleeting expressions on Mr R's face, or even his attempts to hurt her, might be gestures, albeit distorted, of his desire for relationship.

Miss N and Mr R offer classic examples of patients most psychiatrists consider untreatable by psychotherapy. We may admire Fromm-Reichmann's refusal ever to give up on anyone, yet still ask whether she might have used her limited time more expeditiously. I think the reason she did not stems from a case she had taken on twenty years earlier, soon after her arrival at Chestnut Lodge.

Hermann Brunck, a brilliant young economist, had been sent to the Lodge specifically to be Fromm-Reichmann's patient. His psychotic break had been sudden, he had the support of friends and family, and his intellectual background and recent emigration from Germany made him seem especially likely to benefit from treatment with someone like her.

We know these details—and can use his real name here—because sixty years later, his wife, Hope Hale Davis (1994) wrote a memoir excoriating Fromm-Reichmann and blaming her for Brunck's subsequent death. Her book is the only known instance of one of Fromm-Reichmann's cases being recounted from the vantage point of a family member, and it is the only published account that is entirely critical of her clinical work.

Although Fromm-Reichmann treated Brunck for a much shorter time than she did either Miss N or Mr R, he remained a potent symbol of both frustration and possibility for her, precisely the kind of patient she considered potentially reachable by the style of intensive psychotherapy she had pioneered. But she was robbed of the chance to succeed with him. Against Fromm-Reichmann's strenuous objections, Davis had him transferred to a hospital where he could get insulin shock treatments; several months later, he hanged himself with his own belt in his room there. Failing to reach Brunck while he was still in her care seemed to challenge Fromm-Reichmann to try even harder with other patients from then on. His was the type of loneliness she most wanted to assuage, and understanding it more fully became ever more critical to her.

Brunck had been brought up in a cultured and prosperous family like Miss N's (albeit not one as rich as hers), and he knew the proprieties expected of a man of his social class, especially in relation to an older woman professional like Fromm-Reichmann. Even in highly deteriorated states, he struggled to retain the gallantries of that former life. But Brunck's suspiciousness was acute and his regression extreme—he rarely ate or slept, and was often found by nurses to be huddling in a corner of his room, naked and covered in his own excrement.

When Fromm-Reichmann first approached him, he continued to mumble incoherently and did not even appear to register her presence. But after she did everything she could think of to convey a sense that she was on his side—including sitting down on the floor next to him— Brunck suddenly broke through the grip of his own isolation, covered himself with a blanket and said quietly: "Even though I have sunk as low as an animal, I still know how to behave in the presence of a lady".

Such moments of relatedness were, however, fleeting; most of the time, he trusted no one, his mind filled with conspiracies against him. He thought that kitchen workers were sending obscene messages in the way they positioned the foods on his plate, so he rarely ate. He tried to slit his throat while shaving; on a weekend visit, he lunged at his wife with a knife. Yet Fromm-Reichmann thought this might be part of a therapeutic regression, a process that, however dramatic or disturbing, had the potential to bring about some dissolution of his defences, a precondition for effective treatment. When Brunck was removed from Chestnut Lodge prematurely, she lost her chance to create a relational bridge strong enough to reach him.

And sixty years later, Davis was still blaming her. Even though she had been the one to insist on Brunck's transfer, she remained furious at Fromm-Reichmann for not saving him. Davis and Brunck had been married for only a few years in the 1930s, and she had three other husbands, both before and after him, but was still deeply attached—six decades later—to the possibility that Fromm-Reichmann could have broken through Brunck's abject loneliness quickly enough to save him.

Since "quickly enough" for Davis meant in less than seven months, we can shake our heads at her naïveté about the complexities of intensive psychotherapy with a patient that disturbed.

Yet Fromm-Reichmann herself clearly thought that, with more time, she might well have reached Hermann Brunck. Was this misplaced hope, arrogance, or denial on her part? And regardless of whether or not she was right about him, what does this tell us about loneliness and Fromm-Reichmann's assumptions about the needs and capacities of someone as regressed and cut off as Brunck clearly was?

One thing it tells us is that she herself felt the loneliness of not being able to reach him, of his not trusting her for more than a few moments, on a handful of occasions, over the course of those seven months. Whenever she recounted those moments, Fromm-Reichmann made them sound iconic, citing his "I know how to behave in the presence of a lady" among other pithy quotes, and giving them an outsize significance, perhaps unwarranted, given how infrequently they occurred. The Hasidic tradition, again, offers a way of understanding this. As one of the Baal Shem Tov's disciples famously said: "A story must be told in such a way that it constitutes help in itself" (Buber, 1956, p. v). By highlighting the rare moments when Brunck seemed to reach out, was Fromm-Reichmann telling the story of his case so as to "constitute the help" she was unable to provide while he was still alive?

Brunck may have been deeply suspicious and frightened, but he was also capable of being articulate and sensitive, epitomising the type of patient that Fromm-Reichmann considered treatable. But a person who felt himself to be as persecuted and as frightened as he did, who trusted almost nothing anyone said, and whose wife, in her frequent letters and visits, routinely deceived him, cannot ultimately be considered a good candidate for psychotherapy. Increasingly locked inside a tightly woven web of fears and fantasies, he had to have experienced the "real loneliness" that Fromm-Reichmann wrote about. And despite her desire to be "his comrade in overcoming the dangers of his sickness", as she put it (an interesting choice of words for a patient who was an ardent communist), she had to have felt cut off and alone when her dogged attempts to break through his elaborate defences failed to work.

In the case of both Brunck and Mr R, extreme suspiciousness directly blocked Fromm-Reichmann's attempts at relationship. Mr R wore earplugs or left sessions early, sometimes after only a few minutes. Brunck mumbled or masturbated as if she were not present. Neither of them trusted what she said or the promises she made, and Mr R constantly protested (and clearly resented) her taping their sessions "for research purposes". Even Miss N, for all her superficial wit and charm, rarely allowed even a moment of genuine connection. She knew she wasn't even supposed to be there and behaved accordingly.

Fromm-Reichmann never assumed that she could succeed with every patient, and these cases offer painful examples of the challenges she faced. They also show us how her preoccupation with loneliness, as a distinct form of suffering, led to her search for opportunities to break through to those with the greatest need for the healing power of human relationship. Throughout both her life and her work, Fromm-Reichmann struggled to find that "We", that emergent collaborative creation that could offer a refuge to both analyst and patient. When she caught even a glimpse of it, as she clearly did with Brunck, she tried even harder to get past whatever psychological impediments were preventing the connection that might allow healing to occur.

Conclusion

As a woman and an observant Jew at a time of intense anti-Semitism, and as a refugee forced to flee her native Germany before the Nazis could apprehend her, Frieda Fromm-Reichmann knew loneliness from the inside. And although she had warm relationships with many friends, relatives, and colleagues, her interpersonal style remained that of the therapist, which meant she never felt fully known by anyone. This internal isolation, present since childhood, was exacerbated in her sixties, when the hereditary deafness that had afflicted both her parents became a further source of separation and aloneness for Fromm-Reichmann. She didn't suffer the utter desolation of her patients, nor did she minimise the differences between her loneliness and theirs, but these personal experiences did make the whole issue particularly compelling for her. This intensity of focus is perhaps what continues to make her work so stimulating as we struggle to grasp the crucial significance of loneliness in human psychology.

References

Alberti, F. B. (2019). *A Biography of Loneliness: The History of an Emotion*. Oxford: Oxford University Press.

Bennett, B. (2020). *The Vanishing Half: A Novel*. New York: Riverhead.

Buber, M. (1923). *I and Thou* (revised English translation by Walter Kaufmann). New York: Charles Scribner's Sons, 1970.

Buber, M. (1956). *Tales of the Hasidim: The Early Masters*. London: Thames & Hudson.

Buechler, S. (1998). The analyst's experience of loneliness. *Contemporary Psychoanalysis, 34*(1): 91–113.

Carel, H. (2016). *Phenomenology of Illness*. Oxford: Oxford University Press.

Davis, H. H. (1994). *Great Day Coming: A Memoir of the 1930s*. South Royalton, VT: Steerforth.

Freud, S. (1917e). Mourning and melancholia. *S. E., 14*: 237–258. London: Hogarth.

Fromm-Reichmann, F. (1959). Loneliness. *Psychiatry: Journal for the Study of Interpersonal Processes, 22*: 1–15.

Hornstein, G. A. (2000). *To Redeem One Person Is to Redeem the World: The Life of Frieda Fromm-Reichmann*. New York: Free Press/Simon & Schuster.

Hornstein, G. A. (2011). *Bibliography of First-Person Narratives of Madness in English* (5th edn.). www.gailhornstein.com/works.htm.

Hornstein, G. A. (2017). *Agnes's Jacket: A Psychologist's Search for the Meanings of Madness* (revised edn.). New York: Routledge.

Moustakas, C. E. (1961). *Loneliness*. Englewood Cliffs, NJ: Prentice-Hall.

Paul, L. A. (2014). *Transformative Experience*. Oxford: Oxford University Press.

Rogers, A. G. (2006). *The Unsayable: The Hidden Language of Trauma*. New York: Random House.

Spence, D. P. (1982). *Narrative Truth and Historical Truth: Meaning and Interpretation in Psychoanalysis*. New York: W. W. Norton.

Von Witzleben, H. D. (1958). On loneliness. *Psychiatry: Journal for the Study of Interpersonal Processes, 21*: 37–43.

Woolf, V. (1930). *On Being Ill*. London: Hogarth.

CHAPTER 16

Loneliness and being alone: the contributions of two British analysts

Lesley Caldwell

Introduction

In the conditions imposed by the COVID-19 pandemic, loneliness and solitude have been frequently documented aspects of the present lives of many for whom staying alive and keeping others safe have meant distancing themselves from their most significant interactions, while confined to domestic spaces, large or small, shared or unshared. As the incidental contacts that contribute to the physical and emotional fabric of daily living—colleagues, tradespeople, shopkeepers, neighbours, cleaners, the postman—became threats to survival, isolation emerged as an everyday matter for all. Individual responses have been widely divergent but how aloneness is lived has assumed a particular urgency.

Psychoanalytically, the shift from traditional ways of treating patients in the consulting room to distanced sessions created a particularly intense set of losses for analyst and patient alike, and a need to address the worsening psychological health of many. Faced with these losses and the mourning that has accompanied them, there has been an outpouring of creative activity leading to new ways of thinking about future practice. At such a time, a rereading of well-known papers by the psychoanalysts Donald Winnicott and Melanie Klein may provide further inspiration in encountering experiences, clinically and in everyday life, which are familiar but have currently assumed a particular urgency.

General context

The shared institutional and personal histories of these two prominent members of the postwar British society make the existence of papers given approximately around the same time, on ostensibly similar topics, of particular interest. Both show their authors' consistent approaches to the human condition and the tasks facing the human infant, while highlighting a kind of implicit dialogue which deepens a realisation of how their related trajectories shaped and continue to shape psychoanalysis, then and now.

There is no doubt that Winnicott's and Klein's accounts of the neonate and of human nature represent divergent assessments of human subjectivity and its origins, deriving from very different suppositions about early life and the weight to be assigned to innate and environmental factors. In following the priorities of British object relations theory, both contributions are firmly located in the infant, but the infants they discuss are very different beings with lives shaped by very different ways of sustaining internal conflicts and the place of the external world in that negotiation. Winnicott's "The Capacity to Be Alone", published in 1958, and "On the Sense of Loneliness", Klein's paper given to the 1959 IPA congress in Copenhagen and at a scientific meeting in London in February 1960, published posthumously in 1963, are the primary sources. Their titles already establish different fields of inquiry. Where Winnicott introduces the idea of a capacity, an ability to receive or contain or take in usually related to mental activity, Klein takes up the vaguer notion of a sense with its associations of a physical impression, feeling, or perception. Since Winnicott elsewhere posits an originary aloneness (1988, p. 150) such a claim is also considered, especially through his idea of the incommunicado self (1963). For Winnicott the self's encounter with itself is the central resource in meeting the aloneness that remains a human constant.

Klein's paper offers a very moving description of confronting the impact of loneliness as a lifelong activity, and recent archival work by Jane Milton (2018) demonstrates a deep interest in this topic, psychoanalytically and personally. Her paper, which as Meira Likierman (2001) has pointed out, frequently uses the word "painful" and refers to the conflicts of development as "suffering", depicts a human individual who is lonely from the start,

> battling first to integrate himself, and then to keep his good object … her outlook now intimates that we are the victims of the worst part of our nature. This is why loneliness is partly tragic, since some of it is brought on the individual by himself, and by the destructive processes that have made it impossible to keep within a safe good object. Because of this, loneliness gives added impetus to our search for social ties. It creates a great need to turn to external objects and so drives some of our quest for object relations. (Likierman, 2001, p. 195)

The relentless impact of the death drive for all, and an innate disposition towards a weak ego in some, means that such moves are often destined to disappointment.

Like many commentators, I read Klein's paper as venturing a dialogue with Winnicott in its less rigid adherence to her model of infantile development and a greater recognition of the environment. As Kristeva (2001, p. 261) states:

> We have here a good example of the back and forth exchange between Klein and Winnicott, an example that displays the originality of both analysts as well as their debt to each other.

While Winnicott situates the capacity to be alone in a world of ecstasy, Melanie never distanced herself from a tone of desolation that strikes at the very heart of the serenity she had gained.

Personal and intellectual links

Winnicott became interested in Klein's work in the 1930s and his second analysis was with Joan Riviere, one of her close associates. Klein supervised him (1935–40) and at her request he analysed her son though he resisted her wish to supervise the case as well! She later analysed his second wife, Clare. She left London at the outbreak of war and when she returned in December 1940, Winnicott arranged a consulting room above his own for her, which he apparently repeated on subsequent occasions (Grosskurth, 1986, p. 254). At the time of the Controversial Discussions (1942–44) he was one of five Kleinian training analysts, though his was a minimal participation, and he was already insisting that at the beginning there was only a baby–mother relationship. The depth of this challenge to her theory of internal objects was elaborated over succeeding decades.

For someone who so valued loyalty and allegiance, and whose own history, both personal and psychoanalytic, had been so difficult in terms of belonging and acceptance, Winnicott's 1945 paper, "Primitive Emotional Development" must have appeared as a betrayal and there was a growing distance between them, confirmed by his absence from the 1952 *Festschrift* for her seventieth birthday. Although he was further alienated by her paper on "Envy" (1957) he remained an attentive reader of her work and continued to endorse her significance for him personally, and for psychoanalysis in general (1962a, 1962b, 1963).

Klein was less open, and after their parting, she scarcely mentioned him. In her 1952 papers, "Some Theoretical Conclusions Regarding the Emotional Life of the Infant" (1952a) and "On Observing the Behaviour of Young Infants" (1952b), topics riddled with the "Winnicott effect", he is ignored.

At the heart of their disagreement was the weight she assigned to the destructive instincts and the death drive, the existence of a rudimentary ego, and an awareness of self and other from the beginning, and her lack of attention to the environment. The Kleinian infant, driven by anxiety and persecution before coming to accept the existence of these contradictory affects as located in the same person, is plagued by internal conflicts that structure an inner world of unconscious phantasy existing independently of external care. For Winnicott, the paediatrician, it is the ordinary maternal care provided from the start that produces the conditions for the growth of that self. These different models of human subjectivity and its origins lead to very different understandings of the analyst's role, the analytic relationship itself, and the place of loneliness in human life.

The capacity to be alone

This paper identifies a capacity its author proposes is achieved in the first months of life as the infant comes to recognise separateness. For Winnicott, being, and the associated affect of aliveness located in the body and bodily movement, form the foundations of the psyche, a central aspect of mental health and a major aim of psychoanalytic practice. This human aliveness initially depends on an environment of which the baby is unaware, but where infantile omnipotence and its subsequent loss are constitutive of individual internality and exteriority. Built up through successive experiences of another's unrecognised separateness over time, the internalisation of reliability guarantees the foundations of health and enables the development of the capacity to be alone, a different dimension from a person actually being alone. Ultimately, the mother's presence may only be there associatively, in terms of "a cot, a pram, or the general atmosphere of an immediate environment" (Winnicott, 1958, p. 30). His argument links early development and the transference. What the mother's presence enables for two people, child and mother/other, can come to exist in the mind of the baby, and has a parallel in the patient's ability to be alone in the analytic session, for Winnicott an essential of treatment.

For those who do not have it, the actuality of aloneness is enormously difficult, but this is not Winnicott's focus. In proposing a capacity located in an earlier, "less sophisticated" stage than the period psychoanalysis traditionally characterises as enabling people to be alone in a contented relaxed way, he hypothesises an experience of being alone when not alone, when "the baby's ego immaturity is balanced by the ego support of the mother" (Winnicott, 1958, p. 32).

His term "ego relatedness", which refers to a self-relationship to the ego, gathers in a cluster of the earliest experiences inscribed in the baby through a relationship in which the other does not yet exist. First introduced in "Primary Maternal Preoccupation" (Winnicott, 1956), "ego relatedness" proposes a state where the mother "feels herself into the infant's needs, that is body needs, which become ego needs as psychology emerges out of the imaginative elaboration of physical experience" (Winnicott, 1956, p. 304). In normal conditions, an initial formlessness leads to a growing awareness of presence and aloneness. Reliability, consistency, and continuity enable the imprint of the other through a repetition leading to the internal representation of a mother/other whose "memory" sustains her absence over growing time periods. Once gained, such a capacity remains a potential to be drawn upon throughout life.

His account is derived from clinical work in the transference and a theory of infantile development which begins from an untroubled state of unintegration which has similarities with primary narcissism and the oceanic feeling of *Civilization and Its Discontents* (Freud, 1930a). The processes of integration can start almost immediately but, unlike Klein, Winnicott discounts pathology and wonders "whether there can be a value in thinking of *ecstasy* as an ego orgasm" (1958, p. 35), that is, a particular state of affective union which enables the baby to come to a positive recognition of the mother as a person and not as "the symbol of frustration".

> As we grow older
> The world becomes more
> Complicated
> Of dead and living. Not the intense moment
> Isolated, with no before or after,
> But a lifetime burning in every moment …

—Eliot (1940)

Eliot's line, "A lifetime burning in every moment" echoes Winnicott's continuing interest in an aliveness that derives from the infant becoming human through a fantasy of ecstatic union, a union however that rests on "an essential aloneness. At the same time this aloneness can only take place under maximum conditions of dependence ..." (Winnicott, 1988, p. 150). In his paper, "Communicating and Not Communicating Leading to a Study of Certain Opposites" (1963), he introduces the "incommunicado self"—permanently inaccessible, unknowable, *formlessly present* at the core of every human being, before wish or desire comes into being, yet informing conscious and unconscious states of company and solitude, contributing to a person's capacity to live both creatively and alone.

The incommunicado self asserts the origins of the person as anchored in aloneness, but it is introduced in a paper on communication that insists that interiority and the psyche are constituted through human sociality and the earliest environment. Elsewhere, Winnicott illustrates this contradiction and its place in the psychology of the individual through an analogy with the physical situation of pregnancy where, until birth, the baby is both connected to and separated from the mother by:

> a set of substances, the amniotic sac, the placenta, the endometrium .... In the most intimate contact there is a lack of contact so that essentially each individual retains absolute isolation always and for ever. (Winnicott, 1988, p. 157)

The identificatory practices and wishes with which we cement our relations with others, our identities, and our very selves, shaped by the experience of being with another and being alone continually confirm that self through relations with others and in solitude. This is a vision of human possibility with significance for the individual and for the communicative possibilities of the analytic relation, where Winnicott (1963) not only raises the value of not communicating with another, but he also insists on its necessity and inevitability. However later states of aloneness and solitude are lived may depend on the initial state of oneness between mother and baby, but aloneness is always their foundation.

> Shadowing all object relating is a fundamental primary aloneness which is inevitable and immovable, the absolute core of one's being is wordless, imageless solitude which cannot be reached by insight or introspection, but only by living. (Bollas, 1989, p. 21)

In Bollas's distinction between insight and living it is the capacity for being in a potential space, an internal resting place, that is the foundation for the adult's lifelong encounters with self and other.

Although mothers speak often to their babies and in doing so lay down the template for the centrality of speech in human communication, the medium of communication between mother and baby is initially a non-verbal exchange in which the baby requires a degree of responsiveness for human subjectivity to emerge: a capacity to communicate must be learned and encouraged. Effectively Winnicott proposes two classes of human beings: those who have learned to communicate and to relate to others, and those who have not; only the first group has a choice about actually communicating in its extended meanings. The capacity to be alone is embedded in these earliest encounters and coexistent with that essential aloneness. It is illustrated in the analytic session where a patient's silence is both an achievement and a complex communication. In insisting that "significant relating and communicating is silent" (1963, p. 184), and wondering how a patient communicates "that he or she is not communicating" (1963, p. 188), Winnicott offers another possible aspect of what being alone means for a patient who, though silent, may be communicating with himself or herself in the analytic environment provided. The analyst's empathic responses are essential in finding the kind of communicating the patient needs at any one moment, whether verbal or silent. Analytic communicating depends on the recognition of aloneness and how it has been registered in the patient through early care.

An untroubling original formlessness and the encounter with the external world continue to be formative factors in infantile experience and its later effects. Non-communication is part of "creative living"—a manifestation of the individual's *being*, of living immediately in the world that need not to be converted into words … we can only really *be* when we are not forced to communicate this special non-verbal domain of shared experience that allows us to be alive in the world, through a level of rich non-representational communication (Goldberg, 2017).

Goldberg here echoes Milner's postscript to *On Not Being Able to Paint* (1950), where she discusses how "awareness of the external world is itself a creative process, an immensely complex creative interchange between what comes from inside and what comes from outside, a complex alternation of fusing and separating" (Milner, 2010, p. 171). The analyst and the patient work in the transitional arena where self and other are accepted as coexisting, where the creative process depends on the continuing encounter between self and other and self and self. Psychical dynamics and the mental space they assume continuingly shape relations with the self and with others, but, like the capacity to be alone, they depend on a prior profound quietness and aloneness sustained through a kind of unconscious emotional geography. Winnicott's approach to how the human infant comes to be human rejects a foundational moment of trauma and anxiety in coming to recognise the separateness of self and world, of self and other.

On the sense of loneliness

The fundamentally tragic formulations of Klein's last paper offer some recognition of the environment alongside the anxieties of a primitive ego threatened with being destroyed by the conflict of the life and death instincts. As Meira Likierman movingly describes, "Her writing thus ends with a lonely human being rather than an envious destroyer driven by original sin" (2001, p. 192). Klein (1963, p. 301) describes a state of closeness with the actual mother, a "ubiquitous yearning for an unattainable perfect internal state" linked to the earliest unconscious relation which she claims variously as "the foundation for the most complete experience for being understood", an "understanding without words" that can never be filled, the result of which "derives from a depressive feeling of an irretrievable loss".

It certainly envisages a bond that is rare in Klein's writing, one that Milton (2018), with some justification, describes as idealised. Nonetheless, despite the poignancy of her account, the ruthlessness and sadism of the earliest ego remains. The capacity to tolerate anxiety depends on the comparative innate strength or weakness of that ego faced with the excessive splitting of both object and ego to deal with the death instinct. The projective and introjective mechanisms that provide both the good external object and the good part of the self with a degree of protection from an aggression always understood as destructive also contribute to "a sense of being alone regardless of external circumstances, of feeling lonely even among friends or receiving love" (Klein, 1963, p. 300).

In the clinical situation, Klein includes a range of responses as possible defences against loneliness (1963, p. 311): extreme dependence on the mother, the desire for independence, the preoccupation with the past, especially in the old, and "the conflict between male and female elements in both sexes" (p. 306). She understands the latter conflict as deriving from a wish for identification, related to admiration and envy for both sexes, and she illustrates it through two dreams of a male patient which involved his relationship with his analyst, his mother, and his own "feminine part". Her interpretation about "the splitting of his destructive and envious feelings into his feminine side diminished his sense of loneliness" (p. 308).

These mechanisms are exaggerated in the schizophrenic who feels himself alone, confused, and besieged by uncertainty and lack of trust, and in the manic depressive, whose capacity for depressive affect, though stronger, is impeded by a limited capacity for reparation and keeping alive the good object. Where loneliness in the schizophrenic centres on being in bits, for the manic depressive it is centred in the incapacity to maintain an inner and an external relationship with a good object (Klein, 1963, p. 305). These insights are secondary to the universal fear of death and the reduced omnipotence accompanying integration and a growing sense of reality that add to the experience of loneliness for all.

As part of the life instincts, integration leads to the strengthening and establishment of a good internal ego through introjection, but the projective mechanisms through which the baby deposits destructive impulses continue to make the mother a source of anxiety even when early persecution is largely overtaken by depressive type functioning. Moreover, loneliness accompanies both persecutory and depressive anxiety as does the infant's innate drive towards integration, the process of coming together which Klein, and Winnicott, both regard as the resolution of the baby's initial state. Here it too is a source of anxiety, since it is never completed and the resultant incomplete understanding of the self provides yet another potential for loneliness, that is, integration too presents problems for certain patients. The sense of belonging or rather, possibly *never* belonging to a group or person (Klein, 1963, p. 302) further links integration and loneliness. The projected parts of the self are also experienced as lost and "the lost parts too are felt to be lonely" (p. 302).

Her statement that "lessened omnipotence contributes to the pain of integration because it means a diminished capacity for hope" (p. 302) reinforces her melancholic assessment of human possibility and the amassing of examples of the inevitability of loneliness only adds to this bleakness. It is in complete contrast to Winnicott's insistence on an initial infantile omnipotence and the parallel he draws between unintegration in the baby and a state of relaxation in the adult (1958, p. 34). For him integration is a process that the baby moves in and out of without concern and the healthy adult inhabits without anxiety.

Klein acknowledges Winnicott's account though she ignores the relative weight of internal and external presence that he makes central when she describes being able to "picture the presence of the mother" as more possible in the second year "when the child's reality sense increases and he can interpret sounds in the house as the presence of the mother". Winnicott's insistence on very early experience as the condition of arriving at unit status is not referred to but she does emphasise the relation between child and external world as vital. In considering the mother's actual relation to her child she argues for "a constant interaction between the internal and external world persisting throughout life" and regards loneliness as "assisted by a strong ego, a decrease in omnipotence, a happy relation to the first object, and successful internalisation so that love can be given and received" (Klein, 1963, pp. 312, 310).

The response of colleagues

Milton's archival study (2018), which records four versions of the loneliness paper from its presentation at the IPA congress in Copenhagen in 1959, notes the extended dimensions of her interest and its personal associations. Perhaps because under the rubric of loneliness Klein includes several mental states that relate variously to paranoid or depressive states, Milton agrees with O'Shaughnessy's description that the published paper is incomplete (1984), but she links it to Klein's continuing work on the topic and her ambition to publish a book on loneliness. Among the sources she cites are letters from Elliott Jaques and Wilfred Bion recording their responses to the paper and offering comments that widen the terms of Klein's argument. Significantly, both analysts suggest she expand her study of the non-pathological aspects of loneliness. For Jaques, it is her tentative links between loneliness and belonging that offer the most interesting direction for further work:

> … greater integration implies acceptance of loss and hence toleration of a certain amount of loneliness. I think you will find however that what you have written also includes the notion that the capacity for greater toleration of loneliness in itself reinforces feelings of belonging and the capacity to allow oneself to belong, that is to say, to commit oneself to good objects. (Quoted in Milton, 2018, p. 932)

In his first letter, Bion introduces "the new learning experience" involved in any shift from paranoid–schizoid to depressive position and a frequent reluctance in facing this as a way of discussing loneliness especially as it regards the physical limitations of age and their echoes of youthful incapacity. In a second letter a month later, he too suggests separating out ways of speaking of loneliness to introduce the "normal loneliness which is an accompaniment of a capacity for integration and synthesis" (quoted in Milton, 2018, p. 935). For Bion such a loneliness is

> essential to the really creative person and that loneliness may not be painful or misplaced … some people may choose to live in contact with the unsynthesised and incoherent with a view to bringing synthesis and coherence. (Milton, 2018, p. 936)

Indirectly, Bion's view resonates with Winnicott's notion of an essential aloneness.

In that Klein's colleagues encourage her to consider the possibility of a normal loneliness, and what it enables, they not only encourage the shifts Klein herself is in the process of making, but possibly contribute indirectly to linking her theoretical claims and her own personal history.

Overall, Klein's paper undoubtedly conveys a powerful sense of desolation and as Maria Torok et al. (1998) argue, it gains even more from a recognition of Klein's life, her family's painful social history and persecution, her own difficult early history, and the later distress of the death of her son and her wounding relations with her daughter, Melitta, another "little Mel" and its cruel extension to the public world of psychoanalysis. Grosskurth states sympathetically that "few professional women have been subjected to as much distilled malice and rumour accepted as fact" (1986), all of which contributes to the mood Kristeva (2001) identifies in the paper written in Klein's final years.

Conclusion

Both Klein and Winnicott centre on the human infant but their very different theories of that infant derive from profoundly contrasting views of the human condition. There is no mention of solitude in Klein's account, nor does she introduce the possibility of the creative aspects of loneliness. She "regards life as 'a quest to allay loneliness … a yearning to have a sense of being mentally accompanied on our life's journey'" (Likierman, 2001, p. 192) and the yearning that becomes apparent in her paper points to her own struggles in life and perhaps her own assessment of its achievements and its difficulties.

Winnicott's notion of an essential aloneness from the beginning contains the roots of an ecstatic encounter with both self and world which depends on an aliveness at the core of the personality. He does not directly address the matter of loneliness at all. Rather, in its concern with the essential resources that enable a lifelong encounter and negotiation of the pleasures and difficulties of the conflict at the heart of being, Winnicott's work on being alone supports Clare Winnicott's claim that "the 'essential clue' to his work is to be found 'in his own personality, in his way of relating and being related to, and in his whole style of life'" (1989, p. 2).

These papers are primarily focused on psychoanalysis and psychoanalytic theory, and yet they both open towards a wider field. Klein describes the sheer range of emotions gathered under the rubric of loneliness and how psychoanalysis may strengthen the individual's ability to accept its presence through an encounter with the world of love. Winnicott offers a deeper understanding of the dynamics of the analytic relation and a respect for the complexity of the communication between analyst and patient and what this can enable. Both are illustrations of the value of psychoanalysis in confronting the complexity of psychic reality and its place in enlarging what makes life worth living, whatever the conditions.

References

Bollas, C. (1989). *Forces of Destiny.* London: Free Association.

Eliot, T. S. (1940). East Coker. In: *Four Quartets.* London: Faber & Faber, 1941.

Freud, S. (1930a). *Civilization and Its Discontents. S. E.*, *21*: 57–146. London: Hogarth.

Goldberg, P. (2017). Questions and thoughts on Winnicott/Bion inspired by Lesley Caldwell's "A Psycho-analysis of Being". *British Journal of Psychotherapy*, *34*(2): 240–247.

Grosskurth, P. (1986). *Melanie Klein: Her World and Her Work.* New York: Random House.

Klein, M. (1952a). Some theoretical conclusions regarding the emotional life of the infant. In: *Envy and Gratitude and Other Works 1946–1963* (pp. 61–93). London: Hogarth, 1975. [Reprinted London: Karnac, 1993.]

Klein, M. (1952b). On observing the behaviour of young infants. In: *Envy and Gratitude and Other Works 1946–1963* (pp. 94–121). London: Hogarth, 1975. [Reprinted London: Karnac, 1993.]

Klein, M. (1957). Envy and gratitude. In: *Envy and Gratitude and Other Works 1946–1963* (pp. 176–235). London: Hogarth.

Klein, M. (1963). On the sense of loneliness. In: *Envy and Gratitude and Other Works 1946–1963* (pp. 300–313). London: Hogarth, 1975. [Reprinted London: Karnac, 1993.]

Kristeva, J. (2001). *Melanie Klein.* New York: Columbia University Press.

Likierman, M. (2001). *Melanie Klein: Her Work in Context.* London: Continuum.

Milner, M. (1950). *On Not Being Able to Paint.* Portsmouth, NH: Heinemann. [Reprinted Hove, UK: Routledge, 2010.]

Milton, J. (2018). From the Melanie Klein archive—Klein's Further Thoughts on Loneliness. *International Journal of Psychoanalysis*, *99*(4): 929–946.

O'Shaughnessy, E. (1984). *Explanatory Notes to Klein, M.: Envy and Gratitude and Other Works 1946–1963.* London: Hogarth.

Torok, M., Sylwan, B., & Covello, A. (1998). Melanie Mell by herself. In: L. Stonebridge & J. Phillips (Eds.), *Reading Melanie Klein* (pp. 51–80). London: Routledge.

Winnicott, C. (1989). DWW: a reflection. In: C. Winnicott, R. Shepherd, & M. Davis (Eds.), *Psychoanalytic Explorations, D. W. Winnicott* (pp. 1–18). London: Karnac.

Winnicott, D. W. (1945). Primitive emotional development. *International Journal of Psychoanalysis*, *26*: 137–143.

Winnicott, D. W. (1956). Primary maternal preoccupation. In: *Collected Papers: Through Paediatrics to Psychoanalysis* (pp. 300–305). London: Tavistock, 1958.

Winnicott, D. W. (1958). The capacity to be alone. In: *The Maturational Processes and the Facilitating Environment* (pp. 29–36). London: Karnac, 1965.

Winnicott. D. W. (1962a). A personal view of the Kleinian contribution. In: *The Maturational Processes and the Facilitating Environment* (pp. 171–178). London: Karnac, 1965.

Winnicott, D. W. (1962b). The beginnings of a formulation of an appreciation and criticism of Klein's Envy Statement. In: C. Winnicott, R. Shepherd, & M. Davis (Eds.), *Psychoanalytic Explorations, D. W. Winnicott* (pp. 447–457). London: Karnac.

Winnicott, D. W. (1963). Communicating and not communicating leading to a study of certain opposites. In: *The Maturational Processes and the Facilitating Environment* (pp. 179–193). London: Karnac, 1965.

Winnicott, D. W. (1988). *Human Nature.* London: Free Association.

CHAPTER 17

Traumatic aloneness in children with narcissistically preoccupied parents

Jay Frankel

C hildren of narcissistically preoccupied parents often suffer from a particular form of what Ferenczi (1932) called "traumatic aloneness" (p. 193). This chapter will describe the ways that these parents emotionally abandon their children, how this can be experienced by these children, how these children (and later, adults) typically defend themselves from their intolerable feelings, and what this suggests for analysts' ways of engaging the adult patients these children may become.

I will start with a few words from the novel *Perfume: The Story of a Murderer*, by Patrick Süskind (1986), which captures what it feels like when no human response comes back from other people. The novel's main character, to whom the author gives the last name Grenouille—frog—gave off no human scent at all: the cause of his being essentially unseen. In Süskind's words:

> From his youth on, he had been accustomed to people's passing him and taking no notice of him whatever, not out of contempt—as he had once believed—but because they were quite unaware of his existence. There was no space surrounding him, no waves broke from him into the atmosphere, as with other people; he had no shadow, so to speak, to cast across another's face. Only if he ran right into someone in a crowd or in a street-corner collision would there be a brief moment of discernment; and the person encountered would bounce off and stare at him for a few seconds as if gazing at a creature that ought not even to exist, a creature that, although undeniably *there*, in some way or other was not present—and would take to his heels and have forgotten him. (p. 152)

Grenouille, however, had a superhuman *sense* of smell, and trained himself in the skills of a perfumer. At long last, he concocted a scent that mimicked a human scent. It *did* get people to notice him. But anticipating the day his potion would run out, he dreaded "a long slow death, a kind of suffocation in reverse, an agonising gradual self-evaporation into the wretched world" (p. 191).

Süskind, here, makes the crucial link between the absence of human response by others and the intolerable feeling that one doesn't really exist as a human being. And he adds two further links to the chain. The first is the feeling—very frequent, in my clinical experience—that not existing for others reveals something terribly, shamefully wrong about oneself: "[R]aised without love, with no warmth of a human soul", he felt he was "an abomination within and without ..." (p. 248). This often leads to a further reaction: *rejecting* the feeling of not existing, and the terrible shame and badness, through a compensatory narcissistic reaction that insists not only upon one's existence but one's *specialness* (Frankel, 2018). This compensatory reaction can take on angry, cruel, or even grandiose, paranoid, or manic elements. Süskind writes:

> And suddenly he knew that he had never found gratification in love, but always only in hatred—in hating and in being hated ... For once, just for once, he wanted to be apprehended in his true being, for other human beings to respond with an answer to his only true emotion, hatred. (pp. 240–241)

Indeed, Grenouille gets his revenge on human society—on a truly grand scale—and on himself.

Dramatic rejections and abandonments run through his fantastical novel, but Süskind does not elaborate the unspectacular things that real parents do, in the real world, to make their children feel unseen—certainly not as the particular persons they really are. Here is what they do and how their children are likely to react, in brief outline—to be given more life in the clinical vignettes that follow.

First, these parents, much of the time preoccupied with their own struggles, insecurities, anxieties, and depression, unconsciously use their children to fulfil a self-object function, in Kohut's terminology: they don't respond to their child as the child really is, but as the child the parent *needs* the child to be, overlooking many aspects of the real child—a kind of exploitation of the child, though often unconscious, in order to regulate their own intolerable states. Faimberg (2005) describes these parents as *intruding* "bad" aspects of themselves into their children and *appropriating* "good" aspects for themselves. They get angry at the child for things the parent has projected into the child, which may not be part of the child at all; and they see the child's admirable qualities and accomplishments mainly as reflections of the parent, not as originating in the child. Despite the parent's apparent involvement—or really, over-involvement—with the child, the parent is actually engaged with a *misperception* and is blind to the real child—its own kind of emotional abandonment. And indeed, these children are likely to feel intensely alone and different from other people.

The emotional abandonment is often followed by the parent's refusal to own their destructiveness towards their child, whether this refusal takes the form of outright denial or is implied by the parent's behaving "as though nothing has happened" (Ferenczi, 1933, pp. 162–163). Ferenczi (1933) called this tactic "hypocrisy" (p. 158); and in many cases, it does simply involve lying. But these parents are human beings who, like less preoccupied parents do, to a lesser extent, and like all human beings, seek refuge from their unconscious anxieties by unconsciously activating defences; so the term *hypocrisy*—which suggests more awareness and intent to deceive than is sometimes true—is not always quite right. In any case, the child is likely to perceive, at least unconsciously, the parent's selfishness or aggression, even when the parent does not see it herself, or denies it.

Disavowal by the parent—in fact, a second level of abandonment, in which the parent refuses to recognise the child's perceived reality—sends the message that the parent has done nothing wrong. Yet the child knows in her gut that something bad has happened. But the most important thing to the still-immature and dependent child is the security of feeling that she has a good parent who loves her (Fairbairn, 1943). So, unconsciously, she pushes aside whatever true perception she has of the parent's aggression and dishonesty, and tries to preserve an image of a loving, involved parent (see Freyd & Birrell, 2013). One terrible result is that the child's trust, both in other people and her own perceptions, is undermined (Dimitrijević, 2020).

A child who fears emotional abandonment becomes desperate to please her parents and make them love her, and she submits to her parents' wishes in extreme ways (Ferenczi, 1933; Frankel, 2002). She tries to become exactly what she senses they want her to be.[1] Ferenczi (1933) called this "identification with the aggressor"—an identification with the inner object the aggressor projects onto the child. And the child typically complies, not only in behaviour but also inwardly. She is likely to deny her own perceptions when these contradict her parents' views; she virtually eliminates her independent thinking, which could open the door to critical thoughts; and she stifles feelings she senses could push her parents away and creates feelings they want her to have (Frankel, 2002, 2018). Her compliance includes going along with her parents' disavowal of their hurtful and damaging behaviour towards her. The child understands that the bad feeling must come from somewhere, but she dares not blame her parents. Her only real choice is to blame herself (Frankel, 2015). She wonders: What did *I* do wrong? What's wrong with *me*? She feels there *must* be something wrong with her (Dimitrijević, 2020); and she is likely to concretise this feeling by fastening onto some quality, or qualities, of her own that she identifies as her core defect.

Children also often respond to the *pain* behind the parent's attack or exploitation. Ferenczi (1933) wrote about the "terrorism of suffering"—the parent's display of suffering to her devoted, worried child, who is helpless to make her parent feel better in any lasting way. The child is unable to help because, in most cases, the suffering of such a parent had deep roots long before the child was born, even if the parent blames the child; and the young child cannot see that this is so, because she is still dependent on the parent and because she lacks life experience. Winnicott (1960) talked about the child needing to make sense of the parent's "gesture", through

---

[1] Think of Süskind's character Grenouille, who was exquisitely sensitive to the smell of others, but gave off no scent himself. The unseen children I am talking about are exquisitely sensitive to others' *needs and emotions*; and they try to comply with what others need or want them to be, and to make their real selves even more invisible.

compliance, when the parent does not make sense of the child's spontaneous gesture (p. 145); the child's effort to help her suffering parent is certainly a prime example.

But the result can be an unendurable, traumatising feeling of compassion in the child,[2] along with a crushing sense of responsibility—if not for causing the parent's suffering in some way that she doesn't understand, then at least for healing it—a job far beyond the child's capacity. The result, readily observable in patient after patient and hour after hour, is what I (Frankel, 2015) have called "the persistent sense of being bad" (also see Fairbairn, 1943; Ferenczi, 1933). In addition to the feeling of guilt, the child, and later the adult she grows up to be, feels shamefully defective—that there is something wrong or missing in herself, and that this wrong thing is the source of the parent's suffering, that it accounts for the child's failure to heal the parent, and explains why the parent doesn't seem satisfied with the child as she really is. The feeling of shameful defect takes the form of feeling less than other people, and poorly equipped for full membership in human society (see Sullivan, 1953). It leads to vicious self-criticism and self-flagellation, and even self-hatred.

This terrible feeling of compassion often causes the child to become a compulsive caregiver (Bowlby, 1980), repeatedly trying to undo the (imagined) effects of her (imagined) failures and inadequacies. In addition to more recognisable caregiving behaviour, compulsive caregiving can entail excessively accommodating the parent (Brandchaft, 2007; Frankel, 2002)—in other words, the child's unbearable compassion reinforces her identification, submission, and compliance with her suffering parent: her identification with the aggressor. The child tries to placate and defuse the parent's aggression and absorb the parent's pain, in order to calm and soothe the parent. The child tries, by way of this accommodation, not just to shield herself from overwhelming pain and fear, but even—hope against hope—to help the parent feel well enough to give the child the care she so desperately needs. The child's heroic efforts to cure the parent (see Ferenczi, 1932, pp. 80, 89, 99) reflect her fantasy that if she herself were perfect, her parent would be happy, or she would be able to heal her parent's pain, and that she would finally be free from her crushing shame. These feelings of failure, and the futile pursuit of perfection as the antidote, often persist throughout someone's life.

Feelings of guilt, and the imperative to take care of her parent, undermine the child's feeling that she is entitled to try to get her own needs met or pursue her own destiny. And feelings of shameful defect make the child doubt even her *capacity* to psychologically separate and function as an autonomous person.

But the child can be, and often is, driven to defy her internalised sense of badness and her compulsion to accommodate—an apparent U-turn. Her counter-reaction can be dramatic or hidden, but it involves an underlying omnipotent fantasy that denies the vulnerability and helplessness the child feels when she is starved of connection and belonging, and of her need

---

[2] See Figley's (1995) parallel concept of "compassion fatigue", which refers to a form of secondary traumatic stress in healthcare professionals and other adult caregivers.

to be seen and responded to as the person she really is.[3] In the omnipotent fantasy, the child idealises the aggressor; she feels a specialness, and a sense of kinship and belonging to her very special family, through this identification. The omnipotent idealisation often focuses on some aspect of the aggressor that the child sees as a form of strength.

Children naturally identify with and idealise their parents; but when an identification must continuously push away both the unrelenting pressure of traumatic feelings and a continuing parade of contrary evidence, a child's identification may become brittle and rigid, and she is likely to get more and more committed to her identification and hostile to the realities it belies. Maintaining this kind of strained identification often requires the relatively extreme defences found in narcissistic states: paranoid splitting, projection, and hatred; manic superiority, contempt, and excitement; and sadistic control and cruelty (Frankel, 2020)—though these may be disavowed and hide behind milder guises. As such children move into adulthood, these defences may present themselves in subtle, familiar hues that blend—almost—into unremarkable social life: people prone to fits of temper, for example, or to outrage, or who tend to be argumentative, or are arrogant, nasty, smug, dismissive, or disdainful; those who rush to idealise others, or throw themselves into a rigid, aggressive identification and blind loyalty to some movement or group; those who wantonly seek attention. The narcissistic compensation can also be hidden (cf. Bach, 2006)—for example, people whose friendly façade hides secret vengeful fantasies, or whose apparent submissiveness is coloured by contempt. All these expressions of rage *may* be ways to bolster oneself by aligning with an idealised person, group, or image. They all *are* attempts to hide one's urge to submit to others, and to deny the inner sense that something is wrong with oneself.

Therapeutic implications

These formulations about the frequent consequences of early parental emotional abandonment have led me to a particular clinical attitude, and to see certain therapeutic elements as especially important in working with such patients. While clinical sensitivity will often lead analysts in the general direction I propose, I think spelling this out will help analysts be more attuned to what these patients need from them.

First, analytic neutrality or anonymity, as some more conservative analysts apply these concepts, can easily feel to such patients like detachment—yet another abandonment (Dimitrijević, 2020). I think that patients who easily feel abandoned *need to sense their analyst's responsive presence*, and the analyst may need to facilitate this.[4] People cannot be expected to make

---

[3] The child's anxiety about, and attack on, her own vulnerability is at the core of what Sullivan (1953) called "malevolent transformation".

[4] Cf. Killingmo's (1989) elaboration of how patients who, at the moment, functioning at a level of "deficit pathology"—for example, their current clinical manifestations mainly reflect some form of environmental failure, rather than inner conflict—require responses from the analyst that affirm and legitimise their experience, rather than seeking to discover its unconscious meaning.

themselves vulnerable and engage in meaningful self-reflection under what feels like a repeat of earlier traumatic conditions. (Some analysts might be surprised at the need to spell this out.) What an analyst does, specifically, to establish this kind of felt presence will depend on the patient and the clinical moment. Also, the analyst's responsive presence must be balanced against the patient's need for space at any given time.

In a little more detail: the analyst should respond to the patient as a suffering person—with kindness and empathy; often, this means more kindness and empathy for the patient than the patient can muster towards himself. More precisely, the analyst should show interest and empathy for what it was like to be the struggling child the patient was in the family he grew up in—a child whose fear and vulnerability the patient still feels ashamed of and hates, perhaps due to his loyalty to his inner objects who hate these parts of him—and what it's like to still partly feel like that child, even as an adult. This entails, first, *seeing*, and later sensitively *exploring*, the patient's early emotional abandonment; it includes seeing the parents' disavowal of their withdrawal, which pressured the child—and still pressures the adult patient—not to notice what was done to him, much less accept the truth of it and think about it. Even patients who see their parents' abandoning behaviour clearly may not let themselves feel how frightening and upsetting it was, and how much it shaped their development; but the analyst must not join her patient's denial.

In the same vein, the analyst should empathically explore the patient's terrible burden of shame—a virtually universal legacy of childhood abandonment. These patients are ashamed that they were vulnerable as children, and of their vulnerabilities now; of having had needs in childhood that their parents did not respond to, and of the longings for love and care that persist—even though, as adults, they partly know this self-flagellation is fed by enduring childhood perceptions (see Fairbairn, 1943; Ferenczi, 1933; Frankel, 2015). I have often found it helpful to let patients know that, on some level, children naturally feel an abiding shame about being emotionally abandoned, and that they very often feel somehow to blame for their parents' turning away from them. Knowing this may help counteract these patients' feeling of being abnormal or defective—the ideational anchors of shameful feelings. I offer patients this reassurance even as we also explore how their particular feelings of shame developed in their own lives.

I also express my scepticism about, and question, the reflexive self-criticism that patients often struggle with. As I've noted, children, in an omnipotent way, imagine themselves responsible for the trauma that befell them—that, for some elusive reason, it was deserved—so they can feel a sense of control in a situation where they were, in fact, helpless; in their fantasy, taking blame may also appear to be a path to restoring a feeling of closeness to their withdrawn parents (see Fairbairn, 1943).

Patients may try to prove their badness by behaving badly towards their analysts. Analysts should try not to let themselves be pushed out of a position of kindness and empathic interest by their patients' aggression (see Ferenczi, 1931, p. 132, on patients "spoiling the game"—a very gentle characterisation for what can sometimes be extremely demanding and provocative behaviour), which could implicitly confirm the patient's feeling that he is bad, as well as reinforce his belief that people in caregiving roles, despite their efforts to appear benevolent, are in fact selfish and mainly concerned with their own needs. The analyst must hold fast to a position of dedication to the patient's best interests—perhaps an unfamiliar experience for the patient. I have often found it helpful to spell out this dynamic, too, for such patients—a move that, in itself, demonstrates the analyst's continued commitment to the patient's welfare. Patients overwhelmed by, and helpless towards, their internalised traumatising parents need an ally—someone who can see both the disavowed faults in the parents, and the good in the patient, from outside the patient's identification that blinds him to both.[5]

Playfulness is a universal way of empathically connecting with other people (see Frankel, 1998)—and some other animals too—of establishing a bond of shared humanity, a sense that we are all, in Sullivan's (1947) words, "much more simply human than otherwise". As such, a little playfulness at the right time—and on a broader level, simply enjoying a moment with a patient and letting it show—may also underline that a patient's struggles are "simply human" and no cause for shame.

An additional way of being a responsive and freeing presence for the patient—and closely akin to the acknowledgement of shared humanity inherent in playfulness—is an *attitude of humility* in the analyst about her own ideas and perspectives, not least the possibility that the analyst herself may have feelings and motives that elude her own awareness. Such an attitude contrasts with the requirement, in the early lives of many of our patients, that they go along with their parents' story about the family, especially parents' disavowal of their own failings, vulnerabilities, selfish intentions, and disregard of the child's needs—what Ferenczi (1933) called "hypocrisy". More recently, psychologist Jennifer Freyd (e.g. Freyd & Birrell, 2013) documented, in her research, what she termed "betrayal blindness"—how children go along, even in their own subjective experience, with their family's self-serving, false story about the family's destructive behaviours towards the child. Jay Greenberg (1986) has talked about the need for analysts to be, to some extent, "new objects" for their patients; it seems to me, in light of the central role Ferenczi gives parental hypocrisy in his theory about the damage caused by familial childhood trauma, that honesty and, especially, humility—not needing to be right, or acknowledged as right, about either the patient or one's own motives—are most essential for analysts striving to be new, and good, objects for their patients.

Nothing in these attitudes requires the analyst to attack or compete with the patient's parents, though she may not be able to avoid challenging the parents' views. She must be careful not to attack people the patient still loves, remains loyal to and protective of, and continues to identify with. Rather, the analyst is trying to create the necessary conditions for the patient's *own* disavowed perceptions to emerge, and to draw the patient's attention to them, so the patient can discover his own perceptions and come to understand his long-ago—and still

---

[5] See Irwin Hoffman's (2009) discussion of the analyst's "responsibility to combat destructive introjects and to become an inspiring, affirmative presence in the patient's life" (p. 617).

ongoing—decision to, in some way, dissociate them. The goal here is ultimately to separate from the family story he has bought into, to his own great detriment. She is trying to help him see his parents, himself, and his life story with own eyes, and be able to think for himself about it, outside the blinders of his compulsory identification.

Trying to rediscover the patient's actual traumatic reality does not mean ignoring his fantasy life and how his experience of himself and the world, and his ways of engaging the world, have been shaped by his fantasies. But fantasy itself generally seems to be a way to cope with trauma by denying the traumatic events, along with the feelings they aroused and the needs they violated, as I described above. Fantasies express identifications that offer a sense of safety and belonging, by denying bad parts of needed objects and vulnerable parts of oneself. Analytic exploration of fantasy should never lose sight of the traumatic realities the fantasy has been designed to cope with, and how it has been structured to do this.

An important caveat: it may be easy to *mis*understand the idea that the analyst strives to be present and responsive in a way the patient can feel, or different from the parents of childhood, to mean that the analyst should take on some kind of good-parent role. Michael Balint (1979) pointed out the great danger of an analyst presenting herself as even slightly omnipotent, the way a parent looks to a young child. Confidently "knowing" the "right" answers, intervening to shield patients from life's slings and arrows, or otherwise "saving" or infantilising them carries the risk, for narcissistically injured adult patients, of encouraging a destructive "malignant regression", in some sense an addiction to the analyst, that can undermine a patient's strivings for autonomy and growth and doom his chance of recovery. Analysts may naturally be, or choose to be, different from a patient's parents—dependably present; place the patient's interests above one's own needs in the moment, and the patient's preferences above one's own; exercise self-discipline and humility; and listen closely and non-judgementally, for example. Sometimes an analyst may let her caring feelings towards a patient show. Much of this is simply inherent in, or flows from, any version of good analytic technique. But providing these essential conditions for growth is different from trying to make up for patients' childhood emotional abandonment by taking on a quasi-parenting role or otherwise trying to relieve them of responsibility for their own lives. In whatever ways an analyst's sensitivity is expressed, the analyst needs to treat her patients like adults and to respect their strivings for autonomy, not just their needs to regress.

Further, taking on a compensatory good-parent role would likely (and perhaps unwittingly) reflect the analyst's own unconscious fantasies, and—given the traumatic impact, for these patients, of having had parents who confused their children's needs with their own—might, on some level, introduce a traumatic echo that triggers a compulsion to idealise and identify with the analyst, and comply with his sense of what the analyst needs (see Ferenczi, 1933).

How does the traumatic impact of parents' emotional abandonment, and their disavowal of this, unfold later in their children's lives, in more detail? And what does this require of their analysts? The following three brief constructed examples are based on patients whose lives and inner experience I've been privileged to observe at close range, and are, I believe, true to the emotional realities of their lives and their treatments.

Stephanie

Stephanie is a married woman in late middle age, a successful academic in the humanities, and an only child. She had a depressed, angry mother who shamed her young adolescent daughter, especially when her daughter expressed the self-doubts and social insecurities so typical of that age group. Father was also depressed, but in a withdrawn way, and seemed to be perpetually struggling, unhappy, and unfulfilled. Early on, Stephanie came to believe that the simple fact of her having been born had placed an overwhelming burden of responsibility on her father from which he never recovered—that her very existence in the family was the cause of his being unable to pursue the career success and happiness he certainly would have found, had she not come into the world.

As an adult, Stephanie is often depressed and self-critical. She sometimes feels she does not want or even deserve to live. She feels like a terrible disappointment to those who depend on her, at work and at home, despite considerable evidence to the contrary. But she also often feels others' expectations as an unfair burden and resents them; and it gradually emerged that this resentment echoes a deeper, lingering resentment and criticism towards her parents, which she can sometimes be uncomfortably aware of, despite lifelong efforts to minimise her own needs and avoid making demands, and to excuse the most troubling aspects of her parents' behaviour.

It also became clear that Stephanie's efforts to sanitise her parents' image *required* that she stifle her anger towards them and turn it against herself, and blame herself for her family's unhappiness, especially her father's despair. Stephanie's pervasive self-blame centred on her failure to be perfect. In her fantasy, her perfection would have relieved father of the burden of his disappointments and depression, and finally freed him to be happy and show his love for her unreservedly. Mother, too, would have been happy, and would have given her the love and care she had been deprived of. If only she had been perfect, she would have become a happy adult. And so she hated herself for not living up to the standard of perfection and saw her failure to do so as the source of her whole family's misery. In this way, her parents' depression became a source of great personal shame. As an adult, Stephanie has felt that falling short of even the most trivial goal was yet one more proof of her shameful personal failure. She has blamed herself for every problem and believed that not having been perfect in every imaginable way, in many areas of her life, was what has stopped her from finding peace and happiness.

Along with exploring and interpreting Stephanie's expressions of self-hatred, including her efforts to push me away, I have felt it was crucial that I persist in my *affective* engagement of her, quiet though it may sometimes have been—that I not get pushed away when she tells me she is worthless and bad for people, and withdraws. During long silences, I have often commented on what she shows but does not tell—"You look tired—or maybe more than tired"—in other words, I see you, I hear what you're not saying, I care about what you feel, and I am thinking about what you feel. I have not hidden my concern for the child she was and the ways she still suffers.

But during dark sessions, I have also tried to notice little breaks in the clouds—to welcome the freer self tentatively peeking out from behind her compulsory misery—even when she seems uncomfortable with this freer part of herself. I have not hidden my enjoyment of who she is as a person and that I find it gratifying to work with her.

Similarly, I have felt free to pick up on her occasional playfulness, often in a way that includes an interpretive element. For instance, she began a session before my vacation by asking, jokingly: will you miss me? I laughed and said that her question was a minefield—any answer would be bad. Either I *would* miss her, indicating that I'm over-involved and that my good feeling for her reflects a personal problem and is therefore disqualified; or that I *would not*, meaning that she is unlovable. She recognised the dilemma she had created and laughed—a moment of contact and mutual appreciation, and an affirmation of our shared humanity. Plus, we shed new light on something important: how her attempts to reach out to people are engineered to confirm her feelings of worthlessness. A little later in the session, Stephanie noted that she had recently started to loosen up her unforgiving attitude towards herself and started to explore this shift with a sense of helpful psychological distance.

Stephanie's case makes clear that when children feel pressed to overlook the negative aspects of their emotionally abandoning parents, they become unable to disentangle and separate themselves from their families' emotional troubles, and to mourn their own lost childhoods. Instead, they take the family's pain, depression, and shame onto themselves and develop a brittle, idealising identification with their families (see Bowlby, 1980). Precisely because children are immature and need to feel they have strong and loving parents, no other choice is possible when families emotionally abandon their children (Fairbairn, 1943). A child who builds her character upon the cornerstone of an internalised sense of badness must resist the attractions of new, affirming experiences and fight off any good feeling about herself, since these could pull her away from the identification and denial she clings to, and open her up to the pain of facing her unmourned traumas. But with time and work, an emotionally present, attuned, and responsive therapist can help someone begin to release their grip on this death spiral and live more fully.

Samantha

Samantha, a thirty-year-old elementary school teacher, is the daughter of a successful businesswoman. Samantha's mother is loving but considers her daughter's work a waste of her talent. Mother has little respect for women who choose traditional female professions, and she believes Samantha has the smarts, savvy, and stomach to succeed in the tough world of business. Even though Samantha is well into adulthood, mother, now as earlier, seems unable to accept Samantha as an autonomous person with different sensibilities and interests from what mother might wish and who is entitled to choose her own direction in life; though mother seems to consciously feel that she is supporting Samantha. Even though Samantha generally leaves her encounters with her mother feeling depressed and despairing about herself, it is hard for her to see her mother's intentions as anything but supportive.

Mother's emotional abandonment can be seen both in her not responding to or nurturing the person Samantha really is, and in her implicit disavowal that she is doing this. And Samantha submits to her mother's critical view of her rather fully. Perhaps this is because mother's lifelong disavowal has essentially placed Samantha under orders not to notice, much less to defend herself against, mother's attacks. Can we expect more self-confidence and assertion from a child who lacks both affirmation for who she is, and also validation for her feelings and perceptions, from the very person whose reflection is the medium for every child's developing sense of self?

Mother's attacks cut deep. While Samantha can briefly feel good after getting approval for a job well done (which happens often) or validation on a more personal level, she quickly reverts to her default feeling that she is fundamentally a hopeless failure, that something is inherently wrong with her (at times she focuses on her small breasts), and that she is essentially unlovable, undesirable, and disappointing. If she fails to achieve absolute perfection in anything, no matter how well she does it or how difficult or unfamiliar the task, she criticises herself mercilessly and sees herself as a loser. She has been unable to free herself from her mother's way of defining her and sees neither success nor happiness in her future. Samantha's submission has still left her some space to live her own life as she sees fit, but not to enjoy it.

Additionally, Samantha had been the butt of social exclusion by the in-crowd in her early teenage years—more fuel to the fire of her feeling somehow different from, and less than, other people. Her depressed feelings sometimes make it hard for her to get through the day.

The extent of Samantha's devotion to her mother's negative view of her can be seen in her dogged justifications, in therapy, of why she is a hopeless case, and her anger when I raise questions about this. But there have been times, as our work has progressed, that the tone of the sessions has become brighter, and Samantha has been able to see herself in a more positive way and imagine a more hopeful future. Examining her present-day interactions with her mother has made it more difficult for Samantha to blind herself to mother's unresponsiveness to who she really is, and easier to see how she has embraced mother's harsh judgements. These insights have seemed important in allowing the dark clouds to part, if only briefly.

It also began to appear that mother's rigid insistence that *her* way was the *only* way was a means for mother to deny her own deep insecurity and lack of self-acceptance, and that mother unconsciously tried to rid herself of these feelings by projecting them into Samantha. In this light, Samantha's accepting her mother's projections, taking on mother's disavowed anxieties, self-doubts, and depression as her own, and repeatedly exposing herself to mother's critical "advice", can be seen as Samantha's unconscious strategy to save her mother by siphoning mother's pain into herself.

As I saw it, Samantha's devotion and her terrible compassion for her mother have kept her even more tightly tied to her self-flagellation and depression and have been major obstacles to therapeutic progress. This perception led me in a particular direction. I felt it was important that this woman, who felt so alone, should feel me as caring and an ally; and in fact, I felt like one. And while I have not talked about these feelings, I have also not hidden them. And I have not let myself get pushed away by the angry (at both herself and me) shell she constructed around herself to demonstrate how worthless, unlovable, and disappointing she was. I have tried to stay in empathic contact with the vulnerable, emotionally deprived child Samantha had been, and in a way still was, whom she herself despised.

Further, my choice of words and tone of voice have let Samantha see that I took her side even when she did not—even when she has refused to see mother's attacks and defended mother's disavowals. I have focused on details of mother's "support" and advice and encouraged Samantha to think about what was going on inside her mother's head, and about her mother's story about her own benevolence. I have shared my thoughts about mother's fragility (contrary to Samantha's conscious view of mother as unshakable), about how mother's "bad" projections into Samantha were a way to regulate mother's own self-esteem, and how Samantha's "accepting" shame has been a way to comply with and take care of mother—but I have shared these as my thoughts and have taken Samantha's scepticism seriously. I have also let Samantha know that shame and self-doubt are expected reactions to emotional abandonment and to a parent's disavowal of her own aggression towards a child.

I have been rather active in sharing my thoughts because I felt that a quiet, purely exploratory approach could leave Samantha feeling alone, at the mercy of overwhelming, hostile internal objects (see Hoffman, 2009), and thus helpless against her impulse to identify with these objects. I thought she would need an ally and advocate, so she would be able to feel she had space to think.

But when Samantha has detected my personal feelings about her mother's treatment of her, behind exploratory and interpretive comments that I presented in a more neutral-sounding way, I have acknowledged what I felt. And I have added that I thought that my feelings could complicate Samantha's exploration of her own feelings towards her mother. I think it is important that analysts can acknowledge how their own attitudes can affect their patients' freedom to explore and to find their own relation to the important people in their lives—and especially so with patients, like Samantha, whose difficulties were compounded by parents' denial of feelings that the child nevertheless sensed, on some level, and certainly reacted to.

Jane

Jane, an engineer, grew up in a working-class family. Unlike Stephanie and Samantha, Jane had a childhood that included outright physical abuse—her father regularly slapped her hard in the face. But Jane felt that her parents' emotional disconnection was at least as disturbing, and she tried to think of her father's slaps as evidence of his wish for emotional contact. When, as a child, Jane faced some kind of physical risk or danger, father often appeared indifferent or even seemed to enjoy her fear. Jane now believes that her father needed her to feel pain and fear. Mother, often preoccupied with her own concerns, typically minimised Jane's upset feelings and told her that her perceptions of upsetting family events were mistaken.

Jane's parents' disengagement from her feelings made her feel unseen and unwanted. She wondered what was wrong with her—there *must* be something bad about her, or why would they treat her like that? As an adult, she can feel inwardly driven to criticise herself. Everything about her is somehow wrong—her perceptions of other people, what she thinks and feels. Even her unhappiness is evidence that her feelings are different from how she is "supposed to" feel and from what others feel. These trains of thought easily push her into a sad and lonely place which she has a hard time finding her way out of. She believes that no one really wants to hear or share these feelings, and that people will eventually turn away from her. Unless others' interest and concern are genuine and unmistakable, she cannot bear even to think about painful moments in her life and blocks them out.

Jane's self-blame seems a holdover from her efforts to salvage the image of her parents as emotionally involved with her and loving, and to blame herself for feeling uncared for—which she was implicitly pressured to do by their disavowal of their disconnection from her. Of course, seeing her parents as loving contradicted much of her own experience of them. As a girl, Jane had been willing not only to endure but to justify the pain and fear her father forced at her, so she could see him in a good light—a pattern that echoes in her current life, for instance in her efforts to excuse the slipshod work of colleagues she depends on.

These days, Jane's sense of being defective comes to the fore during heated arguments with her husband, but it can even come up when little things go badly. She gets angry at herself, and sad. She also gets confused about her marital fights—she denies her upsetting perceptions of her husband, and then her painful feelings make no sense to her. Getting confused was a trick Jane learned early, from colluding with her parents' disavowal of their own hurtfulness and disengagement. On rare occasions, when Jane is alone after an unresolved fight with her husband, she slaps herself, usually in the face, as self-punishment—just as her father had done to her. Jane feels that attacking herself is a way to protect her husband from her anger. Somewhat similarly, her submission to father's threatening behaviour during childhood may have been, in her thinking, a way to take care of him, and also a tactic to feel emotionally connected to him.

But during marital arguments, when Jane's husband minimises or belittles her feelings, as her mother had done, or when her husband's anger evokes the feelings of her father's assaults, Jane often responds with reflexive, unthinking rage, and counter-attacks. She feels on a hair trigger at these times. This reaction seems to be an identification with her rageful father, and also a way to both display and reject her deep-seated belief that her own innate badness is the real problem in her marriage.

With Jane, I've sometimes been a little playful, which has invariably felt like it created a moment of contact. When she's described painful or especially problematic moments, I've made a point of saying something rather than listening silently, and I often let her see my personal response. I've been gentle, but present and active, in exploring her inner experience of her childhood mistreatment, when our sessions have led there, to help her feel less alone and better able to face what had happened to her, and to be able to think more clearly about how these experiences shaped her view of herself, her parents, and others later in her life. I have paid particular attention to the enduring shame that has its roots in her childhood trauma, and now and then have shared a few details from my own life, to help her see her vulnerability as "simply human" rather than different and shameful.

As with Samantha and Stephanie, we see Jane still busy protecting her parents' disavowal of their emotional destructiveness. For all these women, this requires clinging to the belief that it is they themselves who are bad or broken. But Jane's case description most clearly illuminates how a persistent feeling of being bad can evoke a compensatory aggressive reaction, though such a reaction can also be seen in Stephanie's and Samantha's cases and is hardly pervasive in Jane's. This angry backlash helps someone drown out and deny painful feelings of fear and badness, even as she complies with her parents' requirement, now internalised, that she make herself both guilty party and victim.

Conclusion

These cases demonstrate how clinical phenomena like depression, masochism, and narcissism can be understood as different expressions of a multifaceted dynamic response to a very common trauma—specifically, identification with the aggressor, in its various aspects, as a reaction to traumatic aloneness in children of narcissistically preoccupied parents. Based on what I've observed over many years of clinical practice and heard from supervisees and colleagues, the broad clinical framework I've described here applies to a great many of our patients.

With such patients, the analyst must pay special attention to establishing a responsive presence. She must see, and explore, the patient's early emotional abandonment, and examine its enduring consequences—perhaps especially the shame that is its universal, and terribly damaging, outcome. It can help to let the patient know that shame is a natural consequence of emotional abandonment. It is also important not to let oneself be pushed away by a patient who feels unworthy. Additionally, playfulness, alongside an attitude of humility, foster a bond of shared humanity, undercut a sense of shameful difference from other people, and help free patients from their destructive identifications with the aggressor—and, ultimately, from their traumatic aloneness.

References

Bach, S. (2006). *Getting from Here to There: Analytic Love, Analytic Process.* Hillsdale, NJ: Analytic Press.

Balint, M. (1979). *The Basic Fault: Therapeutic Aspects of Regression.* London: Tavistock.

Bowlby, J. (1980). *Loss: Sadness and Depression.* New York: Basic Books.

Brandchaft, B. (2007). Systems of pathological accommodation and change in analysis. *Psychoanalytic Psychology, 24*: 667–687.

Dimitrijević, A. (2020). Silence and silencing of the traumatized. In: A. Dimitrijević & M. B. Buchholz (Eds.), *Silence and Silencing in Psychoanalysis* (pp. 198–216). Abingdon, UK: Routledge.

Faimberg, H. (2005). *The Telescoping of Generations*. New York: Routledge.

Fairbairn, W. R. D. (1943). The repression and the return of bad objects. In: *Psychoanalytic Studies of the Personality* (pp. 59–81). London: Routledge & Kegan Paul.

Ferenczi, S. (1931). Child-analysis in the analysis of adults. In: M. Balint (Ed.) & E. Mosbacher and others (Trans.), *Final Contributions to the Problems and Methods of Psycho-Analysis* (pp. 126–142). New York: Brunner/Mazel, 1980.

Ferenczi, S. (1932). *The Clinical Diary of Sándor Ferenczi*. J. Dupont (Ed.); M. Balint & N. Z. Jackson (Trans.). Cambridge, MA: Harvard University Press, 1988.

Ferenczi, S. (1933). Confusion of tongues between adults and the child. In: M. Balint (Ed.) & E. Mosbacher and others (Trans.), *Final Contributions to the Problems and Methods of Psycho-Analysis* (pp. 156–167). New York: Brunner/Mazel, 1980.

Figley, C. R. (Ed.) (1995). *Compassion Fatigue: Coping with Secondary Traumatic Stress Disorder in Those Who Treat the Traumatized*. New York: Brunner-Routledge.

Frankel, J. (1998). The play's the thing: how the essential processes of therapy are seen most clearly in child therapy. *Psychoanalytic Dialogues, 8*: 149–182.

Frankel, J. (2002). Exploring Ferenczi's concept of identification with the aggressor: its role in trauma, everyday life, and the therapeutic relationship. *Psychoanalytic Dialogues, 12*: 101–140.

Frankel, J. (2015). The persistent sense of being bad: the moral dimension of identification with the aggressor. In: A. Harris & S. Kuchuck (Eds.), *The Legacy of Sándor Ferenczi: From Ghost to Ancestor* (pp. 204–222). New York: Routledge.

Frankel, J. (2018). Psychological enslavement through identification with the aggressor. In: A. Dimitrijević, G. Cassullo, & J. Frankel (Eds.), *Sándor Ferenczi's Influence on Contemporary Psychoanalytic Traditions* (pp. 134–139). London: Routledge.

Frankel, J. (2020). Election diary. *Kateksis, Bulleteng for Norsk Psykoanalytisk Forening, 2*: 5–23.

Freyd, J. J., & Birrell, P. J. (2013). *Blind to Betrayal*. New York: John Wiley & Sons.

Greenberg, J. R. (1986). Theoretical models and the analyst's neutrality. *Contemporary Psychoanalysis, 22*: 87–106.

Hoffman, I. Z. (2009). Therapeutic passion in the countertransference. *Psychoanalytic Dialogues, 19*: 617–637.

Killingmo, B. (1989). Conflict and deficit: implications for technique. *International Journal of Psychoanalysis, 70*: 65–79.

Sullivan, H. S. (1947). *Conceptions of Modern Psychiatry*. New York: William Alanson White Psychiatryy, Psychoanalysis & Psychology Foundation.

Sullivan, H. S. (1953). *The Interpersonal Theory of Psychiatry*. New York: W. W. Norton.

Süskind, P. (1986). *Perfume: The Story of a Murderer*. J. E. Woods (Trans.). New York: Vintage International.

Winnicott, D. W. (1960). Ego distortion in terms of true and false self. In: *The Maturational Processes and the Facilitating Environment* (pp. 140–152). London: Hogarth Press and the Institute of Psycho-Analysis.

CHAPTER 18

The clinical encounter with the lonely patient: trauma and the empty self

Charles Ashbach

> Sensations, feelings, insights, fancies—all these are private and, except through symbols and at second hand, incommunicable. We can pool information about experiences, but never the experiences themselves. From family to nation, every human group is a society of island universes.
>
> —Huxley, 1954

Introduction

This chapter addresses some of the factors and elements involved in understanding and working with patients suffering from states of intense loneliness, both intrapsychic and interpersonal. I'm organising this work principally around elements and dynamics central to the circumstances of early attachment. Both the attachment literature (Fonagy, 2001) and object relations theorising (Bion, 1967; Fairbairn, 1952; Grotstein, 2009; Klein, 1935) emphasise the vital importance of the earliest connections between mother or mothering figure and infant for the well-being of the patient's personality. As Melanie Klein (1963, p. 301) emphasises, the foundation for the most complete experience of being understood is achieved through the establishment of the link between the unconscious of the mother and the unconscious of the child. I hope to be able to demonstrate that states of chronic loneliness point to failures, deficits, and traumas, of both obvious and subtle forms, that have interrupted the normal processes of attachment and have forced the subject to take on events that he is unable to manage. As Ogden (2014, p. 205) observes, this subject "short-circuits" the primitive agony of his original failed experience of establishing the primal, psychic-emotional tie to his object by generating primitive defence organisations, usually psychotic, autistic, or schizoid in nature, that substitute a self-created inner reality for external reality thus foreclosing his actual experience of life events.

The consequences of this foreclosure lead to a complex and paradoxical psychic state where the subject has "experienced" (gone through) psychic and emotional experiences that he "did not experience", for example, were never organised within his "unit self" as a whole person, living in a body. This traumatic condition gives rise to a particular type of obscuring and defensive consciousness that blocks his actual life experience, which has become "unbearable", leading to what Ogden describes as an "unlived life." It is this experience of an unthinkable catastrophe, along with the associated anxieties and dread that are unfelt in the past and therefore projected into the future as an event the subject anticipates and fears: the unfelt and "unlived" past lives become the threat of the catastrophic future.

My working assumption is that for individuals who have experienced the tragedy of "unlived" life (a cut-out or unrepresented experience) a distorted sense of self-organisation emerges that we come to know as a comprehensive system of emptiness and loneliness. In "Mourning and Melancholia", Freud (1917e) uses the dynamic of the loss or inaccessibility of the primary object to explain the emergence of melancholic depression. Following his arguments and theorising, I see six central factors contributing to the subject's depression and/or loneliness: 1) the shattering or loss of the patient's central psychic structure occurring due to object loss and to the object's unavailability; 2) the splitting of the self and the replacement of the original internal system of object relations with a narcissistically influenced system that enables the subject to create an ideal version of self and object while at the same time, in another register, a devalued and debased sense of self and object; 3) the increase in primitive emotionality, especially of intensely ambivalent states of love and hate, leading to distrust, insecurity, and paranoia; 4) the diminishment of reality testing and the development of a sadistic form of the superego making relationships increasingly difficult to establish; 5) the creation of a false self shell (Winnicott, 1978, p. 212) that protects against retraumatisation and leads to feelings of the inauthenticity of the self; and, 6) the subject's preference for an internal, psychic retreat (Steiner, 1993) characterised by the idealised, delusional experience of protection, comfort, and libidinal gratification provided by an imagined perfect object rather than risk the frustrating and problematic experiences of actual contact with the real world of relationships and experience. As Freud says: "… people never willingly abandon a libidinal position, not even indeed, when a substitute is already beckoning to them" (1917e, p. 244), and it is the patient's preference for his secret and self-constructed and libidinally gratifying, narcissistic internal world that makes the challenge of making contact with and treating him so daunting and complex.

The difference between the depressed patient and the lonely patient can be traced to what Fairbairn (1952) describes as a schizoid structure of internal objects. Where the depressed subject seeks to engage and annoy the objects within his environment, in a noisy, demanding, and often "dramatic" and pugnacious way, to compel them to repair the damage done by their abandonment and to magically reconstitute his lost childhood, the lonely patient has internalised his version of ideal objects within the depth of his unconscious in a schizoid mode. These objects become psychically frozen and are held to with a sense of hidden desperation; and though he has relationships with some figures in his external environment—a spouse, children, boss, or colleagues—there is always a measure of psychic-emotional distance employed to protect him from the dangers of both engagement and rejection. The subject clings to the internal ideal and holds actual relationships at a significant and scorned distance. While the "withdrawn" or introverted version of the lonely patient seems easier to identify, the less obvious form of loneliness, as a background emotional context or psychic field, often is hidden behind the patient's false self façade (Winnicott, 1960) or behind the apparently satisfactory life he is living. The true nature of the patient's internal world is often not revealed until encountered in his resistances, discontinuities, and in the anomalies emergent in the therapist's countertransference. He oscillates between an aloof indifference that leaves the therapist feeling unwanted and unnecessary, and a surprising experience of intrusion or invasion when he begins to feel some measure of his need or desire. The shift in the patient's emotional state, facilitated by projective identification, leads to the therapist's feelings of extensive confusion in the countertransference.

Treatment considerations

An effective treatment process is built upon establishing an alive, intersubjective, authentic, and emotional connection with the patient so that a level of trust and understanding may be established where the lurking injuries, defences, and adaptations stored in the background of the subject's consciousness may be brought forward into the containment structures of a sturdy but sensitive system of the transference and countertransference. The psychic field created by the interpenetration of the patient's and the therapist's *subjectivity and consciousness* is the true location of the treatment and the centre of the therapy effort (Ferro, 2006) and *our understanding of it*. It builds upon Balint's (1979, p. 66) idea that the foundation of the infant's personality is created by means of an "inter-penetrating, harmonious mix-up" between infant and mother that substantiates the baby's being (narcissistic wholeness) and primal self. The shocks and discontinuities of the trauma and impingements of the subject's early life significantly distort and, in some cases negate, through violence and chaos of object loss or object inaccessibility, the subject's experience of ego integration and symbolic function and thus have imposed significant limits on his ability to "learn from experience" (Bion, 1962). When this primal "mix-up" condition is negated or compromised, according to Balint, the subject suffers a "basic fault" (p. 21) in his character that places him outside the realm of empathy and outside a common emotional language.

The therapist working with such a patient is confronted with both *psychic presences*, as memories of events that were recorded, as well as *psychic absences*, understood to exist within a void created by forces and experience that overwhelmed the subject and annihilated the links that might have allowed his experience to be encoded as lived and significant. These "erased" memories and emotions exist within the body–mind as elements that press ever forward, seeking, somehow, to be inscribed in consciousness. Clinical work challenges the therapist to develop ever more sensitive capabilities to be able to discern and connect to an individual who has taken up a deeply withdrawn and in many ways inaccessible self-experience. This subject does not experience pleasure and pain in ways common to most other patients and the therapist has to encounter some shocking signal that might alert him to the hidden, traumatised self that is both present and absent from the therapeutic encounter. Bion (1970, p. 9) speaks about the subject's inability to "suffer" (carry) pain in order to be able to "suffer pleasure" and the therapist needs to "participate" in the suffering and confusion that is at the core of the psychic field created by both partners in the treatment in order to achieve a state of "emotional unison" with the patient (Ferro & Civitarese, 2015, p. 99). The use of the psychic field perspective allows for the interpenetration of subject and object as the most reliable means available to discern and experience the uniqueness and specificity of the intrapsychic and emotional content and dimensions of the patient's turbulent being. As Civitarese (2013, p. 220) has said: "It is my belief than an emotional connection can only be born out of living—or better, out of the suffering—the same things, out of a moment of intersubjective connection between two separate objects."

These patients have encoded their trauma within their being, at a narcissistic level, what Grunberger (1979) describes as a coenaesthetic dimension of the body-self (p. 248) and in a state of consciousness that is not easily identifiable. It is not the unconscious or pre-consciousness of Freud's topographical model but a paradoxical state that exists *next to*, *behind*, or *below* traditional states, or within other registers of the psyche–soma that are not clearly defined, for example: "cut-out consciousness" (Davoine & Gaudilliere, 2004); "zones of non-existence" (Bion, 1970, p. 20); "consciousness without a subject" (Winnicott, 1974); the "not repressed unconscious" (Lacan, 1955, p. 200), or "the unlived life" (Ogden, 2014, p. 214). The patient, because of the unknown and unfelt aspects of his problems, expresses these elements almost exclusively in the form of *resistances* and *disturbances in the setting*, for example, acting-out, inscriptions, crises, and various forms of therapeutic "passion plays" (Grotstein, 2000, p. 220) in order to represent, actualise, or dimensionalise the felt nature of the seeming "invisible" chaos and torture that has unsettled his being and disrupted his world. As Davoine and Gaudilliere (2004) describe it: a psychic and emotional catastrophe has broken the patient's conceptualisation and experience of *time*, *causality*, and *meaning* and has driven him out of the conventional, shared version of reality and into states of mind that are traumatically timeless, terrifying, and unchanging.

Winnicott (1974) says that such patients face the experience of unrepresented "primitive agonies" (p. 104) which carry the dread of madness and trauma that push against the thin membrane of his false self, with the dark, threatening shadow of "breakdown" always closing in although the patient projects it into the future as a "possible" or future catastrophe. He warns the therapist against the danger of assuming the patient's problems are neurotic and colluding in such an assumption is likely to lead to an impasse of frustrating and painful futility. This patient, because of his narcissistic injury, works relentlessly to convince the therapist that he is a "relatively healthy person", and that we must join him in his desperate definition of himself.

With these elements in mind, I represent the goal of treatment as helping the patient "descend" into the psychic-emotional dimension of life constituted by the treatment relationship and away from the unlived zone of unrepresented, unexperienced psychic-emotional numbness of idealisation and persecution. There is no "cure" to move towards, in the sense there is no global transformation of the self, only the step-by-step process of solving innumerable, small, specific problems through the intersubjective suffering of each conflict within the treatment partnership that leads to the gradual expansion of the patient's symbolic and emotional capacity, offering him an ever more realistic and robust understanding of who he is and what has happened to him. Hope, as a central element of the treatment, is developed through the gradual and successful working-through of specific issues leading to the reduction of the dread of aloneness; the transformation of a sadistic superego; the metabolisation of some infantile fixations; and ultimately to the experience that the therapeutic relationship offers a genuine opportunity for the repair of the self and his objects, to whatever extent possible.

Because of the nature of the subject's experience, partially represented and partially non-represented, the work of listening, containment, reverie, and interpretation must undergo an adaptation that focuses on the "here and now" of the transference. Bion (1997) emphasises that where the patient's psyche is unable to get hold of compelling memories, thoughts, and experiences the therapeutic work should focus on the immediacy of elements emerging in the present moment of the session, especially if they are felt to be "stray" or "wild" (p. 27). Any attempt to speculate about "possible" or "imagined" events in the search for the reconstruction of lost experience provides a poor foundation for helping the patient encounter the actual, missing experiences that lie hidden or unrepresented. As Bion (1967; 1992, p. 381) says: "The only point of importance in any session is the unknown. Nothing must be allowed to distract from intuiting that." His primary advice: the therapist should avoid the pressures of "memory and desire" so that the evolution of the session may be observed "while it is taking place" (p. 382). Here we are interested in widening and deepening the psychic field in the moment of the session so that one's full attention and experience is committed to the unfolding of the body and mind of both participants.

The case of Richard

Richard, a sixty-year-old man, presented himself in treatment seeking help with feelings of lack of fulfilment in his work and feelings of extreme frustration in the third year of his second marriage. He had been in psychotherapy for nine years with his therapist who had recently died of cancer. He presented as a professional and attractive man surrounded by an atmosphere of calm confidence, who impressed me as charming and congenial with an extremely articulate way of introducing his ideas. He worked very pointedly to have me experience his intelligence and charm and was discreetly very proud of having attended prestigious universities for both undergraduate and graduate degrees and of having attained substantial professional success and prestige. His intelligence and enthusiasm for the therapy process produced an unusual eager and positive feeling in me about the possibilities for the success of the treatment and we began with two sessions per week. The treatment has been ongoing for seven years.

The opening phase of the treatment was focused on the story of his family with special reference to his older brother, Billy, who was grievously injured in a car accident when he was five years old. He sustained cerebral injuries that left him cognitively compromised and partially paralysed on the left side. His mother was driving the car. Richard was born two years later. The tragedy of the accident drove his mother, who already suffered from anxiety and paranoid ideation, into a state of paranoid depression and she reacted by closing off her home and family against the world. She seemed captured by her grief and operated as a "dead mother" (Green, 1986) with a total preoccupation with her eldest son's tragically compromised circumstances.

No one outside the family was ever allowed in the house and Richard was never able to have friends over to play or to study. All contacts had to occur outside the crypt of his home. His mother wouldn't let him play baseball or football and wrapped a tight web of prohibition around his yearning for athletics and adventure. His one outlet was running, which he pursued with relish when he was in middle school and continued through high school and college. The many sessions of narrating the trials and tribulations of being with his brother failed to elicit any substantial emotional response in him. He spoke about the sorrow he said he felt but I could not experience him feeling it. I frequently felt heartbroken at the thought of Billy's experience of being *treated* in such a cold, mechanical way, as if he had no one to confirm the pain of his experience or the burden of having to carry such deficits. The mother insisted that Billy was not to be "pampered" or "babied." I sometimes experienced feelings of hatred towards his mother as Richard recounted such stories and I asked about him feeling tortured and constrained by her rules and declarations; he responded that while he felt frustrated with her, he did not experience a sense of fury or outrage.

Richard had the capacity to frustrate the people in his life, especially at work, with his tardiness in regard to turning in important projects and his billing, and his constant carping about his wife's extravagant and expensive addiction to high-fashion shopping. He spoke about disagreements and confrontations with colleagues and his wife but when I enquired about the person's response to his opposition he said: "I don't say those things to people, I'm not rude. This is just what I'd *like* to say." His *fantasies* about engaging with others had the same sense of reality as actually speaking with them. Yet it was clear that he felt a very strong sense of frustration and aggression towards people, but the articulation of such negative feelings was something that seemed well beyond his emotional capacity to manage.

I began to understand that he had a particularly slippery style of communicating. He told me how his mentor at his company had commented on his "fondness for the irrelevant" and when I asked him about his evasiveness in the treatment, he said it was his way of keeping a lot of things in mind at the same time. At other times, I experienced him as dull or even stupid, but it was clear that some regressive element had lowered his emotional and cognitive functioning. He did not appear to be actively uncooperative, just helplessly passive. Nonetheless I began to experience feelings of frustration, tediousness, and boredom in working with him while at other times I felt defeated by what I experienced as his perverse delight in frustrating me. He provocatively misunderstood my interpretations, took words or ideas out of context, and attempted to disturb and arouse me with his passivity, confusion, and apparent lack of comprehension. He did not seem to be able to make use of what I was able to offer him or of what he produced from his insights and ideas.

When I began to have ideas of referring him to another therapist, I realised I was having a flight reaction and took the case to supervision. It became clear in those discussions that the annihilation of his feelings and emotional experiences, which I recognised to be his zone of non-existence (Bion, 1970), were brought to life in the struggle of the transference relationship which replicated his experiences with his mother. He did feel pain, agony, frustration, and fury but he needed our transference relationship to provide a measure of "figurability" (Oliner, 2013), to provide a shape through which he might experience the lost experiences inside him and thereby to be able to bring them to life. My impatience had caused me to over-function, and this had the effect of triggering his envy and making him feel small and helpless. He had "gotten under my skin" through his use of projective identification and cast me into the role of the demanding, know-it-all mother. Consequently, there was no possibility for him to come out from his psychic retreat with me occupying the position of such an unempathetic and insensitive figure. My supervisor's suggestions: wait, proceed very slowly, resist the invitation of offering too much, and carry the patient's criticisms without resorting to interpretations that might accuse him of the errors of his misunderstandings.

In the therapy sessions that followed the supervision, I was once again able to maintain the necessary psychological separation from him, had a greater sense of independence and freedom, and felt less a captive of the transference. (Later I came to understand that he had used me as a "scapegoat surrogate" (Ashbach et al., 2020) to carry the intense feelings of guilt and shame for him.) Having understood my countertransference, I was able to contain Richard once again as my patient and was able to think about his psychic experience and not become absorbed and distracted in his life problems. In one particular session, as he spoke of a memory of his brother's frustration with getting dressed and struggling to button his shirt, with his "one good hand", I felt his sorrow and loneliness having to witness this sad spectacle and said: "Richard, I think I understand how your mother was never able to be a partner to Billy. She never said to him: 'Billy, let me help you with your buttons, it'll be easier if we do this together.'" He looked at me with such pain and agony in his face and then broke down and wept, fully and vulnerably, for the first time in the treatment, and I felt a great sense of relief that this experience, finally understood and shared by me, had given me the foundation to speak "for him", on his behalf, as his agent, and articulate something that he had often felt but could never dare imagine to speak. This moment seemed to announce a different form of containment and I felt that my emotional reverie and identification with his sorrow showed him that he had an ally in me rather than some stranger looking in from the outside. I began to understand how terribly alone and lonely he was in his family, in his marriages, at work, and in his therapy experiences.

The dream

In the week after the emotional breakthrough, he told me the following dream:

> I'm walking down the street of my old neighbourhood and came upon my childhood home. It was generally as I remembered it but slightly embellished, as if the scene was airbrushed [his term], with a neatly mown lawn surrounded by a white picket fence defining the front of the house. As I behold this version of our house, I hear sounds from the rear and go to investigate. Upon entering the backyard, I see plumes of dark grey smoke and flares of fire coming out of the kitchen windows. This is very puzzling, and I stand still to listen for any sounds and to see if anyone is inside. I don't hear anything or see anyone and after a few minutes I turn and go back to the front of the house and stand there for a while and look, but now, from this perspective, I don't see any sign of fire or smoke. Everything seems perfectly normal. Gradually I walk away and feel strangely indifferent.

He said this was a recurring dream and he had dreamt it several times over the past twenty-five years. The previous dreams presented in the treatment were all fragments and again Richard was alone, as in almost all of those dreams, so the specificity and detail of this dream was special. Further, he thought the front of the house reflected his mother's "delusions" (his word) about the rightful place she thought her family should have in the world. He grimaced as he said: "There was such a dark cloud in our family and no way to tell anybody about it." I asked why he didn't call the police or fire department in the dream, and he answered that it never occurred to him. I asked if there were any people present at any point in the dream and he said no: "I was all alone. I'm always alone in my dreams." I thought of the house as reflecting his psychic retreat: part self-idealisation—the front of the house, and part of the ongoing trauma of his familial disaster and the rage he continues to feel—at the back. I thought his ability to empty his experience of emotion, as Green (1986) describes in conditions of blank anxiety or blank psychosis, reflected a loss experienced on a narcissistic level, below the level of the ego (p. 146). I felt that he had used the dream to "tell" me of the psychic annihilation he had initiated to protect himself from the feelings of madness, emptiness, and loneliness that followed were bearable compared to the agony of his unfelt experience. The dream provided us with a set of metaphors that revealed that certain psychic experiences were represented but in highly symbolic forms. I suggested the "fire" was a way to approach his aggression and I saw how it was destroying his ability to gain nurturance by destroying the "kitchen" of his experience and why so little sustenance could be derived from the treatment. Then, in a moment of unusual insight and humour, he said: "Next you'll be telling me the treatment is the fire department." I said: "Hopefully we'll be able to help you deal with the flames." We both laughed. Of course, the reparation necessary to relieve him of his guilt and shame would have to wait for a future phase of the process of working-through because one can't begin to rebuild the self until the fire of hatred has been extinguished and transformed into grief.

The flattening of Richard's symbolic capacity was related to his desire not to know and especially not to feel both his hatred for his loved object mother as well as a flight from the agony of Billy's suffering that caused him feelings of extreme guilt. In addition, his identification with his mother's overflowing narcissism put pressure on his capacity to feel normal. As Wurmser (2007, p. 1) points out: the patient in such traumatic circumstances is burdened by a sense of the narcissism of "omnipotent responsibility" where he feels it is his sole task to repair and renew the damaged objects at the centre of his love and for Richard that meant both his mother and his brother.

I became increasingly aware of keeping my therapeutic "zeal" in check because each sign of my ambition seemed to fill him with a sense of how disappointed I was with his present condition, as if he could do nothing right. His movement away from the burning house in his dream suggested that he must not be pushed to take on a psychic task that might make him feel "forced to death by the analysis" (Riviere, 1936, p. 144). I also recognised that as a result of my participation in Richard's trauma and conflicts I came into contact with a new appreciation of my own loneliness that I had not been aware of.

Part of the recovery process for the lonely patient is the necessity to grieve the loss of contact with figures of significance and love and that involves feelings of great vulnerability and helplessness. The impact of our growing relatedness seemed to decrease some of his need to believe in his own magical self-sufficiency, but each moment of real encounter had to be internalised with some measure or element of emotional significance. He and I could only handle brief moments like that. By staying in the moment-to-moment experiences of the here-and-now of the transference, I was less likely to lose contact with Richard and more likely to remain able to contain his shifting but subtle moods and reactions. And likewise, the sense of the ongoing nature of the "fire" within provided me with a metaphor through which I might be able to represent, in a more attuned and sympathetic way, the primitive edge of the experience of psychotic elements that continued to worry Richard about his sanity.

Gradually Richard was able to talk about his hopelessness and pessimism about never getting "better." He said that although he felt better about our work he didn't know if he could continue to hope that the relief that he longed for would ever show up. I pointed out to him that he had never before spoken about his fears of not having a better life and perhaps this was some evidence that he actually had begun to feel his desire to save the "house" that had continued to burn across all these years. He sighed and said: "I think I really do want that fire to stop."

Summary

In this chapter I have described how an understanding of the catastrophe of object loss or object inaccessibility, as described in Freud's (1917e) study "Mourning and Melancholia", helps the therapist to encounter the complex network of internal objects, as both presences and absences that are shattered as a result of such a catastrophe. Unable to protect the self from the impact of this trauma, the subject is unable or unwilling to record these events and instead establishes a realm of empty, unrepresented experience that Ogden (2014) describes as "unlived life".

An alternative system of self and objects is created and stored in a special category of consciousness that exists behind, below, or within normal states of consciousness. The task of making contact and establishing a treatment relationship is challenged by the unusual nature of such psychic and emotional experience. Loneliness is seen as the consequence of such early developmental losses and the restructuring of the self, utilising schizoid modes of psychic experience and defences, often accompanied by psychotic or autistic modes, to enable the subject to withdraw into a psychic retreat (Steiner, 1993) which might allow him to avoid the dangers of intimate contact and therefore of retraumatisation.

The use of an analytic field theory perspective (Ferro & Civitarese, 2015) offers clinically useful possibilities for making emotional contact with individuals who have suffered trauma and abuse in their developmental lives.

References

Ashbach, C., Fraley, K., Koehler, P., & Poulton, J. (2020). *Suffering and Sacrifice in the Clinical Encounter.* Bicester, UK: Phoenix.

Balint, M. (1979). *The Basic Fault: Therapeutic Aspects of Regression.* New York: Brunner/Mazel.

Bion, W. R. (1962). *Learning from Experience.* London: William Heinemann. [Reprinted in *Seven Servants*, New York: Jason Aronson, 1977.]

Bion, W. R. (1967). *Second Thoughts.* New York: Jason Aronson.

Bion, W. R. (1970). *Attention and Interpretation.* London: Tavistock. [Reprinted in *Seven Servants*, New York: Jason Aronson, 1977.]

Bion, W. R. (1992). *Cogitations.* London: Karnac.

Bion, W. R. (1997). *Taming Wild Thoughts.* London: Karnac.

Civitarese, G. (2013). The inaccessible unconscious and reverie as a path to figurability. In: H. Levine, G. Reed, & D. Scarfone (Eds.), *Unrepresented States and the Construction of Meaning.* London: Karnac.

Davoine, F., & Gaudilliere, J.-M. (2004). *History Beyond Trauma.* New York: Other Press.

Fairbairn, W. R. D. (1952). *Psychoanalytic Studies of the Personality.* London: Routledge.

Ferro, A. (2006). *Mind Works: Technique and Creativity in Psychoanalysis.* London: Routledge, 2008.

Ferro, A., & Civitarese, G. (2015). *The Analytic Field and Its Transformations.* London: Karnac.

Fonagy, P. (2001). *Attachment Theory and Psychoanalysis.* New York: Other Press.

Freud, S. (1917e). Mourning and melancholia. *S. E., 14*: 237–260. London: Hogarth.

Green, A. (1986). The dead mother. In: *On Private Madness* (pp. 142–173). London: Hogarth. [Reprinted London: Karnac, 1997.]

Grotstein, J. S. (2000). *Who Is the Dreamer Who Dreams the Dream?* Hillsdale, NJ: Analytic Press.

Grotstein, J. (2009). *At the Same Time and on Another Level, Vol. 1: Psychoanalytic Theory and Technique in Kleinian/Bionian Mode.* London: Karnac.

Grunberger, B. (1979). *Narcissism.* Madison, CT: International Universities Press.

Huxley, A. (1954). *The Doors of Perception.* New York: Harper Brothers.

Klein, M. (1935). A contribution to the psychogenesis of manic-depressive states. In: *The Writings of Melanie Klein, Vol. 1, Love, Guilt and Reparation* (pp. 262–289). New York: Delacorte.

Klein, M. (1963). On the sense of loneliness. In: *Envy and Gratitude and Other Works*: 1946–1963 (pp. 300–313). New York: Delacorte.

Lacan, J. (1955). *The Seminars of Jacques Lacan: The Psychoses: 1955–1956*. New York: W. W. Norton.

Ogden, T. (2014). Fear of breakdown and the unlived life. *International Journal of Psychoanalysis, 95*(2): 205–223.

Oliner, M. (2013). "Non-represented" mental states. In: H. Levine, G. Reed, & D. Scarfone (Eds.), *Unrepresented States and the Construction of Meaning*. London: Karnac.

Riviere, J. (1936). A contribution to the analysis of the negative therapeutic reaction. In: A. Hughes (Ed.), *The Inner World and Joan Riviere: Collected Papers*. London: Karnac, 1991.

Steiner, J. (1993). *Psychic Retreat: Pathological Organizations in Psychotic, Neurotic and Borderline Patients*. London: Routledge.

Winnicott, D. W. (1960). The theory of the parent-infant relationship. In: *The Maturational Processes and the Facilitating Environment* (pp. 37–55). New York: International Universities Press, 1974.

Winnicott, D. W. (1974). Fear of breakdown. *International Review of Psycho-Analysis, 1*: 103–107.

Winnicott, D. W. (1978). *Through Paediatrics to Psychoanalysis*. London: Hogarth.

Wurmser, L. (2007). *"Torment Me, but Don't Abandon Me": Psychoanalysis of the Severe Neuroses in a New Key*. Lanham, MD: Rowman & Littlefield.

CHAPTER 19

Shame and its cover-up: the self-enclosed prison of isolation

Peter Shabad

> And it is just in that cold and loathsome half-despair and half-belief—in that conscious burying oneself alive for grief for forty years ... all that poison of unsatisfied desires that have turned inwards—in that fever of hesitations, firmly taken decisions, and regrets that followed almost instantaneously upon them—that the essence of that delight I have spoken of lies.
>
> —Dostoevsky, "Notes from the Underground" (1864)

As fundamentally interdependent creatures, we human beings cannot help but offer ourselves for acceptance in search of a sense of belonging. Elsewhere (Shabad, 2010), I have written that we are born with a passion to creatively give of ourselves, to "contribute-in" as Winnicott (1954–55) puts it, to the Other. Each expressive gesture of a newborn, for example—every movement of her limbs, every plaintive cry emerging from her mouth, each bowel movement—is a creative communicative gesture, whether voluntary or involuntary, that is meant to be received and heeded by an Other. These spontaneous gestures, or what Winnicott (1954–55) also called "gift gestures", do not convey only "I want" but also the longing to "be wanted".

A receptive response from a parent mirrors back the special contribution that the child is making, providing her at once with both a sense of belonging and significance as an individual who has something of unique value to offer. This open-hearted receptivity of the parent becomes its own return gift back to the child conveying that she has something good inside that has worth to someone else, and thus enables the child to feel worthy enough to receive something good as well. Specifically, the rhythms of the child giving, the parent receiving the child, and then most crucially, *the child receiving back and internalising the gift of the parent's receptivity* propels development forward.

It is precisely this open-heartedness that becomes difficult to retain and is often inverted when people are ambushed by significant relational disruptions or the cumulative traumatic build-up of chronic frustration and disappointments. In the wake of experiences of vulnerability and suffering, we are so exquisitely sensitive to the touch of rejection that we instinctively cover up our shame of exposure by forming a self-conscious, enclosed relationship with ourselves. Little do we know that in doing so, we relegate ourselves to a self-imposed prison of exile and isolation.

More than anything else, we wish to be accepted for who we feel ourselves to be, but how can we be accepted if we are afraid to show ourselves and never really be known? It is this problem of shame and its cover-up that often leaves us with a sense of loneliness indefinitely.

Rejected vulnerability and the dark underbelly of shame

When parents do not accept or recognise a child's offering to any significant degree, the child is stopped short in his tracks and evicted from the containing context of the relationship. He is suddenly exposed in all his naked vulnerability. This experience of exposed vulnerability to a broken relational connection gives way immediately to a reflexive shift from an unselfconscious perspective of looking out at the world from within to a self-consciousness, *as if* one were now looking at oneself from the vantage point of an outside onlooker. The child compensates for the disruption of expectant responsiveness from an Other by splitting mind from body and projecting mental activity into the relational void to cover up her vulnerability and form a self-enclosed relationship with herself.

Significantly, these projections of what we imagine the Other is thinking about us are always informed by the experiences of sudden disruption that gave rise to shame in the first place. The process through which we take in rejection and then shame ourselves thus involves a defensive shift of identifications from one's own vulnerability to an identification with the environmental disruption. Here is Winnicott (1949) describing the child's reaction to *erratic mothering*: "One can observe a tendency for easy identification with the environmental aspect of all relationships that involve dependence, and a difficulty in identification with the dependent individual" (p. 247).

This process of identifying with rejection accords also with Freud's (1917e) description of melancholia as a reaction to experiences of being insulted, injured, and ignored: "In melancholia, the occasions which give rise to the illness extend for the most part beyond the clear case of a loss by death, and include all those situations of being slighted, neglected, or disappointed" (p. 251). As "the shadow of the object falls upon the ego", the identification and introjection of the source of environmental rupture inverts an active outward movement towards the outside world into an enclosed melancholic self-preoccupation.

Self-consciousness, born of disruption, will be necessarily tinged with the tendency to disrupt. The problem is, as Phillips (1995) writes,

Because the mind comes in afterward—after the trauma—it always runs the risk of being a preemptive presence. The mind object, that is to say, has always unconsciously identified with the traumatic agent (or rather, event) that first prompted its existence. *The mind that attempted to repair—to compensate for—the trauma becomes the trauma itself.* (p. 238, original italics)

Perhaps most damagingly, the closed mental system of self-consciousness perpetuates a lonely desolation. To the extent that a central feature of an observing consciousness is to analyse an object into its constituent parts, self-consciousness has a deconstructive effect on the constructed holism of our creations. The created products of our self-revelations, both verbal and non-verbal, that provide us with a sense of kinship to other persons become subject to the nihilistic doubts cast by the second-guessing of self-consciousness. When our creative animus is thus paralysed, it is difficult to construct a bridge of generalisability from our unique experiences to the lives of others. Caught in an internal web of our own making, we become locked in an internal prism of wondering whether our experience is nothing but our experience. In this most isolated of worlds, we lose a sense of belonging to the common fabric of human experience beyond our self-preoccupations. Whereas we are born as semi-circles in search of an Other to complete us, in the aftermath of exposed vulnerabilities turned into shame and self-consciousness, we close the circle upon ourselves such that we now imprison ourselves in covered-up isolation.

The problem of omnipotence: blaming the victim in oneself for one's suffering

When we suffer as children, especially with regard to the insidiousness with which chronic experiences of rejected vulnerability can be introjected in the course of development, we are not always aware of what is triggering our emotional pain, let alone able to convey it in words to someone else. This lack of communication of what we are experiencing while we are experiencing it frequently transforms contained experiences of suffering into trauma and the necessity to cover oneself up. The resulting sense of isolation is often a subtle destroyer of the sense of the real.

Children, in particular, don't interpret that their frustrations, disappointments, and misfortunes are occurring by chance, but instead they take on the burden of responsibility for "creating" rather than "finding" their sufferings. As Winnicott (1960) notes insightfully: "There is no trauma outside of omnipotence" (p. 37). When a child embraces his mother and expects her to reciprocate with a smile and a hug, but instead she remains tight-lipped, sad, and oblivious to him, his sense of being rejected automatically boomerangs as a sense of having done something wrong to make her unhappy.

Through the lens of omnipotence, the child reacts to expectant hopes that are disappointed or rejected to a significant degree—*not by admitting the limitations of our powers,* but as a punitive sign reflecting back to him a sinfulness about those desires. The child's omnipotent burden of responsibility for the misfortunes she or he encounters backfires because now when bad things happen to the child, she or he interprets the limitations and inability in effecting a more successful outcome to desires as a *failure* or *fault*; otherwise, why would the child be punished with misfortune? As Ricoeur (1967) states: "If you suffer, if you are ill, if you fail, if you die, it is because you have sinned" (p. 31).

On the surface of it, this automatic reactivity to a rejecting parent resembles guilt ("I must have done something wrong"), but it does not at all resemble the remorsefulness of a guilt in which one suffers the pangs of one's own conscience. This type of reflexive guilt resembles shame more than it does remorse. Whereas the remorse of guilt is concerned with making amends towards another person who one believes one has injured, shame is focused much more on punishing oneself for injuring the other person in the first place. When committing a mistake, the individual with excessive shame is more likely to browbeat herself endlessly for letting the "cookie crumble" or "spilling the milk".

Significantly, Freud (1917e) observes: "The melancholic does not behave in the same way as a person who is crushed by remorse and self-reproach" (p. 246). Indeed, as Nietzsche (1887) vividly describes how the person with "bad conscience" torments himself mercilessly: "This uncanny, dreadfully joyous labor of a soul voluntarily at odds with itself that makes itself suffer out of joy in making suffer" (p. 87).

Inasmuch as shame is based on omnipotence, it not only targets one's actions but tyrannises desire itself in all its manifestations of thinking, feeling, and imagining. The omnipotence of wish-magic places a heavy burden of responsibility on our inner life for the practical consequences that must necessarily follow. We must always be on the lookout for harbouring nasty thoughts and hurting the people we love; having lust in our hearts is dangerous and judged as morally wrong because of leading inevitably to lustful actions. We must constrain our imagination, and watch what we think or feel or say for fear of where it may lead. Any bad lurking within must remain unimaginable, unthinkable, and unspeakable.

Furthermore, since shame always emerges *only after* experiencing the outcome of relational disruption, the dissociative shift from a lived-in psyche–soma to disembodied mind also occurs in time from an embodied present to a disembodied *omniscient* future. From this projection of our consciousness onto the all-knowing vantage point in the future, the experiences of traumatic victimisation once lived through with an unknowing prospective time orientation are reframed, distorted, and judged after the fact of their occurrence through the retrospective omniscience of twenty-twenty hindsight. When our life choices do not turn out as we would have liked, or our relationships go wrong, we may berate ourselves mercilessly after the fact for how we should have known better. The echoes of these regretful self-accusations pervading one's mind have the oppressive effect of transforming endured sufferings into shameful feelings of failure, weakness, and ineffectiveness.

It is unfortunate that human beings turn on themselves with self-loathing of their "badness"—as if they had done something terribly malicious when they have just been exposed to the human frailties and limitations we all share with one another. When the various layers of memory are peeled away, the moral basis for the self-contempt of shame is frequently elusive because it was not one's malice that was coded as evil, but one's own experience of being victimised by fate and misfortune. In this reflexive, non-rational fashion, children transform the inevitably tragic elements of their experiences that lie outside their control such as deaths, losses, or even a mother's chronic depression into their own shame. There is a heavy cost to pay in sacrificing a sense of one's own self-image as good, however, when taking on one's misfortunes as one's own burden of shame; the victimising powers that be such as God, fate, or one's parents are not at fault; the enemy now lies within. Through the constructed prism of the rationalised rules and standards of our harsh superegos—our own very personal tyrannical Gods—we "blame the victim" in ourselves retroactively for being victims of an unfortunate fate.

Whether we have big elephant ears, a large protruding nose, uncontrollable adolescent pimples, parents who never stop bickering, or an abusively alcoholic father, we hound ourselves mercilessly for our all-too-human flaws and weaknesses, as if we had committed the worst of transgressions. When a person is raped or sexually abused or subject to an ethnic slur, the self-shaming victim blames herself rather than the abuser for bringing on her experience of victimisation in the first place. The self-cruelty of shame is like a tragic misunderstanding in which the police have apprehended the wrong person for a crime he did not commit. To the extent that one has not done anything really wrong but feels as if one had, the source for the sense of badness that undergirds shame is like an elusive phantom that is difficult to catch.

Kierkegaard (1844) has described self-imposed prison as "inclosing reserve", and suggests it is animated by the "demonic" element in us: "The demonic does not close itself off with something, but it closes itself up within itself, and in this lies what is profound about existence, precisely that unfreedom makes itself a prisoner" (p. 124). The self-enclosed person searches fruitlessly within the insulated safety of his own being for the wellspring of self-renewal, but it is not to be found there. It is precisely because of the misdirected failure to find the ground of a new beginning within that this individual is caught in the demonic grip of endless repetition, not unlike a dog chasing its own tail. In this sense, Descartes's dictum "I think therefore I am" should be more accurately amended to "I think therefore I am … I think therefore I am … I think therefore I am."

The self-enclosed person is so intent on covering up his sense of shame, he is not able to open up and risk the exposed vulnerability that is intrinsic to the participatory give-and-take with an Other. Kierkegaard (1844) states that the demonic tendency towards self-enclosure is always haunted by an "anxiety about the good" (p. 123), a needed openness to relationship that is not being lived out. Kierkegaard states:

> The demonic is unfreedom that wants to close itself off. This, however, is and remains an impossibility. It always retains a relation, and even when this has apparently disappeared altogether, it is nevertheless there, and anxiety at once manifests itself in the moment of contact. (p. 123)

The transformation of aloneness into loneliness: the self-negating voices within

Since in one's self-enclosure one cannot gain relief from these burdens through an open give-and-take of loving and being loved, the need for relationship continues to haunt one through the "anxiety about the good", until finally emerging in the collapsing of oneself into a dependent relationship with a stronger Other who will know better.

The problem is that since such persons have not *been received* sufficiently and feel unlovable, they also cannot *receive* love easily. When compliments or praise or even love should come their way, they often go unrecognised and disbelieved. Nineteen people may be explicitly loving and accepting of these persons without it really registering internally; it is only the non-acceptance of the twentieth person which resonates with their own sense of being unlovable.

A wife may desperately long for love from her husband, and she may even "know" that he means it when he says that he loves her, but because she feels unlovable, she cannot fully believe that he loves her. In her shame, she feels unworthy of the love that she craves, but nevertheless continues to crave the love of which she feels undeserving and cannot let herself receive. Indeed, in her desperation, the more she craves love from her husband, the more she is likely to see his declarations of love as coerced because of her begging rather than as a proffered love from his free agency.

Without the capacity to internalise, people may become helpless or without help. They continue to be bound in dependence to others precisely because they cannot take in whatever may be offered to them. And as their incompleteness as an individual becomes painfully and humiliatingly obvious, such individuals may feel more unworthy to sustain themselves or to stand alone, if only temporarily.

As clinicians, we often hear our patients speak of their dread of being alone. These individuals are so intent on not being with themselves that they often compromise the quality of the company they keep. Perhaps this is because when human beings are alone, they are not really alone. The human psyche is peopled with myriad images, voices, and memories of real and fantasied relationships, all of which influence how a person copes with the experience of being alone. Solitude is never a neutral experience.

Children who have been rebuffed in their attempts to contribute to their parents' lives often carry those experiences of rejected vulnerability into adulthood as negative self-shaming introjects, where they often surface in solitude. When these persons find themselves alone, a sense of unacceptability conspires with a chorus of self-castigating voices to declare incessantly that they are not worthy or good enough to fit into the lives of others, such that aloneness comes to signify the loneliness of isolation and exile. It is not aloneness that is unbearable, but the relational meaning of rejection recast as a punished exile of isolation that is superimposed on the experience of being alone that is difficult to bear.

The empty spaces and times that permeate aloneness may be dreaded as an infinite void of meaninglessness that separates one from the life-sustaining contact with someone who will reassure the lonely person that she is good enough. Alternatively, solitude can be welcomed as a potential opportunity to use the freedom of time and space to actively shape one's life and relationships. One's experience of solitude and the relative self-acceptance or self-condemnation permeating one's consciousness of being alone thus also shape one's experience of freedom.

For the innumerable individuals whose offerings to parents have been rebuffed and relegated to the self-enclosed impotence of worrying about others, consciousness is weighed down with a burdened sense of one's inadequacy. Freedom of choice is not very enlightening when each thought and each decision occurs under the critical, self-doubting eye of a perfectionistic consciousness that does not tolerate failure. For many, the kind of freedom exercised under the coercive pressure and threat of punishment for making a wrong move resembles submission to a demanding autocrat. It is no wonder then that in such circumstances, human beings would opt, as Fromm (1941) points out, to escape from freedom. For perhaps in that escape, they are seeking a freedom from cares and shame with which their self-consciousness is burdened. Instead of actively expressing and living a passionate freedom of self-determination, such individuals, in their desperation to take flight from themselves, reactively attempt to shape themselves according to the designs of external moral authority.

The distinction between active and reactive is a central aspect of Rank's (1936) character typology, in which he distinguishes between normal, neurotic, and creative character types. Rank (1936) suggests that normal character types erase their uniqueness as individuals by surrendering themselves to larger groups. Such individuals conform to their peers and adhere closely to the conventional norms of their society.

For such "normal" persons, the collective illusions that are constructed through consensus are arbitrary inasmuch as they have been created by human beings, yet they are elevated into sacred truths, as if they are God-given. By bringing heaven down to earth in this way, Dostoevsky's (1864) Underground Man thus states that such "normal" individuals mistake "secondary causes for primary causes" (p. 276).

In this view, it is not only the neurotic who is inhibited by shame and then must look reactively to external authority for guidance of how to live, but the normal type as well. In the process of moulding themselves to the specifications of cultural constructions of "normality", innumerable individuals cover up the authenticity of their uniqueness because of their shame and self-consciousness. In the process of fitting themselves as "square pegs" into the "round holes" of their society, they remain unknown to themselves and others, and thereby never fully break out of their covered-up isolation.

Jerry: the urge to find one's own path

Jerry is an intelligent, articulate twenty-year-old man who came for psychotherapy because he had just been suspended during his sophomore year from the highly prestigious university where he had been matriculating. Since Jerry had not been going to class regularly and had also not completed assignments and term papers on time, he had received failing grades or incompletes on all his classes.

Jerry's parents accompanied him into the first session, and while Jerry remained silent and fidgeted uncomfortably, his mother grilled me about my religious beliefs. She made it clear that my level of religiosity (as opposed to secularism) mattered to her far more than the particular religion to which I belonged. While Jerry's father remained silent, Jerry spoke only intermittently in response to my questions. I was determined to give Jerry the respect and dignity of talking to him. Jerry's mother went on at length about her concerns that Jerry was suspended from his university and provided a roadmap of what they were hoping Jerry would get out of therapy. I then suggested that for the last half of our session Jerry and I speak alone while they go to the waiting room.

When I asked Jerry how he understood his predicament, he said that he lacked confidence in expressing himself. As the youngest of children, he said that he was much more in the habit of listening to his older siblings rather than speaking, and that he preferred it that way. In a similar way, when he attempted to write a term paper, his thinking would freeze when faced with a blank sheet of paper.

From the first sessions onwards, Jerry insisted that he had been excited about the prospect of taking his courses at the beginning of the semester, and that he looked forward to doing the required reading. When, for example, he saw on the syllabus that Dante's *The Divine Comedy* had been assigned, he was excited because he had wanted to read the book for a while. When the time came, however, to actually do the readings and write papers, he would instead find himself surfing the internet and binge-watching Netflix. He insisted that he had no conscious intention to engage in those activities, but that they were just "impulsive" actions.

Jerry experienced tremendous shame about his inability to keep up with the norms set by his older siblings. He brooded about his own inadequacies. Given that he is a very bright young man, it is not surprising that he emphasised the virtues of rationality and could not understand how he could be sidetracked from his own plans by impulsive actions that led to his suspension. Indeed, in reacting with great distaste for the arbitrary moods and whims that governed his mother's domineering authority, Jerry had come to place a great premium on the guiding principles of rationalism to make decisions. As Jerry discovered to his consternation, however, the emotional life that he had dismissed for being so irrational kept ambushing him at the most inopportune times and thwarting life plans.

Over the course of therapy, Jerry provided numerous examples of his mother's rules with which he either complied (he was forced to break up with a girlfriend during his junior year in high school) or bypassed without her knowledge. Often when he talked about her, he would punctuate his narrative with sardonic chuckles and a cynically mirthless laughter. The presence of Jerry's mother as a predominant figure in his mind was vividly dramatised in our third session together. With ten minutes left in the session, his cell phone rang; he glanced at the phone and said: "I have to get this." He listened for two minutes and then after he hung up, he suddenly broke into tears. We both understood at that moment how suffocating his mother's presence had become in Jerry's mind and life.

The first months of therapy were characterised by some tension and conflict about how Jerry understood the original problem and needed a solution for which he sought out therapy. He viewed his deviation from the expected norm of doing his schoolwork and graduating from college as an impulsive, irrational departure from how he had planned to live his life. I responded to Jerry that he also had resentments and rebellious desires that were embedded in his non-compliant "impulsivity". That impulsivity had always been prohibited by the authoritarianism of Jerry's mother, and now was dismissed by Jerry himself. His actions seemed compulsive to him precisely because Jerry could not let himself know what he was doing, otherwise the sentry of "rationality" in Jerry's consciousness would not have allowed him to indulge his pleasures. Jerry remained unconvinced.

Jerry often would become silent during our early sessions, claiming that he did not have a lot to say. I wondered to myself whether Jerry felt comfortable and trusting enough to express himself during sessions. I began to realise that my adamant persistence that Jerry acknowledge the motivated aspects of his "deviant" impulsivity for which he was suspended was a moralistic judgement by an authority figure in the image of his mother. Through the boycott of his silence in sessions, he was, in part, transferring his cynicism about his mother's rigid authority to me, not without reason. In one session, I wondered out loud whether I had contributed to some of the tension between us because, like his mother, I had been too stubbornly opinionated about what I was saying. Ironically, by acknowledging my role in contributing to our tensions, I also somewhat differentiated myself from Jerry's mother in his eyes.

There were other important ways in which I was able to earn Jerry's trust as someone who was on his side, especially when I did not automatically ally myself with the therapeutic aim of returning Jerry to the "normality" of academic success. When Jerry asked whether I thought he should apply for reinstatement to his university for the following year, I replied that I was somewhat concerned about him repeating his "impulsive" behaviour of watching YouTube videos and Netflix instead of completing his assignments since he did not yet understand why he did that in the first place. When I asked him how he felt about returning to school, he acknowledged his own ambivalence. He then immediately said that he had an urge to go on a months-long hike on a well-known trail in the United States. My ears perked up at the mention of his spontaneous "urge" because already in our first session, he had said that he felt most himself when he was engaged in the simple activity of walking.

So, here then was a clear choice between returning to a pre-set plan of culturally sanctioned academic and career success, or for he and I to take his spontaneous "urge" of embarking on the trail more seriously. I recognised that for most of his life, Jerry had gone through the robotic motions of following orders and complying with authority, and had then attempted to adhere to the most rational way of implementing his plans for an abstractly successful future. Yet those plans were all head and no heart; Jerry existed, but he was not yet an embodied self who participated in his own life.

After listening to Jerry describe how going on the months-long hike would help him overcome his stranger anxiety as he learned to rely on himself while meeting new people whom he encountered, I realised that he viewed the marathon trip as an opportunity to give rebirth to himself, to conceive and discover himself perhaps for the first time. He also saw the trip as a way of giving himself a powerful boost of self-confidence that he sorely needed. Such self-confidence seemed to be precisely what "Jerry the doctor" ordered for himself the patient because he was paralysed by shame and self-conscious dread of making mistakes no matter what choices and decisions he made.

Whereas early in life, Jerry complied with his mother's authority and judgements, now through the introjection of those judgements, he had become his own worst critic. As we explored Jerry's experience of self-consciousness and problems with decision-making more deeply, he spoke contemptuously of people who blabbered on pointlessly and wondered sometimes whether he too had any real purpose in expressing himself out loud. I noted that perhaps in hating and attempting to distance himself from his mother's narcissism of taking up too much social space without purpose, he had gone too far to the opposite extreme and had paralysed his own self-expressiveness in the process.

When Jerry first came for treatment, he felt terrible about himself because in his self-conscious paralysis, he was attempting to fit the "square peg" of his own uniqueness into the "round hole" of conventional academic norms. I have largely supported his spontaneously creative urge to embark on his own "path" both literally and metaphorically. Indeed, most recently Jerry's parents decided to discontinue paying for any more of his sessions because they did not see the "progress" that they had envisioned. I told Jerry I would be willing to see him for a greatly reduced fee if he felt that he was benefiting from the therapy and wished to continue. He thanked me and decided to accept my offer. I have followed Rank's (1936) therapeutic recommendation of attempting to help Jerry replace his self-consciousness of his difference with a self-acceptance of his individuality with regard to his unique difference.

After completing his lengthy trek of 1100 miles of four and a half months on October 1, Jerry called me to schedule a session when he returned. I immediately saw a difference in the way he held eye contact with me. He seemed to speak with less hesitation and more confidence. He also said that as soon as he returned from the hike, he wanted to call high school friends with whom he had long been out of touch because he now felt that he had accomplished something that he could talk about.

When we actually spoke about the hike itself, he said that for the first month he ruminated much about his failures of the past and worries about the future, but that changed when he got to the higher altitude mountains. He had a major transitional moment when he saw the sun rise one day. As he persevered through his hike, he realised also that he could rely on himself to persevere through adversity. In general, Jerry's walking journey literally has helped him ground his life and transform shame into a self-respect for his accomplishment. Jerry says now matter-of-factly that he is ready to apply himself to his studies.

Given that Jerry had closed himself off from relationships with others by self-consciously viewing himself from the outside in, from the vantage point of an alienated, disembodied mind, it is not surprising that his regained access to his embodied desires had a healing effect on his self-confidence. Even though in our sessions, Jerry had emphasised the virtue of the "rational" mind, he also was quite ashamed that he never had accomplished anything on his own in his life. Whether he tried to follow his older siblings in their footsteps or closely adhere to the dictates of his mother, he did not really know what *he* wanted for his own life, except to embark on this long hike. His sense of accomplishment at the end and his newly gained self-confidence now allowed him to identify himself with the subjectivity of his desires. Once any human being does just that, he will spontaneously free himself from the prison of self-enclosed isolation and open up to others.

References

Dostoevsky, F. (1864). Notes from the underground. In: *Great Short Works of Fyodor Dostoevsky* (pp. 261–377). D. Magarshack (Trans.). New York: HarperCollins.

Freud, S. (1917e). Mourning and melancholia. *S. E., 14*: 243–258. London: Hogarth.

Fromm, E. (1941). *Escape from Freedom*. New York: Avon, 1972.

Kierkegaard, S. (1844). *The Concept of Anxiety*. Princeton, NJ: Princeton University Press, 1980.

Nietzsche, F. (1887). *The Genealogy of Morals*. W. Kaufman (Trans.). New York: Vintage.

Phillips, A. (1995). The story of the mind. In: E. G. Corrigan & P. E. Gordon (Eds.), *The Mind Object* (pp. 229–240). Northvale, NJ: Jason Aronson.

Rank, O. (1936). *Will Therapy* and *Truth and Reality*. New York: Alfred A. Knopf.

Ricoeur, P. (1967). *The Symbolism of Evil*. Boston, MA: Beacon.

Shabad, P. (2010). The suffering of passion: metamorphoses and the embrace of the stranger. *Psychoanalytic Dialogues, 20*(6): 710–729.

Winnicott, D. W. (1949). Mind and its relation to the psyche–soma. In: *Through Paediatrics to Psychoanalysis* (pp. 243–254). New York: Basic Books, 1975.

Winnicott, D. W. (1954–55). The depressive position in normal emotional development. In: *Through Paediatrics to Psychoanalysis* (pp. 262–277). New York: Basic Books, 1975.

Winnicott, D. W. (1960). The theory of the parent–infant relationship. In: *The Maturational Processes and the Facilitating Environment* (pp. 37–55). New York: International Universities Press, 1974.

CHAPTER 20

Strengthening the human bond: in psychotherapy, "doing We" is more important than intervention

Michael B. Buchholz

> Theoretical clarity does not necessarily aid in therapy; it may be harmful. Clinical practice does not appear to derive from theory in any straightforward fashion.
>
> —Levenson, 1983, p. 7

Introduction

Again and again I wonder that former authors in psychoanalysis and psychotherapy clearly and distinctly articulated ideas which gain their dynamic and power only today. The quote from Levenson, one of the leading "relationalists" of his time, is a profound insight. It frees us from conceptualising psychotherapy and psychoanalysis in terms of technical vocabulary like "intervention", "measuring", "outcome" and related concepts; maintaining psychotherapy or psychoanalysis can be described as cause (or influence) and effect emanating from one side towards the other.

These technical terms apply in health policies, but not in the treatment room. However, at the end of this chapter I will try to make clear that there is a chance to observe "outcome" *in* and during individual sessions.

The reason to keep apart the sphere of clinical verifiability from the treatment room is simple. It is language. Or better, "talk-in-interaction". Talk—this includes silence, of course (Dimitrijević & Buchholz, 2021). Bion, in his Los Angeles lectures in 1975 (transcribed by Aguayo) would agree with Levenson. He also adds another point:

> What I feel sometimes is that the attempt to think of it in terms of the past or infancy or so on, becomes more of a liability than an asset because it hides the fact that one is dealing with a person, a mind, a character or a personality there in front of you. And it is curious you see if you start thinking of what the person may feel—while one is thinking about that, time passes and one is not able to listen to the patient or observe what is going on ... while you are wondering about the patient's past, the present goes on flying through; or while you are wondering either about what you are going to do, or what the patient is going to do or what is going to happen to the patient, something is happening and one fails to notice what is happening.... It is just a sort of theory or a hunch that one puts forward to ease one's self ... (Aguayo, 2013, p. 68)

What we deal with is not a "dis-order", termed in more than 500 diagnoses, it is a person. A thinking, feeling, observing person. And suffering, of course.

For more than a decade we observe how medical technology intrudes in the spheres of psychotherapy. However, all these efforts try to rule out the fact that we do not treat "diagnoses", but persons. Recently, we were reminded by prominent researchers:

> As Sir William Osler (1906), father of modern medicine, wrote: "It is much more important to know what sort of a patient has a disease than what sort of disease a patient has." The accumulating research demonstrates that it is indeed frequently effective to tailor or match psychotherapy to the entire person. (Norcross & Wampold, 2018, p. 1890)

Similar insights could be traced as far back as Hippocrates. They are formulated in the same way by behaviour therapists, humanistic therapists, and many others. To find out the "sort of a patient" and, as I would add, what "sort of a therapist" people meet in the treatment room to talk with. Nothing else. Tailoring psychotherapy to the entire person is, according to these authors, clearly outlined as "inventing" a psychotherapy for each patient anew. This is said to be what good clinicians do. I conclude that there are two reasons why theory alone cannot guide us through the jungle of clinical interaction: the practice of talk-in-interaction *and* the fact that we treat persons.

If this holds true, we can unburden ourselves from many theoretical debates and look at what happens in the treatment room. We acquire a new task: observation. And document our observations as the primary non-positivistic data to help psychoanalysis to become a science of observation again. I do not think of observations confused by our too bad memories. I think of observing audio recordings while protecting them in the service of our patients' anonymity and integrity. To open our talk-in-interaction data has a highly convincing power for everyone. Person and talk—this is the task for the future.

To say it frankly: to observe includes exchange of gazes, smells, listening to prosody, observing race, dress code, hesitations, socio-economic status, and many other things—this is "talk-in-interaction", not only an "exchange of words", as was Freud's famous formula. The little miracle is that it does not require questionnaires, but attentiveness. We observe this mutually in a very short time. And try to hold our minds open for errors and recognising prejudice. Before the first words are spoken we unavoidably enter a process of what was termed "a meeting of minds" (Aron, 1996), an apt formula for the treatment of loneliness.

What I described in these few words is a kind of "doing together"; it is observable for third persons as it is for the two participants. They can ignore or deny it, nevertheless it happens. Why is it an event of minds? The reason is that this happens not unidirectionally—I observe you or you observe me. No, it's more extended right from the start: I can observe you observing me and I can recognise how you observe me doing this. I observe your behaviour and you mine, but we are not behaviourists. Unavoidably, both of us constitute what has been named an interpersonal "field" (Baranger & Baranger, 2008). Sociological authors have named this practice "mutual monitoring":

> Persons must sense that they are close enough to be perceived in whatever they are doing, including their experiencing of others, and close enough to be perceived in this sensing of being perceived. (Goffman, 1963, p. 17)

Careful observations of children at the very early age of two to three months (see Dimitrijević, Chapter 10 this volume) have documented that children do these things—they enjoy viewing mother's face. But what is more is that they enjoy being observed, to share attention, to engage in a common play of smooth touches and gaze exchange. Mutual monitoring begins very early and it can never be really given up, as it is the indispensable basis of our sociality. Michael Tomasello, who summarises his observations of chimpanzee and human babies, writes:

> A partial list of the most important uniquely human psychological outcomes would include such things as joint attention, perspective-taking, cooperative/referential gestures, conventional linguistic communication, role reversal imitation, conformity, instructed (pedagogical) learning, recursive thinking, cooperative problem solving, coordinated decision-making, dual-level collaboration, joint commitment, paternalistic helping, a sense of fairness and justice, second-personal protest, enforcing and creating social norms, active impression management, a sense of shame and guilt, and a conception of moral identity. (Tomasello, 2019, p. 341)

Third persons can observe the listed forms of mutual monitoring; however, what remains the property of the participants is that they do this as persons thinking about others as thinking persons. This is the full meaning of "meeting". This is an essential antidote against loneliness. It refers to both, meeting by talk-in-interaction and as person. Psychotherapy cures by perceiving and being perceived. Like in a mother–baby relationship, this mutuality is a practice of "doing We"; it is done by observable practices and nevertheless it establishes mind-meeting. "Doing We" has many aspects. I will later describe only one, the emergence of *common ground*.

Meeting of minds—some history

Many authors have coined the term "meeting of minds". This term has an interesting history. It wanders back and forth between the different fields, between social sciences and psychology. The first author was Hans Loewald, psychoanalyst in New York:

> Understanding would seem to be an act that involves some sort of mutual engagement, a particular form of the meeting of minds. (Loewald, 1979, p. 165)

Leading social scientist in those days, Jerome Bruner, adopted this term. Having observed that interior intellectual work is almost always a continuation of a dialogue, he included joint attention:

> At its most sophisticated level, joint attention is, in effect, a "meeting of minds." It depends not only on a shared or joint focus, but on shared context and shared presuppositions. (Bruner, 1995, p. 6)

It was Lewis Aron (1996) who took over the term and added the observation that in psychoanalysis states of loneliness can show up as "solitude à deux" or as "dynamic solitude", terms he takes from other authors.

Recently, a leading linguist made similar observations in a book titled *Relationship Thinking*:

> So when we study human interaction, we are studying the mind, in the real sense of that word: an interpretative system that is distributed through and across people, places, and times. (Enfield, 2013, p. XVIII)

The distinction between "mind" and "behaviour" is far less sharp than we were trained to assume. Enfield is very consistent:

> A fundamental claim of the approach outlined in this book is that any sequence of "communicative action and subsequent response" is by nature a unit, not a conjunct. The sequence cannot be derived from independently established concepts "communicative action" and "response". This is because neither may be defined without the other. (Enfield, 2013, p. 28)

To separate action from response would be like to describe a kiss as something you give me and I give you—as if these were two distinct individual acts. No, this is not a conjunct, it is a unit. It is "doing We" and Enfield maintains that this is the methodological stance we should take when we begin to study how psychoanalysis helps to cure loneliness.

Such ideas and conceptions come very close to what psychoanalysts had described. One prominent author, Thomas Ogden, had described "the analytical third" as constituting the two persons in the treatment room:

> The analytic third is a creation of the analyst and analysand, and at the same time the analyst and analysand (*qua* analyst and analysand) are created by the analytic third. (There is no analyst, no analysand, and no analysis in the absence of the third.) (Ogden, 1994, p. 17)

And he goes a step further when he maintains that there are not only two persons in the treatment room but three: "The analytic process reflects the interplay of three subjectivities: that of the analyst, of the analysand, and of the analytic third" (Ogden, 1994, p. 17).

Now, we see more clearly why "theory" in psychotherapy and psychoanalysis may be misleading. They constitute both as only two. There must be a "something more" (Bruschweiler-Stern et al., 2002), which cannot be grasped with technical and individualistic concepts.

However, there are problems with "the analytic third". How can we avoid reification of the "third"—is it an "object"? Is it atmosphere? Is it co-creation? What, precisely, is it?

> … I consider it crucial not to reify the Third, but to consider it primarily as a principle, function, or relationship (as in Ogden's (1994) view), rather than as a "thing" in the way that theory or rules of technique are things. (Benjamin, 2018, p. 23)

Clearly, Benjamin identifies the problem—is it a principle? A function? A relationship? Of course, not a "thing".

What I want to propose here is to follow linguist Enfield's proposal when we observe human interaction in the treatment room that "in one move" we observe "mind", too. What is observable is both talk-in-interaction *and* the conclusions participants draw from that. It is my aim here to use a new method in psychotherapy research, "Conversation Analysis" (Peräkylä et al., 2008), in order to take a step forward in microanalytically observing how "the third" is created by two participants and what kind of "talk-in-interaction" they use to move to a higher level: not only to observe (and talk about) each other, but to observe their common relationship and to transform their "relationship thinking" in a "thinking relationship" creating two participants in *dynamic solitude* or *solitude à deux* (Aron, 1996, p. 152). Both concepts proceed from Winnicott's "capacity to be alone" (see Caldwell, Chapter 16, this volume), a conceptual and an observable process altering loneliness into solitude.

Common ground

Common *ground* is produced by talking; it's not the common *world* we think to live in. The construction of a common *ground* in the treatment room by talk-in-interaction is what I want to study here in detail in order to cure or, at least, alleviate loneliness.

Common ground is a linguistic term (Buchholz, 2016, with further references), but I will avoid linguistic jargon here. Common ground requires five components: a) a joint focus of attention, b) both sides take into account what the other side can be assumed to know;

c) utterances are tailored accordingly, d) contributions must be selected from a richer pool of possibilities to respond, and e) participants listen. This is an overall description of common ground activities. These components already show that psychological ("attention") and conversational ("utterances") components and a mixture of both ("tailoring of utterance") constitute common ground, unique for a single dyad, although both use practices (talk) and knowledge stores (words, symbols, reports, and narratives) which are commonly available. But this conception does not yet include the vertical perspective indicating the step to a thinking relationship.

Common ground—outlined so far—is a concept that has the potential to overcome a conceptual conflict in the process research dealing with the working alliance. Introducing "Working alliance" (WA) at the start of this century (Safran & Muran, 2000), WA advanced to a central concept of the psychotherapeutic endeavour. It strongly conflicted with the idea of (independent) "intervention" (from outside) which was not fully ruled out in psychotherapy research and clinical conversation (Lepper, 2015). The number of WA studies grew very fast. How could "ruptures" of the WA become explained? Are they typical for specific disorders? Answers to these questions were guided by a search for the right "intervention", ruptures were ascribed to patients in an *individualistic* fashion, the idea of "doing We" vanished. The conceptual conflict is precisely seen by the originator in a recent summary:

> We have also found it useful to define ruptures by specific patient communications or behaviors—even though, we have always considered a rupture as something co-constructed by patient and therapist, as an interaction between their respective personality configurations and immediate needs (Safran & Muran, 2000). (Muran, 2019, p. 3)

Can ruptures be defined by specific *patient* communications or as *co-constructed* by patient and therapist? Both views strongly oppose each other—this dilemma remains unsolved if it is studied in individualising terms of "personality configurations" and "needs". You cannot explain cooperation (and its failures) simply by studying one person and then *adding* the other person. What is needed is a concept of common ground for "doing We".

Data, method, and a conceptual proposal

My method of choice is conversation analysis (CA) (Peräkylä et al., 2008). This method observes the details of (therapeutic) interaction with a microscopic eye and has produced a lot of interesting results.

My examples, not in a casuistic manner, are well transcribed from the audio record of psychoanalytic sessions, analysed by CA and published elsewhere with further observations. They are taken from our CEMPP-Project (Conversation Analysis of Empathy in Psychotherapy Process), conducted under my supervision and that of Horst Kächele. We transcribed and compared treatments from the Munich Psychotherapy Project (Huber & Klug, 2016) of three different psychotherapy schools (psychodynamic psychotherapy, psychoanalysis, and CBT). Of each therapy we had a session from the beginning, middle phase, and end phase (Alder, 2016; Buchholz et al., 2017; Dittmann (now: Franzen), 2016; Dreyer & Franzen, 2021). However, here I am not interested in comparisons between psychotherapy schools.

Most people intuitively understand a simple typology of relationships which I present here as *metaphorical mathematics*. A couple's states can be typologised in equations such as:

$1+1 = 0+0$ Together both participants are reduced to "zero"; for example, talkative people sometimes discover that they have nothing to tell each other, that they feel "nullified" by the other's presence. It was a surprise when two linguistically powerful philosophers, Martin Heidegger and Ernst Cassirer, met in Davos, Switzerland, in 1927. The audience discovered that they had nothing to tell each other.

$1+1 = 1+0$ One person leads or dominates, the other person is silenced (Buchholz et al., 2021), a very often observed constellation in couples of every kind.

$1+1 = 1+1$ Both are in a state of rivalry; the overall question "Who decides?" (e.g. to talk next) they think is the problem, while observers add "Who decides who decides?" as the relevant, but not definitely answered question ruling the couple's interaction.

$1+1 = 2$ Both are in a state of agreement or harmony; they deeply agree without secret reservations; consolation and tension reduction is tolerated.

$1+1 = 3$ Both individuals view themselves involved in a superordinate order of which they become elements; like, for example, common efforts, a shared idea, or a spiritual experience, or a common conviction. They realise an insight from philosopher Gadamer (1960, p. 387), that having a "good conversation" means being able to let the conversation lead you. Interestingly, what was described as "dyadic state of mind" between mother and baby on a preverbal level (Tronick, 2007) comes very close to Gadamer's formulation.

This is not a typology of couples. Rather it estimates momentary states in a couple's relationship. There is an element of yielding to the power of a good, helping conversation without fearing other dimensions of power which are more easily realised in other forms of talk. "Good conversation" in this sense overcomes individualistic loneliness and connects two people while approaching and tolerating a state of solitude.

Regrettably, power dimensions are not very often described in CA (exceptions are Stevanovic & Peräkylä, 2014; Winefield et al., 1989) and underestimated or ignored in most clinical papers, too.

I assume a *resonating membrane* as embodied experience for both participants, from which *metaphors for the ongoing interaction* may emerge. If proposed *and* accepted, the resonating membrane constitutes with gentle and casual coercion a "We" experience and a moment of mutual understanding. And, such metaphors operate as *observing* the relationship from a superordinate level. Under fortunate circumstances such a metaphor runs again and again through sessions (Dreyer, 2021). Indeed, individualistic restrictions can be overcome when I add further dimensions—time and vertical design—to the common ground. CA authors write, that meaning "… lies not with the speaker nor the addressee nor the utterance alone as many philosophical arguments have considered, but rather with the interactional past, current, and projected next moment" (Schegloff et al., 1996, p. 40).

Common ground includes a dimension of time. While an actual utterance is produced in the present, it can refer to the past and project the future (next step). References to the past (of common interaction) can become so rich that outsiders cannot follow easily. Projecting the future points to a horizon of expected responses and sometimes opens to surprise in responses. When responses refer to what has been said before (e.g. as a quotation, "You said, that …"), a response comes as observation, binding together projecting the next moment *and* referring to the past. One of them might be to talk of past organisation of cooperation and then to talk about thinking of organising cooperation leading to higher levels of conversation—and the whole process starts again. A restart, now from a higher level. The name for this line of reasoning is recursion (Corballis, 2011). Recursion is the tool to build up a vertical architecture of talk and restructuring the past of the common ground.

What is recursion? A classical illustration for recursion is the alphabet of twenty-six letters. To write them down again and again creates the library of Babylon—repeating the same produces endless new meaning. However, to conceptualise repetition only, as Freud did, is only one half of a (hampered) creative process (Buchholz, 2019). The task is to be spelled "re-petition"—a patient who needs release from the constraints of repetition through inclusion in mindful cooperation with another person in order to change (individualistic) loneliness into (common) solitude.

To illustrate, think of an analyst framing an utterance with "Yesterday in our session you said that …" The analyst refers to the *past* laid down in the common ground; at the same time, he realises an actual interaction (*presence*) in order to project a next utterance (*future*) which comes as a higher level observation (*vertical design*). This is my conversation analytic spelling of the "analytic third"; it's a conversational process-in-time.

Conversation analysis of speech formats like narration and report

While doing "talk-in-interaction", therapists are hearing words with the aim to visualize (Buchholz, 2015), explore, and articulate a patient's experiential world. A well-known example is that therapists sometimes sense a patient's anxiety which the patient does not sense; any attempt to address their anxiety will be responded to by denial and, worse, withdrawing from the relationship.

Looking at the "talk-in-interaction" one can observe how such patients inform the therapist not by emotional *narration* with increasing tension and a narrative climax, but by an emotionally flat *report*. Other formats are arguing, reflection, comments etc.

Shallowness of a report is sequentially produced by stringing together single events, a pause follows and, with particles like "and then", the next event is added. On the contrary, in *narration*, the listener is involved by opening remarks which attract and guide the listener's attention ("Want to know what happened to me yesterday?"), an imaginative stage is presented ("On the so-and-so street I met X"), embellishments follow ("He came straight at me"). These elements in combination constitute a narrative tension curve and the recipient feels urged to utter little tokens, indicating attentiveness and recipiency of increasing tension. At the climax of the narrative the recipient feels urged to utter some "change-of-state" tokens ("Really? Did he say this to you?", "Incredible", or "Did he?") indicating that his or her state of information was changed. By applying physiological measures it could be shown (Nissen-Lie et al., 2021; Voutilainen et al., 2018) that therapists are called upon to "share the emotional load" as Peräkylä et al. (2015) titled this phenomenon: after the recipient utters a change-of-state token, the teller's physiological tension is reduced, that of the recipient increases. To include the distinction of narration/report enables CA to analyse "larger chunks" (Buchholz et al., 2021; Buchholz & Kächele, 2017), which are often met from session to session.

Transcription rules—simplified

[ ]	begin and end of overlapping utterances
=	contiguous utterance
(.)	micro pause (0.3 seconds max.)
(1.2)	length of pause in seconds
:	elongation
,	fall in pitch
;	slight rise in pitch
?	rising in pitch (not necessarily a question)
WORD	loud speech
Word	accentuation
talk	surrounds quiet talk
hhh	exhalation
.hhh	inhalation
><	surrounds talk spoken faster
<>	surrounds talk spoken slowly
Wo(r)d	laugh particle
( )	approximation of what is heard

Here I use a transcribed example of a twenty-eighth psychoanalytic session with a female *reporting* patient and a female therapist. The patient sought therapeutic help because of compulsively thinking of fat men exposing themselves in front of her (Buchholz & Reich, 2015). This is the beginning of the session:

```
1    ((recording in progress))
2    (31)
3    ?: ((slight cough))
4    (6)
```

```
 5   P: I managed to while away the hours really well
        yesterday (2) and (3) I don't remember (-) having any
        obsessive thoughts? (2) nor when I was somehow driving
        home (2) and then (2) <I was at HOMe for some time> and
        um (2) then I drove to Landsberg with a (girl)friend
        (3) a:nd (-) there we met two kind of:: (1) old friends
        of ours and went to the swimmingpool for a bit and (1)
        after the weather wasn't so good then um (1,5) went
        into town for a bit as well >got something to eat< and
        them um (..) an icecream afterwards an::d (1,5) yeah
        and I was really (1) able to unwind again.
 6   (4)
 7   P: well, I::
 8   T:    °>mhm<°
 9   P: didn't notice, that somehow something was coming (2)
        something somehow was creeping up on me, that was all
10   T: °good°
11   P: somehow really=really far away
12   (15)
13   T: strictly speaking you didn't while away the hours,
        you actually ENJOYed them!
14   P: yeah exactly haha ((laughs)) that's right! that was
        bad wor(h)d(h)ing haha ((laughs))
```

The patient reports her last days: how she managed to keep herself free of unwanted thoughts. In her reporting, she uses particles like "and then", often producing a series of various events. A new distinction can be observed: she reports her "told self" (past experiences), while she speaks (doing the talk in the presence of the therapist) as if she reports another person's improvement of a medical condition. Her "performative self" (Deppermann, 2015; Deppermann et al., 2020), positions herself as if she were a kind of therapeutic assistant informing the chief therapist about the state of someone else. The formula for her "told self" is 1+1=1+0. Positioning her performative self submissively, she can use the report format.

After reporting, a pause follows (line 6). Her reporting is acknowledged by the therapist (line 10). The therapist, then, after a reflective pause, restarts the conversation with an utterance like a translation ("strictly speaking"), bringing up an emotional meaning of the patient's report: "you actually enjoyed", uttered with hearable pleasure. The patient immediately agrees and laughs. Emotions become present as does a common laughter, transcending lonesome reporting. The therapist did not address the "told self", but the "performative self's" feeling of relief. With a single "formulation" the therapist created relief from these defences; both share joy for a moment, about the correct interpretation and giving up a defensive position. The relationship formula alters to 1+1=2. Their relationship is implicitly observed and calmed.

STRENGTHENING THE HUMAN BOND   329

The conversational operation is described as "lexical substitution" (Rae, 2008) or as "formulation" (Antaki, 2008). Questions remain: how does the therapist know what to do? John Rae refers to the occidental tradition that you can never know what is in another person's mind. This is true. However, it is not necessary to fully know what is in another person's "mind", but sometimes conversation plays ideas back. Harvey Sacks, founder of CA, argued (Sacks & Jefferson, 1992, pp. 166f.) that you cannot do conversation without a silent dimension which he termed "my mind is with you"—always running silently along. This minimal therapeutic utterance succeeds, and both burst out in some laughter establishing a *resonating membrane* between the two. Report is changed to a narrative format, generating a moment of *shared sensitivity*. Loneliness is overcome.

My next example is meant to illustrate a richer process of shared sensitivity. Horst Kächele tape-recorded several therapies, now available from the Ulm Textbank (Mergenthaler & Kächele, 1988). A young student in his early twenties suffered from several obsessive-compulsive actions he felt obliged to do. The session starts in the following way:

```
1    (( Rustling of fabrics))
2    P: so, it's not you beginning; ((snorting with
     laughter))
3    (1,2)
4    P:.h
5    T: °hm.°
6    (2,8)
7    P: °mhm,°
8    (2,5)
9    T: °is this important for you, or; (1,2) °if I would
     [begin°,
10   P: [.h no:] no:, (-)
11   P: I was just thinking today, I'm not going to say
     anything today. ((grin in his voice)) at the beginning
     ((laughingly)) (-)
12   and look what happens, .h=
13   T: =mhm;
14   (1,9)
15   P: ((clearing his throat))
16   (3,1)
17   T: so it's more kind of a [TEST
18   P: [yeah;, (--) °really°]
19   T: a: little bit (1,8) little bit of a wrestling match
20   (2,0)
21   P: °hm ne;°
22     (2,2)
```

In the service of establishing a common ground (Buchholz, 2016), interactions start with a pointing gesture (deixis)—either using one's index finger, gazes, chin, or other body part pointing to something. Or, on a more elaborate level, pointing with words to interactive events. The "object" of pointing creates a common reference: it can be perceived as perceivable by both. Pointing is the first level of constituting "common ground". The patient points to an announcement while making a paradoxical announcement: he will not begin—to *say* this is paradoxical. Nevertheless, talk-in-interaction unavoidably starts with pointing. Besides the distinction between "told self" and "performative self", which constitutes the paradox here, the first words can be paraphrased as solicitation: "Look at me while I am pointing at you who does not begin."

Karl Bühler, a German psychologist and linguist stated that the "deictic" (pointing) gesture includes a tacit claim; pointing is not only directed to a physical, mental, or interactive "object" in the world, but unavoidably has self-referent dimensions: "here, now, I". This triplet Bühler named the "origo".

> My claim is that if this arrangement is to represent the deictic field of human language, three deictic words must be placed where the O is, namely the deictic words *here, now* and *I*. ... There is nothing conspicuous about the phonetic form, about the phonematic impress of the words *now, here, I;* all that is peculiar about them is what each of them demands: the first demands, look at me, an acoustic phenomenon, and take me as a mark of the moment; as a mark of the place, says the second; and the third, as a mark of the sender (or characteristic of the sender). (Bühler, 1934, pp. 117*f.*)

Unavoidably, the exposition of "origin" is the start (line 2): the patient pointing to an observation (the pause, during the rustling of fabrics). His statement includes a silent expectation: the therapist should begin. This is made impossible, as the patient did begin.

Lines 3–8 then show how pointing is taken over into another mode of conversation: some utterance of hearable silent in-breathing by the patient (line 4), silent confirmation tokens are exchanged by therapist and patient interrupted by pauses, unavoidably, which confirm that *mutual monitoring* constitutes common ground. Both mutually recognise each other's contributions, mutually confirm to perceive each other as "origins" (I, here, now), what constitutes them as participants of the same conversation.

From "pointing" to "conversational" is a next step (level 2). Both can continue conversationally. A question (line 9) adds a value ("important"). Level 3 establishes a linking with further conversational stuff. By pointing to "this" an anaphora is produced, defined as "recourse to what has been said or anticipation of what is yet to be said in the context, whether the reference is explicitly formulated or not" (Bühler, 1934, p. 189). The anaphora transforms "the context itself into a deictic field" (Bühler, 1934, p. 439). It opens a possibility to use the other's origin (I, here, now) as another possibility to speak from; as if *I* were *you*. Bühler has named this as "phantasmatic deixis". Often in quotations, the "I" circulates as that of the recipient, not of the speaker—a source of many misunderstandings, but also a source of deepening mutual monitoring.

Pointing to the value of "this" addresses the patient's I-element of the "origin" and in alignment with the question he responds in explicating his up-to-now silent expectation project: to "look what happens". He links to other conversational stuff and reveals his project a step further. His project is to turn roles and identify himself with a kind of experimenter who "looks what happens" on the therapist's side. The roles of experimenter (therapist) and guinea pig (patient) shall be altered.

This role rotation is commented upon by the therapist who finds a humorous reply after some short pauses and silent utterances. His comment is a first metaphor: "test"—testing the therapist is a name he gives to the patient's project. Spoken from the patient's "origin" the patient laughingly agrees. A new metaphorical level (4) is achieved, a vertical architecture of the interaction by metaphorically commenting on what the patient said is established.

Both role parts of the metaphor—being tested and testing—are agreed; the metaphor observes their interaction. After a pause again (line 19) the therapist produces another metaphor, "wrestling match", which is accepted by the patient after a pause, adding a tag. This second metaphor is an observation of a description of an interaction—we see the vertical design clearly.

Why can the metaphor be created and accepted? My proposal is to again assume an embodied sensory membrane mediating the interaction in a certain way: what one part feels can be taken as the role complement of the other. Testing and being tested can be turned around and around, the result of which were a fight between who is tester and who is tested. Pointing to this easily imaginable interactive "doing We" the new metaphor "wrestling match" recursively observes their common interaction. The "wrestling match"-metaphor cannot be dismissed. It observes a truth about the preceding interaction and reduces its complexity. Recursively, the four-step process started again taking the metaphor as to point to another metaphor ("test"). Before I show how this works in my next example, I want to summarise the model.

The extended common ground model

On level 1, (verbal) *pointing* gestures create a "common ground" with the result of joint attention (often uttered by small tokens) which prepare the floor for the next level. ("A butterfly— there!" This is "pointing" to an object, assuming the listener as cognitively addressable, directing attention and anticipating response).

On level 2, observations can be referred to not only as sensual, but as conversational elements including perception, memory, and cognitive inference ("Oh yes, rare at this time of the year"— exclamation, agreement confirms perception + beginning of *conversational* enrichment).

On level 3, higher procedures of *linking* with further conversational elements are possible ("I saw a big one last year ...", analogical reasoning of the type "event A behaves to B like event C to D"). On this level most of conversational work is done.

On level 4, *metaphors* and *analogies* are created as observation for the common relational activity ("we talk about butterflies here as if we were experts" accompanied by mimic-expressive and other embodied activities such as laughing together). Metaphors are cognitive "tools" based on "image schemas" (Lakoff, 1990); here their target domain is the common relationship: "we *are* experts"). If confirmation of a proposed metaphor (for the experienced interaction) is delivered the resonating membrane is perceived as being perceived. This goes beyond the exchange of words, touches embodied feeling dimensions (by words!), and a silent agreement is reached that *exchanging information* is not the whole stuff of participants' conversation. Here, loneliness for moments is overcome; not by exchange of information, but by shared sensitivity expressed in words.

Metaphors that aptly describe an interaction require some *creativity* from outside the inter-action itself, from participants' cognitive-emotional domains (Ricoeur, 1981) based on the *resonating membrane* of participation. Thus, participants create a "dyadic state of consciousness" (Tronick, 2007). The equation 1+1=3 is established for a moment; neither can avoid viewing themselves as wrestlers. Participants operate for a moment as individual elements of a higher order system. The *resonating membrane* informs participants if the metaphor fits or not. A deep (conversational) ecology (Orsucci, 2001) is created. My following example shows what this looks like.

Recursion—an interactive spiral

This is a session from a psychoanalysis with a young woman in her mid-twenties. She felt unreal and complained that she was equally friendly to all people because she could not really feel anything. After her parents' divorce, when she was eleven years old, she lived with her mother and a younger brother in a state of "connected loneliness", as she said. One night, when she felt alone, she opened the door to her mother's sleeping room, discovering her mother in sexual intercourse with an unknown man. Shocked, she developed suicidal thoughts, and was never sure what kind of a relationship her mother and she shared. Did they share anything at all? When she left home for her professional training, she had telephone calls with her mother three times a day, a routine that continued beyond the beginning of her analysis.

The following session (number 120) starts with a surprise. She had told me several weeks before that for the first time in her life she had a boyfriend. Both wanted to go away for a long weekend. But she doubts: shouldn't she let her mother know? Or her brother? Or her girlfriend with whom she shares "everything"? Should they know about the boyfriend or the town to which they travel? Wouldn't they become envious or jealous? Or blame them for not being informed? She is so happily looking forward to the journey together, but to travel without informing mother, brother, and girlfriend—it seems to her that nobody knows where she is.

```
46  P: But nobody really knows where I am
47  (0.3)
```

STRENGTHENING THE HUMAN BOND 333

```
48   T: I do! I know it too
49   P: YES! YOU know it too, but=
50   T: °(h) (h) ((silent laughter))
51   P: =Yes right You know that (.) I forget this anyhow
        sometimes (.) for me >it's so self-evident that you
        know< that (-) that (.) as if I have incorporated this
        (2) as if you=you were my second HEAD °although (.)
        this would be beautiful then I would think more°
52   (7)
53   P: or as if I have four EARs (.) so to speak
54   (6)
55   T: which is (.) °a beautiful metaphor°
56   P: Four EARs?
57   T: ((laughing softly))
58   (2)
59   T: °ya°
60   T: (4)
61   T: Well then these are ears
62   (0.4)
63   P: °h:m°
64   (0.3)
65   T: which would listen to your own listening again
66   (1)
67   P: Yea:hh
68   T: °can I put it that (.) [way?°
69   P: [Yeah (.) so (-) an=then I also thought about (-)
        and a mouth quasi (.) an auxiliary mouth
70   T: HM::!
71   (7)
72   P: °Ya!°
73   (1)
74   P: °so I would understand that°
75   (6)
76   T: the auxiliary mouth (.) that's [me
77   P: [oh yeah (.) of course
78   T: °hmhm°
```

While she muses about nobody knowing where she is alone, her definition of our relationship follows the formula 1+1=1+0—she speaks, the listening therapist is "overlooked". As the therapist (line 48) points to his knowing (level 1) the formula for the relationship changes to

1+1=1+1. The patient's strong confirmation (line 49) enters level 2 of common ground. After confirming mutual monitoring she reasons about her forgetting that he knows about her plans and welcomes her knowledge; level 3 of common ground (linking) is achieved. This remembered experience is endowed with a positive value ("it's so self-evident that you know") and via the metaphor of incorporation (line 51) she achieves level 4 and creates a metaphor for the common relational activity. The equation 1+1=3 is achieved. The therapist is experienced "as if" he were her second head—again endowed with a positive value ("beautiful") and it would make her think more.

After some silence (line 52), the two-head metaphor is extended to "four ears" in an "as if" mode—which makes a restart on common-ground level 1 (*pointing*) possible, *but now within a relationship equation of 1+1=3*. She extends the "two heads" metaphor to a "four ears" metaphor and adds, "so to speak" (line 53). She is in touch with her *resonating membrane* and makes it feelable for me, the therapist. After some silence, I add a value ("beautiful metaphor"), both exchange some confirmation (lines 56–60) about still inhabiting metaphorical common ground. In touch with the resonating membrane, the therapist extends the metaphor (lines 61–65), positioned on the other side.

To listen to one's own listening has been described in the clinical literature as of psychoanalytic (Buchholz, 2015; Faimberg, 1996) and of systemic origin (Levold, 2019). It is a classical description of recursion, applying an operation onto itself. In line 76 the therapist, recurring to level 1, points to the "auxiliary mouth" and the patient confirms conversationally that he is right in his understanding of things. The session continues:

```
79   P: Yes I believe because I do not perceive you in that
        sense as an individual human being, which you are of
        course, but always within this framework of analysis
        here and also in this room I think
80   T: °hm°
81   (4)
82   P: and I do not even have to say that (.) so when I
        for example anyhow (1.3) if=I (.) I have said to Petra
        ((a girlfriend)) (1) or I have sometimes Petra told
        things I say- then which even Mama doesn't know (.)
        does nobody know and I've told her that and there she
        said (.) Yes and (.) and Mr. Buchholz knows it and then
        I yes=yes of course! (1) so (-) this is (.) I don't
        mention this anymore because for me it's clear that you
        know
83   (3)
84   P: at least that what I say here
```

```
85   (4)
86   T:  °hm!°
87   (2)
88   T:  and there's still maybe one or the other thing you
         do not tell then (-) if it became audible
89   P:  Ya::!
90   T:  then, by my auxiliary mouth it would again become
         hearable to your ears
91   P:  Yes, probably I should talk out exactly the things I
         do not say here
92   T:  °hm°
```

The patient reasons about a difference: the therapist as "individual human being" and him "within this framework" (line 79). To establish this difference indicates what psychoanalysts call "transference"; it can become analysable in the sense, that it is *pointed* to—level 1 of common ground within a relational equation of 1+1=3.

The patient cognitively *compares* her everyday-relationships to the special relationship with her therapist ending with the remark "for me it's clear that you know". After a short pause she diminishes that statement by adding that the therapist can know only "what I say here" (line 84) indicating that she actively silences other topics. Again, the therapist utters a token, embedded in two pauses (lines 85–87). He takes up the mouth-ear metaphor and creates actively a reason which might cause the patient not to tell more, but actively keep the silence; "it would again become audible to your ears" (line 90).

This type of analysis is two-pronged. It uses a metaphoric equation (1+1=…) to indicate the relational state and it uses the common ground-theory described here and elsewhere (Buchholz, 2016) in order to assess the level of common ground. The common ground scheme operates recursively altering the relational states. "Doing We" is embedded in the common ground of "doing analysis" with a strong curative component for her loneliness.

As a test of the validity of this complex theory I now turn to an example where therapeutic interaction obviously failed.

Determining why the relational state fails

The following material was first published in Alder (2016). In the fourth minute of a third session, a female patient announces that she wants to talk about a dream with her female therapist:

```
193  P:  .hhh (---) ((coughs)) WELL (-) that was the one
         thing (1.3) and the other (.)
194  tonight I had a dream
```

I summarise what happens in the next ten minutes. The therapist interrupts the patient because she, the therapist, has pain related to a nail, and she gets up to fetch a pair of scissors. Having finished her little operation, she invites the patient to continue her talk about dreams, extensively explores the patient's interest in dreams, and finally declares that she herself does not believe in dreams and adds her own example of an anxiety dream in the night with the advice, best is to stand up, read a book, and sleep again. Then she gives way for the patient to tell her dream:

```
451 P: I have temporarily I dreamed that I (1) well either
       I had burned hands and thus
452 I couldn't work at all or I've (--) been somehow (1.1)
453 I don't know in the jungle I was (.) naked and in need
    of help
454 and then someone passed by looked at me and left again
455 T: [mhmh]
456 P: .h (-) well like (-) one cannot even help me now;
```

Alder (2020) analyses this example as allusion. The dream narrative alludes to the ongoing interaction in a very surprising match.

"Burned hands" or "burned fingers" are in English and German a phrase that indicates having done something risky or wrong. She could not work in the jungle of this interaction, she exposed herself by sharing a dream, and had to hear that the therapist was not interested in it. She is in need of help and experiences someone passing by, looking at her, ending this phrase with "one cannot even help me now". The helper passes by, after some exploration of her emergency. The patient dreamt this after two sessions with the therapist. For the therapist such a dream must have been a riddle. Why?

Two reasons can be named: a) the recursive scheme of establishing a common ground in four steps was not passed, and b) a resonating membrane could not be established. Thus, the dream appears as a metaphorical riddle coming from nowhere. Nevertheless, the dream elements seem to allude to elements of the interaction. But without the recursive interaction, neither the meaning of the dream ("told self") nor of telling the dream ("performative self") can be securely determined. The therapist's rejection of dreams defines the relationship as 1+1=1+0; the patient's telling the dream is a response to this definition, in my metaphorical mathematics: 1+1=0+1. This sheds light on why the patient dropped out after this session. She was left alone.

Conclusion

For me, this is an example of why mutual interests between CA and professional psychotherapists should be enhanced. I want to end with some recommendations.

First, if therapists understand treatment outcome not as something at the end of therapy, but as something they can immediately observe in and during the session, they will be in a better state of "doing We" in order to cure loneliness.

Second, such process observation is opposed to the current overestimation of diagnoses. Loneliness is no disorder, but a very influential mental state missing a resonating membrane. Therapists should learn to distinguish resonating membrane from usual "emo-talk" beginning every sentence with "I feel ..." or some equivalents.

Third, my examples show that to "stand in"—not "above"—the situation *as a participant* opens the therapist's mind and senses for what can and should be said—and what better not. To "stand above" is a hidden metaphor for the power dimension in therapy.

Fourth, everything that can be said can be framed in at least two ways; as direction or question, as violation or as support, as contrast or as resonance. Frames are most often ignored; they guide how a speaker wants a remark to be understood. "I want to inform you that ..." frames the same content differently than "I want to tell you that ...". Often, therapists begin with "Yes—but ..." and this eludes self-observation. *Form beats content.* Premeditated choosing of what to say produces pauses, silence becomes a reflective moment-of-talk (Levitt & Morrill, 2021). Selection among alternatives re-establishes the sense of agency.

Fifth, being aware of the "situation" is highly important for recognising its gestalt (Buchholz, 2020) and it supports the cure of loneliness.

Sixth, therapists are a part of a process which they cannot fully steer or determine, a function which was ascribed to traditional theory. Becoming aware of the highly important role of conversation pervades all psychotherapies; a "communicative turn" is under way. I do not mean the overall communicative "noise" that can be met everywhere, which strongly contributes to loneliness. A therapeutically meaningful conversation is something highly special. I hope I am contributing to making this distinction clearer.

References

Aguayo, J. (2013). Wilfred Bion's "Caesura"—from public lecture to published text—(1975–1977). In: H. B. Levine & L. J. Brown (Eds.), *Growth and Turbulence in the Container/Contained: Bion's Continuing Legacy* (pp. 55–74). Hove, UK: Routledge.

Alder, M.-L. (2016). Dream-telling differences in psychotherapy: the dream as an allusion. *Language and Psychoanalysis*, 5(2): 19–26.

Alder, M.-L. (2020). *Allusives Sprechen in Psychotherapien*. Berlin: Humboldt-Universität zu Berlin. https://doi.org/10.18452/21288.

Antaki, C. (2008). Formulations in psychotherapy. In: A. Peräkylä, C. Antaki, S. Vehviläinen, & I. Leudar (Eds.), *Conversation Analysis and Psychotherapy* (pp. 26–43). Cambridge: Cambridge University Press.

Aron, L. (1996). *A Meeting of Minds—Mutuality in Psychoanalysis*. Hillsdale, NJ: Analytic Press.

Baranger, M., & Baranger, W. (2008). The analytic situation as a dynamic field. *International Journal of Psychoanalysis, 89:* 795–826.

Benjamin, J. (2018). *Beyond Doer and Done To: Recognition Theory, Intersubjectivity and the Third.* New York: Routledge.

Bruner, J. S. (1995. From joint attention to the meeting of minds. In: C. Moore, P. J. Dunham, & P. Dunham (Eds.), *Joint Attention: Its Origins and Role in Development* (pp. 1–14). Hoboken, NJ: Taylor & Francis, 2014.

Bruschweiler-Stern, N., Harrison, A. M., Lyons-Ruth, K., Morgan, A. C., Nahum, J. P., Sander, L. W., Stern, D. N., & Tronick, E. Z. (2002). Explicating the implicit: the local level and the microprocess of change in the analytic situation. *International Journal of Psychoanalysis, 83:* 1051–1062.

Buchholz, M. B. (2015). Listening to words, seeing images—metaphors of emotional involvement and the movement of the metaphor. *Psychoanalytic Discourse, 5(1):* 20–38.

Buchholz, M. B. (2016). Conversational errors and common ground activities in psychotherapy—insights from conversation analysis. *International Journal of Psychological Studies, 8(3):* 134–153. https://doi.org/10.5539/ijps.v8n3p134.

Buchholz, M. B. (2019). Re-petition in (therapeutic) conversation: a psychoanalyst's perspective using conversation analysis. In: J. R. Resina & C. Wulf (Eds.), *Repetition, Recurrence, Returns: How Cultural Renewal Works* (pp. 85–108). Lanham, MD: Lexington.

Buchholz, M. B. (2020). Seeing the situational Gestalt—movement in therapeutic spaces. *Gestalt Theory, 42(2):* 1–31. Retrieved from DOI 10. 2478/gth-2020-0011.

Buchholz, M. B., Bergmann, J. R., Alder, M.-L., Dittmann (now: Franzen), M. M., Dreyer, F., & Kächele, H. (2017). The building of empathy: conceptual "pillars" and conversational practices in psychotherapy. In: M. Kondo (Ed.), *Empathy—An Evidence-based Interdisciplinary Perspective.* https://intechopen.com/books. Open Access: InTech. https://doi.org/10.5772/intechopen.69628.

Buchholz, M. B., Buchholz, T., & Wülfing, B. (2021). Doing contrariness: therapeutic talk-in-interaction in a single therapy session with a traumatized child. *Frontiers in Psychology, 12.* https://doi.org/10.3389/fpsyg.2021.545966.

Buchholz, M. B., Ehmer, O., Mahlstedt, C., Pfänder, S., & Schumann, E. (2021). Speaking that silences. A single case multi-method analysis of a couple's interview. In: A. Dimitrijević & M. B. Buchholz (Eds.), *Silence and Silencing in Psychoanalysis: Cultural, Clinical, and Research Aspects* (pp. 333–397). Abingdon, UK: Routledge.

Buchholz, M. B., & Kächele, H. (2017). From turn-by-turn to larger chunks of talk: an exploratory study in psychotherapeutic micro-processes using conversation analysis. *Research in Psychotherapy: Psychopathology, Process and Outcome, 20:* 161–178. https://doi.org/10.4081/ripppo.2017.257.

Buchholz, M. B., & Reich, U. (2015). Dancing insight. How a psychotherapist uses change of positioning in order to complement split-off areas of experience. *Chaos and Complexity Letters, 8(2–3):* 121–146.

Bühler, K. (1934). *Theory of Language: The Representational Function of Language.* D. F. Goodwin & A. Eschbach (Trans.). Foundations of Semiotics series. Amsterdam, PA: John Benjamins, 2011.

Corballis, M. C. (2011). *The Recursive Mind: The Origins of Human Language, Thought, and Civilization.* Princeton, NJ: Princeton University Press. Retrieved from http://worldcat.org/oclc/670238275.

Deppermann, A. (2015). Positioning. In: A. de Fina & A. Georgakopoulou (Eds.), *The Handbook of Narrative Analysis* (pp. 369–386). Chichester, UK: Wiley Blackwell.

Deppermann, A., Scheidt, C. E., & Stukenbrock, A. (2020). Positioning shifts. From told self to performative self in psychotherapy. *Frontiers in Psychology, 11*. https://doi.org/10.3389/fpsyg.2020.572436.

Dimitrijević, A., & Buchholz, M. B. (Eds.) (2021). *Silence and Silencing in Psychoanalysis: Cultural, Clinical, and Research Aspects.* Abingdon, UK: Routledge.

Dittmann (now: Franzen), M. M. (2016). Moving closer. A conversation analytic perspective on how a psychotherapeutic dyad works on closing their encounters. *Language and Psychoanalysis, 5*(2): 46–61.

Dreyer, F. (2021). *Gestaltorientierungen in der Psychotherapie. Rekurrente Orientierungen am Modell und ihre therapeutische Wirksamkeit* (Dissertation). Freiberg, Germany: Albert-Ludwigs-Universität, Freiburg.

Dreyer, F., & Franzen, M. M. (2021). How to move on after silences. Addressing thought processes to restart conversation. In: A. Dimitrijević & M. B. Buchholz (Eds.), *Silence and Silencing in Psychoanalysis: Cultural, Clinical, and Research Aspects* (pp. 275–306). Abingdon, UK: Routledge.

Enfield, N. J. (2013). *Relationship Thinking—Agency, Enchrony, and Human Sociality: Foundations of Human Interaction.* New York: Oxford University Press.

Faimberg, H. (1996). Listening to listening. *International Journal of Psychoanalysis, 77*: 667–677.

Gadamer, H.-G. (1960). *Wahrheit und Methode. Grundzüge einer philosophischen Hermeneutik (Gesammelte Werke, Band 1, 1990).* Tübingen, Germany: J.C.B. Mohr (Paul Siebeck).

Goffman, E. (1963). *Behavior in Public Places: Notes on the Social Organization of Gatherings.* New York: Free Press.

Huber, D., & Klug, G. (2016). *Münchner Psychotherapiestudie. Psychotherapeut,* 1–6. https://doi.org/10.1007/s00278-016-0139-7.

Lakoff, G. (1990). The invariance hypotheses: is abstract reason based on image schemas? *Cognitive Linguistics, 1*(1): 39–74.

Lepper, G. (2015). A pragmatic approach to the study of therapeutic interaction: toward an observational science of psychotherapy process. In: O. C. Gelo, A. Pritz, & B. Rieken (Eds.), *Psychotherapy Research* (pp. 517–536). Vienna: Springer Vienna.

Levenson, E. A. (1983). *The Ambiguity of Change.* New York: Basic Books.

Levold, T. (2019). Hören 1. und 2. Ordnung. Warum Zuhören mehr ist als Wissen, was gesagt worden ist. *Kontext—Zeitschrift Für Systemische Therapie Und Familientherapie, 50*(1): 24–42.

Levitt, H. M., & Morrill, Z. (2021). Measuring silence: the pauses inventory categorization system and a review of findings. In: A. Dimitrijević & M. B. Buchholz (Eds.), *Silence and Silencing in Psychoanalysis: Cultural, Clinical, and Research Aspects* (pp. 233–250). Abingdon, UK: Routledge.

Loewald, H. W. (1979). Reflections on the psychoanalytic process and its therapeutic potential. *Psychoanalytic Study of the Child, 34*: 155–168.

Mergenthaler, E., & Kächele, H. (1988). The Ulm Textbank Management System: a tool for psychotherapy research. In: H. Dahl, H. Kächele, & H. Thomä (Eds.), *Psychoanalytic Process Research Strategies.* Berlin: Springer.

Muran, J. C. (2019). Confessions of a New York rupture researcher: an insider's guide and critique. *Psychotherapy Research*, *29*(1–2): 1–14.

Nissen-Lie, H. A., Orlinsky, D. E., & Rønnestad, M. H. (2021). The emotionally burdened psychotherapist: personal and situational risk factors. *Professional Psychology: Research and Practice*. Advance online publication. https://doi.org/10.1037/pro0000387.

Norcross, J. C., & Wampold, B. E. (2018). A new therapy for each patient: evidence-based relationships and responsiveness. *Journal of Clinical Psychology*, *74*(11): 1889–1906. https://doi.org/10.1002/jclp.22678.

Ogden, T. H. (1994). The analytic third: working with intersubjective clinical facts. *International Journal of Psychoanalysis*, *75*: 3–19.

Orsucci, F. (2001). Happiness and deep ecology: on noise, harmony, and beauty in the mind. *Nonlinear Dynamics, Psychology and Life Sciences*, *5*(1): 65–76.

Peräkylä, A., Antaki, C., Vehviläinen, S., & Leudar, I. (Eds.) (2008). *Conversation Analysis and Psychotherapy*. Cambridge: Cambridge University Press.

Peräkylä, A., Henttonen, P., Voutilainen, L., Kahri, M., Stevanovic, M., Sams, M., & Ravaja, N. (2015). Sharing the emotional load. Recipient affiliation calms down the storyteller. *Social Psychology Quarterly*, *78*(4): 301–323. https://doi.org/10.1177/0190272515611054.

Rae, J. (2008). Lexical substitution as a therapeutic resource. In: A. Peräkylä, C. Antaki, S. Vehviläinen, & I. Leudar (Eds.), *Conversation Analysis and Psychotherapy* (pp. 62–79). Cambridge: Cambridge University Press.

Ricoeur, P. (1981). The metaphorical process as cognition, imagination, and feeling. In: M. Johnson (Ed.), *Philosophical Perspectives on Metaphor*. Minneapolis, MN: University of Minnesota Press.

Sacks, H., & Jefferson, G. (1992). *Lectures on Conversation*. G. Jefferson (Ed.). E. A. Schegloff (Intro.). Oxford: Basil Blackwell, 1995.

Safran, J. D., & Muran, J. C. (2000). *Negotiating the Therapeutic Alliance—A Relational Treatment Guide*. New York: Guilford.

Schegloff, E. A., Ochs, E., & Thompson, S. A. (1996). Introduction. In: E. Ochs, E. A. Schegloff, & S. A. Thompson (Eds.), *Interaction and Grammar* (pp. 1–51). Cambridge: Cambridge University Press.

Stevanovic, M., & Peräkylä, A. (2014). Three orders in the organization of human action: on the interface between knowledge, power, and emotion in interaction and social relations. *Language in Society*, *43*(02): 185–207. https://doi.org/10.1017/S0047404514000037.

Tomasello, M. (2019). *Becoming Human: A Theory of Ontogeny*. Cambridge, MA: Belknap Press of Harvard University Press.

Tronick, E. Z. (2007). *The Neurobehavioral and Social-Emotional Development of Infants and Children*. New York: W. W. Norton.

Voutilainen, L., Henttonen, P., Kahri, M., Ravaja, N., Sams, M., & Peräkylä, A. (2018). Empathy, challenge, and psychophysiological activation in therapist-client interaction. *Frontiers in Psychology*, *9*: 530.

Winefield, H. R., Chandler, M. A., & Bassett, D. L. (1989). Tag questions and powerfulness: quantitative and qualitative analysis of a course of psychotherapy. *Language in Society*, *18*(1): 77–86.

Index

age, xxii–xxiii, 169, 174–175, 177–178, 182, 187–189, 203–209, 214–220, 229, 321

Akhtar, Salman, xviii, 32, 109–110

Alberti, Fay Bound, xxi, xxv, 63, 259–260

aloneness, xvii, xix–xx, xxiii–xxiv, 7, 11, 14, 20, 61, 77, 85, 104, 114, 122, 125–126, 128, 130, 142, 170, 187–188, 194–195, 197, 231, 255–258, 265, 267–268, 270, 271–272, 275, 279, 292, 299, 312 *see also* constructive aloneness; essential aloneness

Alzheimer's Disease (AD), 123, 217, 221

anaclitic depression, 173, 257

analytic third, 322–323, 326

anger, 193, 215, 241, 246, 251, 262, 287, 289, 291

anima mundi, 91–93

animus, 309

anxiety, 21, 35, 40–41, 100, 110, 112–114, 122, 174, 181, 189, 192, 206, 215, 216–218, 221, 228–230, 232, 246–247, 257, 269, 272–274, 283, 300, 302, 311–312, 315, 326, 336

Ariés, Phillipe, 58–59, 61–62

Aron, Lewis, 322

art, xvii, 6, 59, 62–63, 71, 73–75, 77, 82, 89, 92–5, 99–101, 103–106, 108–117, 123–124, 127–131, 134–136, 138, 140, 142–143, 256–257

art therapy, 74, 123, 129, 131, 136, 142–143

as-if, 333–334

asceticism, 19–21, 79

Asperger's syndrome, 246, 252

attachment, 27, 126–127, 129, 133, 159, 170, 179, 182, 185–186, 188–189, 192–193, 195, 207, 227–228, 231–232, 295 *see also* disorganised attachment; insecure attachment; secure

Augustine, 7, 61, 71

autism spectrum disorder (ASD), 169, 192, 217

autonomy, xxii, 6, 8–9, 11, 57, 100, 134, 174–176, 180–181, 208, 286

Bach, Johann Sebastian, 73, 85–86, 101, 116

Balint, Michael, 129, 286, 297

Beebe, Beatrice, 109, 159, 189, 191–192

Beethoven, Ludwig van, 73, 78, 91, 104–105, 112, 115–117

Bernardus Claraevallensis, 79, 82

Beutel, Manfred E., 170, 202–206, 208

Bion, Wilfred R., 148, 154–155, 157, 163, 252, 274–275, 295, 297–299, 301, 319

Bipolar Affective Disorder, 112, 218

bliss(ful), iii, xix, 3, 6–7, 74, 93, 114, 124

body/bodily, xvii, xxii, 3, 5, 13–14, 19, 37, 61, 133–134, 140, 153, 163, 171, 174, 229–230, 269–270, 296–297, 298–299, 308, 330

body-self, 298

Bollas, Christopher, xxii, 38–39, 271

borderline personality disorder (BPD), 43, 231

Bowlby, John, xvii, 126–127, 179, 185, 188–189, 192, 214, 282, 288

brain development, 171, 190, 229

342   INDEX

brain imaging, 214, 233–234
Brunner, Jerome, 322
Buber, Martin, 258–259, 261, 264
Buecker, Susanne, 204–205
Bühler, Karl Ludwig, 26, 330
Burton, Robert, 67, 83
bystander, 33, 39–40, 42, 47–49, 52–53

Cacioppo, John T., xix, 123, 126, 137, 201–203, 206,
         213–216, 218–219, 212, 227, 231–234
calcified paranoia, 38
capacity to be alone, 12, 14, 127, 142, 169, 174, 180,
         241, 243, 268–272, 323
cardiovascular risk (CVH)/cardiovascular disease,
         xvii, 215, 219, 221
child
         abuse, xii, 106, 171, 179, 195–196, 251, 290
         maltreatment, 171, 228, 230
         neglect, xxiii, 3, 73–74, 106, 179, 189, 195–196,
                  228–229, 231, 243, 308
childhood trauma, 130, 179, 196, 241, 250, 284–286,
         288, 292
chronic loneliness, xx, 3, 126, 171, 194, 203, 214–216,
         228, 232, 234, 242, 295
cognitive development, xvii, 174, 176, 178–179,
         228–230
common ground see doing together/doing We
communication, xxii, 8–9, 27, 34, 36–37, 47–52, 94,
         150, 159, 161–162, 169, 175, 218, 241, 260,
         271–272, 276, 309, 321, 324
communitarisation, 8, 12
compulsions, 159, 246, 282, 286, 329
consciousness, 5, 7–8, 11, 13, 25, 58, 64, 94, 133,
         154, 296–298, 304, 308–310, 313,
         315–216, 332
constructive aloneness, 125–126, 257
containment, 135, 246–247, 252, 297, 299, 301
Conversation Analysis, 45, 51, 149, 242, 323–326,
         329, 330–332, 337
coping
mechanism, 11
style, 173–174
copycat effect, 25
coronavirus (COVID-19), xvii, xx, 20–21, 121–123,
         131, 133, 138, 171, 213, 219–220, 267
couch, xviii, 36, 74, 124, 246
countertransference, 248, 258, 297, 301 see also
         transference
creative
         block, 104, 109–111
         loneliness, 122, 125, 257, 275

creativity, xx, 15, 22, 73–74, 80, 82–83, 101, 104–109,
         112–113, 115–118, 122, 127, 130, 169,
         177–179, 182, 202, 257, 332
cultural loneliness, 256

Darwin, Charles, 185, 188
daydreaming, 19, 180
dead see mother
death drive, 185, 268, 269, 272–273
defence, 38–39, 88, 126, 131, 176, 243, 249, 251–252,
         263–264, 273, 281, 283, 295, 297, 304, 328
dementia, 216, 217
dependency, 11, 124, 175–176, 181
depression, 34, 79, 81, 83–84, 110, 115, 123, 129, 131,
         134, 144, 161, 171, 173–174, 176, 181, 206,
         215–217, 220–221, 257, 280, 287–289, 292,
         296, 300, 311
depressive position, 274 see also Bion, Wilfred
         R.; Klein, Melanie
Descartes, René, 8, 39, 94, 311
desolation, 78, 84–87, 95, 246, 250, 265, 269, 275, 309
development, xvii, xx, 11, 14–15, 73, 105, 110, 112,
         125–127, 133–134, 142, 155, 167, 169–171,
         173–182, 189–190, 192, 195–196, 207–208,
         228–231, 242–244, 268–270, 284, 304, 307
developmental functions, 173, 175
deviant, 104, 111, 315
diagnosis, 36, 43–44, 218, 220–221, 246, 320, 337
disability, 217, 218, 220
disorganised attachment, 195
disruption, 308, 310
dissociation, 250–251, 286, 310
doing together/doing We, 242, 319, 321–322,
         324, 331, 335, 337
Dowland, John, 80, 83, 100
dream, 66, 99, 169, 242, 273, 302–303, 335–336
Duby, Georges, 58–59, 61–62
Dürer, Albrecht, 61–62, 79

ego, 5, 7–15, 26, 39, 80, 83–84, 107, 110, 125, 127, 133,
         176, 245, 268–270, 272–274, 297, 302, 308
         see also superego
         development, 176
         relatedness, 127, 270
         rudimentary, 269
         strength, 107, 125, 273
emotional intelligence, 230
empathic attunement, 245
empathy, xi, 177, 179, 197, 259, 284, 297, 324
Enfield, N. J., 322, 323
Enlightenment, 8, 51, 87–88

INDEX   **343**

estrangement, xix, 140, 258
environment, 14, 43, 47, 62, 108, 111, 117, 122,
    125–126, 128, 130, 131, 138, 143, 188, 191,
    202, 208, 227, 231, 243, 250–251, 268–272,
    283, 296–297, 308
environment mother *see* mother
erratic mothering *see* mother
essential aloneness, 257, 271–272, 275
evolution, 170, 185–188, 197, 201, 227, 232, 299

Fairbairn, W. Ronald D., 246, 281–282, 284,
    288, 295–296
false self, 296–298
fantasy, 124, 127, 129, 133, 175–178, 180–181,
    192, 250, 271, 282–284, 286–287
feedback system, 130
Ferenczi, Sándor, 115, 185, 243, 245, 251, 279–282,
    284–286
flight reaction, 301
flow, 113–114
Fonagy, Peter, 231–232, 295
Foucault, Michel, 22, 24, 58, 62
fragmentation, 232, 243, 244, 247
free will, 62
Freud, Sigmund, xviii, 9, 36, 38–39, 63, 66, 73, 83,
    89–90, 92, 115–116, 133, 154, 163, 170,
    179, 185, 192, 260–261, 270, 296, 298,
    302, 308, 310, 320, 326
Fromm, Erich, 313
Fromm-Reichmann, Frieda, 122, 125–126, 197, 241,
    255–265
functional magnetic resonance imaging (fMRI), 214,
    229, 233
fundamental schizoid reaction, 246

gender, xxi, 49, 109, 174, 203–204, 207–208, 216
genetics, 12–13, 217–218, 231
Goffman, Erving, xx, 37, 40, 196, 321
good enough mother *see* mother
Green, André, 300, 302
Greenacre, Phyllis, 129–130, 142
Greenblatt, Stephen, 58–60, 62–65

Hamm, Mark, 36, 42–49, 51–52
Handel, George Frideric, 73, 77, 86
Hawkley, Louise, 123, 174, 202–204, 208, 213, 215,
    219–220, 232, 234
health, xvii–xxi, 21, 29, 112, 122–123, 171, 173–174,
    181, 196, 201, 203–208, 213, 215–221,
    228–230, 243, 246, 267, 274, 282, 298, 319
Hegel, Georg Wilhelm Friedrich, 94, 96

Heidegger, Martin, 11, 325
Heine, Heinrich, 93, 96–97
helicopter parenting, 181, 195
hermit, 19–28, 78, 80, 84, 125–126, 130, 141
heroic solitude, 11
Hildegard of Bingen, 80–81, 100
Hoffmann, Ernst Theodor, 90–92
holding environment, 14, 126, 128, 143
homelessness, 58, 79, 95, 194
Hopper, Earl, 37–39, 41
Hopper, Edward, 138–140, 142
House-Tree-Person Test (HTP), 131, 137
Husserl, Edmund, 6–8, 12–14
hypersensitivity, 234
hypervigilance, 138, 232

id experience, 127
identification, 34–36, 116, 121, 131, 253, 260, 273,
    281–283, 285–286, 288, 291–292, 297,
    301, 303, 308
imaginary friend, 173, 175–182
immune system (immune function), 123, 206, 214,
    219, 229
implicit relational knowing, 191, 196
impulse control, 176, 182, 197, 232
impulsivity, 230, 315
incommunicado self, 268, 271
individual growth, 122
individualism, xxi–xxii, 22, 36, 48, 59, 259
individuation, 12–14, 134, 136, 176
infancy, 229, 320
infantile omnipotence, 270, 274
insecure attachment, 159, 185, 193, 197, 227, 234
inspiration, xviii, 28, 73, 70, 80–81, 104, 107–110, 114
integration, 108, 270, 273–275, 297
intelligence, 196, 198, 229, 230, 299–300
intention reading, 191–192
internal object *see* object
internal working models (IWMs), 192–194, 197
introjection, 273, 308, 316
introversion, 213
isolation, xvii, xix–xx, xxiii, 3–4, 7–12, 21, 24–25, 34, 41,
    61, 73, 77, 79, 82, 96–97, 99, 104, 108, 110–112,
    121, 123–127, 130–131, 133, 138, 143, 161,
    171, 176, 179, 195, 197, 202–203, 213–216,
    218, 220, 227, 232–234, 252–253, 255–258,
    262–263, 265, 267, 271, 307–309, 312–313, 317

Jaques, Elliott, 274
Jaspers, Karl, 4, 10–11
joint attention, 143, 191, 321–323, 331

Kächele, Horst, 188, 324, 327, 329
Kant, Immanuel, 9, 88, 94
Kierkegaard, Søren, 11, 116, 242, 311
Klein, Melanie, 126, 154, 192, 241–242, 267–270, 272–275, 295
knowledge, xxii, 5–6, 8, 26, 41–47, 91, 117, 154–155, 177, 190, 230, 324
Kohut, Heinz, xxii, 110–111, 116
Kris, Ernst, 107–108, 127
Kristeva, Julia, 58, 268, 275

language, xii, xxi, 6, 34, 40–41, 44–46, 60, 63, 66, 95, 97, 126, 147–148, 156–159, 161, 196, 205, 229, 251, 256, 197, 319, 339
Leibniz, Gottfried Wilhelm, 8–10, 13, 91
libido, 129, 185, 296
life instinct, 10, 272–273
Likierman, Meira, 268, 272, 275
linking, 75, 148, 153–155, 157, 331, 334
Loewald, Hans, 322
lone wolf, xxiv, 4, 34–36, 48, 52–53
ludic interpretation, 247
Luhmann, Niklas, 74

Macho, Thomas, 125
manic depression, 273
Maslow, Abraham, 20, 29, 111, 113
Medieval mysticism, 71, 78, 81
meditation, 7–8, 20–22, 28, 84, 88, 92, 95
meeting of minds, 321–323
Meister Eckhart, 71–73, 78–80, 100
melancholia, 73, 83–85, 87, 296, 303, 308
memento mori, 80, 84, 86–88
mental disorder, xx, xxiii, 33–34, 53, 60, 196–197, 206
mentalization, 227, 230–231, 234
Merton, Thomas, 4, 24
metaphoric equation, 325, 334–335
Middle Ages, 59, 61–62, 79–80
Milarepa, 27–29
Milton, Jane, 242, 268, 273–275
Milton, John, 67, 83
minority groups, 205
minus phenomena, 153, 157
mirroring, 8–10, 142, 159, 230, 248
monk(s), 20, 22–23, 25–28, 58, 79–82
morbidity, 171, 202, 206, 213, 215, 216, 218
mortality, xx, 124, 171, 206, 210, 212, 213, 215–216, 218
mother, xxii, 134, 137, 175, 186

and baby, 110, 126–127, 128–129, 136, 142, 169, 187, 189–190, 191, 192, 194, 228, 269, 270, 271, 272, 274, 295, 297, 309, 321, 325
dead, 300
environment, 108–109, 114
erratic, 308
good enough, 128, 180, 245
substitute, 115
Mozart, Wolfgang Amadeus, 74, 78, 84, 87, 89–90, 106, 116–117
mutual monitoring, 170, 321, 330–333, 334

nameless dread, 157, 163
narcissism, xxi, 110–111, 129, 142, 182, 242, 246, 270, 279–280, 283, 286, 292, 296–298, 302–303, 316
narcissistic wound, 246
narrative distortions, 158
negative capability, 252
neglect, xxiii, 3, 73, 104, 179, 189, 196, 198, 228–229, 231, 235–236, 243, 308
neurobiology, 8, 231
neurodevelopment, 218, 228
neurodivergency, 217
neuroendocrine system, 218–219, 232
neuropathology, 217
neuropsychiatric disorders, 228, 238
neurosis, 26, 38
neurotransmitter, 227
new learning experience, 274

object
    choice, 39
    internal, 14–15, 114–115, 126–128, 154, 269, 281, 284, 290, 296, 303
    outer, 129, 154
    transitional, 128, 179–180
object relations (theory), 15, 115, 192, 241, 268, 296
object-loss, 296–297
observation, 40, 45, 59, 192, 320–321, 236, 331–332, 337
Oedipus, 58,
Ogden, Thomas H., 162, 295, 298, 303, 322–323
omnipotence, 9–10, 270, 273–274, 309–310
ostracism, 58

panic attack, 142, 250–251
pantheism, 91, 94
paranoia, 38–39, 44, 153, 155, 156, 216, 296

paranoid–schizoid position, 274
parental
    attunement, 193
    deprivation, 173
    support, 181
parenthood, 170, 185–187, 250
parenting styles, 180–181
peak-experiences, 113
Peräkylä, Anssi, 323–325, 327
perfectionism, 313
performative self, 75, 148, 158–159, 328, 330, 336
persecution, xxiii, 99, 245, 269, 273, 275, 299
persona, 95–96, 98, 262
personal grievance *see* political grievance
physical distancing, 121, 213
physical health, 123, 174, 204–206, 213, 215, 220–221
Piaget, Jean, 175–176
Plato, xxii, 4, 6, 91, 185
playfulness, 108, 129, 285, 288, 291–292
political grievance / personal grievance, 33–35,
    42–43, 45–46, 48
political hopelessness, 99–100
Popa, Elena, 217, 220
prevention, 201, 208
primary
    intersubjectivity, 5, 9, 12–14
    narcissism, 270
    relationship, 243
primitive agonies, 295–296, 298
private self, 4, 57–59, 61–64
projection, 39, 64, 107–108, 125, 139, 176, 283,
    289, 190, 308
projective identification, 297, 301
psychic
    absence, 297
    annihilation, 302
    retreat, 247, 296, 301–302, 304
psychosis, 44, 138, 218, 256, 261, 302
psychosomatic disorder, xxi, 197
public self, 65
Purcell, Henry, 84, 87, 94

quarantine, 121

Rabe, David, 74–75, 147–148, 150, 152, 155, 158, 162
radicalisation model, 42–43, 46, 52–53
Rapoport, David C., 52, 54
rationalism, 87, 91, 314
real self, 262

reality testing, 296
recursion, 326, 332, 334
reflective functioning, 197, 199
regression, 107, 124, 127, 263, 286
regulation, 11, 126, 170, 182, 219, 227, 229–230,
    233–234
relatedness, 126–127, 129, 133, 158, 263, 270, 303
relationship, xviii, xxiv, 7, 9–11, 20, 24, 50–52, 58–59,
    66–67, 73, 100, 110, 114–115, 122, 126,
    129, 131, 133, 143, 147, 150–151, 153–155,
    159, 161, 163, 170–171, 173–178, 180, 182,
    185, 193–195, 197, 201–202, 204–206, 213,
    215–216, 218, 221, 227, 231–232, 243, 245,
    248, 250, 257–260, 262, 264–265, 269–270,
    273, 293, 296–297, 299, 301, 304, 308,
    310–312, 316, 321–326, 328, 332–336
religion, xviii–xix, xxi, 4, 20–26, 28, 32, 52, 59–61,
    64, 72, 74, 83–84, 96, 101, 124, 128,
    185–186, 314
Renaissance, 61–63, 90
resilience, 21
resonating membrane, 325, 332, 334, 336–337
resource, 40, 169, 173, 181, 268, 275
restoration, 99, 118
revolution, 51, 66, 83, 93, 99, 117, 185
reward (system), 186–187, 230, 233, 234
Ricoeur, Paul, 310, 332
Rilke, Rainer Maria, 73–74, 103, 105, 107–109,
    112–116, 124–125, 196
risk factor, 201, 203–205, 208, 213–215, 127, 219–221,
    228, 296, 340
Rogers, Annie, 256
Romanticism, 66, 92–93, 95, 100, 116

Sageman, Marc, 49–51
scapegoat surrogate, 301
Schelling, Friedrich Wilhelm Joseph, 92–96
schizoid, 246, 257, 274, 295–296, 304
schizophrenia, 43, 136, 138, 217–218, 273
Schopenhauer, Arthur, 9–10, 73, 78
Schore, Allan, 230
Schumann, Robert, 90. 93, 95–97, 99
seclusion, xix, 78–80, 124–125, 169, 257
secure
    attachment, 127, 179, 192, 195
    base, 179, 182, 192
Seiden, Henry M., 133–134
self
    -acceptance, 289, 313, 316

346   INDEX

-actualisation, 58, 111
-fashioning, 62
-harm, xviii, 217
-negation, 312–313
-object differentiation, 177, 202
-preservation, 4, 232–233
-regulation, 126, 170, 182, 219, 230, 233–235, 236
sensory processing, 234
separation, xix, xxii, 38, 110–112, 133–134, 136–137,
        139, 176–177, 179–181, 189, 192, 207, 229,
        241, 257, 265, 301
sex, xviii, 43, 55, 112, 115, 136, 152, 170, 185–186, 195,
        216, 219, 250–251, 273, 311, 332
Shabad, Peter, 242, 307
Shakespeare, William, 39, 57–58, 60, 62–67, 83–85,
        109, 116–117, 256
shame, xx, xxiv, 38, 175, 231, 242, 246, 280, 282, 285,
        287–288, 190, 292, 301–302, 307–309,
        312–314, 316–317, 321
silent zone, 33, 47
Simmel, Georg, 51, 56, 100
social
        anxiety, 174, 216, 218, 228
        bond, xx, 41, 44–45, 214, 227
        brain, 170–171, 190, 218, 227–228, 230–231,
                233–234
        cognition, 126, 231, 234
        functioning, 217, 229
        identity, 66
        inhibition, 125
        isolation, xvii, xx, 79, 104, 123, 126, 131, 197,
                202–203, 213–214, 216, 218, 220, 227,
                232–234
        mind, 37–42, 44–45, 47, 51, 53
        neuroscience, 214, 228, 231, 232
        psychology, 33, 36, 47, 208
        reward, 230, 233–234
        skills, xxiii, 169, 178–179, 191, 196, 228–229,
                231, 234
        smile, 188
sociality, 5, 8, 11, 13, 40, 271, 231
socioeconomic (status), xxiv, 203, 215, 259, 320
Socrates, 5–7, 11, 58
solipsism, 9, 22, 27, 147
solitary, xx-xxi, xxiv, 5–7, 11, 14, 22, 61, 67, 77, 88,
        92, 103–104, 108, 124, 142, 163, 193, 217,
        244, 257
solitude à deux/dynamic solitude, 322–323
somatic memories, 250
somatoform disorder, 197–198
Sophism, 6
Spaaij, Ramón, 34–36, 42–49, 51–52

splitting, 154, 249, 273, 283, 296, 308
Steiner, John, 247–248, 296, 304
Stern, Daniel, 158–159, 191
stigmatisation, 170, 196
stimuli, 171, 189, 227, 232–233
stress, 20, 174, 207, 214, 216, 218–219, 229–230,
        236, 282
structural theory, 39
subjecticide, 39
subjectivity, 8, 10, 12–13, 24, 268–269, 271, 297, 317
suicide, xviii, xxv, 34, 47, 50, 110, 115, 123, 161, 208,
        213, 216–217, 222, 224
superego, 83, 107, 133, 248, 296, 299, 311
supervision, 24, 301
support, 170, 202, 218, 220, 230
symbolic representation, 131
symbolisation, 180
symptoms, xxi, 33, 123, 169, 174, 206–207, 215,
        217–218, 228, 231, 234, 243, 246, 251, 260

talk-in-interaction, 45, 319–321, 323, 326, 330
Target, Mary, 232
Taylor, Majorie, 175
technologies of the self, 19, 22, 26, 28
terrorism, 32–36, 42, 49, 52–53
        of suffering, 281
threat surveillance, 233
timing, 248–249
told self, 75, 148, 158–159, 328, 330, 336
Tomasello, Michael, 191–192, 321
topographical model, 298
transference, 241, 248, 261, 270, 297, 299, 301, 303, 335
        see also countertransference
transformative experience, 257, 265
transient loneliness, 203, 298, 214
transitional object see object
trauma, xviii, 34–35, 37, 43, 130, 133, 179, 181–182,
        188–189, 196–197, 207, 229, 241–243,
        250–253, 272, 279, 282–286, 292, 295–298,
        302–304, 308–310
truth, 5–7, 9, 11, 79, 154, 284, 313, 331
typology of relationships, 325

uncanny, 73, 80, 87–89, 92–93, 95–96, 98, 133,
        241, 257, 260, 310
unconscious, xviii, 5, 9, 14, 33–34, 38–41, 64, 66,
        91–92, 107, 110–111, 121, 127, 131, 133,
        137–138, 149, 155, 159, 161, 192, 195, 238,
        269, 271–272, 280–281, 283, 286, 289,
        295–296, 298, 309
unintegration, 108, 127, 161, 270, 274
urbanisation, 59

violence, 32, 34, 37–42, 126, 262, 297
von Witzleben, Henry, 258

well-being, 121–122, 201, 205, 216, 220, 295
Weltschmerz, 93
Winnicott, Donald W., 12, 14–15, 74, 103, 107–109, 127–128, 130, 174, 179–180, 182, 192, 241, 244, 267–276, 281, 296–298, 307–309, 323
withdrawal, xix, 14, 21, 28, 33–34, 36, 44, 47, 53, 84, 88, 126, 174, 181, 206, 216, 218, 221, 230, 232, 243–245, 249, 260, 284

Wittgenstein, Ludwig, 40, 147
Woolf, Virginia, 255–256
working alliance, 324
working memory, 229, 234

Yeats, William Butler, 4, 19–20, 24, 27, 31

zero zone, 33, 43, 46–47, 52
Zimmermann, Johann Georg, 67, 87–88
zone of non-existence, 298, 301